About t

Nick Redfern works full time as an author, lecturer, and journalist. He writes about a wide range of unsolved mysteries, including Bigfoot, UFOs, the Loch Ness Monster, alien encounters, and government conspiracies. His many books include *Control, Assassinations, The Alien Book, The Zombie Book, The Bigfoot Book, The Monster Book, Cover-Ups & Secrets, Area 51, Secret History, Secret Societies, The New World Order Book, Time Travel: The Science and Science Fiction,* and, with Brad Steiger, *The Zombie Book: The Encyclopedia of the Living Dead.* He also writes regularly for *Mysterious Universe.* He has appeared on numerous television shows, including History Channel's *Monster Quest, Ancient Aliens,* and *UFO Hunters;* VH1's *Legend Hunters;* National Geographic Channel's *The Truth about UFOs* and *Paranatural;* the BBC's *Out of This World;* MSNBC's *Countdown;* and SyFy Channel's *Proof Positive.* Nick lives just a few miles from Dallas, Texas's infamous "grassy knoll" and can be contacted at his blog: http://nickredfernfortean.blogspot.com.

For some five decades, award-winning writer **Brad Steiger** was devoted to exploring and examining unusual, hidden, secret, and otherwise strange occurrences. A former high school teacher and college instructor, Brad published his first articles on the unexplained in 1956. He subsequently wrote more than two thousand articles with paranormal themes. He was the author or coauthor of more than 170 books, including *Real Vampires, Night Stalkers, and Creatures from the Darkside; Real Ghosts, Restless Spirits, and Haunted Places; Conspiracies and Secret Societies;* and with his wife, Sherry, *Real Miracles, Divine Intervention, and Feats of Incredible Survival.* Brad's *Otherworldly Affaires* was voted the Number One Paranormal Book of 2008 by Haunted America Tours. Brad died on May 6, 2018, at the age of 82.

Other Visible Ink Press Books by Nick Redfern

The Alien Book: A Guide to Extraterrestrial Beings on Earth
ISBN: 978-1-57859-687-4

Area 51: The Revealing Truth of UFOs, Secret Aircraft, Cover-Ups, & Conspiracies
ISBN: 978-1-57859-672-0

Assassinations: The Plots, Politics, and Powers behind History-Changing Murders
ISBN: 978-1-57859-690-4

The Bigfoot Book: The Encyclopedia of Sasquatch, Yeti, and Cryptid Primates
ISBN: 978-1-57859-561-7

Control: MKUltra, Chemtrails, and the Conspiracy to Suppress the Masses
ISBN: 978-1-57859-638-6

Cover-Ups & Secrets: The Complete Guide to Government Conspiracies, Manipulations & Deceptions
ISBN: 978-1-57859-679-9

The Monster Book: Creatures, Beasts, and Fiends of Nature
ISBN: 978-1-57859-575-4

Monsters of the Deep
ISBN: 978-1-57859-705-5

The New World Order Book
ISBN: 978-1-57859-615-7

Runaway Science: True Stories of Raging Robots and Hi-Tech Horrors
ISBN: 978-1-57859-801-4

Secret History: Conspiracies from Ancient Aliens to the New World Order
ISBN: 978-1-57859-479-5

Secret Societies: The Complete Guide to Histories, Rites, and Rituals
ISBN: 978-1-57859-483-2

Time Travel: The Science and Science Fiction
ISBN: 978-1-57859-723-9

The Zombie Book: The Encyclopedia of the Living Dead
with Brad Steiger
ISBN: 978-1-57859-504-4

Other Visible Ink Press Books by Brad Steiger

Conspiracies and Secret Societies: The Complete Dossier of Hidden Plots and Schemes
with Sherry Hansen Steiger
ISBN: 978-1-57859-767-3

Haunted: Malevolent Ghosts, Night Terrors, and Threatening Phantoms
ISBN: 978-1-57859-620-1

Real Aliens, Space Beings, and Creatures from Other Worlds
with Sherry Hansen Steiger
ISBN: 978-1-57859-333-0

Real Ghosts, Restless Spirits, and Haunted Places, 2nd edition
ISBN: 978-1-57859-401-6

Real Miracles, Divine Intervention, and Feats of Incredible Survival
with Sherry Hansen Steiger
ISBN: 978-1-57859-214-2

Real Monsters, Gruesome Critters, and Beasts from the Darkside
with Sherry Hansen Steiger
ISBN: 978-1-57859-220-3

Real Visitors, Voices from Beyond, and Parallel Dimensions
with Sherry Hansen Steiger
ISBN: 978-1-57859-541-9

Real Vampires, Night Stalkers, and Creatures from the Darkside
ISBN: 978-1-57859-255-5

Real Zombies, the Living Dead, and Creatures of the Apocalypse
ISBN: 978-1-57859-296-8

The Werewolf Book: The Encyclopedia of Shape-Shifting Beings, 2nd edition
ISBN: 978-1-57859-367-5

The Zombie Book: The Encyclopedia of the Living Dead
with Nick Redfern
ISBN: 978-1-57859-504-4

Also from Visible Ink Press

Alien Mysteries, Conspiracies, and Cover-Ups
by Kevin D. Randle
ISBN: 978-1-57859-418-4

Ancient Gods: Lost Histories, Hidden Truths, and the Conspiracy of Silence
by Jim Willis
ISBN: 978-1-57859-614-0

Angels A to Z, 2nd edition
by Evelyn Dorothy Oliver and James R. Lewis
ISBN: 978-1-57859-212-8

Armageddon Now: The End of the World A to Z
by Jim Willis and Barbara Willis
ISBN: 978-1-57859-168-8

The Astrology Book: The Encyclopedia of Heavenly Influences, 2nd edition
by James R. Lewis
ISBN: 978-1-57859-144-2

Celebrity Ghosts and Notorious Hauntings
by Marie D. Jones
ISBN: 978-1-57859-689-8

Censoring God: The History of the Lost Books (and other Excluded Scriptures)
by Jim Willis
ISBN: 978-1-57859-732-1

Demons, the Devil, and Fallen Angels
by Marie D. Jones and Larry Flaxman
ISBN: 978-1-57859-613-3

The Dream Encyclopedia, 2nd edition
by James R. Lewis and Evelyn Dorothy Oliver
ISBN: 978-1-57859-216-6

The Dream Interpretation Dictionary: Symbols, Signs and Meanings
by J. M. DeBord
ISBN: 978-1-57859-637-9

Earth Magic: Your Complete Guide to Natural Spells, Potions, Plants, Herbs, Witchcraft, and More
by Marie D. Jones
ISBN: 978-1-57859-697-3

The Encyclopedia of Religious Phenomena
by J. Gordon Melton, PhD
ISBN: 978-1-57859-209-8

The Fortune-Telling Book: The Encyclopedia of Divination and Soothsaying
by Raymond Buckland
ISBN: 978-1-57859-147-3

The Government UFO Files: The Conspiracy of Cover-Up
by Kevin D. Randle
ISBN: 978-1-57859-477-1

Hidden History: Ancient Aliens and the Suppressed Origins of Civilization
by Jim Willis
ISBN: 978-1-57859-710-9

Hidden Realms, Lost Civilizations, and Beings from Other Worlds
by Jerome Clark
ISBN: 978-1-57859-175-6

The Horror Show Guide: The Ultimate Frightfest of Movies
by Mike Mayo
ISBN: 978-1-57859-420-7

Lost Civilizations: The Secret Histories and Suppressed Technologies of the Ancients
by Jim Willis
ISBN: 978-1-57859-706-2

The Illuminati: The Secret Society That Hijacked the World
by Jim Marrs
ISBN: 978-1-57859-619-5

The New Witch: Your Guide to Modern Witchcraft, Wicca, Spells, Potions, Magic, and More
by Marie D. Jones
ISBN: 978-1-57859-716-1

Nightmares: Your Guide to Interpreting Your Darkest Dreams
by J. M. DeBord
ISBN: 978-1-57859-758-1

The Religion Book: Places, Prophets, Saints, and Seers
by Jim Willis
ISBN: 978-1-57859-151-0

The Sci-Fi Movie Guide: The Universe of Film from Alien to Zardoz
by Chris Barsanti
ISBN: 978-1-57859-503-7

The Serial Killer Next Door: The Double Lives of Notorious Murderers
by Richard Estep
ISBN: 978-1-57859-768-0

The Spirit Book: The Encyclopedia of Clairvoyance, Channeling, and Spirit Communication
by Raymond Buckland
ISBN: 978-1-57859-790-1

Supernatural Gods: Spiritual Mysteries, Psychic Experiences, and Scientific Truths
by Jim Willis
ISBN: 978-1-57859-660-7

Unexplained! Strange Sightings, Incredible Occurrences, and Puzzling Physical Phenomena, 3rd edition
by Jerome Clark
ISBN: 978-1-57859-344-6

The Vampire Almanac: The Complete History
by J. Gordon Melton, PhD
ISBN: 978-1-57859-719-2

The Vampire Book: The Encyclopedia of the Undead, 3rd edition
by J. Gordon Melton, PhD
ISBN: 978-1-57859-281-4

The Witch Book: The Encyclopedia of Witchcraft, Wicca, and Neo-paganism
by Raymond Buckland
ISBN: 978-1-57859-114-5

Please visit us at VisibleInkPress.com

WEREWOLF STORIES

STORIES

Shape-Shifters, Lycanthropes, and Man-Beasts

Nick Redfern and Brad Steiger

VISIBLE
INK
PRESS

DETROIT

WEREWOLF STORIES

Shape-Shifters, Lycanthropes, and Man-Beasts

Visible Ink Press®
43311 Joy Rd., #414
Canton, MI 48187-2075

Visible Ink Press is a registered trademark of Visible Ink Press LLC.

Most Visible Ink Press books are available at special quantity discounts when purchased in bulk by corporations, organizations, or groups. Customized printings, special imprints, messages, and excerpts can be produced to meet your needs. For more information, contact Special Markets Director, Visible Ink Press, www.visibleink.com, or 734-667-3211.

Managing Editor: Christa Gainor
Art Director: Alessandro Cinelli, Cinelli Design
Cover Design: John Gouin, Graphikitchen, LLC
Typesetting: Lumina Datamatics, Inc.
Image Editor: Gregory Hayes
Proofreader: Larry Baker
Indexer: Shoshana Hurwitz

ISBN: 978-1-57859-766-6 (paperback)
ISBN: 978-1-57859-829-8 (hardcover)
ISBN: 978-1-57859-830-4 (eBook)

Cataloging-in-Publication Data is on file at the Library of Congress.
10 9 8 7 6 5 4 3 2 1

Contents

Introduction

Sightings of upright, hairy creatures have been seen deep in the heart of the mysterious forest from time immemorial. I even had my own experience in 2002. It occurred while I was in a state of paralysis in my bedroom—and I was half awake. That I was unable to move didn't do any good.

Because I am someone who believes that the phenomenon of sleep paralysis has an external, supernatural aspect to it, rather than being due solely to the mysteries of the mind, I feel it is relevant to share the story here. In other words, it was not just a dream. It was around four o'clock in the morning, I was awake and yet not awake, and I couldn't move. I was suddenly aware that something was slowly heading down the corridor of my duplex that linked the bedroom to the living room.

That "something" was nothing less than a humanoid figure with the head of a huge wolf and enormous fangs. It was attired in a long, flowing black cape. Not just that: it emitted strange and rapid growling noises that seemed to be an unintelligible language. And the creature, whatever its origin was, seemed mightily pissed off about something. As it closed in on the room, I made a supreme effort to move my rigid, paralyzed form and finally succeeded, just as the beast entered the bedroom. In an instant, it was gone, and I was wide awake. It was a bizarre and terrifying situation. And for a couple of days, there was a hard-to-explain, menacing atmosphere in the home. It was a one-time experience; the vile creature never returned.

There's yet another thing, too, that made me become very enthusiastic about the idea of beastly man-creatures. I grew up in a small village in central England called Pelsall that is very old; its origins date back to 994 CE. More important and relevant to the subject at hand, Pelsall is located only about a five-minute drive from the site of what ultimately became one of the most controversial, weird, and some say paranormal events of the early twentieth century. It was focused upon a man named George Edalji.

Edalji, who was the son of a priest, lived in a nearby old town called Great Wyrley. He was thrust into the limelight in 1903 when he was convicted, sentenced, and imprisoned for maiming and mutilating horses in the area—reportedly in the dead of night and, some believed, for reasons related to some kind of occult ritual. Collectively, the horse slashings and deaths generated not only a great deal of concern at a local level but also anger, fear, and a distinct mistrust of the Edalji family, whom the locals had consistently frowned upon ever since they'd moved to the area years earlier.

Such was the publicity given to the case of George Edalji that none other than the creator of Sherlock Holmes, Sir Arthur Conan Doyle himself, took careful notice of the case, its developments, and the outcome for Edalji. Actually, Conan Doyle did far more than merely take notice. Fully believing that there had been a huge miscarriage of justice in the Edalji affair, he highlighted it, wrote about it, and even loudly complained to the government of the day about it—events that, combined with the work of others, ultimately led to Edalji's early release from prison.

For me, growing up practically on the doorstep of where all of the old bloodthirsty carnage occurred decades earlier, the weirder aspects of the matter were the most fascinating. And, I hasten to add, there were a great deal of them. Stories did the rounds locally for years suggesting not only that Edalji was not the culprit, but that the attacker wasn't even human! A giant, monstrous bird, a large ape trained via hypnosis, and an equally well-trained group of wild boars were all proposed as viable candidates for the attacks. Notably, also in whispered words, there were rumors that Edalji was, by night, a rampaging werewolf.

As a kid, I was fascinated by werewolves, both in fiction and fact.

And there's another thing—a last piece of information that I find very intriguing: as a kid, I was fascinated by werewolves, both in fiction and fact. I don't know why. But my fascination for werewolves started around the age of five or six, and it's never gone away. So you can see why I was excited to work on this collection of tales, *Werewolf Stories:*

Shape-Shifters, Lycanthropes, and Man-Beasts, culled from the files of cryptozoology specialist Brad Steiger and my own research. Along the winding path I'll be looking at the world of shape-shifting, Witchcraft, the occult, psychedelics, multidimensions, and everything else that surrounds the domain of the werewolf. Of course, it would have been great to have worked on the book directly with Brad. Sadly, as most of you will know, it was not destined: Brad died at the age of 82 on May 6, 2018. I hope I will be able to reach Brad's standards and make this volume one of the most formidable beasts of all.

The book that you are about to read deals with a subject that many people might assume falls solely into the domain of folklore, mythology, and legend. They would, however, be wrong. Shape-shifting, for most people, provokes imagery of centuries-old tales of savage, murderous werewolves and of big-bucks movies, such as *An American Werewolf in London*, *Underworld*, *Dog Soldiers*, and *The Wolfman*. The topic is much broader than that, however. As incredible as it may seem, shape-shifters are not merely the stuff of Hollywood or urban tales of the "friend of a friend" variety. Rather, they are menacingly real. And they are not all of the "man turns into wolf" variety, either; shape-shifters come in all kinds and sizes and have done so for countless millennia.

While the traditional image of the werewolf is, without a doubt, the first thing that springs to mind when a discussion of shape-shifters takes place, the truth is that there is a veritable menagerie of such infernal things in our midst. Werecats, were-tigers, were-hyenas, and werecoyotes also lead the monstrous list. Then there are the ancient beliefs that those who died violent deaths — or those who were, themselves, murderers — were often destined to return to our plane of existence in the forms of hideous beasts, including wild and savage ape-like animals, fearsome black dogs with glowing or blazing red eyes, and mermaid-like things. There are also beings from other worlds: aliens, extraterrestrials, and Men in Black. Even the legendary monsters of Loch Ness in Scotland are believed — in certain monster-hunting quarters — to be paranormal beasts that have the ability to alter their appearance at will — as are vampires, who, the old legends suggest, can transform into the likes of bats and wolves.

Collectively, all of these "things" amount to an absolute army of otherworldly creatures and half-human monsters that have plagued and tormented us since the dawn of civilization. And they show zero signs of slowing down. The things you thought were only fit for campfire tales, late-night stories intended to thrill little children, and entertaining monster movies are, in actuality, creatures of the real world. Of our world.

Shape-shifters are everywhere: they lurk in the shadows, in the deep woods and expansive forests, in dark and dank caves, and in the murky waters of our lakes and rivers. Maybe even, after sunset, in the recesses of your very own backyard, patiently waiting to pounce. And many of them like nothing better than to terrorize and torment us, the human race.

With that all said, it is now time to take a wild and weird road trip into the mystery-filled domain of creatures that many will assure you simply do not exist. I am here, however, to tell you otherwise. Shape-shifters are disturbingly real. And you are about to meet them, in all their savage and sinister glory. As you read this book, and as day becomes night, keep those silver bullets close at hand. *Very* close. You know—just in case …

Nick Redfern, 2023

Animal Ancestors

The belief in animal-man beings goes back to the dawn of humankind's curiosity about its place in the natural scheme of things. In *The Algonquin Legends of New England*, C. G. Leland repeats a common Native American myth that states that in the beginning of things, humans were as animals and animals were as humans. The mythologies of the aboriginal people of South America echo the same belief: in the beginning, people were animals but were also humans. That is to say, the spirit-stuff that would one day evolve into a human found its first physical expression in the shapes of animals.

Numerous legends from Indigenous tribes across North America tell of wolf-men, bear-men, cougar-men, and other were-creatures. Stories of women who gave birth to man-beasts are common, as are accounts of men who took animal brides. Ancient cultures throughout the world formed totem clans and claimed an animal ancestor as the progenitor of their clan. Although it is always hazardous to make cross-cultural

The oldest known statue is believed to depict the figure of a human with the head of a lion, hand-carved from mammoth ivory during the upper Paleolithic, sometime between 35 to 41 millennia ago.

generalities about any subject, it seems safe to suggest that there is a commonality of belief among shamans from nearly every known tradition that all creatures on the planet are relatives.

Donna Kay Barthelemy, who spent five years with a cross-cultural shaman studying the ways of many different traditions, agrees. In the shamanistic tradition, she writes in her article "Shamanism as Living System":

> All creatures are called "relatives," and are considered sisters, brothers, grandparents. … Non-human relatives are considered "people" and are prayed for … the birds (winged ones), the trees (tall-standing people), the plants (green-growing people), the four-leggeds, the creepy crawlies, as well as the two-leggeds.

Perhaps because of our species's association with wolves—which according to recent research began over 140,000 years ago—many tribes in Europe and the Americas believed that their ancestors truly had been wolves.

Many Native American tribes contain legends that tell how the first tribes that ever existed were wolf-people. At first, according to these traditions, the wolf-people walked on all fours. After a time, it seemed a good thing to begin walking upright and—very slowly at first—become human. So a toe was formed, then a couple of fingers, smaller ears and teeth, and so forth, until they gradually became perfect human beings. Some mourned the loss of a tail, but it was agreed that such an appendage made sitting difficult—and besides, one could always "borrow" one from those spirits who had chosen to remain in wolf, coyote, or fox forms. After a time, clans began to form around the belief that certain animals other than wolves had been ancestors of their families. Some admired the grace of the deer, the strength of the bear, the prowess of the cougar, and so forth, and clan demarcations were established within the tribes.

Sources:

Barthelemy, Donna Kay. "Shamanism as Living System." *Quest*, Summer 1995.

Leland, C. G. *The Algonquin Legends of New England; or, Myths and Folk Lore of the Micmac, Passamaquoddy, and Penobscot Tribes.* New York: Houghton, Mifflin, 1884.

Steiger, Brad. *Totems — The Transformative Power of Your Personal Animal Totem.* San Francisco: HarperSanFrancisco, 1997.

Anubis

Anubis is the jackal-headed Egyptian god of the underworld, the judge of the dead. Sometimes known as the Great Dog, Anubis was mated to Nepthys, the underworld counterpart of the goddess Isis. Dogs were greatly revered in ancient Egypt, and Anubis had a place of great honor in the pantheon of gods. For Christians in the Middle Ages, images of Anubis reinforced folk legends of werejackals that attacked unwary desert travelers. Although some ancient cults saw Anubis as a conduit for healing, others believed that the priests, with their dog-headed masks, were assuming the pagan god's role as judge of the underworld and were stealing the souls of those hapless victims that they only pretended to cure.

Sources:

Gaynor, Frank, ed. *Dictionary of Mysticism*. New York: Philosophical Library, 1953.

Appearance of Werewolves

When werewolves are free of the awful curse that dominates their existence during the nights of the full moon, they appear as ordinary men and women — perhaps a bit nervous or restless, perhaps somewhat melancholy, but essentially normal in every aspect of their physical appearance. They can walk about in full sunlight and need not fear crucifixes or holy water. Most of the contemporary folklore describing the transformation of human to werewolf is influenced by such Hollywood films as *The Wolf Man* and *Curse of the Werewolf*, which depict the end result of the process of shape-shifting as a two-legged, hairy, fanged, wolflike entity, lusting for blood and flesh. The werewolf continues to walk upright, rather than move on all fours, and is still recognizable as a humanoid creature. During the transmutation, articles of clothing may be ripped or shredded and shoes discarded, but the werewolf remains barefooted and clothed as he seeks his prey under the full moon.

Such films as *An American Werewolf in London*, *An American Werewolf in Paris*, and the series of motion pictures based on *The Howling* returned to the descriptions of werewolves of ancient legend by portraying a beast that is more wolf than human. In the classic accounts, once the transformation into wolf has occurred, it is difficult to detect any differences between the werewolf and the true wolf without careful examination. The werewolf that has undergone a complete shape-shifting process is somewhat larger than a true wolf, often has a silvery sheen to its fur, and always has red, glowing eyes.

The werewolf of ancient tradition runs on all fours and has discarded all vestiges of clothing before the process of transmutation begins. If the shape-shifter should be killed while in the form of a wolf, he or she would return to human shape and be naked. When those individuals who have become werewolves against their will are not under the power of the curse that forces them to become ravenous beasts, they experience all the normal human emotions of shame and disgust for the deeds that they must commit under the blood spell. They may long for death and seek ways to destroy themselves before they take the lives of more innocent victims. However, they soon discover to their dismay that the Grim Reaper can only be summoned to their door by certain means — and self-destruction is not one of them. On the other hand, those who have become werewolves of their own choice and who sought the power of transmutation through incantations, potions, or spells revel in their strength and in their ability to strike fear into the hearts of all who hear their piercing howls on the nights of the full moon.

Sources:

Douglas, Drake. *Horror!* New York: Collier Books, 1966.

Spence, Lewis. *An Encyclopedia of Occultism*. New Hyde Park, NY: University Books, 1960.

Apuleius, Lucius (c. 125–c. 180)

Lucius Apuleius lived in North Africa around the middle of the second century. Although he wrote in Latin, he was very familiar with the popular Greek romances of his time. His passion for Greek philosophy expressed itself in a book of philosophical extracts, which included an essay on Plato and another on the theology of Socrates. Although he was very prolific, the books of Apuleius failed to enter the classical canon of authors because of his vocabulary and involved syntax; thus he is remembered primarily for his *Metamorphoses*, often referred to as *The Golden Ass*.

In nearly all of his prose, Apuleius displays a kind of obsession with the supernatural, Eastern religions, and magic. His *Apologia* is written as his legal defense for the accusation that he had cast spells on his wife and her family. In *The Golden Ass*, he describes the salves that

In a sixteenth-century engraving depicting a scene from Apuleius's Metamorphoses, *the protagonist, transformed into an ass, eavesdrops as an old woman tells the tale of Cupid and Psyche.*

wizards and Witches used to transform themselves into animals. In one episode, he tells of peering through a crack in a door and watching a Witch named Pamphile take off her clothes and remove from a chest several small boxes that contained various ointments:

> She anointed her whole body, from the very nails of her toes to hair on the crown of her head, and when she was anointed all over, she whispered many magic words to a lamp. … Then she began to move her arms, first with tremulous jerks, and afterwards by a gentle undulating motion, till a glittering, downy surface by degrees overspread her body, feathers and strong quills burst forth suddenly, her nose became a hard crooked beak, her toes changed to curved talons. …

To Apuleius's spying eyes, Pamphile was no longer Pamphile but had become an owl. As he continued to watch in astonishment, Pamphile uttered a "harsh, querulous scream, leaping from the ground by little and little" until at last "she stretched forth her wings on either side to their full extent and flew straight away."

After such a demonstration, Apuleius decided that he must apply the ointment to his own body and become an owl, just as Pamphile had done. After he had thoroughly applied the salve to every part of his body, Apuleius began to flap his arms and eagerly anticipated the appearance of feathers that would signal his transformation into an owl. But to his great surprise and disappointment, his skin hardened into a leathern hide covered with bristly hair.

"The palms of my hands and the soles of my feet became four solid hoofs, and from the end of my spine a long tail projected. My face was enormous, my mouth wide, my nostrils gaping, my lips pendulous, and I had a pair of immoderately long, rough, hairy ears." Instead of an owl, Apuleius found that the ointment had transformed him into an ass.

Sources:

Spence, Lewis. *An Encyclopedia of Occultism*. New Hyde Park, NY: University Books, 1960.

B

Balls of Light That Change
into Creatures

It is apparent that that shape-shifting beings do not confine themselves to animal-human hybrids. Furthermore, it is possible that some UFO encounters might not be what they initially appear to be—that is, face-to-face confrontations with extraterrestrials from faraway worlds. We must consider that they may actually be carefully stage-managed, manipulated events. Perhaps our presumed aliens are, in reality, shape-shifters from our own world—entities that toy with our minds and assume the role and appearance of ETs.

When people ponder on the matter of extraterrestrial encounters, they typically think of so-called alien abductions and the Grays, those diminutive, large-headed entities with eerie, black eyes that are near-hypnotic in nature. Back in the latter part of the 1940s and the early 1950s, however, things were very different. Back then, the Grays were in the sights of precisely no one. That is not to say people weren't encountering aliens; they most assuredly were. Back then, however, they were known as the Space Brothers. They were very human-looking aliens—sometimes slightly shorter in stature than us, and other times reaching heights of around seven feet. They sometimes wore long robes and other times wore silver outfits, similar to the clothing worn by fighter pilots. And their message was always the same: they were deeply concerned by our growing nuclear arsenals and wished us to lay down our weapons and live in peace and harmony with one another.

Among the more well-known of the contactees were George Adamski (whose 1952 book, *Flying Saucers Have Landed*, became a huge hit not just with UFO devotees but also with the public), George Van Tassel (who attracted significant FBI attention as a result of his UFO claims), and Frank Stranges (who maintained that human-like ETs had infiltrated the Pentagon). And then there were the lesser-known contactees, one of whom is central to the story related here. His name was Orfeo Angelucci. Although a fairly minor cog in the contactee wheel, Angelucci wrote a number of books that were well received, although they failed to sell in large quantities. They included *The Secret of the Saucers* and *Son of the Sun*. The nature of Angelucci's experiences are not unfamiliar ones.

A Warning from the Shape-Shifters

According to the man himself—who was born in 1912 and worked for a flooring company in New Jersey—it was in 1946 that his otherworldly experiences began, which Angelucci reveals in *Son of the Sun*. Angelucci had a big interest in science and aviation and, in August 1946, launched a large balloon array into the skies of Trenton, New Jersey. The balloons were filled with different kinds of mold, the reason being to determine if mold was affected by exposure to different altitudes, temperatures, and air pressure. Angelucci further maintained that it was this experiment that caught the attention of the Space Brothers, who specifically chose him to further their agenda on Earth.

Although Angelucci claimed numerous encounters with the cosmic brothers (and sisters, too), it was not so much the encounters that were significant but the means by which the entities from the stars manifested before him. It is important to note that although Angelucci stressed that it was in the summer of 1946 that aliens first took note of his work with high-altitude balloons, it was not until 1952 that the cosmic ones met with him, face to face. By this time, Angelucci had moved to Los Angeles, California. The night of May 23, 1952, was when everything changed for Angelucci. The day had started out as a strange one, even before the ETs arrived on the scene. From the moment he woke up, Angelucci felt agitated and worried; he had a strange sense that the day was going to turn out very weird.

At the time, Angelucci was employed by the Lockheed Aircraft Corporation—which, interestingly enough, had also employed ufologist George Van Tassel, albeit in the 1940s—and was working a night shift. It was shortly after midnight on the evening in question that Angelucci got in his car and drove home. He didn't know it then, but he was about to have a most interesting detour and experience. It was as Angelucci crossed a bridge over the Los Angeles River—a bridge that was eerily empty of any other vehicles at the time—that he caught sight of a large, blue-colored ball of light that was clearly shadowing him. The circle of light, about the size of a beach ball, took a sudden turn and appeared directly in front of Angelucci's car. Shocked to the core, Angelucci slowed his car to practically a walking pace and watched, amazed, as two small green balls of light emerged from the larger one and floated toward him.

Via telepathy, a booming voice informed Angelucci that he had indeed been watched ever since the day of that fateful balloon launch back in 1946. Angelucci was about to ask a question when the two balls closed in on each other and then merged into one larger green light. In mere seconds, the ball changed into the disembodied images of a man and a woman—as Angelucci came to learn, the floating heads of a pair of aliens who could pass for you or me. Like many contactees, Angelucci was asked—in a slightly bullying and patronizing fashion—to spread the word of the supposedly utterly benevolent ETs. "We'll be back," they said when all was over. The ball of light raced into the sky, and Angelucci, a nervous character at the best of times, raced home.

The aliens were good to their word and arranged another meeting, again late at night, under Los Angeles's Hyperion Avenue Freeway Bridge. Angelucci patiently waited and finally noticed a pair of small balls of green light approaching through the darkness. *They* were coming. The lights transformed into one single light, described by the man of the hour as something resembling a huge

Angelucci's numerous encounters were significant in the means by which the entities from the stars manifested before him as speaking balls of light.

"soap bubble" that gave off a "pale glow." A chummy chat about the universe, destiny, life, death, and even the afterlife followed—although the chat was a strange one, given that Angelucci found himself speaking to a ball of light that spoke back to him. Suddenly, the light was gone, and Angelucci was left to do nothing stranger than head back home.

> *Neptune warned Angelucci that our solar system had been the home to numerous earlier civilizations that had destroyed themselves, and that unless humans changed our dangerous ways, we would surely be next.*

Three weeks later, under cover of overwhelming darkness, Angelucci was back at the bridge—as were the two green lights. This time, they shape-shifted into the forms of a man and a woman whose appearance, said Angelucci, put them both at around the age of 35. The male entity, named Neptune, warned Angelucci that our solar system had been the home to numerous earlier civilizations that had destroyed themselves, and that unless humans changed our dangerous ways, we would surely be next on the long and sorry list of casualties. It was for that very reason, Neptune said, that Angelucci should write books about his experiences and get the word out to the public—which he duly and faithfully did, right up until his death in 1993 at the age of 81.

Finally, it should be remembered that W. Y. Evans-Wentz, a native of Trenton, had a similar series of experiences in 1910, in Ireland, involving two supernatural entities that manifested out of a pair of glowing balls of light. Indeed, when one compares the 1910 Ireland case, described by Evans-Wentz in *The Fairy Faith in Celtic Countries*, with Angelucci's experience in 1950s-era Los Angeles, one sees very little difference between the two. They practically mirror each other. That both Evans-Wentz and Angelucci were born in Trenton, New Jersey, makes the story even more bizarre.

Bosco, the Mysterious Morphing Ball of Light

In July 1952, an encounter similar to those of Orfeo Angelucci was reported by a man named Karl Hunrath, who at the time lived in Racine, Wisconsin. It is a story that is told in a declassified Federal Bureau of

Investigation (FBI) file of 1953 titled "Karl Hunrath" and in an article from me titled "Kidnapped by a Flying Saucer?" On the morning of July 22, Hunrath complained to his local police department about something strange that had occurred just a few hours earlier, in the dead of night. Who knows what the cops thought of it all, but it basically went as follows.

In the early hours of a Sunday morning in July, Hunrath's bedroom was flooded with a blinding white light. He immediately sat upright, and as his eyes finally adjusted to the light, he saw in the corner of the room a floating ball of light that had a diameter of about four feet. Hunrath could only stare in shock and awe. Then, something amazing and terrifying happened: the glowing ball transformed into a well-dressed man in black, and Hunrath found himself temporarily paralyzed.

The "man" proceeded to pump Hunrath's right arm full of chemicals, which rendered him into a distinctly altered state of mind, and proceeded to tell Hunrath that he had been chosen to play a significant role in the alien mission on Earth. A very groggy Hunrath could only look on from his bed as the somewhat foreign-sounding, but perfectly human-appearing, alien told him: "I am Bosco. You have been chosen to enter our brotherhood of galaxies."

The suit-and-tie-wearing Bosco advised Hunrath that the brothers from beyond were deeply worried by the warlike ways of humans and so determined to take action against the dastardly elements of humanity that wanted to spoil everyone else's fun. There was not to be any *The Day the Earth Stood Still*–style ultimatum for one and all, however. Nope. The aliens wished to recruit sympathetic humans to aid their righteous cause. Perhaps more accurately, they wanted to get someone else to do their dirty work while they lurked safely in the shadows. As Hunrath quickly came to realize, he was now one of the chosen few. But there was more. Bosco, via what Hunrath said were "occult techniques," downloaded into his mind countless amounts of data on how to build a terrible weapon that had the ability to destroy aircraft — specifically, the aircraft of the U.S. military, which the Space Brothers viewed as being just about as dangerous to world peace as the dastardly commies.

"I am Bosco, and that will be its name, too," boomed the alleged alien, in reference to the device that he wanted Hunrath not just to build but also to deploy. Far too stunned and drugged to move, Hunrath could only watch in a mixture of befuddlement and shock as Bosco then turned on his heel and left for his — one might be inclined to assume after an experience like that — flying saucer. There was no amazing "Beam me up" type of exit for Bosco, however. For a ball of light that shape-shifted into a human-like extraterrestrial, Bosco had a very down-to-earth means of making good his departure: he pulled back the curtains of Hunrath's bedroom window, clambered out, and vanished into the depths of the early-morning blackness of Hunrath's front yard.

The now-declassified FBI file — titled "Karl Hunrath" — reflects that Hunrath had assured the police there was no way he would even consider building Bosco and letting it loose on the world. Special agents of the bureau were not quite so sure, however. The neighbors were soon complaining of strange noises coming from Hunrath's garage day and night, and at least three or four times per week he had a visitor who stayed for hours on end. Checks of the man's license plate by the FBI revealed the visitor was a local: Wilbur J. Wilkinson — a subservient, Igor-like lackey to Hunrath's escalating Dr. Frankenstein. On a morning in early August, FBI agents made an unannounced visit to Hunrath's place of residence, demanding to be shown what it was that he and Wilkinson were working on in the garage. Weapon or not, to the FBI it appeared to be nothing more than "a collection of radios, and speakers and cables strung together." The somewhat bemused agents said their farewells and left. Had they been born into today's world, they might just as well have texted their boss: "Hunrath/Bosco: WTF?"

Whether Hunrath may have anticipated getting such a visit is unknown. But we can be sure that Hunrath was now a man on a mission. And with the bureau boys snooping around, Hunrath had no choice but to head for pastures new. There was only one way he was going to achieve his goal of fame and fortune and do the right thing by brother Bosco. It was time to say "adios" to both Wisconsin and the FBI and head to where all the alien action was then taking place: California. Hunrath and Wilkinson soon hooked up with the major players in West Coast ufology at the time. These included such contactees as George Adamski and George Hunt Williamson, along with a number of UFO researchers and investigative groups. All was going well until November 1953. That was when things came to a mysterious and ominous end.

It was early on the morning of November 10th that Hunrath and Wilkinson rented a compact aircraft from a local airstrip. They headed off for what they claimed to several colleagues, just 48 hours earlier, would be a face-to-face meeting with a group of extraterrestrials connected to Mr. Bosco. Although the pair was seen taking off from the airstrip and headed in a direction that would have set them on a course for Palm Springs and Joshua Tree, California, they were never seen again. Despite extensive searches by the emergency services, Hunrath and Wilkinson were not found. No wreckage of the aircraft was ever found, either. Wilkinson's wife never heard from her husband again. They were gone—forever.

The strange stories of Orfeo Angelucci and the Hunrath–Wilkinson affair could be considered just a couple of odd but engaging UFO encounters except for one thing. Their experiences with the morphing balls of light parallel nearly exactly those of W. Y. Evans-Wentz in early twentieth-century Ireland. In that case, however, there was no extraterrestrial component—just fairy-like entities.

This raises an important question: Are the balls of light native to our world rather than extraterrestrial? Probably, yes. That being so, perhaps their incredible ability to shape-shift allows them to toy with, manipulate, and tantalize the human race—for bizarre and obscure reasons that, for all we know, might be born out of a decidedly deranged sense of humor. Maybe they simply enjoy passing themselves off as hair-covered hominids, ETs, or fairies—and amazing and terrifying us in the process—for one simple reason: *because they can.*

Sources:

Angelucci, Orfeo M. *Son of the Sun*. Los Angeles: DeVorss, 1959.

Redfern, Nick. "Kidnapped by a Flying Saucer?" *Mysterious Universe*. April 6, 2012. http://mysteriousuniverse.org/2012/04/kidnapped-by-a-flying-saucer/.

Redfern, Nick. *Shapeshifters: Morphing Monsters and Changing Cryptids*. Woodbury, MN: Llewellyn, 2017.

Baring-Gould, Sabine (1834–1924)

For many werewolf enthusiasts, the first book that they may have read on the subject is *The Book of Were-Wolves* (1865) by Sabine Baring-Gould. Perhaps a good many admirers of this classic work that tells tales of lycanthropes remain unaware that the Rev. Baring-Gould stood at his writing desk to produce more than 1,240 separate publications. The Anglican priest, who was born in Exeter, England, is revered as a writer of hymns, and those who sit in their Sunday pews and gustily sing the popular "Onward Christian Soldiers" and then lower their voices to harmonize on "Now the Day Is Over" would undoubtedly be shocked to know that the composer of such Christian standards was also fascinated by werewolves.

Sabine Baring-Gould's The Book of Were-Wolves *is a thorough collection of prior myth and legend, like a meta-analysis of transformation tales through the ages and around the world.*

In addition to shape-shifters, Baring-Gould also wrote a collection of ghost stories called *Guavas, the Tinner* (1897), the popular *Curious Myths of the Middle Ages* (published in two parts, 1866 and 1868), *Devonshire Characters and Strange Events* (1908), and *Cornish Characters and Strange Events* (1909). Balancing his interest in the strange and unknown is his 16-volume *Lives of the Saints* (1872–77).

In 1864, Baring-Gould, who was serving as the curate at Horbury Bridge, West Riding Yorkshire, fell in love with Grace Taylor, the 16-year-old daughter of a mill-hand in his parish. After the lower-class girl had spent two years acquiring middle-class manners, Baring-Gould married her on May 25, 1868. Together they had 15 children, all but one of whom lived to adulthood. When Grace passed away in 1916, Baring-Gould commissioned a gravestone that bore the Latin motto *Dimidium Animae Meae* ("Half of My Soul"). He never remarried.

Baring-Gould regarded his collection of folk songs as the crowning achievement of his eclectic miscellany of literary works. *Songs and Ballads of the West* (1889–91) is remembered as the first collection of folk songs for the mass market. In 1895, he released *A Garland of Country Songs*, and in 1907, collaborating with Cecil Sharp, he produced *English Folk Songs for Schools*, which remained a music-class staple in British schools for over 60 years.

Rev. Sabine Baring-Gould died on January 2, 1924, and was buried next to his wife, Grace.

Sources:

Beckley, Timothy Green, and William Kern. *Big Book of Werewolves*. New Brunswick, NJ: Global Communications, 2008.

Colloms, Brenda. "Baring-Gould, Sabine (1834–1924)." *Oxford Dictionary of National Biography*, Oxford University Press, 2004. https://natpmail2. netcore.co.in/fmlurlsvc/?fewReq=:B:JVI2PTk5Nip6MT4iPCplaDE8PTY-8PSp/ZWtibXh5fmkxPWlvOWhuamptOjloP29qPT5oOT1pOzppaTw4aDw/ NTs9OjhpPjo0bip4MT06ND07ND0/PTUqfWVoMT8/RT1fbllhPDw/ NDw7IT8/RT1fblljPDw/NDw7Kn5vfHgxZ2NgbXx8bX5tZm0iZ0xgeWFlY-m1oIm9jYSpvMTU8KmRoYDE8&url=http%3a%2f%2fwww.oxforddub. com%2fview%2farticle%2f30587.

Basques of Louisiana and the Loup-Garou

by Alyne A. Pustanio

Though it was founded as the New Galvez colony in 1778 by Governor Bernardo de Galvez, the old parish below New Orleans became known by the name of its founder's patron, St. Bernard. Its close proximity to the city—extending as it does directly from the old barracks to the south and east along the Mississippi River where it meanders toward the swamps and the Gulf of Mexico—made St. Bernard Parish more a suburb of New Orleans, and although rural in aspect, its families and history are closely connected to those of the city.

At a spot along the riverbank, just across the lower boundary of Orleans Parish at the St. Bernard Parish line, was located a thriving slaughterhouse. The largest of its kind in the city, these abattoirs had been in full operation from the earliest years of the nineteenth century, supplying New Orleans and the surrounding areas with the finest quality meat and poultry to be had. Though local pigs, fowl, and even deer were processed through these slaughtering yards, the real money was in beef, especially the Texas cattle that were deposited into pens along the Mississippi River by ship and the herds that came down from the north in the Mississippi River drives.

The host of butchers who dispatched the animals lived nearby; their makeshift huts of old ship hulls and tattered canvas dotted the flat, dry riverbanks known to locals as the "batture." These slayers were Basque, a mix of Spanish and French, and came originally from Europe's mountainous Lower Pyrenees region. They made their living and earned their table's fare in the abattoirs with skills as sleek and refined as their work could boast. In fact, the men were so well known for their bloody craft that people traveling from New Orleans through St. Bernard Parish would make a point of stopping by the abattoirs to see the butchers at their work. And they worked hard, spending most of their day smeared up to their knees and elbows in blood and offal.

In the evenings the Basquemen would retire to their humble shacks, the flickering embers of their fires sparking into the indigo darkness of the New Orleans nights, glowing clay pipes illuminating their swarthy, deeply lined faces as soft laughter and songs in their unique language drifted languidly over the river's ebbing tides.

The Basquemen seldom ventured far from the batture. Some of them had wives, mostly French women of the lower caste, though some had taken Native American brides. Often young boys and girls—Basque children—were seen playing in the encampment, astonishing the locals by frolicking naked together along the batture, swimming, playing, and even drinking in the blood-polluted waters. Occasionally one or two of the wives would appear in the great market of New Orleans, replenishing supplies that could not be obtained elsewhere. Sometimes one or two of the Basquemen might be glimpsed drinking and sampling the tenderloin or fighting with a Kentiauk flatboatman in Gallatin Street. The Kentiauk was always the worse for wear from such encounters as the Basque butchers were exceptionally strong, and "bet the Basque" was a going phrase.

By and large the slaughterhouse men and their kin kept to themselves, and the locals did not often intrude upon them.

But by and large the slaughterhouse men and their kin kept to themselves, and the locals did not often intrude upon them. Truth told, most families who lived nearby kept their distance and avoided altogether straying near the batture or the abattoirs after nightfall. Fortunately, the families and others who knew of the butchers heeded that gut instinct, for the Basquemen, it was said, kept a well-guarded secret, though rarely, over the long years, had there been much evidence of it.

Yet sometimes circumstance and fate conspire against secrecy, and because of this the men of the abattoirs are forever woven into the tapestry of haunted Old New Orleans. It was about the time of the war with the English that people first began to talk. Before then the swampy wilderness of St. Bernard Parish was sparsely populated. The pockets of civilization were centered mainly around the plantations and belonged to many of the most prominent families of New Orleans—the Villeres, the McCartys, the Dreux, and of course the great landowner, Bernard Marigny. The swampy lands of St. Bernard—called the "Oxen Lands" because of the animals used to tame and farm it—were a vast, mysterious swath of the unknown to the nearby New Orleanians. Because it was removed from the mainstream of city life and yet provided ample access to the Mississippi River, St. Bernard Parish was chosen as the place most appropriate for the bloody work of animal slaughtering.

In the earliest days indentured and some enslaved servants were impressed to work in the slaughterhouses, but the product was shabby, and plantation owners placed too high a value on their enslaved workers as property to have them worked nearly to death in the brutal conditions of the slaughterhouses. The Filipinos were thought to be untrustworthy for the task; most would work only as long as it took to cut up enough meat to fill a lugger boat and then make a hasty escape. In the end the

In the early 1800s, the City of New Orleans had not yet sprawled to encompass the surrounding plantations, swamps, and bayous shown in this period map.

only reliable source of labor to be found was the immigrants from the Pyrenees, the Basquemen, and so the abattoirs quickly became the exclusive territory of these silent strangers.

Then the British once again brought war to America, and they had New Orleans directly in its sights. The army was pressuring men everywhere to fight; warships lined the Mississippi River levees, overflowing with newly recruited sailors; in secret, Captain Jean Lafitte was swelling his ranks with privateers, both willing and unwilling. All of these men had to be fed somehow, and with no supplies coming through the British blockades, General Jackson's army had been ordered to buy or confiscate cattle and other animals wherever they were found. Some wily farmers made deals for their herds; others protested angrily. But at the abattoirs, soldiers seized whatever animals remained alive.

In December of 1812, as the troubles with the British escalated and began to suck New Orleans into the war, a particularly cold winter set in; this and the animal seizures finally brought work at the abattoirs to a complete standstill. The Basquemen learned what news they could from pirates and smugglers who passed through on larger errands and disdainfully accepted the charity of the church when it was offered, but, caught as they were between two great warring forces, the Basquemen and their families were soon left to fend for themselves to pass that brutal winter.

In New Orleans, amidst the rumors of war there arose another strain of murmur; taverns, inns, brothels, and hostels were fluttering with tales of strange happenings in the outlying regions—events that had nothing to do with battle. Priests and upstanding citizens tried to quell the rumors by characterizing them as fables made up by Native Americans to stir the population with superstition and fear. Nonetheless, the rumors grew, and soon a palpable fear took hold at what might be happening in St. Bernard Parish.

First a boy was found, no more than nine years of age. He had been sent out to herd his family's geese in against the freezing weather. When his father and brothers found him, he was unrecognizable. He had been torn to pieces; many body parts were missing, and there was blood everywhere. The boy's head, his face frozen in a mix of fear and horror, was found floating in the icy water of a mule trough nearby. Not one goose had been harmed.

Then a family living near the barracks lost three daughters. They had been sent out on their daily chore of milking the family's two remaining cows. The mother was the first to hear their bloodcurdling screams amidst the wild, frightened bovine lowing. The father, running in from a nearby field, prevented his wife from entering the barn—a wise choice, for such a bloodbath met his eyes that he burst from the barn in a screaming fit. Down the center of the barn was a trail of blood littered with chunks of flesh, mixed in with hair and shredded clothing. The daughters had been dragged away, and one cow lay torn into bits in its stall.

Many suggested renegade soldiers were to blame; others blamed the nearby Native American population. But these ideas were quickly dismissed because whatever was killing the people of St. Bernard Parish was, from all appearances, feeding on them as well.

Native Americans and Kentiauk tradesmen appeared in the markets carrying tales of strange creatures being seen in the land. Wolves, the Kentiauks said, larger than any ever seen, were moving in packs along the riverbanks. The Indians had another name for the beasts: "windigo" they called them, skin walkers, men who took on animal form to prey on humankind. Still, although the citizens of New Orleans were concerned about their neighbors in the outlying parishes, and gruesome though the news of the killings was, no one could venture out to investigate. The city was locked in a state of war, and until the battle had been fought, whatever its outcome, nothing could be done about the grisly attacks. But following General Andrew Jackson's great victory over the British at the Battle of New Orleans, there appeared even more evidence that the tales of the Indians and Kentiauks might have borne some truth: the graves of many soldiers buried in the fields of St. Bernard Parish after the battle had been found disturbed and the remains dragged from their coffins and partially devoured on the spot. This, pronounced everyone from priest to shaman, could only be the work of the loup-garou.

The Basque butchers would certainly have been acquainted with the superstitions surrounding the "loup-garou"; the man-wolves were well known in the lore of France.

The Basque butchers would certainly have been acquainted with the superstitions surrounding the "loup-garou"; the man-wolves were well known in the lore of France. Indeed, some of the Basquemen or their ancestors might have encountered these same beasts, and although familiar with regularly subduing and dispatching powerful animals, the Basquemen would have recognized the werewolf as a formidable foe.

In both the Old and New Worlds, the wolf was known as an animal of great power, sometimes weighing twice as much as the average full-grown man. The wolf was swift and could easily travel more than one hundred miles in a day. In addition, the wolf's sharp eyes and hearing, and its movement in packs with others of its kind, gave it a tremendous advantage over its prey. A hunter of deadly efficiency, wolves avoided contact with humans as long as food remained plentiful. But in the bare months of winter or other lean times, the wolf grew bolder, often invading and attacking whole villages. Unlike the dog, the great servant of humanity, the wolf recognized no master, and inevitably this rebelliousness would appeal to some humans.

The Basques of the Pyrenees were known by their French countrymen and other neighbors as a particularly rebellious lot, a quality that had long set them apart and for all the wrong reasons. Over the years strange tales arose to explain the rebelliousness and insular nature of the Basque people. In the fear-ridden years of constant warfare and religious persecution, it was not inconceivable for those trying to understand the Basques to make the leap from fact to fancy. Therefore in Europe they had long been known as cursed with the evil charge of the loup-garou, and though they coexisted with men by the light of day, in the dark hours of the night, the wolfmen devoured human flesh.

In an attempt to quell public excitement and growing suspicion about the butchers, several Capuchin monks of the St. Louis church volunteered to visit the Basquemen. The monks found the men hard at work in the St. Bernard abattoirs, where, since the great victory at the Battle of New Orleans, the holding pens once again overflowed with steady shipments of cattle. The monks found the Basquemen welcoming, in their fashion, and were encouraged when all the men and their families attended an evening mass that was held on the battures.

The womenfolk took great pains over the monks' comfort, feeding them and preparing crude but tidy overnight lodgings. The monks found the Basque children happy and well fed; indeed, the whole settlement appeared to be a group of thriving, hard-working, charitable, and faithful people. The monks' findings, which were quickly disseminated among the common folk of the city, did much to stem the growing tide of superstitious fear that previously had held sway. And as the city prospered in the days following the battle, the memories of the cruel winter slayings faded and were all but forgotten.

But, in fact, the monks and anyone who had an interest in knowing the truth had all been duped. As the Native Americans and the Kentiauk frontiersmen had suspected, and as some had feared, a colony of werewolves had indeed taken up residence in the abattoirs of St. Bernard.

> *As the Native Americans and the Kentiauk frontiersmen had suspected, and as some had feared, a colony of werewolves had indeed taken up residence in the abattoirs of St. Bernard.*

Suspicion arose again in the 1820s, though this time it was confined to the plantations located nearest the busy abattoirs. Over a period of several months in 1821 and 1822 (another cold winter), plantation owners were complaining more frequently to the local constables of the disappearance of livestock—in particular, the valuable oxen used to plough the fields for planting the major crops of sugar and cotton. Without the strength of those great beasts of burden, productivity, and in turn the harvest, was greatly impacted.

The enslaved population were whispering among themselves about the disappearance of the livestock; they had their own explanations, and their local rootworkers were busy trying to determine the true culprit behind the strange events. Soon almost every enslaved person was wearing some kind of talisman or "gree-gree." Then, one cold morning, news spread like wildfire from plantation to plantation of a strange event that allegedly had occurred at the abattoirs the night before.

"Ah see'd it, ah tells yo! Ah see'd it with my own eyes!" Thus began the story of old Jerome, a man enslaved at the old Villere plantation who had been making his way home from what he called "a churching" meeting when he had the most terrible fright of his life. Those around him insisted his previously graying hair had turned an even lighter shade. "Ah knows it!" Jerome said, rubbing his hand over his hair. "Yo hair'd be white, too, if you'da seen what ah seen!" Pressed by his owner and the local constable to relate exactly what he had seen, Jerome went on to tell a fascinating tale.

Jerome was walking westward on the Shell Beach road toward the Villere plantation that he called home. The road took him past a place he didn't like to go by at night. This was the dilapidated mansion of the old Countess, a reclusive Russian woman who everyone said had lost her mind shortly after her arrival here over a decade ago and who lived in the ramshackle remains of her plantation house with only her maid for company.

In sunlight, the long alley of moss-hung oaks and the brace of dark pecan trees rustling over the fading whitewash of the melancholy old mansion had a storybook appeal, as if at any moment a princess would emerge upon the gallery surveying the distant river. But when night fell, the place exuded an entirely different atmosphere: fog-shrouded starlight intermingled with the darkness under the trees, and a foggy miasma floated from the land and lingered around the roadside.

As Jerome approached the old plantation, the frosty stillness of the night seemed to draw in close; his breath, now heavy, hung in a moonlit mist about his head. Eyes glancing from left to right, he picked up his pace to put as much distance between himself and the "old Russian place" as possible. Thinking that whistling might help to lighten his uneasiness, Jerome broke out in a torrent of notes from nameless, half-remembered tunes. Sweat broke on his brow and the hairs on his neck began to rise

Le Loup-Garou, *an engraving by French artist Maurice Sand, was exhibited in Paris at the 1857 Salon at the Académie des Beaux-Arts.*

as Jerome became aware of someone walking along the road ahead of him; Jerome was surprised to find it was a woman.

"Lawd, ma'am," he said as he came up behind her. "Yo sho' gives me a skeer, ah tells yo!" He laughed but the woman made no reply, nor did she turn or in any other way acknowledge him. She was small, slightly built, wearing a cloak and large bonnet against the cold, and Jerome noticed she carried a basket over her arm.

"Sho' is cold out'cheer!" he said now, flapping his arms around himself. Still the woman made no reply. "Den I guess, since we be headin' de same way, yo won't mind me walkin' by you?" The woman shook her head, indicating that she would not. Jerome and the strange woman walked along in silence for what seemed an eternity. The trees grew closer in on either side of the road indicating that they had reached a less-traveled portion; a steady rise meant they were toiling up a low hill.

"Ma'am, is yo' sure yo' alright?" Jerome asked, but suddenly his attention was drawn to something in the road ahead. There, in a patch of wintry starlight where the trees were thinner, were the hulking forms of what Jerome at first mistook for dogs. Taking a few steps closer, down the side of the low hill, it was clear to Jerome that these were like no dogs he had ever seen before. The cold, sobering realization came over Jerome that he was watching two huge wolves at work over some prey, and at the same time he was aware that the strange woman had not slowed her pace but was walking right toward the wolves.

"No, no, no—ma'am!!" Jerome cried and caught up to her. "Don't yo' be gwon near dem wolfs, now! Dey liable tear yo' to pieces!" The woman stopped but did not turn around. Then, for the first time since he had encountered her, she spoke. "Would you hold my basket?" said a sweet, strangely detached voice.

Jerome took the basket from the woman and watched as she moved to untie her bonnet. "Thank you," she said then, and Jerome felt his blood run cold. The voice was coming from the basket, and in the instant he realized this, Jerome watched the bonnet fall away, revealing empty space where a head ought to have been!

Instinctively, he dropped the basket, and to his horror he watched as a woman's head rolled out. Yet the head did not appear to be human. Its wild, once-blond hair was soaked red in blood, its eyes two flames, and a mouth full of razor sharp teeth snapped as the head circled Jerome's feet.

Standing guard over their prey — animal? human? Jerome could not tell — their hackles rose, their bloodied fangs glistened in the dim light, and they stood to their full werewolf height, ready to fight off the vampire creature.

Then, suddenly, all the clothes that had contained the woman's body fell away, revealing a hairless, winged creature, like a great bat. Together with the head, it flew at the wolves. As soon as the creature revealed itself, the wolves in the road ahead became aware of it and stopped their eating. Standing guard over their prey — animal? human? Jerome could not tell — their hackles rose, their bloodied fangs glistened in the dim light, and they stood to their full werewolf height, ready to fight off the vampire creature.

"Oh, lawd, lawd, lawd, lawd!" Jerome was crying as he fell on all fours and crawled into the underbrush.

Jerome escaped as quietly as he could from that horrible place and decided to head back to the still shack as quick as he could. Instead, he was met by a constable out on other business who apprehended him and took him to the nearest home, Highland. It was from there that Jerome's owner came to fetch him, but he was obliged to wait until the sun was fully risen before Jerome could be coaxed into a wagon heading home.

The constable accompanied the men as far as the spot where Jerome's alleged encounter with the battling werewolves and vampire occurred. Strangely, and unfortunately for Jerome, there was no evidence to be found of the event. Jerome's owner rewarded what he considered "drunken, lying insolence" with confining the man to the kitchen by a chain and making him peel endless heaps of potatoes. But Jerome didn't mind. Anything was preferable to what he had seen the previous night.

As had happened during the Battle of New Orleans, the Civil War and the occupation of the city by Union forces did much to impede the livelihood of the Basquemen. Consequently, there were numerous reported sightings of large wolves in the distant areas of the parish, along with the disappearance and mutilation of livestock nearby. But unlike the Battle of New Orleans, the Civil War would bring lasting change to the economic and cultural landscape, in particular with the Emancipation

Proclamation and the freeing of the enslaved. A flood of new labor entered the local market, and in New Orleans especially this was exacerbated with the arrival of first the Irish and then the Sicilians offering a wide variety of cheap, skilled labor. The Basquemen could no longer hold their monopoly over the abattoirs; they suffered greatly through the great snowfalls of 1895 and then World War I. Then, during the years of the Great Depression and the Works Progress Administration, the old abattoirs were finally closed.

Even the great Mississippi River seemed set to conspire against the Basques. Each year the waters encroached more and more upon the shoreline, eking away the batture little by little, eventually forcing the Basquemen to abandon their homes and move inland. Because it was against their nature to assimilate, the Basquemen ultimately moved on, some say into the wilderness regions north of Baton Rouge, others claim into the mountains of the Ozarks.

Whatever their fate, the departure of the Basquemen from the batture truly was the end of the butchermen's culture along that part of the river. It also produced a notable drop in the encounters with werewolves there for many years to come. A drop in sightings, that is, but not an end; it is entirely possible that some remnant of the butchering werewolves still haunts the old areas of St. Bernard Parish to this day.

Bear People

It requires little imagination to understand why the bear became a favorite totem animal wherever they coexisted in the same environment as primitive humans, and why so many clans claim direct descent from an ancestor who was originally a bear. Among all ancient people who encountered the bear and who left some kind of record of those meetings, the powerful, lumbering giant was held in the greatest respect as the one who knew all things, the one who could speak directly with the gods.

When the bear walks upright on its two hind feet, it appears very much like a stout, powerfully built man with short, bandy legs. When it moves through the forest on the hunt, it seems to saunter in a leisurely manner, confidently assured that no one will challenge its majesty. Many tribal

Among the old tribes of Northern Europe, the warriors known as the Berserkir wore bearskin shirts into battle in dedication to the Goddess Ursel, the She-Bear. To wear the bearskin in battle was to become one with the bear's indomitable spirit.

shamans address the bear reverently as "Grandfather," and there is a widespread belief that the spirit of the bear never dies. It is common for traditional Native American medicine priests to adopt "bear" as a part of their name, and shape-shifting shamans frequently take the form of a bear because of its supernatural powers.

Among the old tribes of Northern Europe, the warriors known as the Berserkir wore bearskin shirts into battle in dedication to the Goddess Ursel, the She-Bear. To the Vikings, the bear symbolized the lone champion, prepared to fight to the death in single combat against all odds. To wear the bearskin in battle was to become one with the bear's indomitable spirit.

In the opinion of a number of scholars, the eighth-century saga of Beowulf, the Swedish hero who defeats the monster Grendel and its hideous underwater troll mother, is an example of the "Bear's Son Cycle" found among the folklore of European, Asian, and Native American people. In these sagas, the child has a bear for one of his parents and acquires the strength of a bear to fight supernatural beings for the good of his people.

Writer and researcher Paul Dale Roberts sent a contribution that tells of his meeting with a man who was part Chinook and Modoc Native American and who claimed to shape-shift into the form of a black bear. "Minash," as he wished to be called, lived in Washington State before relocating to California.

Minash said:

> I used to be a hunter and when I fell into a ravine, I startled a mother black bear and her cubs. She swiped my shoulder. [Minash at this time raises up his sleeve to expose three scars.] These are from the mother black bear. I was lucky she didn't kill me. I went home, the worse for wear. I was looking in the mirror and placing hydrogen peroxide antiseptic on my bleeding wound. It was bleeding profusely, and I was cussing underneath my breath. I was mad as hell and wanted to go back out there and kill that mother bear and her cubs. That is when it happened. My spirit guide, an Indian man from long ago, probably a shaman of sorts, appeared in the mirror behind me. He placed one hand on my shoulder, smiled, and vanished. Before I knew it, I felt an inner peace. I no longer wanted to kill those bears. I looked into the mirror and my eyes changed; I had the eyes of a black bear. I looked again, and I had become a bear.

When asked if anyone had seen him change, Tana, Minash's female companion, answered Paul's question by saying that she had seen him change twice. Minash said that he could not change at will but that it happens on special occasions. For example:

> One time my friend was changing his car tire and somehow had his leg underneath his jacked-up car, and the jack got loose and the flat tire pinned his leg. He was screaming. All of a sudden, I shape-shifted into a black bear and lifted the car off his leg. He looked at me and was astonished. He later told me that he saw me shape-shift into a black bear when I lifted the car. He said the shape-shift was only for a minute or so, enough time for me to lift up the car. He now thinks he was delirious during the time from the excruciating pain and imagined what he saw.

Later, after his interview with Minash and Tana, Paul Dale Roberts considered the possibility that one could be a shape-shifter and move from a human body and transform into an animal:

> Could it be that somehow certain people have DNA molecules that interact with our own reality and on the atomic level interact with still another reality? In one reality we are humans, and in an alternate reality, our molecules on the atomic level change—and we discover we are now an animal, such as a bear, wolf or even a bat. Perhaps ancient gifts from our ancient gods were once bestowed upon certain individuals. It is my theory that shape-shifters' ancestors served a purpose of transforming from human to animal and that certain selected humans in our present time carry this unique DNA that contains the properties of transforming from human to animal. The DNA that these unique humans possess places them from our reality into another alternate reality, a reality that their ancestors are too familiar with. Energy cannot be destroyed, but it can be altered, so on the sub-atomic level, on the quantum level, our own bodies are pure energy and changing from a human to a werewolf should not be any kind of problem at all. Of course these are my thoughts, my theories. I just think that if there are stories, legends and myths of normal human beings transforming into animals, there must be some kind of foundation of truth to all of these stories.

Sources:

Davidson, Ellis H. R. *Gods and Myths of the Viking Age*. New York: Barnes & Noble, 1996.

Russell, Jeffrey Burton. *Witchcraft in the Middle Ages*. Ithaca, NY: Cornell University Press, 1972.

Spence, Lewis. *An Encyclopedia of Occultism*. New Hyde Park, NY: University Books, 1960.

Beast of Bray Road

Linda Godfrey (1951–2022), a journalist and prolific author, was one of the key figures in the field of research and writing in the world of werewolves, dogmen, skin walkers, and shape-shifters. Not only that, but Linda was someone who didn't just do her work from the internet: road trips and expeditions were essential for her work. With that established, let's take a deep look at the werewolf-driven work Linda did over the course of 30 years. She began her first account with these words: "The story first came to my attention in about 1991 from a woman who had heard rumors going around here in Elkhorn, Wisconsin, and particularly in the high school, that people had been seeing something like a werewolf, a wolflike creature, or a wolfman. They didn't really know what it was. But some were saying it was a werewolf. And the werewolf tag has just gotten used because I think that people really didn't know what else to call it." A phenomenon—an undeniably dangerous and sinister one—was growing. As a journalist, Linda wanted the answers to the creepy riddle.

Though first reported as early as 1936, the Beast of Bray Road didn't join the ranks of popular cryptids until reporter Linda Godfrey began her research in 1991.

Linda said to me: "I started checking it out. I talked to the editor of *The Week* newspaper here, which I used to work for. He said, 'Why don't you check around a little bit and see what you hear?' This was about the end of December. And being a weekly newspaper, we weren't really hard news; we were much more feature oriented. I asked a friend who had a daughter in high school about the story, and she said, 'Oh yeah, that's what everybody's talking about.' So I started my investigations and got one name from the woman who told me about it. She was also a part-time bus driver."

Things began to change radically when none other than U.S. government employees got involved in the enigma. Linda said of this angle: "In my first phone call to the bus driver, she told me that she had called the county animal control officer. Of course, when you're a reporter, any time you have a chance to find anything official, that's where you go. I went to see him, and sure enough, he had a folder in his file drawer that he had actually marked 'Werewolf,' in a tongue-in-cheek way.

"When you have a public official, the county animal control officer, who has a folder marked 'Werewolf,' that's news."

"People had been phoning in to him to say that they had seen something. They didn't know what it was. But from their descriptions, that's what he had put. So, of course, that made it a news story. When you have a public official, the county animal control officer, who has a folder marked 'Werewolf,' that's news. It was very unusual." Indeed, it was unusual; it's exceedingly rare that a government agency will investigate the sighting of something that looks like a werewolf.

That local authorities in the area *did* get involved made it almost inevitable that the story would grow. And grow. A name grew for the beast that people were seeing, too: the Beast of Bray Road, named for the primary road that runs through the city of Elkhorn. The story was a journalist's dream. Indeed, Linda quickly realized this was a mystery that wasn't going away:

"It just took off from there, and I kept finding more and more witnesses," said Linda, expanding: "At first they all wanted to stay private. I remember talking about it with the editor, and we thought we would run the story because it would be over in a couple of weeks. The story was picked up by Associated Press. Once it hit AP, everything broke loose, and people were just going crazy. All the Milwaukee TV stations came out and did stories, dug until they found the witnesses, and got them to change their minds and go on camera, which some of them later regretted. And which I kind of regret, because it really made them reluctant, and kind of hampered the investigation." There was more to the story, it seems — something that sounded incredible: Wisconsin had a real-life werewolf in its midst. Everyone in the area was talking — or at least whispering:

"They were all mostly saying they had seen something which was much larger than normal, sometimes on two legs and sometimes on four, with a wolfish head. Some described it as a German shepherd–like head, pointed ears, very long, coarse, shaggy, and wild-looking fur. One thing they all mentioned was that it would turn and look at them and gaze fearlessly or leer at them, and it was at that point that they all got really frightened. Everybody who has seen it — with the exception of one — has been extremely scared because it's so out of the ordinary. It was something they couldn't identify and didn't appear to be afraid of them. It would just casually turn around and disappear into the brush. It was never just out in the open where it didn't have some sort of hiding place. There was always a cornfield or some brush or some woods. So, that was pretty much the start of it."

That may have been the start, but things soon grew: the local folks were in a state of terror, and more and more people were seeing this "animal anomaly."

"Once that got out," Linda told me, "other people called me and got in touch with me, and I sort of became the unofficial clearinghouse. And we called it the 'Beast of Bray Road' because I've always been reluctant to call it a werewolf. The original sightings were in an area known as Bray Road, which is outside of Elkhorn." It wasn't long before folks around town were trying to figure out what the creature—or creatures—might be.

"Everybody seems to have an opinion about this that they are eager to make known and defend," Linda explained. "I personally don't think there are enough facts for anybody to come to a conclusion. I have a couple of dozen sightings, at least. A few of them are second-hand, and they date back to 1936. And they aren't all around Bray Road. Quite a number are in the next county, Jefferson. I've had a woman write me who insists it's a wolf. And I think a lot of people subscribe to that theory: yes, it's definitely a wolf and can't be anything else. But that doesn't explain the large size."

The monstrous matters got bigger: "We've had all sorts of theories: mental patients escaping or some crazy guy running around. A hoaxer is another theory—that it's somebody running around in a werewolf suit. One or two could have been that, but I tend to have my doubts about that, because the incidents are isolated and not close together. One of the sightings was on Halloween, but that's also from one of the people who got a really good look at it, and they're sure it wasn't a human in a costume. Otherwise, most of them have been in really remote locations where, if they were going to hoax, the person would have to have been sitting out there in the cold just waiting for somebody to come along. So if it's a hoaxer, my hat's off to them. But I tend not to think that's the case. I don't rule it out completely because once publicity gets out, things like that can happen."

Eventually, things changed—and to an incredible degree: another of the menacing monsters appeared on the scene. *Now there were two of the things*. Linda detailed this incredible development to me:

"Two hunters quite a bit farther north saw what looked like two 'dog children' standing up in the woods. They were too scared to shoot when they saw them. The creatures were not tall; they were juvenile-looking, standing upright, which is what scared the men. But outside of this encounter, it's a single creature. Most of the sightings I receive aren't recent, and so people can't remember too well what the moon was like. But most of the sightings occur around the fall when the cornfields get big and there's really good hiding cover. So, that's anywhere from late August through November. And I've had some sightings from the spring. But there are other theories as well for what is going on."

> *"Occasionally I'll get letters from people who say they are lycanthropes themselves, and their theory is that this is an immature, real werewolf and it cannot control its transformation."*

While some people were sure the area had a werewolf in the area, there were more than a few alternative ideas. Linda reeled them out to me: "Occasionally I'll get letters from people who say they are lycanthropes themselves, and their theory is that this is an immature, real werewolf and it cannot control its transformation, and that's why it allows itself to be seen occasionally. They are completely convinced of that. And there are people who believe it's a manifestation of satanic forces, that it's a part of a demonic thing. They point to various occult activities around here.

"There are also people who try to link it to UFOs. Then there's the theory it's just a dog. One woman, a medium, thought that it was a natural animal but didn't know what it was. And there are a lot of people out here that do wolf-hybridizations, and I've thought to myself you'd get something like that. But that doesn't explain the upright posture. Then there's the theory that it's a creature known as the Windigo or Wendigo, which is featured in Indian legends and is supposedly a supernatural creature that lives on human flesh. But none of the descriptions from the Windigo legends describe a creature with canine features."

Linda wasn't done. Before she knew it, Bigfoot was on the scene, more or less: "There's another possibility: I think a lot of these people are seeing different things. And that when they heard somebody else talk about something, there's a tendency to say, 'Oh, that must be what I saw.' There's really no way to know. And there are differences in some of the sightings. I've had people ask me, 'Are you sure this isn't Bigfoot?' Most of the sightings really don't sound like what people report as Bigfoot. But a couple of them do. There's one man who saw it in the 1960s in a different area of the county, who insists positively that he saw a Bigfoot and doesn't want anyone saying he saw a werewolf. And the terrain around here isn't really the typical sort of Bigfoot terrain of forests where people usually report these things. We do have woods and a big state forest, but it's a narrow band of forest. It's a lot of prairie, which is not what you would think a Bigfoot would live in. But you never know. I've also had the baboon theory, which I find extremely unlikely."

Of her first book on the subject, *The Beast of Bray Road* (2003), Linda said to me: "Part of the angle of the book is looking at this as a sociological phenomenon and how something that a number of people see turns into a legend. And it has become that, a little bit. Personally, I'm still happy to leave it an open mystery. I don't have a feeling that it has to be pinned down." Linda's thirty-some years of investigations continued until her death in 2022.

Sources:

Redfern, Nick. Interview with Linda Godfrey.

Beauty and the Beast

The most famous of the ancient beast marriage tales that has survived into modern times is "Beauty and the Beast." Stories of a human married to an animal are popular in folklore throughout the world, and in many cultures it is the union between animal and human that produces the tribe or the clan that perpetuates the legend.

The version most familiar to contemporary audiences is the one recorded by Madame Le Prince de Beaumont in her *Magasin des Enfans* (1756). In this telling, Beauty is the youngest of three daughters of a merchant who is traveling away from home in a desperate effort to reestablish his failing business. While on his journey, he is caught in a terrible storm and seeks refuge in a castle. During his stay, he is provided with all the blessings of hospitality, but he sees no one. The next morning as he is leaving, he admires his unseen host's magnificent garden, and his thoughts turn to Beauty. Before he left home, the two oldest daughters begged for elegant gowns and expensive gifts, but all Beauty wished from her father was a rose. Surely, he imagines, no one could object to his taking just one rose from the garden.

British illustrator Warwick Goble's 1913 illustration depicts the moment Beauty returns from her prolonged absence to discover the Beast close to death.

The enraged Beast suddenly appears, prepared to slay the merchant for such a breach of etiquette. When he hears the frightened man's explanation, he agrees to let him go on the condition that one of his daughters must return to his castle. If this demand is not met, Beast will hunt him down and kill him.

Beauty volunteers, and her purity of heart allows her to overlook Beast's monstrous appearance. She is treated with the greatest of courtesy and respect by the Beast, and she stays with him until she looks in Beast's magic mirror and sees that her father is very ill. She is granted her wish to return to visit her father for only one week. The weeks go by, and Beauty stays with her father until she has a vision in which she sees that Beast is dying. Beauty rushes back to the castle and promises to become Beast's wife, and her love dissolves a curse that had transformed a handsome young man into an ugly monster.

Many scholars have stated that in the original version of the tale, the beast was a werewolf. While there is no folklore that suggests a werewolf can be redeemed by the love of virtuous maiden, the tale could represent love and compassion as antidotes for the bestial impulses within all humans. Variations of "Beauty and the Beast" abound throughout the world. In certain regions of the Middle East, Beast is a boar, complete with large, curved tusks. Among some African cultures, he is a crocodile.

"Beauty and the Beast" has become such an integral archetypal element within the psyche that it has been filmed at least seven times, including the award-winning Walt Disney animated version released in 1991 and Disney's 2017 live-action adaptation starring Emma Watson and Dan Stevens. A contemporary interpretation of the story, transforming the Beast's castle to a subterranean world beneath New York City, became a successful television series (*Beauty and the Beast*, 1987–1990) starring Linda Hamilton and Ron Perlman.

Sources:

Gaskell, G. A. *Dictionary of All Scriptures and Myths*. Avenel, NJ: Gramercy Books, 1981.

Hazlitt, W. C. *Dictionary of Faiths & Folklore*. London: Studio Editions, 1995.

Larousse Dictionary of World Folklore. New York: Larousse, 1995.

Becoming a Werewolf

There are two basic ways by which one might become a werewolf: voluntary and involuntary.

According to the ancient Greeks, any skilled sorcerers who so chose could become a werewolf. Throughout history, self-professed werewolves have mentioned a "magic girdle," which they wear about their middles, or a "magic salve," which they apply liberally to their naked bodies. Others tell of inhaling or imbibing certain potions.

Magical texts advise those who wish to become a werewolf to disrobe, rub a magical ointment freely over their flesh, place a girdle made of human or wolf skin around their waist, then cover their entire body with the

Among other ways to voluntarily become a werewolf, it is said that one method involves drinking water from the track of a wolf.

pelt of a wolf. To accelerate the process, they should drink beer mixed with blood and chant a particular magical formula.

Some werewolves claimed to have achieved their shape-shifting ability by having drunk water from the paw print of a wolf. Once this had been accomplished, they ate the brains of a wolf and slept in its lair.

One ancient text prescribes a ritual for the magician who is eager to become a shape-shifter. He is told to wait until the night of a full moon, then enter the forest at midnight. Then, according to the instructions:

> Draw two concentric circles on the ground, one six feet in diameter, the other fourteen feet in diameter. Build a fire in the center of the inner circle and place a tripod over the flames. Suspend from the tripod an iron pot full of water. Bring the water to a full boil and throw into the pot a handful each of aloe, hemlock, poppy seed, and nightshade. As the ingredients are being stirred in the iron pot, call aloud to the spirits of the restless dead, the spirits of the foul darkness, the spirits of the hateful, and the spirits of werewolves and satyrs.

Once the summons for the various spirits of darkness have been shouted into the night, the person who aspires to become a werewolf should strip off all of his clothing and smear his body with the fat of a freshly killed animal that has been mixed with anise, camphor, and opium. The next step is to take the wolf skin that he has brought with him, wrap it around his middle like a loincloth, then kneel at the boundaries of the large circle and remain in that position until the fire dies out. When this happens, the power that the disciple of darkness has summoned should make its presence known to him.

If the magician has done everything correctly, the dark force will announce its presence by loud shrieks and groans. Later, if the would-be werewolf has not been terrified and frightened away by the Dark One's awful screams and groans, the entity will materialize in any number of forms, most likely that of a horrible half-human, half-beast monster. Once it has manifested in whatever form it desires, the Dark One's force will conduct its transaction with the magician and allow him henceforth to assume the shape of a wolf whenever he wears his wolf-skin loincloth.

By far the most familiar involuntary manner in which one becomes a werewolf is to be bitten or scratched by such a creature. In the same category would be those men and women who were transformed into werewolves by being cursed for their sins or by being the victim of a sorcerer's incantations.

Another involuntary means of becoming a werewolf, according to some old traditions, is to be born on Christmas Eve. The very process of one's birth on that sacred night, so say certain ecclesiastical scholars, is an act of blasphemy since it detracts from the full attention to be given to the nativity of Jesus. Thus, those born on that night are condemned to be werewolves unless they prove themselves to be pious beyond reproach in all thoughts, words, and deeds throughout their lifetimes.

Sources:

Eisler, Robert. *Man into Wolf.* London: Spring Books, 1948.

Spence, Lewis. *An Encyclopedia of Occultism.* New Hyde Park, NY: University Books, 1960.

Berserks

Since earliest times, levelheaded persons have observed that when a man becomes absolutely filled with rage, he is no longer quite human. One may say that he has given the control of his reason back to the beast within — or one might say that the enraged man is "beside himself," that he has become something more than himself. Either the beast within or some other supernatural power has now endowed the angered, raging man with more strength and more deadly determination to work harm against his enemy than he had before he became so angry — so berserk.

Among the old tribes of northern Europe, the warriors known as the Berserks (in Old Norse, Berserkir) were so filled with the savage joy of battle that they tossed aside their armor and wore only bearskin shirts into battle in honor of the Goddess Ursel, the She-Bear. To the Germanic tribes, the bear was a masterful martial artist, and the angered she-bear protecting her cubs was the most formidable challenge a warrior could ever face. The bearskin shirts were worn in the hope that the wearers could absorb the great beast's fighting prowess and her enormous endurance and strength.

Those Viking Berserkirs who considered the wolf to be their totem donned a wolf coat and charged into battle howling like wolves, giving warning to the enemy that they were a cross between man and beast and that they would soon change their shapes and become even more vicious in their attack.

The oldest reference to Berserks is in a poem composed to honor the Norwegian king Harald Fairhair after his victory at Hafrsfjord about 872. In the thirteenth century, the skald (poet) Snorri gives a detailed account of Berserks in action at the beginning of his *Ynglinga* saga 6:

> Odin's men went (into battle) without armour and were as wild as dogs or wolves. They bit their shields and were stronger than bears or bulls. They killed many men but they themselves were unharmed either by fire or by iron; this is what is called berserksgangr (berserk-fury).

Snorri indicates the connection between Odin and the Berserks and Ulf-heonar (wolf skins), stating that they are "his warriors." It should be noted that in addition to being the father of the gods and the god of war, Odin/Wodan is also the god of cult ecstasy. His very name confirms this, Rudolf Simek points out, since in Old Norse it means "fury." Simek continues, "The berserk-fury bears all the traits of ecstatic states of consciousness: insensitivity to fire and pain (as well as not bleeding) are phenomena known from shamanic trances." Therefore, in his opinion, the concept of Berserks and the wolf skins originates "in special forms of old masked cults in Scandinavia, which manifest themselves in the existence of masked bands of warriors dedicated to Odin."

Sources:

Davidson, Ellis H. R. *Gods and Myths of the Viking Age.* New York: Barnes & Noble, 1996.

Simek, Rudolf. *Dictionary of Northern Mythology.* Translated by Angela Hall. Rochester, NY: Boydell & Brewer, 1993.

Bigfoot and a Baby

Stan Gordon is one of the world's leading figures in the field of Bigfoot investigations, particularly cases that are steeped in mystifying high strangeness. In October 1973, Gordon investigated a very weird case that was focused upon the late-night landing of a brightly lit UFO in a rural part of Pennsylvania; it's a case that appears in Gordon's 2010 book *Silent Invasion*. As a group of concerned and inquisitive locals reached the area of farmland where the UFO touched down, they heard what seemed to be, oddly enough, a crying baby.

As the curious investigators got closer, they could see a significantly sized dome-like object sitting in the darkness of a large pasture. If that was not enough, to their horror, they beheld a pair of large and lumbering Bigfoot looming out of the shadows that proceeded to head toward them. Panic immediately erupted, and the group scattered, firing their guns at the beasts as they did so. The bullets had no effect, and no evidence of a baby—in distress or otherwise—was ever found. Of course, their concern for the baby was the key thing that prompted them to approach the UFO—which, in all likelihood, was the goal of the sly, mimicking monsters in their midst.

Elsewhere, Bob Carroll, who I chatted with at the October 1996 Staffordshire UFO Conference in Cannock, England, had a very similar encounter in January or February of either 1972 or 1973 at Bridge 39 on England's Shropshire Union Canal—the very location that spawned the diabolical Man-Monkey in January 1879, as described elsewhere. It was the early hours of the morning, and Carroll, a truck driver, was driving to the nearby town of Newport, where he was due to make a 6:00 a.m. delivery, having picked up a pallet of paint from a depot in the city of Leicester the previous evening. Everything was completely normal until he approached that damned bridge.

Stressing that everything was over in a few seconds, Carroll said that it was his natural instinct to slow down as he reached the bridge. As he did so, he was shocked to see from his cab a hair-covered humanoid race out of the trees, cross the bridge, and head down to the old canal. Carroll was amazed by the incredible speed and apparent agility of the beast as it bounded across the road and was quickly lost to sight. He estimated that the creature was four and a half to five feet tall at most, that it had dark fur, and that it looked very muscular. Stressing that he had always been a gung-ho type, Carroll quickly pulled over to the side of the road, turned on his truck's hazard lights, and ran back to the scene of his bizarre and brief experience.

On reaching the canal bridge, Carroll quickly peered over both sides; however, the total lack of light made it fairly impossible for him to see much. But there *was* one other odd thing that Carroll was keen to relate—something that, by now, will be as familiar as it is disturbing.

As he leaned over the bridge, he heard what he was absolutely sure were the loud and distressing cries of a baby. In fact, he said, the cries were *too* loud—almost ear-splitting and echoing. Despite feeling that he needed to help the "baby," Carroll almost immediately developed a feeling that this was no baby. Rather, he felt, it was a creature that is known locally in the area as the Man-Monkey, an ape-like creature that is said to be able to change its form into multiple other creatures and was cunningly trying to lure him down to the canal for an encounter of the fatal kind. Carroll, probably very wisely, did not act upon the beast's macabre ruse. It may well have been a decision that saved his life.

Sources:

Redfern, Nick. Interview with Bob Carroll, September 1996.

Black Dogs

While the Somerset region in England has a tradition of a large, benevolent black dog that accompanies lone travelers as a kind of protector and guide, the vast majority of black dog folklore depicts the dark canine as an ominous creature that forebodes death to those who behold it.

Great Britain seems to have more than its share of demonic hounds. In Sidney Paget's iconic illustration for The Hound of the Baskervilles, *Sherlock Holmes and Dr. Watson catch sight of the tale's title character.*

Great Britain, especially, seems to have more than its share of demonic hounds. The very glance from the devilish eyes of the black hound of Okehampton Castle on Dartmoor means death within the year. The Black Dog Woods in Wiltshire are haunted by a black dog whose appearance signals a death before Christmas. Knaith, Lincolnshire, is a site where many frightened travelers have seen a large black dog with a woman's face.

According to an old story that is often told in England, a terrifying thunderstorm descended on Bungay on Sunday, August 4, 1577. The storm transformed the day into a darkness with rain, hail, thunder, and lightning beyond all imagining. Fearing the worst, a number of the townsfolk gathered in St. Mary's Church to pray for mercy.

As the lore tells it, it was while the people knelt in fear and prayed for deliverance that a large black hellhound manifested suddenly in their midst. Without any challenge from the cowering congregation, the massive black hound charged many members of the church with its terrible claws and large fangs. According to a verse taken from a pamphlet published by Rev. Abraham Fleming in 1577, "All down the church in midst of fire, the hellish monster flew, and passing onward to the quire, he many people slew."

After the hellhound had finished ravishing St. Mary's Church and chewing up a good number of its members, tradition has it that the creature next appeared in Blythburgh Church. Its appetite for human flesh had merely been whetted by its attack on the people of Bungay, for it viciously mauled and killed more churchgoers at Blythburgh.

According to the accounts of the hellhound's attack at Bungay, the beast used more than its teeth and claws to kill. Fleming testified that in some instances, the monster wrung the necks of two churchgoers at the same time, one victim in each of its paws as it stood upright.

At Blythburgh, the hellhound burst through the church doors, ran into the nave, then dashed up the aisle, killing a man and a boy. In addition to leaving bodies strewn about before it departed the church, the monster left numerous scorch marks about the church — marks that people swear can still be seen to this day.

For over four hundred years, Newgate prison has been haunted by the Black Dog, which appears shortly before executions. According to legend, in 1596 a man named Scholler was brought into the prison to face accusations of Witchcraft. Before the man could even come to trial, starving prisoners had killed and eaten him. Not long thereafter, the Black Dog appeared, its huge canine jaws eager for revenge. Whether the phantom hound was the spirit of Scholler returned in another form or his familiar come to avenge its master, the cannibalistic prisoners were so terrified of the apparition that they murdered their jailers and escaped. According to the legend, however, the Black Dog hunted down each one of the men who had dined on Scholler. Then, its mission of revenge completed, it returned to Newgate to haunt the prison walls.

In August 1977, before serial killer David Berkowitz was sentenced to 365 years in prison, he stated that he had been ordered to kill his victims by demons speaking through his neighbor's black Labrador.

Sources:

Gaskell, G. A. *Dictionary of All Scriptures and Myths.* Avenel, NJ: Gramercy Books, 1981.

Steiger, Brad. *Real Monsters, Gruesome Critters, and Beasts from the Darkside.* Canton, MI: Visible Ink Press, 2011.

Wright, Bruce Lanier. "Hell Hounds and Ghost Dogs." *Strange Magazine* 19, Spring 1998.

Boguet, Henri (1550–1619)

In 1598, Perrenette Gandillon, a werewolf, was seen attacking two small girls who were picking strawberries near a village located in the Jura Mountains. When the girls' 16-year-old brother came to defend them with a knife, the werewolf grabbed the knife away from him and slashed his throat. Enraged villagers, hearing the cries and sounds of struggle, cornered the werewolf and clubbed it to death. Amazed, they beheld the grotesque beast in its death throes turn into the nude body of a young woman they recognized as Perrenette Gandillon.

In his *Discours des Sorciers* (1610), Henri Boguet, the eminent judge of Saint-Claude in the Jura Mountains, writes that an official investigation of the matter led to the arrest of the entire Gandillon family, and he states that he personally examined and observed them while they were in prison. According to his testimony, the Gandillons walked on all fours and howled like beasts. Their eyes turned red and gleaming; their hair sprouted; their teeth became long and sharp; their fingernails turned horny and clawlike.

Antoinette Gandillon freely admitted to being a werewolf and said that she had had intercourse with Satan when he assumed the form of a goat.

Her brother, Pierre, was accused of luring children to a Satanic Sabbat, where he turned himself into a wolf and killed and ate them. Pierre's son, Georges, confessed that he had become a wolf by smearing himself with a special salve. When the Gandillon family hunted, they said that they ran on all fours to bring down their victims. Antoinette, Pierre, and Georges were convicted as werewolves by Judge Boguet, and they were burned at the stake in 1598.

As a judge, Boguet was known for his cruelty, especially toward children. He had no doubt that Satan gifted Witches with the ability to change shape into a variety of animal forms, especially the wolf, so that they might devour humans, and the cat, so they might better prowl by night. In another of the cases recounted in *Discours des Sorciers*, he tells of eight-year-old Louise Maillat, who in the summer of 1598 was possessed by five demons: wolf, cat, dog, jolly, and griffon. In addition, the little girl was accused of shape-shifting into the form of a wolf.

Sources:

Masters, R. E. L. *Eros and Evil*. New York: The Julian Press, 1962.

Trevor-Roper, H. R. *The European Witch-Craze*. New York: Harper & Row, 1967.

Bridges

All across the world, one can find tales of strange creatures that lurk on, around, and below ancient bridges. More than a few of those tales revolve around the world of the shape-shifter. They appear to have a particular liking for bridges — something worth keeping in mind should you find yourself crossing an old bridge late one night when the moon is full.

Her name might be inclined to provoke laughter and amusement in some quarters, but there is nothing to joke about when it comes to the matter of the Donkey Woman of San Antonio, Texas. She is a terrifying shape-shifter who haunts a particular old bridge in a suburb of San Antonio known as Elm Creek. Her strange story is one that began in the latter part of the nineteenth century. As the old tale goes, the woman in question resided with her family in a run-down wooden shack on the edge of the creek in question. They earned their living from raising chickens, pigs, and goats and selling them to the local folk. Life was hard, but the woman, her husband, and her two children — a boy and a girl — got by and, by all accounts, had a happy life. That is, until one day when a certain man arrived on the scene, and tragedy and death soon followed in his ominous wake.

Bridges around the world have earned a reputation for being places where things mysterious and magical can happen.

Although the family did not know the man, they were fully aware of his reputation—that of a cruel, spoilt local tyrant. In his early twenties, the man didn't need to work: his father was a powerful figure in a nearby community who had a large house, acres upon acres of land, and a great deal of money, much of which went to the son. He was a disturbing character who got his kicks from hurting and even killing animals. When the man happened to be riding near the family home one particular morning, he caught sight of their pet mule doing nothing but happily munching on the grass of the small field that the family owned.

The man brought his horse to a standstill, jumped off it, and began punching the mule's face and body. When the mule cried out, both husband and wife ran to the field to see what on earth was going down; their first thought was that the mule was being attacked by the likes of a mountain lion or something similar. When, however, they saw the young man assaulting their mule, they quickly retaliated with a barrage of rocks, several of which caught the man on the arms and back. He immediately turned his attention away from the mule and vowed that they would pay for their actions—ironically, actions that his crazed character had provoked in the first place. And pay they did, unfortunately.

In the early hours of the following morning, as the landscape was blanketed by darkness, a group of men hired by that aforementioned spoilt tyrant stealthily descended on the family home. They torched it as the family slept. Such was the speed with which the old wooden building burned that the two children were unfortunately burnt to death. As for their father, he received a bullet to the brain, which killed him instantly. The woman, meanwhile, was fried to a crisp and just about managed to stagger her way to Elm Creek, into which she plunged, never to be seen again. At least, not in human form.

In the immediate years that followed, reports regularly surfaced of sightings of a frightening-looking woman with the head of what appeared to be a donkey. She would prowl around the area where her dead family had lived and her destroyed home once stood. That the skin of the strange woman was described as blackened, burnt, and smoldering is a solid indication that this was the spectral form of the murdered woman. There was, however, another aspect to this saga that revolves around the matter of shape-shifting.

A local rumor—which persists to this very day in the Elm Creek area of San Antonio—suggests that the donkey woman returned from the grave as not simply a woman with a donkey's head but as a combination of human and mule. As the story goes, the spirit form of the woman, angered by what was done to her family and their pet mule, returned to our plane of existence in the form of what might most accurately be termed a mule-woman. She has most often been seen at what is called Elm Creek Bridge. Could it be the case that after death, we can come back and shape-shift into the form of something that is half-animal and half-human? That is precisely the theory that circulates among those who live in the Elm Creek area and who take the legend of the animal-woman very seriously. Even in the twenty-first century, shape-shifting in South Texas is perceived as being all too real. Perhaps the people of the area know something the rest of us do not.

C

Cambrensis, Giraldus (c. 1146–1220)

Until the end of the eighteenth century, Ireland was known in England as "the Wolfland," a country that abounded with accounts of werewolves. As early as the twelfth century, Giraldus Cambrensis (in his account *Topographia Hibernica*) tells of a priest who was met by a wolf in Meath who beseeched the cleric to accompany him to be with his dying wife.

The wolf explained that they had been natives of Ossory, whose people had been cursed for their wickedness by St. Natalis to change their shapes into that of wolves for a period of seven years. The priest was at last persuaded to give the she-wolf the sacrament when she was able to turn her skin down a little and reveal that she was an old woman.

Sources:

Eisler, Robert. *Man into Wolf*. London: Spring Books, 1948.

Cannibalism

There are a number of serious scholars who believe that we are all descended from carnivorous lycanthropes. Although humankind may have begun as peaceful tribes of fruit-collecting, seed-planting, root-digging agriculturalists, climatic changes at the end of the last pluvial period forced our ancestors to become meat-eaters—and sometimes meat could only be found in the flesh of other humans. While child-bearing women and children huddled in their caves or huts, human wolf packs attired in wolf skins hunted down whatever meat entered their territory—animals or slain members of other tribes. Thus it is thought by some that all humans bear the genes of the werewolf, the man-beast who will eat even his fellows to become the fittest to survive.

At the same time, some scholars argue, there exists an atavistic sense of guilt within the collective human psyche that our species so freely

Ingrained in our history and even our DNA, cannibalism appears often in our myths, legends, and literature. In one tale, the Arcadian king Lycaon served his own son's flesh to Zeus, who in turn transformed the man into a wolf—the origin story of the term lycanthropy.

partakes of the flesh of other beings to increase the bulk of our own flesh. Thus, while the eating of all flesh is at best a necessary evil, to taste human flesh would be the most abhorrent of taboos.

Of course, the strict vegetarian may consider the consumption of any creature's flesh to be as bad as cannibalism, but for some unbalanced minds, breaking the ancient taboo of dining on the meat of one's own kind may represent the greatest single act of rebellion against the rules of established decency, proper social behavior, and ecclesiastical doctrines. And, in a sense that is extremely sickening to the sensitive mind and the weak of stomach, there may also be a great empowerment in eating the flesh of one's enemies. How better to gain the strength of a mighty foe than to eat his flesh and absorb his prowess? And how better for a werewolf to achieve the strength of a dozen men than to eat a dozen men? Furthermore, as frightening as it may seem to the sensibilities of twenty-first-century idealists, we still have any number of cannibals among us.

> *For some unbalanced minds, breaking the ancient taboo of dining on the meat of one's own kind may represent the greatest single act of rebellion against the rules of established decency.*

In July 1970, tall, bearded Stanley Dean Baker contacted Detective Dempsey Biley of Monterey County, California, and the resident FBI agent at the substation and convinced the astonished officers that he had a rather unique problem. "I am a cannibal," Baker confessed.

Baker explained that he had killed and dismembered a young social worker, James Schlosser, who had made the fatal mistake of giving him a ride outside of Yellowstone Park. He admitted murdering Schlosser while he slept, then cutting out his heart and eating it.

Investigating officers discovered a blood-stained survival knife near a riverbank and noticed a patch of ground saturated with blood. To their disgust, the officers found what appeared to be human bone fragments, pieces of flesh, teeth, and what appeared to be the remains of a human ear. Informants came forward to relate ghastly accounts of Baker's demonic activities around his home base of Sheridan, Wyoming. A teenage boy told of devil worshipping rites that had occurred in the Big Horn Mountains. He testified that small wild animals had been eaten alive and human blood had been drunk.

In 1993, Omaima Nelson testified before a court in Orange County, California, that after she and her husband Bill quarreled, she struck him in the head 24 times with an iron, then stabbed him with a knife. Next, the 24-year-old woman hacked his body into pieces with a meat cleaver, cut all the flesh from his bones, and ground the leftovers in the garbage disposal. Twelve hours later, she fried her husband's hands and feet, baked his head in the oven, and stored it in the refrigerator.

When these tasks were completed, she told court-appointed psychiatrist David Sheffner, she barbecued her husband's ribs. She sat at the table and commented that the ribs were sweet and delicious — nice and tender.

In January 1998, South African police in Johannesburg found the mutilated remains of three children with their heads and feet hacked off and feared that 12 other missing children had met a similar fate. Certain tribal shamans in South Africa reportedly seek human flesh to add special potency to their mystical potions. The flesh of children is thought to be the most powerful.

Sources:
Eisler, Robert. *Man into Wolf*. London: Spring Books, 1948.
Steiger, Brad. *Bizarre Crime*. New York: Signet, 1992.

Cannibalism in the U.K.

Jon Downes, director of the Centre for Fortean Zoology, notes of the wild men seen in the counties of Devon and Cornwall: "From the Cannibals of Clovelly to the Brew Crew of Treworgey, the whole area has attracted people who wish to live outside of our recognized society; and these people have often degenerated into a wild and lawless existence, sometimes even reverting to a surprisingly primitive lifestyle." They are not of the hairy and subhuman variety, such as true werewolves, but they are, by definition, men living wild, sometimes *very* wild, and in quite recent times. Thus, in their own odd and unique ways they have become staple parts of the legend of the British wild or wolf man. Here we will focus on the alleged cannibals among them.

Preserved in an eight-page chapbook in the Pearse-Chope collection at the Bideford Library in Devon is a sensational and controversial story of one John Gregg and his assorted family of murderers and thieves. The text is estimated to date from the latter part of the eighteenth century and recounts the story of how the Gregg family took up residence in a cave near Clovelly on the north coast of Devon in the 1700s, and where they were to live for an astonishing 25 years.

So the legend goes, during this period they passed their time by robbing more than a thousand unfortunates and merrily devoured the corpses of all those they robbed. Such was the horror the story generated that even the king himself—along with 400 men—allegedly resolved to bring to an end their prehistoric-like and abominable existence. The cave was supposedly discovered and reportedly contained, according to the chapbook, "such a multitude of arms, legs, thighs, hands and feet, of men, women and children hung up in rows, like dry'd beef and a great many lying in pickle." Gregg's distinctly less-than-charming family was found to consist of a wife, eight sons, six daughters, 18 grandsons, and 14 granddaughters all begotten by incest, many said to have been as mad as hatters, and all of whom were taken to Exeter and on the following day executed at Plymouth without trial.

It was suggested *very* convincingly by A. D. Hippisley-Coxe, in his 1981 book *The Cannibals of Clovelly: Fact or Fiction*, that this bizarre

Clovelly Harbour, in southwest England's County Devon, was the setting for fantastic tales of cannibalism. The likely truth was only slightly less grisly: that the stories served as a smokescreen to ward off discovery of murderous, thieving smugglers.

and horrific tale was simply that: a tale, and one created to ensure that the superstitious locals kept away from the myriad local caves used by smugglers at the time. Indeed, the area around Bideford and Clovelly *was* a hotbed for smuggling.

Roughly the same legend appears in a number of other chapbooks, such as *The Legend of Sawney Beane*, which places the scene of the action in Galloway, Scotland. The tale of Sawney Beane was first recorded in 1734 in *A General and True History of the Lives and Actions of the Most Famous Highwaymen* by Captain Charles Johnson, a pseudonym of none other than Daniel Defoe, who had visited north Devon as recounted in his *Tour through the Whole Island of Great Britain* and from where, in 1714, he reported that he "could not find any foreign commerce, except it be what we call smuggling."

So we have a story of people gone wild—horrifically so, in the saga of the Clovelly cannibals—but one so steeped in legend, folklore, and probably a high degree of fabrication that the complete picture will probably never become clear to the point where it satisfies everyone who has sought out the truth of the matter.

Sources:

Redfern, Nick. Interview with Jonathan Downes, Centre for Fortean Zoology, 2012.

Cat Men and Women

There is perhaps no animal on Earth that inspires such lengths of devotion and dedication—and such animosity and abhorrence—as the cat. In European tradition, the black cat is the favorite familiar of the Witch, and during the course of the Inquisition, almost as many cats as Witches were condemned to be burned at the stake.

An old black-letter book titled *Beware the Cat!* (1540) warns that black cats may be shape-shifting Witches. A person might kill a black cat and believe that they have also killed the Witch, but the act does not necessarily guarantee the elimination of the servant of the devil—for a Witch has the power to assume the body of a cat nine times.

> *A person might kill a black cat and believe that they have also killed the Witch, but ... a Witch has the power to assume the body of a cat nine times.*

During the terrible Witchcraft trials of the Inquisition, men and women under torture confessed to kissing cats' buttocks and toads' mouths and cavorting with them in blasphemous ceremonies. Some poor wretches confessed that Satan first appeared to them in the form of a cat, for it was commonly held that cats were allied with the Prince of Darkness in the great rebellion against God.

A Navajo named Manuel told me about his grandfather Esteban's experience with two Witches who could transform their bodies into cats. It happened once in 1909, when Esteban was a 15-year-old shepherd, herding his father's flock of sheep not far from the Arizona–New Mexico border.

One day he stopped at a small hut a few miles from his family's hogan in which two sisters, Isabel and Carmelita, lived alone. The sisters were very courteous to him, and they gave him some cool water and some fry bread. Isabel seemed to be about his age, and Carmelita appeared only a few years older. Since they were very pretty girls and there was little to do in the evenings in the small village, Esteban began to slip out at night to visit them. The sisters were exciting company, and they sang songs that he had never heard anywhere else. As Carmelita played the guitar, the two sisters sang of people with great powers, of Witches and serpent people and shape-shifters.

Although Esteban cherished the secret nocturnal hours he spent with the beautiful sisters, he always left their hut before midnight so he could silently return to his parents' home and be there asleep in his bedroll for his father's morning call to work. Such diligence became increasingly difficult when the girls began to tempt him with promises of what fun he could have if he stayed with them until after midnight.

History and lore teem with feline shapeshifters, including cat people and werecats, often associated with Witchcraft or even the devil himself.

One day, as he daydreamed about the enchanting sisters, Esteban allowed a number of sheep to stray from the herd. By the time he was able to round them up and return them to his furious father, it was late at night — but his desires forced him to set out for the hut of Isabel and Carmelita in spite of the lateness of the hour.

As he knocked on their door, his common sense told him that he was doing a foolish, perhaps even discourteous thing. Isabel and Carmelita might be sleeping. On the other hand, the girls had often said that they stayed up most of the night, playing the guitar and singing.

After knocking unsuccessfully on their door, Esteban cautiously opened the latch and stepped inside. He was disappointed to discover that the girls were not at home — and he was startled to find their hut empty except for half a dozen very large cats that began to yowl fiercely at him the moment he entered the hogan. He knew that Isabel and Carmelita kept no cats. These creatures had to be homeless strays that had invaded their kitchen in search of food. In frustration and disgust, he kicked the cat nearest him and left the hogan.

He had not walked far when he felt a sharp pain in his ankle. The cat that he had kicked had bitten him. And he was startled to see that all six of the stray animals were attacking him.

Esteban received several bites and scratches, but he gave much worse than he received. He dealt several of the cats powerful kicks in their ribs, and he picked up one of their number and dashed its brains out against a large rock.

Frightened out of his wits when he realized that the vicious cats from the evening before were the same Witches he now saw before him, Esteban ran all the way home and confessed everything to his father.

The next evening when he called upon Isabel and Carmelita to inquire where they had been the night before, an angry old woman met him at the door and told him that he was no longer welcome there. Although she wore a shawl, Esteban could see that her head was bandaged. Directly behind her were the shadowy figures of four old hags who glared at him with hatred such as he had never before perceived.

When he protested that he wished to speak with Carmelita or Isabel, he was told that Carmelita did not want to see him ever again and that Isabel had been killed the night before when she fell and struck her head on a rock.

Esteban's senses began to whirl. His ankle began to throb anew with pain as he recalled the large cat that had sunk its fangs into his flesh before he dashed its brains out against a rock. Frightened out of his wits when he realized that the vicious cats from the evening before were the same Witches he now saw before him, Esteban ran all the way home and confessed everything to his father, who immediately ordered a ceremonial "sing" to purify him and to drive away any evil that might have lingered near him in spirit form. Esteban lived forever with the memory of the wrinkled old crones who had used their sorcery to create the illusion that they were beautiful young women instead of shape-shifting Witches.

Sources:

Steiger, Brad. Primary source interview.

Cats That Alter Their Forms

The phenomenon of werecats—people who can transform themselves into cat-like creatures, and cats that have the ability to change their forms—is widespread. Tales of the creatures can be found in such diverse locations as Europe, Asia, Central and South America, and Africa. I have collected a number of notable cases from the United Kingdom, where I lived until 2001.

One such case, a particularly memorable and weird one, came from James. He is a now-retired fireman who encountered just such a creature on a bright summer morning in 1978, and who I met in Exeter, England, in the summer of 2001. At the time, James was living in Exwick, a town in the English county of Devon that is noted for its long history of encounters with phantom black dogs. To what extent that is relevant is a matter of debate, but it is intriguing.

According to James, on the day in question he was out walking with his spaniel, Sammy, on the Haldon Hills, which provide an expansive view of the area, including the nearby city of Exeter. As James and Sammy took a pleasant walk through the hills, they found themselves confronted by a very strange animal. It was Sammy who alerted James to the fact that something weird was about to go down. As they pair took their daily stroll, Sammy suddenly came to a complete halt and began to growl. It was clear she had picked up on something strange. At first, James thought that perhaps she had picked up the scent of a rabbit or a fox—although, as James admitted, Sammy had not reacted like that before when rabbits were around.

In seconds, the cause of Sammy's behavior became apparent: around 50 or 60 feet away a large black animal rose out of the deep grass. At first James assumed it was a black Labrador. It was not. In mere seconds, James realized that what was walking toward him and his faithful pet was a large black cat that resembled a mountain lion. Sammy whimpered, and James's heart thumped. When the animal reached a point around 20 feet from the terrified pair, the huge cat rose onto its back legs, which appeared to physically change as the creature transformed from a four-legged animal to a bipedal one. But, that was not the weirdest part of the story.

As James looked on, pretty much frozen to the spot with fear, the face of the cat began to change and took on a malevolent, human-like appearance. A strange and sinister grin dominated the face, although the beast did nothing more than stand and stare at James and Sammy. James told me it was the terrible grin that finally made him realize that it was time to leave—immediately. As Sammy was only four months old at the time, it was easy for James to scoop her up under his arm and get the hell off the hills. He looked back twice: on the first occasion the cat-human was standing just as it had been 30 seconds or so earlier. On the second look, however, it was gone. By James's own admission, he and Sammy did not take another walk on the Haldon Hills for around three months.

It may not be a coincidence that in 1996, Jonathan Downes, the director of the Centre for Fortean Zoology, investigated a wave of sightings of a strange, large, cat-like animal on the Haldon Hills. Downes related the facts in his 2004 book, *Monster Hunter*. Most of the encounters occurred in the vicinity of an old pet cemetery, which houses the remains of numerous beloved, long-gone old friends. Downes did not solve the mystery, but he did come away from the investigation fully convinced that the Haldon Hills were home to something dangerous and predatory. James's werecat? Don't bet against it.

Sources:

Nick Redfern. Interview with James York, Exeter, England, U.K., 2001.

Ceara, Brazil

There were so many reports of werewolves terrorizing the inhabitants of the rural area of Tauá, in the Brazilian state of Ceará, that fellow Brazilians began calling the region the Werewolf Capital of South America. Seeing the frightful half-man, half-wolf creatures creeping around in the moonlight was terrifying enough, but the people of Tauá also had to endure the beasts stealing their sheep and even breaking into their homes.

On Monday, July 7, 2008, a new moon night, a woman reported seeing a half-man, half-wolf near her home. On Tuesday, a 12-year-old boy told police that he saw a werewolf outside his family home. More instances of werewolf attacks were received on Wednesday, when police received two reports of werewolves stealing sheep.

Some witnesses who saw the werewolves testified that the creatures were very ugly and emitted a strong odor that smelled like sulfur.

Some witnesses who saw the werewolves testified that the creatures were very ugly and emitted a strong odor that smelled like sulfur. Priests reminded their parishioners to remember their prayers and to keep their crucifixes with them at all times.

People recalled that on January 28 in São Sepe, Rio Grande do Sul, a woman told police that she had been attacked at night by a huge dog that had stood on its hind feet and had walked as if it were a man. The victim underwent medical examination at a hospital, where her wounds were confirmed.

On Friday, February 13, a woman in São Paulo encountered a werewolf that attempted to grab her.

In April, the inhabitants of Santana do Livramento, Rio Grande do Sul, were under siege by a mysterious man in a black cape. This dreadful night marauder had so terrified the citizens of the area that Valerio Silveira, a local priest, had distributed "bloodied" crucifixes, painted red, insisting that the holy object would keep people safe from the Black Caped Man.

Marcos Sandro Lira, the regional deputy police officer, told inquisitive journalists investigating the claims of werewolves molesting the people of the area that "people in werewolf masks" were frightening the locals so it would easier to steal their sheep.

Sources:

"Werewolf Scares Inhabitants in Ceara State." Forgetomori. Accessed March 21, 2011. http://forgetomori.com/2008/cripto zoology/a-brazilian-werewolf/.

Children Raised by Wolves

Many of us are familiar with Rudyard Kipling's tale of the boy Mowgli, who was raised by wolves in the jungles of India, through the various cinematic treatments that have been made of the story. In 1942, *The Jungle Book* was made into a captivating live-action feature starring the actor Sabu as Mowgli. In 1967, Disney translated the adventures of the wolf boy into an animated musical version. In 1994, the company filmed the Kipling story once again, this time with live actors and Jason Scott Lee as Mowgli, and in 2016 Disney remade the film yet again, with Neel Sethi starring as Mowgli.

In his *Man into Wolf*, Robert Eisler makes the point that Kipling's *Jungle Book* achieved worldwide success because of the appeal that it makes to archetypal ideas about the human race. He also states that the "wolf cubs" among the Boy Scouts was suggested by the romanticized wolf-boy Mowgli and characterizes such expression as "a curious and harmless revival of atavistic lycanthropic ideas."

In a case of truth that's stranger than fiction, there have been many documented cases of human children raised entirely by nonhuman foster parents, including wolves, pigs, and others.

While the vast majority of people may be skeptical about claims that human infants could be reared by wolves, there are some well-documented accounts of wolves and other animals becoming surrogate parents to human children.

In 1920, the Reverend J. A. L. Singh, an Anglican missionary who supervised an orphanage at Midnapore, India, was beseeched by villagers from Godamuri who sought his help in ridding them of ghosts. More intrigued than alarmed by the superstitious villagers, Reverend Singh journeyed to Godamuri and ordered a tiger-shooting platform constructed in the area where the evil spirits had been seen.

After some time, three full-grown wolves emerged from their lair. The adults were followed by two pups and a ghost—a hideous-looking being with hands, feet, and torso like a human, but a large grotesque head that was more like a giant fur ball than a face. Close at its heels came another awful creature, exactly like the first, although smaller in size.

Reverend Singh suddenly found himself all alone on the tiger-shooting platform. And when he returned to the village, he found no amount of persuasion could convince anyone from Godamuri to return to the lair to capture the terrible ghosts.

Six days later, he returned with help recruited from nearby villages and flushed the wolves out of their den. In a corner of the wolf den, they were forced to kill a female that had stayed to defend the two ghosts, who now faced Reverend Singh with bared teeth. To his astonishment, he could at last see the two evil jungle spirits for what they really were: two young girls who had been raised by wolves.

The missionary took the two wolf-girls back with him to an orphanage at Midnapore, where he first cut the huge, matted mass of hair from their heads and then undertook the arduous task of rearing them as human children. Reverend Singh estimated their ages to be about nine and two. Neither of them was able to utter a single human sound. They walked about on all fours and could not be forced to stand erect. He christened the older girl Kamala, and the younger, Amala.

To his astonishment, he could at last see the two evil jungle spirits for what they really were: two young girls who had been raised by wolves.

The wolf-girls ate and drank canine-fashion by lowering their faces into their bowls. If not attended at mealtimes, they would scamper out to the courtyard and eat with the dogs, fighting with them for the choicest bits of raw meat. From their wolf environment, Kamala and Amala had developed a keen sense of smell, so they could detect the bones and stores of meat that their canine comrades had buried. They not only relished the caches of rotting flesh that the dogs had hidden, but they would chase off any vultures they might spot picking at a choice bit of carrion.

The wolf-girls slept most of the day, then prowled around at night while the rest of the orphanage slept. Whenever the opportunity presented itself, Kamala and Amala escaped for a nocturnal hunt for small game in the surrounding jungle.

It was only after several months that the girls tolerated loincloths. Personal hygiene had been a major problem from the beginning of their stay at orphanage, for toilet training is not required among jungle creatures who follow the instincts of the pack.

Little Amala died 11 months after her capture, and Kamala gave evidence of her first human emotion when she shed a few tears upon the death of her sister. At about that same time, Kamala began to respond to Reverend Singh's patient ministrations, relinquishing some of her ferocious, wolflike ways. With daily massage and measured exercise, she was eventually able to stand erect and to walk in a conventional human manner.

Kamala's table etiquette advanced to the point where she could eat at the table with guests who might be visiting the orphanage. By 1927, her vocabulary included 30 words, and she was helping Reverend Singh by watching the younger children and had begun to attend church services.

Sadly, as Kamala's adjustment to human society improved, her health began steadily to fail. On September 26, 1929, at the approximate age of 17, the last of India's wolf-girls died of uremic poisoning.

In October 1990, welfare workers in Springs, South Africa, discovered a case where the family dog had apparently been given almost full responsibility for the care of Danny, a 23-month-old boy. The child's mother admitted that she had left her son in the kennel to be raised by Skaapie, the dog, because she was an alcoholic and usually too drunk to care for him herself.

Child welfare workers said that Danny scampered about on all fours, barked, and whined. It was obvious to welfare worker Les Lancaster that the boy had spent so much time with Skaapie that he had assumed the behavior patterns of a dog. For her part, Danny's mother said that she provided him with a daily bowl of food, and she was happy that Skaapie had assumed all other maternal duties.

Sadly, when the officials took Danny away from his life in the dog kennel, they also separated him from his devoted, caring surrogate mother. Devastated by the loss of her "puppy," she died two weeks after their separation.

One of the most astonishing cases of surrogate animal parentage was made public in China's Liaoning Province in September 1991 when authorities at the China Medical Institute in Shenyang revealed that 16-year-old Wang Xian Feng had been raised from the age of two to six by pigs. The bizarre situation had been discovered by a botanist searching for rare flowers who happened upon a small girl foraging for food among a herd of pigs. The girl was on all fours, squealing, grunting, and shoving her face into the grass just like the members of her family of swine.

Although at first the child could only grunt and squeal, an expert in dealing with children with learning problems eventually taught little Xian Feng to speak and to behave like a human.

According to the Anshan Psychology Research Institute of the China Medical Institute, they had sent researchers to investigate the botanist's claims, and the members of their team even witnessed the child suckling a sow. Later, they observed her grunting, pushing pigs out of the way, and shoving her face into a trough to eat. At night, she would curl up next to the pigs to share body heat against the cold.

The girl was removed from the swine herd and taken to the Institute for study and observation. Although at first the child could only grunt and squeal, an expert in dealing with children with learning problems eventually taught little Xian Feng to speak and to behave like a human. By the time she was 16, she was evaluated as a sweet, simple, lovable girl by all who knew her.

On December 21, 2007, Moscow police were hunting a snarling, biting "werewolf boy" who escaped from a clinic just a day after he had been found living with a wolf pack in a remote forest in the Kaluga region of central Russia. Although the boy appeared to be about ten years old, a medical examination suggested that he may have been much older. A police spokesman stated that with his claw-like nails and very strong, sharp teeth, the werewolf boy was clearly dangerous to other people.

The boy had been spotted by villagers as he moved about with a pack of wolves searching for food. According to the newspaper *Tvoi Den*, the wolf boy was captured when some villagers found him in a lair made of leaves and sticks.

Sources:

Eisler, Robert. *Man into Wolf.* London: Spring Books, 1948.

Steiger, Brad, and Sherry Hansen Steiger. *Strange Powers of Pets.* New York: Donald I. Fine, 1992.

"Werewolf Boy — Who Snarls and Bites — on the Run from Police after Escaping from Moscow Clinic." *Daily Mail.* Accessed March 21, 2011. http://www.dailymail.co.uk/news/article-503736/Werewolf-boy — snarls-bites — run-police-escaping-Moscow-clinic.html.

The Chindi

Navajo artist David Little Turtle explained the eerie details of the Chindi, a shape-shifter that acts as a kind of avenging angel to those who show disrespect to any of the Earth Mother's creatures.

"It can assume any shape," he said, "or, perhaps more accurately, it can inhabit any living thing. Almost any traditional Navajo has at least one Chindi story to tell. He or she will tell you about coming home at night and seeing a coyote walking on its hind legs."

According to Navajo tradition, one of the ways of knowing that an animal harbors a Chindi is that it will walk upright, like a human. Another sure way of identifying an animal that harbors a Chindi is that its eyes will appear dead. If your headlights hit the animal's eyes and they do not reflect the light, you will know that a Chindi has possessed the creature.

How the Chindi responds to an innocent person depends upon that individual's attitude toward the Earth Mother and whether or not he or she has a good heart.

If a Chindi should have been set against you for any reason, the only way you can stop the energy is to draw a medicine circle around you and sing or say a prayer for protection. "It need not be a Navajo chant," Little Turtle said. "Sing or say aloud any prayer you know. The important thing is your attitude. If the Chindi sees that you have a good heart, the evil energy will boomerang and return to the one who set it upon you."

If a Chindi should have been set against you for any reason, the only way you can stop the energy is to draw a medicine circle around you and sing or say a prayer for protection.

And what about the worst-case scenario? What if a wolf or coyote or fox appears at your door walking on its hind legs and you don't know how to draw a proper medicine circle or sing the right kind of prayer? Can you stop it with a silver bullet?

Little Turtle soberly informed me that there is no kind of bullet that can stop a Chindi. "If you kill the host animal," he explained, "the Chindi will simply enter another animal. And another and another ... until it has worked its vengeance upon you."

The tragic account of the Navajo Long Salt family is the most completely documented story of the Chindi's persistence in exacting vengeance. Incredibly, the avenging spirit pursued the members of this one clan for over one hundred years.

According to Navajo tradition, one of the ways of knowing that an animal harbors a Chindi is that it will walk upright, like a human.

The Long Salt's ordeal began in 1825 when a man of the family became ill because of nightmares that constantly troubled his sleep. He confided in his brothers that he was being visited by the angry spirit of a man that he had killed.

His older brother protested that the man had been their family's enemy for years and that he had been slain in a fair fight. According to tribal law, the killing had been justified.

The tormented man explained that the spirit was restless because he had been struck down before he could sing his death song. They must find a medicine priest to rid him of the troubled spirit, or he would surely die.

The Long Salts sought assistance from an old, blind medicine priest from the Tsegi country who, at their request, held a three-day *b'jene* (sing) over the afflicted brother. After the final day of the ritual, the troubled man sighed his relief and his gratitude that the restless spirit had departed and that he could now sleep peacefully.

For his pay, the blind priest had asked for five butchered sheep from the Long Salts' herd. The requested recompense was surely fair, and the powerful Long Salt clan, who at that time numbered over a hundred members, possessed many sheep. But since the flock was grazing at a considerable distance from the old priest's village, the two Long Salt men assigned the task of slaughtering the sheep decided to substitute five wild antelope in their place. After all, the old man was blind. He wouldn't be able to tell the difference between the animals, and they would preserve five valuable sheep for the family's own use.

The Long Salt elder who awarded the priest the five carcasses was himself unaware that antelope had been substituted for the specified sheep. With the animals' heads cut off and their lower legs removed at the knees, even those at the ceremony rewarding the medicine man were unaware of the deceit that two members of their family had perpetrated.

A few weeks later, an older member of the Long Salt family who had been healthy and without illness died suddenly. Then a very young and robust Long Salt male fell dead for no perceptible reason. As his pregnant wife and other family members sang their mourning songs, an uneasy feeling began to grow that something was not right.

Every few weeks after the young husband's death, a member of the Long Salt family would become ill, begin to waste away, and then died in suffering. To the wiser members of the family, it was becoming increasingly obvious that a Chindi had been set against them. But why?

When at last the two men confessed to substituting the antelope for the sheep, a council of family leaders agreed that selected delegates would meet with the medicine priest and seek to rectify the situation without further delay.

The old priest admitted that he had discovered the deception and had become very angry. He also acknowledged that he had set a Chindi against them with the instructions that the entire Long Salt family should be eliminated one by one.

The representatives of the Long Salts beseeched him to call off the avenging spirit. They tried to make him understand that they, too, had been duped by two deceitful and lazy members of the clan. They did not intend to cheat him. And already many members of their family had been killed by the Chindi.

The elderly medicine priest carefully evaluated their words and deemed them sincere. He told them that he was not an evil man, but he had been forced to uphold his dignity and reputation. He would remove the curse, but he must charge them a price somehow commensurate with the laws of the spirit world that had required him to set the Chindi upon them.

The Long Salt delegates answered that they would not question his judgment. They would pay whatever price he asked to call off the Chindi and to save the lives of their family members.

The old priest called his son to his side, complaining that he was now very tired—too weary to determine a proper compensation. He bade the Long Salts return in ten days. At that time, both parties would agree to the terms of payment. The Long Salts were dismayed, but they knew better than to protest the old man's decision.

On the morning of the tenth day, the delegation from the Long Salts was prompt in keeping the appointment at the hogan of the blind medicine man. But they were greeted by a family in mourning. The elderly priest had passed to the land of the grandfathers three days earlier.

The desperate Long Salts asked the man's son if he had called off the Chindi before he died. To their horror, they were unable to determine if the curse had been lifted. The priest's son could only tell him that he knew that his father had thought much about the problem before he died.

By the time the Long Salt delegation returned home, several members of the family lay ill and dying.

In the August–September 1967 issue of *Frontier Times*, John R. Winslowe wrote that he met the last surviving member of the Long Salts in 1925, a slender teenage girl named Alice, and learned the family's fate:

> Curiously, anyone marrying into the family met the same fate as a blood Long Salt. Alice's mother died when the girl reached seven and she was attending

the Tuba City boarding school at the Indian agency. Alice's father became skin and bones, dying two years later. … The remaining three Long Salts [Alice's two uncles and an aunt] were ill, crippled, and helpless. Friends cared for them, watching them fade into nothing before their eyes.

An aging but determined Navajo named Hosteen Behegade adopted Alice Long Salt and swore that he would protect her from the Chindi's mission to destroy the sole surviving member of once proud and prosperous family. Behegade was incensed that so many people had to die because of the deceit of two lazy men who had tried to deceive an old priest, and he devised a plan to keep moving, to somehow stay one step ahead of the Chindi.

In the winter of 1928, the desperate wanderers found themselves seeking refuge from a blizzard in a hogan three miles from the trading post on Red Mesa. The blizzard developed into the worst snowstorm in years. Surely not even the Chindi could find them amid the deep-piling snow and the fierce howling wind.

The next morning, Alice Long Salt lay dead. The final propitiation had been exacted. At last the Chindi would return to the unknown realm from which it had come, its one-hundred-year mission of revenge completed.

Sources:

Steiger, Brad. Interview with David Little Turtle.

Winslowe, John R. *Frontier Times*, August–September 1967.

The Chronicon of Denys of Tell-Mahre

For centuries now, scholars have puzzled over *The Chronicon of Denys of Tell-Mahre*, written by a leader of the Syrian Jacobites. From what can be determined, the ancient scribe was born in Mesopotamia (now Iraq) and recorded a remarkable account of the appearance of frightening and terrifying creatures just before the reign of the Greek-Byzantine ruler Leo IV, circa 774:

> They fled from no man, and, indeed, killed many people. ... They were like wolves, but their faces were small and long ... and they had great ears. The skin on their spine resembled that of a pig. These mysterious animals committed great ravages on the people in the Abdin Rock region, near Hoh. In some villages they devoured more than one hundred people; and in many others, from twenty to forty or fifty. If a man did pursue them, in no ways did the monsters become frightened or flee. Instead, they turned on the man. If men loosed their weapons on a monster, it leaped on the men and tore them to bits.
>
> These monsters entered houses and yards, and ... climbed in the night onto terraces, stole children from their beds and went off without opposition. When they appeared, dogs were afraid to bark.
>
> For these reasons, the country suffered a more terrible experience than it had ever known before. ... When one of these monsters attacked a herd of goats, cattle, or a flock of sheep, they took away several at one time. ... These monsters finally passed from the land and went into Arzanene [a district in southern Armenia along the borders of Assyria] and ravaged every village there. They also ravaged in the country of Maipherk and along Mt. Cahai and caused great damage.

At this point, several pages are missing from the ancient manuscripts. Many scholars have long maintained that Denys of Tell-Mahre was only writing a fanciful tale. Others debate whether the monsters were packs of aggressive wolves driven by hunger to invade villages or if they were herds of wild pigs who were fiercely unafraid to turn upon those men who sought to hunt them down. There are many such accounts from antiquity that contain descriptions of strange, hairy creatures with glowing eyes that leap on their victims from a dark ambush.

Sources:

Hurwood, Bernhardt J. *Vampires, Werewolves, and Ghouls*. New York: Ace Books, 1968.

Chupacabra

When it first emerged from the shadows in Puerto Rico in the summer of 1995, the chupacabra ("goat sucker"), with its penchant for seizing goats and sucking their blood, immediately fascinated the public at large and created another deadly night stalker to fear. From August 1995 into the twenty-first century, the monster has been credited with the deaths of thousands of animals, ranging from small prey like goats, rabbits, and birds to larger animals like horses, cattle, and deer. While some argue that the creature is a new monster, perhaps even created in some scientist's clandestine laboratory, others point out that such vampiric entities have always existed and have been reported by farmers and villagers in Puerto Rico and elsewhere in the Caribbean and in Central and South America.

Indeed, rather than regarding the chupacabras as a recent arrival in the theater of night stalkers, we need only go back to the accounts of shape-shifting amalgamations of monstrous entities summoned by the alchemists in medieval Spain. It seemed clear to some investigators of the strange and unknown that these beings, slumbering in the psyches of the Hispanic people of Puerto Rico and Central and South America, had found a propitious moment in time and space to resurface. Now these perverse creatures need not follow the selective commands of their alchemical masters to savage their rivals in their smoky laboratories. The creatures were free to attack and feed on whatever victims they might find—human or animal.

Numerous eyewitnesses have described chupacabras as standing erect on powerful goat-like legs with three-clawed feet. The creature is often described as slightly over five feet in height, though some reports list it as over six and a half feet tall. Its head is oval in shape with an elongated

Eyewitnesses have described chupacabras as standing erect on powerful goat-like legs with three-clawed feet. … Its head is oval with an elongated jaw, a small, slit mouth, and fangs that protrude both upward and downward.

The chupacabra has eluded capture or positive photo identification. Supposed pictures and specimens, like this purported chupacabra roadkill in Florida, are usually explained away as conventional animals suffering mange or other conditions.

jaw, a small, slit mouth, and fangs that protrude both upward and downward. Some witnesses have claimed to have seen small, pointed ears on its reptilian-like head and red eyes that glow menacingly in the shadows. Although its arms are thin, they are extremely powerful, ending in three-clawed paws.

Chupacabras appear to have the ability to change colors even though the creature is most often reported to have strong, coarse black hair covering its torso. Through some chameleon-like ability, the creature seems to be able to alter its coloration from green to grayish and from light brown to black, depending upon the vegetation that surrounds it. Another peculiarity of the beast is the row of quill-like appendages that runs down its spine and the fleshly membrane that extends between these projections, which can flare or contract and also change color from blue to green or from red to purple.

There have been reports that the chupacabras can fly, but others state that it is the beast's powerful hind legs that merely catapult it over one-story barns or outbuildings. Those same strong legs enable the creature to run at extremely fast speeds to escape its pursuers.

Within a short time after the night terrors began in Puerto Rico, reports of chupacabras began appearing in Florida, Texas, Mexico, and Brazil's southern states of São Paulo and Parana. In Brazil, the ranchers called the monster *O Bicho*, "the Beast." The descriptions provided by terrified eyewitnesses were also the same—a reptilian creature with thin arms, long claws, powerful hind legs, and dark gray in color.

On May 11, 1997, the newspaper *Folha de Londrina* in Parana state, Brazil, published the account of a slaughter that had occurred at a ranch near Campina Grande do Sul where, in a single corral, 12 sheep were found dead and another 11 were horribly mutilated.

From April to September 2000, more than 800 animals were slaughtered by the bloodsucker in Chile. Some witnesses to the bloody rampages of the creature described it as a large rodent, others as a mutant kangaroo, and still others as a winged, ape-like vampire.

A number of authorities even began to theorize that the chupacabras had been manufactured by some secret government agency for some nefarious purpose. Clergymen issued pronouncements stating that the demonic creatures were heralding the end of the world. UFO enthusiasts theorized that the monsters had been brought here by extraterrestrial aliens to test the planet's atmosphere preparatory to a mass invasion of Earth. Anthropologists and folklorists reminded people that tales of such mysterious, vampire-like monsters had been common in Central America for centuries.

Anthropologists and folklorists reminded people that tales of such mysterious, vampire-like monsters had been common in Central America for centuries.

A widely circulated story stated that Chilean soldiers had captured three chupacabras, a male, female, and cub, that had been living in a mine north of Calama. Then, according to the account, a team of scientists from the National Aeronautics and Space Administration arrived in a black helicopter and reclaimed the chupacabra family. The creatures, so the story went, had escaped from a secret NASA facility in the Atacama Desert of northern Chile where the U.S. space agency was attempting to create some kind of hybrid beings that could survive on Mars.

On August 30, 2000, Jorge Luis Talavera, a farmer in the jurisdiction of Malpaisillo, Nicaragua, had enough of the nocturnal depredations of chupacabras. The beast or beasts had sucked the life from 25 of his sheep and 35 from his neighbor's flock, and he lay in wait with rifle in hand for its return. That night, Talavera accomplished what no other irate farmer or rancher had been able to do. He shot and killed a chupacabra.

Scott Corrales of the Institute of Hispanic Ufology reports that a specialist of veterinary medicine examined the carcass and acknowledged that it was a very uncommon creature with great eye cavities, smooth bat-like skin, big claws, large teeth, and a crest sticking out from the main vertebra. The specialist said that the specimen could have been a hybrid animal made up of several species, created through genetic engineering.

On September 5, 2000, the official analysis of the corpse by a university medical college was that Talavera had shot a dog. A furious Luis Talavera declared that the officials had switched carcasses. "This isn't my goatsucker," he groused as the college returned the skeleton of a dog for his disposal.

In the twenty-first century, chupacabra reports continue from nearly all the South American countries, Puerto Rico, and the Southwestern United States, and frightened and angry people complain that whatever the chupacabra is, it continues to suck the blood from their livestock.

Sources:

Redfern, Nick. Data from seven expeditions in Puerto Rico, 2004–17.

Cleadon Man-Beast

On December 10, 2009, paranormal investigator Mike Hallowell, in an article titled "Cleadon BHM," told of how several days earlier a friend and research colleague, John Triplow, informed Mike of a website that contained "an intriguing BHM [Big Hairy Man] story, not unlike that of the infamous Beast of Bolam Lake," which Mike had "actively investigated with a CFZ [Centre for Fortean Zoology] team in early 2003." Bolam Lake, Northumberland, England, was the site of a Bigfoot-type creature seen in January 2003 by a team from the British-based CFZ, one of the few full-time monster-hunting groups in the world.

What puzzled Triplow—and also deeply flummoxed Hallowell—was that this particular sighting of a large, hairy man-beast allegedly occurred right in the heart of Cleadon village, in the very same year that a large black cat was reportedly prowling around the neighborhood. As for why it so flummoxed Hallowell, let's take a close look.

The idyllic Cleadon Hills have been the site of many bizarre sightings, including the Cleadon man-beast.

Hallowell correctly noted that the Borough of South Tyneside is the smallest Metropolitan Borough in the United Kingdom, comprised of only half a dozen villages and towns, a handful of farms, and, if one is brutally honest, not much else at all—aside, that is, from one significant thing. The area, Mike revealed, is a veritable beacon for bizarre activity. That activity has included ghostly experiences, UFO sightings, two Man in Black encounters, and a confrontation with a strange beast that resembled the infamous Mothman of Point Pleasant, West Virginia, made famous in John Keel's acclaimed book *The Mothman Prophecies*.

As for the story of the Cleadon man-beast, Hallowell said that the witness reported seeing in the darkness of the night in question (the precise date for which has yet to be ascertained) what appeared to be a large, two-legged animal covered in a thick coat of fur. A second individual was there, too—this one undeniably human—apparently out walking their pet dog. Hallowell added that "it seemed more than a little odd to me that this BHM sighting should occur in the same village that had only a short while previously been the setting for the infamous Cleadon Big Cat incident. Two spectacular cryptids in the one village, only a few short years apart?"

It was a most puzzling question, to be sure, and one that Hallowell dug into further as he attempted to resolve the nature of what, exactly, was afoot. As Hallowell asked more and more questions, he discovered something amazing. Both the encounter involving the large black cat and the one that revolved around what might be termed a British Bigfoot occurred on the Cleadon Hills, and the witnesses were people out walking their dogs late at night. This gave rise to several people suspecting that the black cat and the man-beast were one and the same—a nightmarish thing that was taking on multiple grisly forms.

Sources:

Downes, Jonathan. *Wild-Man*. Woolsery, U.K.: CFZ Press, 2012.

Hallowell, Mike. "Cleadon BHM." *Fortean Zoology* (blog). December 10, 2009. http://forteanzoology.blogspot.com/2009/12/mike-hallowell-cleadon-bhm.html.

Coyote People

It must be understood that the coyote has a unique place among the Native American tribes of the Southwest. For many, Brother Coyote participated with the Great Mystery in the very act of creation. For others, humans first assumed the form of coyotes before they evolved to their present physical shape.

It was Brother Coyote who gave the tribes the knowledge of how to make fire, how to grind flour, and how to find the herbs that would bring about healings. But Brother Coyote is also a trickster. While it is true that he brought fire and food and healing wisdom to the tribes, he also brought death. The shamans soon learned that when you ask such a creature to grant you a wish, you must be very careful that there is not some trick attached to it.

Trickster, ancestor, shapeshifter, god: The coyote plays many roles in the legends of North America's first peoples.

The Navajo generally regard the coyote as the very essence and symbol of Dark Side Witchcraft. If a Navajo were to set out on a journey and a coyote should cross his path, he would go back home and wait for three days before he set out again. And once the missionaries told the Navajo about Satan, they were certain that he uses the coyote as his steed to travel about working nocturnal evil.

David Little Turtle, a Navajo artist, told of a shepherd near Window Rock, Arizona, who was out hunting one night when he caught a glimpse of a large coyote running behind a clump of mesquite.

As he walked around the bush with his rifle at the ready, a female voice startled him by shouting at him not to shoot or he would kill a member of his own clan. The shepherd was further astonished when the coyote pulled back its skin to reveal a woman he immediately recognized as one of his cousins.

She promised to conduct a powerful sing for him, and in return, he would promise to say nothing of the incident to anyone. The shepherd had long suspected his kinswoman of being a shape-shifter, but to see her in the act of transforming herself into a coyote had made him feel as though his brain were spinning. Once the Witch had obtained his vow of secrecy, she slipped the coyote skin back over her head and ran off with such speed that she became but a blur of motion.

David Little Turtle said that the Navajo believe in many types of were-animals. Referring to the account of the shepherd encountering his kinswoman as a coyote, he explained that the Witch probably kept the skin of the animal hidden somewhere in a cave or in her home. When she wanted to join with other Witches or move about at night with great speed, she would put on the magic skin.

"Other Witches might keep the hide of a bear, a fox, a wolf, or a mountain lion hidden away for such purposes of night travel," he said. "When they gather together in secret meeting places, the Witches plot against their enemies, initiate new members, and sometimes eat human flesh or have sexual intercourse with corpses."

A Native American psychiatrist in Phoenix explained that the were-creatures in which the Navajos believe are not quite the same as the popular werewolf of European traditions. "Interestingly, though," he said, "it is the wolfmen or the coyotemen who are most common among the North American tribes as in Europe. The difference is that the creatures of various tribal beliefs are more often supernatural entities who are shape-shifters that can assume the form of humans and—at will—can travel many, many miles in the blink of an eye and appear as wolves or as men dressed in wolf's clothing."

A young Navajo woman, a convert to Roman Catholicism, told of her brother's experience while hitchhiking late one night to their grandmother's home:

It was in February and it was pretty cold. It was past midnight, and he just couldn't go any farther. There are these little bus stops on the roads where they pick up schoolchildren, so he was sitting there, debating whether or not to spend the night there or to keep walking the second half of the fifty miles to Grandmother's home.

Then he saw this animal that he thought was a big dog. He wanted some company, so he whistled at it. It came running up to him, then it stood up on its hind legs. My brother was so scared! He said the big dog or big coyote had a man's face—and the face was painted with little white dots and other kinds of signs. Then the thing ran off on four legs, and my brother said it dawned on him what he had seen. He had never really believed in such creatures until then. Now he knew that it was true that some Medicine people really have the power to travel long distances in no time at all in the form of a wolf or a coyote.

My brother did not tell our grandmother about his experience until many months later; because if he had, Grandmother would have become frightened and insisted that we have a sing to chase away any evil spirits.

Sources:

Steiger, Brad. Personal interviews.

Cry-Baby Bridge and the Changing Monster

Most shape-shifting monsters seem to be content with terrifying and tormenting us. But not all of them. Some of these creatures are deeply cunning and are intent on luring us into their nightmarish realms, quite possibly to try to take our lives. Maybe even our souls.

Aside from literal shape-shifting, there is a related aspect to the mystery that is downright eerie and menacing in the extreme. It is the ability of certain monsters—almost always Bigfoot-type creatures—to very closely mimic us. Specifically, they mimic the stress-filled cries of babies. As the following accounts collectively demonstrate, the clear implication is that the beasts mimic the vocalizations of babies in distress to lure us into their environments. Is their ultimate purpose to attack or kidnap us? To kill us? Maybe even to savagely devour us? These are deeply chilling questions.

The small town of Ennis, Texas, was the site of a brief series of such encounters with a Bigfoot-style entity in 1964. Those encounters involved an immense monster, described by the half dozen people who saw it as somewhere between eight and ten feet in height. It is a saga told by the Bigfoot Research Organization in an article titled "Tall Creature Seen by Witness." Notably, nearly all of the encounters occurred at the site of an old wooden bridge, now demolished, that spanned a still-existing creek. Eye-opening is the fact that the bridge became known by the locals as Cry-Baby Bridge because of the disturbing, baby-like wailings that were always heard when the hairy monster was around. Fortunately, despite the voice sounding like the cries of a baby, no one fell for the potentially deadly ruse. All recognized it for what it was: an attempt to reel in the witnesses, for reasons that remain unknown.

Five years later, in 1969, the Ennis Bigfoot was back again—as were the baby-like cries, which continued to haunt the old bridge and those who saw the beast across a period of roughly five weeks. Again, the monster was immense: around nine feet tall. There was a difference, however: the Bigfoot was seen to run on both four limbs and two, despite looking entirely humanoid in shape and stance when upright. That it was able to race through the trees in both dog-like fashion and human-like fashion strongly suggests that a degree of shape-shifting was afoot.

One final thing on this matter: of the several old graveyards that can be found in and around the Ennis area, one is called Cryer Creek Cemetery. Cryer Creek is a town located just a few miles from Barry, Texas. Today, it has a population of under 20, which means the dead significantly outnumber the living. There is a notable story behind the name of the town.

When it was settled in the 1850s by one William Melton, one of the most important things on the agenda was the name of the town. It is eye-opening to note that the name chosen, Cryer Creek, was inspired by local legends. These legends suggested that if one was to walk the old, nearby creeks late at night, one would hear the fear-filled cries of a woman. That there are stories of strange cries amid the local creeks dating back to the middle years of the nineteenth century strongly suggests that Cryer Creek's monstrous mimics were around long before the events of 1964 began.

Sources:

Redfern, Nick. Personal investigations with witnesses, 2006.

"Tall Creature Seen by Witness." Bigfoot Field Researchers Organization. June 28, 1999. Accessed March 25, 2023. https://www.bfro.net/GDB/show_report.asp?id=2396.

Defiance, Ohio

Located in northwestern Ohio, the small and picturesque town of Defiance is home to around 17,000 people and has origins dating back to the latter part of the eighteenth century. In the summer of 1972, Defiance became a hotspot for monster-seekers when locals reported a shape-shifting werewolf in their midst. Thankfully, the beast did not stay around for too long, but from July to August of that year the man-beast left its assuredly creepy calling card, and as a result, the town was quickly under siege. Children were kept indoors after school. The local police carefully combed the neighborhood by day and night. And werewolf fever was just about everywhere in town.

The first encounter occurred on July 25 in the early hours of the morning. The unfortunate soul who came face to face with the creature was a railroad employee working an early shift. As the man switched a train from one track to another on the Norfolk and Western railroad, in the area of Fifth Street and Swift and Co., he was suddenly confronted by

Author Nick Redfern stands near the place where a railroad worker was allegedly assaulted by a werewolf-like creature in 1972, kicking off a rash of sightings and a persisting local legend.

a large, humanoid figure that had apparently been stalking him from the shadows.

Dressed in ragged clothing, covered in dark hair, and with a face that closely resembled that of a wolf or a German shepherd dog, it rendered the man frozen to the spot with overwhelming terror. That was most unfortunate, given that the fanged beast had a large brick in its huge paw, which it used to pound the fear-filled man on his left shoulder. Fortunately for the hysterical man, the beast raced off into the darkness, leaving his shaking victim curled up into a ball on the floor. An interesting point was that the night of the attack was a full moon.

That was hardly the end of things, unfortunately. Rather, matters had just begun. Other railroad employees, including Tom Jones and Ted Davis, had notable tales to tell. According to Davis, as cited by journalist James Stegall for the *Blade*, a Toledo newspaper, "I was connecting an air hose between two cars and was looking down. I saw these huge hairy feet, then I looked up and he was standing there with that big stick over his shoulder. When I started to say something, he took off for the woods."

Jones, also quoted in Stegall's article, was far more concise, describing the beast as "wooly."

The local media was at least partly responsible for the growing controversy. A week later, on August 2, the city's *Crescent News* ran an article titled "Horror Movie Now Playing on Fifth Street," a reference to the location of the initial attack. Then, one day later, on August 3, the newspaper ran a second article, "Wolfman Reports Persist." Its subtitle was suitably spine-chilling: "The Shadow of the Wolfman Stalked Defiance Again Last Night."

August 3 was also the date on which yet another report was made, this time near Deatrick and South Clinton Streets. The single witness, a man, was making his way to the Henry Hotel at around one o'clock in the morning when he developed a deep and unsettling feeling of being followed. Such was his level of terror that after racing to the police station, he spent the rest of the night in the hotel lobby, fearful of what might be waiting for him should he dare to venture outside and into the darkness of the city.

The staff of the *Crescent News* knew a good story when they heard it, hence the August 4 article, "One Wolfman Report Logged." The story was growing by the day. The *Blade*'s article reflected the police's attitude on the matter: "Werewolf Case in Defiance Not Viewed Lightly by Police."

In a city the size of Defiance, it didn't take long before just about everyone had heard of the werewolf in their midst. One such citizen was a woman whose home backed onto the railroads. She was someone very keen to speak to the police when word of the potentially deadly attacks got around. For three nights running, the woman informed the police, she was woken up by the sound of someone violently turning back and forth the knob to her front door. Someone, or some*thing*, was trying to get in the house. Of course, it could have been a burglar, except for one thing: on each occasion, a low and disturbing growl could be heard directly outside.

Police Chief Don F. Breckler urged calm and told the citizens of Defiance not to try to take on the monster themselves but to dial 911 immediately and let the police handle the situation. He added: "We don't know what to think. We didn't release [the details of the story] when we got the first report about a week ago. But now we're taking it seriously. We're concerned for the safety of our people."

> *Wearing a werewolf mask is not a difficult task. Covering one's entire body with fake hair would be far less easy.*

It was also the police who suggested a down-to-earth explanation for the weird affair: that the creature may have been a burglar wearing a werewolf mask to hide his real identity. Not an impossible scenario, but it's important to note that of those who saw the thing at close quarters, all were unanimous on one point: it was covered in hair from head to toe. Wearing a werewolf mask is not a difficult task. Covering one's entire body with fake hair would be far less easy. No wonder many scoffed at the idea of a masked burglar on the loose. Even the police noted this, admitting that, whether the mysterious entity was werewolf or burglar, "there is a lot of natural hair, too." Quite!

When the story reached the media, other people came forward, all claiming that the man-monster had tried to force its way into their homes, always in the early hours, and sometimes leaving deep and long scratch marks on the front doors, which the police were careful to photograph and add to their quickly growing werewolf file.

As the publicity grew, other railroad workers—also working night shifts—came forward to say that although they had not been attacked by the creature, they had certainly seen it. But, for the most part, they had previously stayed silent for fear of ridicule. By now, however, no one was laughing.

It was as a result of this collective body of data that the police were able to put together a composite picture of the sinister shape-shifter. By most accounts, it stood at a height of around eight feet. The hair on its body was coarse-looking and short. And the creature was clothed, which led many to believe the inevitable: that this was a man who, whether by choice or not, was able to take on the form of a werewolf. Of course, the fact that the clothes—jeans and a shirt but no footwear—were always ragged and torn and that the beast was around eight feet in height provoked a theory that in his normal form, the man was of regular height and build, but when the terrifying transformation took place, he grew in size and burst out of his clothes in a style very much befitting Marvel Comics' Incredible Hulk!

Nighttime and early-morning encounters continued into August, as did sightings of the huge beast in the vicinity of the railroad tracks. And then, as mid-August arrived, the beast was gone, never to return. Thus ended what was, without doubt, the weirdest saga in the history of Defiance, Ohio.

Sources:

Doc Conjure. "The Defiance OH Werewolf." *The Demoniacal*, October 24, 2012. http://thedemoniacal.blogspot.com/2012/10/the-defiance-oh-werewolf.html.

Redfern, Nick. Personal investigations, 2006.

Stegall, James. "Werewolf Case in Defiance Not Viewed Lightly by Police." *The Blade* (Toledo, Ohio), August 2, 1972.

"Wolfman of Defiance." 2016. Accessed March 25, 2023. http://www.oocities.org/zoomar1/wolfman.html.

Detecting Werewolves

It's not as easy to detect the werewolves among us as it is to hunt down the vampires lurking in the shadows. Perhaps the most essential difference between the two creatures of the dark side is the fact that the werewolf is not a member of the undead. When lycanthropes are not in the throes of transformation precipitated by the rays of the full moon or the wearing of the magic wolf belt, they walk about the bustling streets of the city or the pleasant country lanes appearing as any normal human. Werewolves have no need to scamper off to a coffin before the rays of the rising sun begin to burn welts into their hide. Werewolves can don shades, lie out on the sunny beach, and work on their tan if that should be their pleasure.

Mirrors offer no problem for werewolves. They can straighten their neckties or apply lipstick without worrying if they are casting a reflection.

Crucifixes are of no concern. Werewolves might even wear the sign of the cross themselves, attend church services, and perhaps even serve as members of the clergy.

Some old traditions do offer certain advice when it comes to detecting the werewolves among us. As early as the seventh century, Paulos Agina, a physician who lived in Alexandria, described the symptoms of werewolfism for his fellow doctors:

- Pale skin.
- Weak vision.
- An absence of tears or saliva, making the eyes and tongue very dry.
- Excessive thirst.
- Ulcers and abrasions on the arms and legs that do not heal, caused by walking on all fours.
- An obsession with wandering in cemeteries at night.
- Howling until dawn.

Many old traditions insist that the hands may provide the biggest giveaway. Check the palms of a suspected werewolf, and if his palms are covered with a coarse, stiff growth of hair, you had better avoid his company

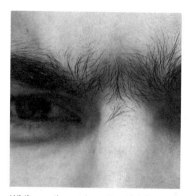

While a unibrow alone shouldn't be cause for alarm, it is on the list of signs that some scholars suggest for detecting werewolves in our midst.

on the nights of the full moon. And while you would rightfully argue that any reasonably intelligent werewolf would be careful to shave the palms—especially a female lycanthrope—if you are observant you would be able to notice that the flesh of their palms would be rough, perhaps even a bit scaly.

Another certain sign of the werewolf, according to a vast number of ancient traditions, lies in the extreme length of the index finger. If you should notice a man or woman with an index finger considerably longer than the middle finger, you have quite likely spotted a werewolf.

Then there is the matter of the eyebrows growing together. If they should meet in the center of the forehead, there is cause for genuine concern that you have encountered a werewolf. Once again, if it is obvious that the area is regularly shaved, beware of walks in the moonlight with this individual.

A good many traditions regard the pentagram, the five-pointed star, as a symbol of Witchcraft and werewolves. Some werewolf hunters of old believed that the sign of the pentagram would be found somewhere on a lycanthrope's body, most often on the chest or the hand. It was also believed that the shadow of the pentagram would manifest on the palm or forehead of the werewolf's next victim and would be visible only to the monster's eyes.

And speaking of the eyes of the werewolf, while they appear normal at all other times, when the curse is upon them, their eyes glow in the dark, most often with a reddish hue.

Perhaps with tongue firmly in cheek, the following test for detecting the werewolves among us was posted on Tina's *Humor Archives on the Internet*. Although some of the items on the list are actually traditional determinants in the folklore of werewolves, others are a bit off the wall. Allegedly compiled by a scholar who has been studying werewolves for 50 years, here, edited and condensed, is Dr. Werner Bokelman's test for determining if your friend or neighbor is a werewolf:

    ↫ Werewolves have extra glands that emit unpleasant odors. Therefore, if your friend or neighbor smells like a mixture of stale hay and horse manure, he or she could be a werewolf.

  ∾ Doctors in Denmark have declared that a certain mark of the werewolf is evidenced when he or she possesses eyebrows that meet in the middle of the forehead.

  ∾ The arms, legs, and bodies of werewolves are extremely hairy, especially the backs of their hands and the tops of their feet.

  ∾ Werewolves reach sexual maturity five years ahead of normal humans, so keep an eye on that neighbor's child who seems unusually attracted to children of the opposite sex at the age of seven or eight.

  ∾ Check the ring finger of both of the suspected werewolf's hands. Experts have determined that a long ring finger is a certain sign of a werewolf.

  ∾ Does your neighbor own large pets that are always disappearing, only to be replaced by others? Because werewolves have demanding appetites that require large amounts of raw flesh, they may be devouring their pets.

  ∾ If you hear strange howling and moaning sounds at night in the neighborhood where there is a full moon but no dogs around, you are quite likely living next to a werewolf.

  ∾ Have you noticed his or her skin slowly changing color? It may take a few hours for a werewolf to transform from human to animal form, and the first sign of the coming metamorphosis is a gradual darkening of the skin.

  ∾ If you spot your neighbor wandering around graveyards and mortuaries and often appearing at the scene of fatal accidents, he or she may be a werewolf scouting for fresh corpses.

  ∾ If you have the courage to be near a werewolf in the daylight, you might follow him into a public restroom to see if his urine is a deep purple in color — another sure sign of a werewolf.

Sources:

Douglas, Drake. *Horror!* New York: Collier Books, 1966.

Hurwood, Bernardt J. *Vampires, Werewolves, and Ghouls.* New York: Ace Books, 1968.

Noll, Richard. *Bizarre Diseases of the Mind.* New York: Berkley Books, 1990.

Diana the Huntress

Throughout the Middle Ages, Diana, the goddess of the wilderness and the hunt, ruled all the dark forests of Europe. Some scholars have declared that the Inquisition was instituted to stamp out all worship of Diana in Europe. The book of Acts in the Bible is filled with the struggles of the early apostles to counteract the influence of Diana, whose temple was one of the Seven Wonders of the World. "Great is Diana of the Ephesians," the tradespeople of Ephesus shouted at Paul and his company, setting in motion a riot (Acts 19). To the members of the Christian clergy, Diana was the Queen of the Witches. To the infamous Witch-hunter and Grand Inquisitor Torquemada, Diana was Satan.

The goddess Diana (Artemis to the Greeks) was the deity of the hunt and the wilderness. She had a twofold nature, being both the Lady of Wild Creatures and Queen of Heaven, but also the Huntress and Destroyer.

From ancient times (to the Greeks, she was Artemis), Diana was the Queen of Heaven, the Mother of Creatures, the Huntress, the Destroyer. While the early Christian fathers felt great satisfaction when the peasantry bent their knee to worship Mary as the Queen of Heaven, in truth, the majority believed that they were really worshipping Diana, the great and powerful goddess of old.

Diana, with her pack of hunting dogs, her stature as the Mother of Animals, the Lady of Wild Creatures, was the patron goddess of those who chose the life of the outlaw werewolf and all others who defied conventional society. She has remained the goddess of the wild woodlands and hunting throughout most of the Western world.

Sources:

Hazlin, W. E. *Dictionary of Faiths & Folklore*. London: Studio Editions, 1995.

Spence, Lewis. *An Encyclopedia of Occultism*. New Hyde Park, NY: University Books, 1960.

Walker, Barbara G. *The Woman's Encyclopedia of Myths and Secrets*. San Francisco: Harper & Row, 1983.

Dog People

The Inuit have a legend about the Adlet, the Dog People, the offspring of a great red dog and an Inuit woman. This beast/human marriage produced five ugly weredogs and five regular dogs, and the disgusted mother set them all adrift on rafts.

The five dogs eventually reached the shores of Europe and begat among them the various white ethnic groups. The weredogs evolved into horrible, bloodthirsty monsters who still haunt the northern icelands in search of human flesh.

Sources:

Larousse Dictionary of World Folklore. New York: Larousse, 1995.

Dogman/Cryptid Conference, Tennessee, 2022

The term "Dogman" is occasionally used as a modern-day name for the centuries-old werewolf. That's right: the creatures that you thought could never live … *do* live. For decades I've followed stories of the werewolf type, and from my perspective, the phenomenon is all too real. Of course, the mystery provokes rolling eyes and shaking heads. Nonetheless, in 2022, a conference on the history of the hairy creatures was held in Paris, Tennessee.

A similar event, called the Dogman Symposium, had taken place in 2016 in Defiance, Ohio, organized by cryptozoologist Ken Gerhard. Among the displays there was a Dogman figure used in the indie movies *Dogman* (2012) and *Dogman 2: The Wrath of the Litter* (2014) by Traverse City, Michigan, filmmaker Rich Brauer.

The more recent 2022 event was organized by Josh Turner, who has had his very own Dogman encounter. When he invited me to speak at his

Author Nick Redfern poses with a head from indie movies Dogman *(2012) and* Dogman 2: The Wrath of the Litter *(2014) at the Dogman Symposium of 2016.*

Dogman/Cryptid Conference, I didn't just say "Yes!" I said, "Hell, yes!" Other speakers joined in, a date was set in August, and the Dogman was unleashed.

The other speakers were ace cryptozoologists—and good mates—Ken Gerhard and Lyle Blackburn, skin walker expert David Weatherly, and just about all the key Dogman investigators there are: Ron Murphy, D. A. Roberts, Joedy Cook, Barton Nunnelly, Bettina Moss, Elijah Henderson, Tony Merkel, Jay Tucker, and Josh Nannochio.

Saturday, August 13, 2022, was a great day. Attendees and participants embraced the mystery, the high strangeness, and the many lectures and displays related to Dogman/cryptid/werewolf phenomena. Things began with cool words for Linda Godfrey (1951–2022), without whom, in all likelihood, the Dogman phenomenon would not be what it is now. Linda really launched the phenomenon in the 1990s, and without her, we wouldn't have what we do now: masses of data, thick case files that Linda generously shared with the Dogman/Cryptid Conference, and much more. Soon the crowd of around 300 people took to their seats. Josh hit the stage and introduced the speakers. And we had liftoff, so to speak.

Theories abounded among the participants as to what the Dogmen might be. It's not surprising, because the creatures are fascinating in multiple aspects: the paranormal, the supernatural, and even the occult. Some are sure the beasts are a form of large wolf that can walk upright. The Dire Wolves, for example, are said to be large and powerful wolves that lived thousands of years ago and were more monster than animal. Another idea is that at least some Dogmen might actually be hairless bears. (Have you ever seen a photo of a grizzly bear without its hair? It looks downright creepy!) There is also the theory that people who think they've seen Dogmen have really encountered Bigfoot creatures. Of course, the fact that wolves have muzzles and the Bigfoot beasts don't provokes some controversy.

David Weatherly, an expert on the skin walker phenomenon, shared his thoughts about the Dogman. David's words included matters relative to the trickster phenomenon, the shape-shifting Djinn, the fear provoked by the creatures, and the skin walkers' notable ability to run on both two legs and four. Both the skin walkers and the Dogmen can provoke illness in people—a sinister phenomenon. More impressive: some of these creatures have been seen running around up to 60 miles per hour. David elaborated on the matter of shape-shifting, including ties to such animals as the crow, the raven, the were-hyena, and multiple other animals that seem to be part flesh-and-blood and part paranormal.

I found it fascinating there was a kind of split between some of the Dogmen enthusiasts. The paranormal angle kept surfacing, as did the theory that these creatures were simply unknown animals that were able to hide themselves to amazing degrees. Burial rites, ancient mounds, and Witches all came into play as the picture of the Dogman grew. One of the questions put to me was whether the Dogmen can jump portals and dimensions. I have no issues answering yes! I've heard of many cases that seem to allow these creatures to exist in our world and what I can only term "elsewhere."

Here is one fascinating issue that I must share with you. I had a very weird experience back in 2002. I was in a state of sleep paralysis in my bedroom. As I believe that sleep paralysis has an external, supernatural aspect to it (rather than it being due to the mysteries of the mind), I feel it's relevant to share the story here. I had gone to bed and then had an extremely curious encounter. It was around 4:00 a.m., and I was awake and yet not awake. And I couldn't move. I was suddenly aware that something was slowly heading down the corridor of my duplex that linked the bedroom to the living room.

That something was a humanoid figure with the head of a wolf. It was attired in a long, flowing black cape. *It emitted strange and rapid growling noises that seemed to be in an unintelligible language.* And the creature, whatever its origin was, seemed mightily pissed off about something. As it closed in on the room, I made a supreme effort to move my rigid, paralyzed form and finally succeeded, just as the beast entered the bedroom. In an instant it was gone, and I was wide awake. After I mentioned this to the audience, a woman came to me and said that she, too, had experienced that "growling language."

My lecture at the conference was on the bizarre werewolf case from the summer of 1972 in Defiance, Ohio, in which a wolfman or werewolf appeared to the local population in July and August and then apparently vanished. (The incident is described fully in the entry called "Defiance, Ohio.")

I also spoke about an entire pack of werewolves reported at the legendary Cannock Chase woods of central England. The woods and forests of England are inviting and picturesque. They are also, however, filled with terrible things that provoke fear and hysteria. One of them—a hideous shape-shifter—plunged a small community into a collective state of fear in 2007.

The Cannock Chase is a large and ancient area of forest in central England; in 1958, it was officially designated as an "area of outstanding beauty" by the local government. While 1958 is not that long ago, it's important to note that the area itself has been a wild and mysterious one not just for decades or even centuries, but for millennia. For example, in the village of Cannock Wood, on the fringes of the Chase, there stands the remains of an Iron Age hill fort that was constructed by the Cornovii people, a Celtic band that held sway over much of the area at the time. It is known locally as the Castle Ring. Numerous reports of creatures resembling Bigfoot, large black cats, and even a Mothman-like entity with fiery eyes have surfaced from the Castle Ring.

The saga began in March 2007 when a local paranormal investigations group, the West Midlands Ghost Club, found itself on the receiving end of something extremely weird and surely unanticipated: a stash of reports of werewolf-like beasts seen lurking among the old gravestones. The story of how the WMGC came to be involved, and the nature of the encounters, is recounted in the group's online article, "But I'm Alright Naaoooowwwwwww!!!!!"

The reports provoked enough interest that Mike Lockley, at the time the editor of the now-defunct local newspaper, the *Chase Post*, gave the story a great deal of ink. Such publicity brought in even more reports. For around three months, the good folk of the Cannock Chase found themselves plunged into a controversy that had at its heart sinister shape-shifting monsters that dwelled among the long dead. It was a controversy that soon aroused terror and hysteria.

The morphing monsters of the Cannock Chase were not typical of the old legends, however. In other words, this was most assuredly not a case of witnesses reporting people changing into werewolves (or vice versa). No, they were wolflike creatures that had the ability to alter their body structure, thus allowing them to walk on either four legs or two.

As the event started to wind down, new friends were made, good food was eaten, and hundreds of people came to realize that there really are strange and sinister creatures that seem to look like werewolves. Furthermore, they are deadly and dangerous and should be avoided whenever and wherever possible. Of course, most of us in the building—including me — would say "screw that" and head off into the woods to find a few of these muzzle-faced monsters!

Here's to the next Dogman gig!

Sources:

Redfern, Nick. August 2022.

WMGC. "But I'm Alright Naaoooooowwwwwww!!!!!" The West Midlands Ghost Club (blog), October 1, 2009. https://westmidlandsghostclub.blogspot.com/2009/10/but-im-alright-naaoooooowwwwwww.html.

Doñas de Fuera

On the matter of fairies and shape-shifting, we have the Doñas de Fuera ("Ladies from Outside") of Sicily, the Italian island of the Mediterranean. Very much like the elementals of England, Scotland, Ireland, and Wales, the Doñas de Fuera were small, humanoid entities that had a somewhat fraught relationship with the local human population.

Although they were described as both beautiful and enchanting, the Doñas de Fuera were not to be messed with. They certainly had their friendly and even helpful sides to their characters, but if they were offended, their wrath ranged from cruel and dangerous to deadly.

The Doñas de Fuera looked human, for the most part, aside from their strange feet, which were described as being circular or paw-like. The latter description is most apt, since the Doñas de Fuera had the ability to turn themselves into cats — of the regular kind and also those that looked like large, black mountain lions. Interestingly, reports of shape-shifting large black cats can be found within the United Kingdom, too.

The Doñas de Fuera of Sicily — small, humanoid entities described as both beautiful and enchanting — looked human, aside from their circular or paw-like feet.

Sources:

Redfern, Nick. Interview with Rosemary Ellen Guiley, 2015.

Dwayyo
by Pastor Robin Swope

The Dwayyo is a large, wolflike, bipedal creature that has been reported primarily in West Middletown, Maryland. The creature first came to prominence within the local population after a story ran in the local paper, the *Frederick News-Post*, in late November 1965. Reporter George May wrote in the article "Mysterious Dwayyo Loose in County" that a young man, named anonymously as "John Becker," heard a strange noise in his backyard, which was situated on the outskirts of Gambrill State Park. Upon going out to investigate the noise, he initially saw nothing, so he headed back in. It was then that he caught sight of the creature. Something was moving toward him in the dark. Becker was quoted as saying, "It was as big as a bear, had long black hair, a bushy tail, and growled like a wolf or dog in anger." The thing quickly moved toward him on its

The first mention of the name Dwayyo comes from a sighting in 1944, when witnesses heard the creature make "frightful screams."

hind legs and attacked him. He fought off the creature and drove it back into the woods, later calling police to report the incident.

According to other sources, this was not the first sighting of the legendary creature. In the 1890s, a local farmer reported seeing a doglike creature nine feet tall at Camp Greentop near Sabillasville, Maryland.

The first mention of the name "Dwayyo" comes from a sighting in 1944 from an area in Carroll County, Maryland. Witnesses heard the creature make "frightful screams," and there were footprints attesting to the claims of the sighting.

But it was not until late 1965 and early 1966 that the creature made headlines when it was frequently sighted across the area. The first time was the incident reported by Mr. Becker. Besides that incident, the *Frederick News-Post* revealed in early December that it had received numerous calls reporting sightings of the creature, so many that the initial reporter, George May, was issued a hunting license for the creature by the County Treasurer's office and rallied a "call to arms" in the December 8, 1965, article "Dwayyo Hunt Tonight." The hunt must have been a bust, since Mr. May wrote a follow-up article the next day called "Dwayyo Hunt Flops." There were also many reports of the creature being sighted in early December at the nearby University of Maryland.

Later, in the summer of 1966, the creature was again sighted on the outskirts of Gambrill State Park. A man referred to only as "Jim A." encountered the Dwayyo as he was heading toward a camp site. It was described as a shaggy, two-legged creature the size of a deer and had a triangle-shaped head with pointed ears and chin. It was dark brown in color, and when approached it made a horrid scream and backed away from the man. Jim described it as having an odd walk as it retreated; its legs "stuck out from the side of the trunk of the body, making its movements appear almost spider-like as it backed away."

It was described as a shaggy, two-legged creature the size of a deer and had a triangle-shaped head with pointed ears and chin.

In the late fall of 1976, another sighting of the Dwayyo took place in Frederick County near Thurmont between Cunningham Falls State Park and Catoctin Mountain National Park. Two men drove off Route 77 and onto a private road so they could "spot deer" with their headlights to see how thick the native population had become before deer season. To their surprise, they did not catch a deer in their lights but instead a different kind of large animal, which ran in front of their car. They described the creature as "at least 6 ft tall but inclined forward since it was moving quickly. Its head was fairly large and similar to the profile of a wolf. The body was covered in brown or brindle colored fur, but the lower half had a striped pattern of noticeable darker and lighter banding. The forelegs (or arms) were slimmer and held out in front as it moved. The back legs were very muscled and thick similar to perhaps a kangaroo. This was not a hominoid type creature; it did not have the characteristics of an ape. It was much more similar to a wolf or ferocious dog. However, it was definitely moving upright and appeared to be adapted for that type of mobility. I was particularly impressed by the size and strength of the back legs, the stripes on the lower half of the body and the canine-wolf-like head."

It was in this same vicinity where the next sighting took place two years later, in 1978, by two park rangers near the Cunningham Falls area, where they encountered "a large hairy creature running on two legs."

According to Aubrey (not her real name), she was driving her old Subaru on Coxey Brown Road near Myersville, Maryland, late in the summer of 2009, when she had an eerie feeling, as if she were being watched. The road was lined with trees, and she was on the outer edge of Gambrill State Park, where the forest was beginning to grow thicker. According to Aubrey, as she turned on Hawbottom Road, where her friend lived, the eerie feeling became overwhelming. The hairs on the back of her neck rose in terror as she sensed the unseen eyes upon her. She wanted to stop the car and take her breath, but she was afraid that she would veer off the road and hit a tree because her nerves were getting so unsteady that she was beginning to shake. But she knew that whatever was watching her and following her was out there, and she took what little comfort she had by being relatively safe inside her rusty car. Still, to prevent a wreck, she slowed down as she headed south, and that was when she saw the creature.

At first it was a blur to the right of her peripheral vision. It was something that was moving through the trees, a shadow that flickered as it went in and out of sight on the edge of her vision. It was a brown smear of color that popped out in contrast to the dull dark gray trees that she passed.

Whatever it was, it bobbed through the underbrush and between the trees to keep pace with her car. She thinks at the time that she was going around 25 miles per hour. She then slowed down once more to take a good look to her right and make sure that she was not seeing things. As her car slowed to a crawl, the brown, blurry smear of color seemed to bound out of the woods closer to the road. With a massive leap, the hazy color became flesh as a huge, doglike animal on two legs emerged from the foliage.

The sight of the fangs, Aubrey wrote, was burned into her memory. A huge mouth grimaced in anger and hate. She could feel the fangs as if they were ripping her skin while the creature stood there panting on the side of the road. Drool dripped from its huge mouth as she heard a loud growl, and she looked into the dark eyes. Darkness took up the entirety of both eyes; there was no white at all. It was if she was staring death and hell head-on in dizzying madness.

Then it leaped, arms outstretched with claws grasping the wind. Instinctively, Aubrey stepped on her gas pedal with all her might. The squeal of her tires made it seem as if her car, too, was screaming in horror at the thing that had emerged from the dark, gloomy forest.

> *The squeal of her tires made it seem as if her car, too, was screaming in horror at the thing that had emerged from the dark, gloomy forest.*

She did not look back. She didn't want to know if the thing was following her. She didn't feel the eyes upon her anymore. She was too shaken to really feel anything at all. When she made it to her friend's house, she sat in the driveway, shaking as she looked around to make sure the creature had not followed her there. The house was also in the woods at the opposite side of the state park.

When she felt safe again, she made a mad dash for her friend's door and banged on it frantically. He did not know what to make of her story. Aubrey knew he did not believe her. He had lived in the woods all his life and he had never encountered what she had seen. He assured her that it must have just been a dog, perhaps a rabid one. Her mind was playing tricks on her.

But the young woman knew what she had seen that late summer day. It was no dog. It was something out of a horror movie come to life before her eyes. Though she told nobody what she felt it really was, she called it a werewolf—that is, until after she did some research in the local college library and came up with the name that others had called it when they, too, saw the forest come alive. She had encountered the Dwayyo.

According to local authorities, there are always rumors of the creature being sighted in the state parks surrounding Frederick County, but few are willing to come forward to make a formal report because they are afraid of ridicule or doubts about their sanity. Aubrey was one of those. Even though the encounter was one of the most horrifying things she had ever experienced, the fear of what others will think of her because of what she saw is even greater. She vows that the creature she saw on Hawbottom Road will not take anything else from her life. "The Dwayyo has taken enough."

Sources:

May, George. "Mysterious Dwayyo Loose in County." *Frederick News-Post*, November 27, 1965.

Eagle Creek, Ohio

Is it possible that there was once a tribe of Native Americans who, a time long ago, worshipped the werewolf—or truly believed that they were werewolves?

On an afternoon in 1949, Kentucky farmer A. C. Ayres was digging post holes in a field on his small bottomland acreage when a metal glint caught his eye. He bent down to examine what appeared to be an old copper wrist band in the wet clay.

While finds like the one Ayres made that afternoon were not uncommon in an area that had once been the home of many Native American cultures and where artifacts were regularly turned up by a farmer's plow, something told Ayres that it was no ordinary find he had made.

Ayres was right in that feeling. He had found the first clue pointing the direction to one of the most macabre archaeological finds ever made

In the spring of 1950, archaeologists uncovered and reconstructed the first evidence of a bizarre wolf-worshipping Indian cult: a man with a full set of wolf fangs protruding from his skeletal mouth.

in North America. The Kentucky farmer had unearthed the first evidence of a bizarre wolf-worshipping Indian cult that had practiced strange rites when the field in which he was standing had been a wilderness.

Ayres decided to call archaeologists at the University of Kentucky, who had made known to farmers in Owen County their deep interest in artifacts from the Ohio Valley Mound Builders who had flourished there in prehistoric times.

The field team that arrived at Ayres's farm became greatly excited when the farmer took them to the site where the object had been found. They observed at once that Ayres had been digging his new post hole on an ancient burial mound built perhaps 1,500 years earlier by a group of people known by anthropologists as the Adena Culture.

In the spring of 1950, archaeologists began probing the area with only a slight hope that any further significant finds might be made. But then digging tools encountered shreds of what appeared to be the decomposing fiber of some organic material suspected to be leather. Proceeding with great care from the small corner of the material that had been exposed, the archaeologists began moving with excited swiftness when portions of a human skeleton began to emerge.

Within hours, the scientists had uncovered the skeletal remains of what had been a large man who had apparently died or been killed at the prime of his life in some remote era.

The body had been encased in tightly bound leather and laid to rest in the mound on a pallet of bark. A second covering of bark had been placed over the corpse. Curiously, the skull of the ancient man had been violently crushed in some manner.

As scientists labored to put all the pieces back together, an amazing discovery was made. Among the bone shards, a skeletal fragment that was not of human origin was found.

Examination showed the alien bone to be the intricately cut jaw of a wolf, carved from the total skull of the animal in such a fashion that a rear, handle-like portion extended forward to a point where the front teeth of the animal still protruded from the upper palate structure.

An object identical to the cut wolf jaw on the Ayres farm had been found almost ten years earlier at another archaeological dig in nearby Montgomery County, Kentucky, by scientists sifting another mound grouping.

Archaeologists had conjectured that the strange wolf tooth artifact had been significant to some ancient Adena religious ceremony, but it remained for the scientists assembling the Ayres skull to discover the macabre use to which the prehistoric tribe had put the sacred instrument.

A reconstruction of the skeletal remains indicated that the man buried in the mound had been no more than 30 years old at death. Piecing together the skull, scientists found the man's four front teeth missing, although the remaining teeth were in perfect condition. Healed portions of the jaw showed that the four missing teeth had been deliberately taken out at some time during the man's life.

When the archaeologists once more picked up the wolf jaw carving, they could not help observing that it fit perfectly into the space where the teeth of the prehistoric man had been removed.

The composite that emerged was one in which a full set of wolf fangs protruded from the skeletal mouth of the Ayres man, giving him, even in death, an appearance that frayed the nerves.

The composite that emerged was one in which a full set of wolf fangs protruded from the skeletal mouth of the Ayres man, giving him, even in death, an appearance that frayed the nerves. How much more frightening the wolf man of Eagle Creek must have appeared on the moonless nights when he stalked the primeval forests of Kentucky.

The discovery set off a flurry of scientific speculation about the meaning of the wolf tooth artifact in the daily life of the ancient culture. Was there a special wolf cult among the Adena? What might their ceremonies have been to require the use of the raw, keen wolves' teeth inserted into the mouths of their priests?

Anthropologists were certain that the body found buried in lonely splendor in the Ayres mound must have been that of a tribal leader or a man of some other great importance. Few Adena people were given the honor of single mound burial, a practice reserved for persons of high rank.

Some knowledgeable observers believed the Ayres man may have given his life in a sacred ceremony designed to propitiate a god, most likely the wolf. Several Indian cultures were known to place victims inside a leather bag, allowing the material to slowly contract and squeeze the life from the body. Often the skull was crushed when this method was employed.

The discovery of the werewolf cult of Kentucky and the Ohio Valley substantiates, in part, a number of tribal legends previously thought to be baseless, in which terrible stories of men who became wolves are told.

Sometimes when the moon is full, those legends say, strange forms stalk the deep woods of the Ohio Valley, and sharp, piercing howls reach toward the sky.

Sources:

Steiger, Brad. *Real Monsters, Gruesome Critters, and Beasts from the Darkside*. Canton, MI: Visible Ink Press, 2011.

Eisler, Robert (1904–1949)

Robert Eisler, author of *Man into Wolf*, had a distinguished and tragic life. Born in Vienna in 1904, he was educated there and in Leipzig and gained his degrees and his doctorates summa cum laude. He was a Fellow of the Austrian Historical Institute, traveled widely, and visited the excavations at Ephesus, Milletus, and Knossos.

From 1925 to 1931, Eisler worked with the League of Nations in Paris and lectured at the Sorbonne on the origins of Christianity. He returned to his native Austria and spent the next six years doing research. In 1938, he had just received a position teaching comparative religion at Oxford when he was arrested by the Gestapo.

After 15 months in Buchenwald and Dachau, he was released and permitted to travel to England to accept the position at Oxford. Although he lectured at the university for nearly two years, the terrible results of the treatment that he had endured in the concentration camps began to take their toll on his body. By now the war was in full fury, and he remained in England, continuing to research and write, until his death in 1949.

The author of many works in German, Eisler had his final achievement in *Man into Wolf—An Anthropological Interpretation of Sadism, Masochism, and Lycanthropy* in which he sought to demonstrate that all violence, from individual rape and murder to collective organized war, stems from an ancestral memory of humankind's prehistoric descent from timid vegetarian to savage, meat-and-blood eating lycanthrope. Eisler was convinced that humankind's collective consciousness—and conscience—had expressed its guilt all over the world in its legends, myths, and psycho-religious rites.

Sources:

Eisler, Robert. *Man into Wolf*. London: Spring Books, 1948.

Elkhorn Monster

As Linda Godfrey (1951–2022) tells in her book *The Beast of Bray Road* (2003), late one winter's night in 1993, Lorianne Endrizzi was driving down Bray Road in Elkhorn, Wisconsin, when she saw what she at first thought was a man crouching at the side of the road. Curious as to what he might be doing on the shoulder of the road, she slowed down to take a closer look. Within the next few moments, she was astonished to see that the being spotlighted in the beams of her headlights was covered with fur and had a long, wolflike snout, fangs, pointed ears, and eyes that had a yellowish glow. The thing's arms were jointed like a human's, and it had hands with humanlike fingers that were tipped with pointed claws.

Lorianne sped off, thinking that the creature was so humanlike that it had to be some kind of freak of nature. Later, when she visited the library, she found a book with an illustration of a werewolf. She said that she was startled to see how much the classic monster of legend resembled the beast that she had seen that night on Bray Road right there in Elkhorn, Wisconsin.

Doristine Gipson, another Elkhorn resident who sighted the creature on Bray Road, described it as having a large chest, like that of a weightlifter. She was certain that she had not seen a large dog but instead a humanlike creature that had a wide chest and was covered with long, brown hair.

A 12-year-old girl said that she had been with a group of friends walking near a snow-covered cornfield when they sighted what they believed to be a large dog. When they began to call it, it stared at them, then stood upright.

As the children screamed in their alarm, the beast dropped back down on all fours and began running toward them. Fortunately for them, the monster suddenly headed off in another direction and disappeared.

"What impressed me most about the first witnesses to the Beast of Bray Road," Linda Godfrey said, "was their almost visible sense of deep fright that was still obvious as they recounted what they saw. They didn't act like people making something up, and in fact, they could hardly bring themselves to tell their stories. I was also impressed by the fact that they all noticed a certain jeering cockiness from the creature as it made eye contact with them. This is a characteristic that has continued to be present in every sighting reported. Even when the witness is some distance away, he or she reports feeling almost more like the observed than the observer. And that is very unnerving to even the most macho, outdoorsy of the witnesses. I was also struck by the fact that the creature apparently was more interested in getting away than in harming anyone.

"Officially, I don't eliminate any sightings that are reported in good faith, as long as the witness felt there was something very strange about it. In much Native American lore, 'spirit' animals are visually

"It's worth noting that people do see ordinary dogs, coyotes, bears, wolves, etc., all the time and the reaction is just, 'hey, there's a coyote' — not, 'heaven help me … it's scaring me to death.'"

indistinguishable from ordinary creatures. So if witnesses think there is something different enough about what they see that they are compelled to report it, I just put it down exactly as they tell it. I feel the more information we have, the easier it will be to see patterns.

"It's worth noting that people do see ordinary dogs, coyotes, bears, wolves, etc., all the time and the reaction is just, 'hey, there's a coyote'—not, 'heaven help me, there's something so unusual it's scaring me to death.' So I tend to trust people's instincts when they say there was something not right about what they've spotted, whether it was size, speed, posture, or even as some have reported, telepathic communication!

"Most people entertain the Hollywood notion of the slathering, tortured soul who transforms bodily under the full moon and must be killed with silver bullets," Godfrey continued. "Others might consider the word to signify a shamanistic shape-shifter who is able to summon the very realistic illusion of another creature. Or perhaps you are talking about the medieval notion of a human who is able to project an astral entity that looks like a wolf (usually while the person is sound asleep) that is able to roam the countryside, kill and eat people and which, if wounded, will transfer the wound to the corresponding area of the human body.

"There are other versions, too. Statements by witnesses such as 'I thought it was a demon from hell' or 'It was something not natural, not of this world,' have indeed made me wonder if something other than a natural, flesh-and-blood animal is roaming the cornfields around here.

"A few witnesses that I detail in my second book, *Beyond Bray Road*, claim to have seen the creature either morphing or materializing. This points to the supernatural, but still doesn't prove that an actual human has changed bodily structure, grown fur and fangs, and then sneaked out for a midnight possum dinner. However, I do consider the possibility. And while I know there are self-proclaimed lycanthropes who insist they do transmute, I haven't yet found the evidence to prove it occurs."

Sources:

Godfrey, Linda. *The Beast of Bray Road*. Madison, WI: Prairie Oak Press, 2003.

Steiger, Brad. *Real Monsters, Gruesome Critters, and Beast from the Darkside*. Canton, MI: Visible Ink Press, 2011.

Endore, Guy (1900–1970)

When Guy Endore attended Columbia University in the early 1920s and his classmates first began to perceive his literary talents—together with his aureole of blond hair—they began to describe him as the present incarnation of the young Percy Bysshe Shelley. Although Endore preferred the sciences, he excelled in the humanities and was a member of a group of young intellectuals who included such future literary luminaries as Clifton Fadiman, Mortimer Adler, Edgar Johnson, and Henry Morton Robinson. It is unlikely, though, that any of his classmates in the Columbia class of 1924 knew that Endore's childhood had known desperate poverty.

When he was just a small boy in Brooklyn, his mother died, and his father sent him, with his brother and three sisters, to a Methodist orphanage in Ohio. Later, family circumstances dramatically improved to the point where their father took them to Vienna. Here, however, rather than offering comfort and peace of mind, Endore's father left his children with a French governess and then mysteriously disappeared.

For five years, the governess fulfilled her responsibility to her vanished employer and saw to it that the young Americans were trained in scholarly ways in the rigorous elementary schools and gymnasia of Vienna. And then the funds ran out. The governess appealed to the U.S. Consulate to intervene, and the Endore children were restored to their father, who had taken residence in Pittsburgh. Guy enrolled in Schenley High School and the Carnegie Institute of Technology in Pittsburgh before his acceptance at Columbia.

Soon after his graduation, he married his wife, Henrietta, and managed to support himself, his wife, and eventually a child by doing translations from French and German. His first book, published in 1929, was a biography of Casanova. His second was a study of Joan of Arc. In 1933, he published the famous horror tale *Werewolf of Paris*.

Endore, his wife, and their two daughters, Marcia and Gita, survived the Depression years by answering Hollywood's call to come to Los Angeles and write scripts for motion pictures. He subsequently wrote scripts for all the major studios and worked on a number of horror films, including *The Mark of the Vampire* (1936). Although Endore's werewolf novel is credited as the inspiration for *The Werewolf of London* (1935) and *Curse of the Werewolf* (1961), it actually bears very little resemblance to either one of the cinematic treatments. Endore's wolf man is based on the actual case of François Bertrand, who was truly more ghoul than werewolf.

Endore wrote a number of novels after his stint at the studios, including *Methinks the Lady* (1946) and *King of Paris* (1956).

Sources:

Endore, Guy. *The King of Paris*. New York: Simon and Schuster, 1956.

Melton, J. Gordon. *The Vampire Book: The Encyclopedia of the Undead*. Canton, MI: Visible Ink Press, 2011.

Enkidu

Perhaps our earliest written record of a man-beast appears on a Babylonian fragment circa 2000 BCE that tells the story of King Gilgamesh and his werewolf-like friend, Enkidu. *The Epic of Gilgamesh* remains to date the oldest known literary work in the world. Although it comprises 12 cantos of about 300 verses each, ancient records indicate that the original epic was at least twice as long as its presently known length.

Pieced together from 30,000 fragments discovered in the library at Ninevah in 1853, the story tells of Gilgamesh, the legendary Sumerian king of Uruk, and his quest for immortality. At first perceiving that the physical aspect of his quest lies in perpetuating his seed, Gilgamesh becomes such a lustful monarch that no woman in his kingdom is safe from his advances. The goddess Aruru, assessing the situation, decides to take matters into her own hands, and she forms the beast-man Enkidu from clay and her spittle to create an opponent powerful enough to challenge Gilgamesh.

In some period art, like this Akkadian cylinder seal where Enkidu (right) battles a lion, Gilgamesh's beastman companion is depicted with bull-like features.

Gilgamesh soon learns of this hairy wild man of the desert who protects the beasts from all those who would hunt in his desolate domain, and the king begins to have uncomfortable dreams of wrestling with a strong opponent whom he could not defeat. Gilgamesh sends a woman into the wilderness to seduce the wild beast-man and to tame him. She accomplishes her mission, teaching him such social graces as the wearing of clothing and other amenities of civilization as they wend their way to Uruk. When Enkidu eventually arrives in the city, the two giants engage in fierce hand-to-hand combat. The king manages to throw the beast-man, but he does not kill him. Instead, the two become fast friends, combining their strength to battle formidable giants and even the gods themselves. It is the jealous goddess Ishtar who causes the fatal illness that leads to Enkidu's death.

Gilgamesh finally abandons his search for immortality when the goddess Siduri Sabitu, dispenser of the Wine of Immortality to the gods, confides in him that his quest will forever be in vain—the cruel gods have decreed that all mortals shall die. Each day should be treasured, she advises, and one should enjoy the good things of life—a wife, family, friends, eating, and drinking.

Sources:

Gordon, Stuart. *The Encyclopedia of Myths and Legends*. London: Headline Books, 1993.

The Reader's Companion to World Literature. New York: New American Library, 1956.

Ethnology of the Werewolf

In the beginning of the thirteenth century, Gervase of Tillbury wrote in Latin in his *Otia Imperialia*: "In English they say werewolf, for in English were means man, and wolf wolf." In Medieval Latin, werewolf was written *guerulfus*.

In Scandinavia, the Norwegian counterpart to *werewolf* is *vargulf*, which, literally translated, is "rogue wolf." In Swedish, *varulf*; Danish, *vaerulf*. The Norse words *Ulfhedhnar* ("wolf-clothed") and *ber-werker* (in German, *barenhauter*) refer to the skins worn by the dreaded Northern warriors when they went berserk, war-mad, running amok among their opponents.

In other regions of Europe, we have the Medieval Norman *garwalf*; in Norman-French, *loup-garou*. In Portugal, *lobarraz*; in Italy, *lupo-manaro*; in Calabria, *lupu-minaru*; and in Sicily, *lupu minaru*.

In the Slavonic languages, the werewolf is called *vlukodlak*, literally "wolf haired" or "wolf-skinned." In Bulgaria, *vulkolak*; Poland, *wilkolak*; Russian, *volkolka* or *volkulaku*; Serbia, *vulkodlak*.

This Belarusian silver commemorative coin depicts Vseslav of Polotsk—a famed Slavic prince, hero, and reputed sorcerer—with a running wolf to acknowledge the fact he was a werewolf.

In modern Greek, the word *brukolakas* or *bourkolakas* can apply to vampires as well as werewolves, since it is adapted from a Slavic word for a creature that flies or attacks by night.

Sources:

Eisler, Robert. *Man into Wolf*. London: Spring Books, 1948.

Simek, Rudolf. *Dictionary of Northern Mythology*. Translated by Angela Hall. Rochester, NY: Boydell & Brewer, 1993.

Spence, Lewis. *An Encyclopedia of Occultism*. New Hyde Park, NY: University Books, 1960.

Exorcism

During his Sunday, March 4, 1990, sermon at St. Patrick's Cathedral in New York City, Cardinal John O'Connor stated that diabolically instigated violence is on the rise around the world, and he disclosed that two church-sanctioned exorcisms had been performed in the New York area within that past year.

Cardinal O'Connor went on to say that the novel *The Exorcist* by William Peter Blatty was a gruesomely authentic portrayal of demonic possession. Perhaps the only exposure that most people have to the concept of exorcism is derived from that popular novel and motion picture—and perhaps the majority of those who read the book or shuddered through the chilling cinematic version believe that such demonic manifestations and such rites of exorcism exist only in the lively imagination of authors of horror novels. Those people could not be further from the truth.

Lorraine Warren and her late husband, Ed Warren, of the New England Society for Psychic Research revealed that they had been present during the two violent exorcisms referred to by Cardinal O'Connor. The first exorcism involved a woman who howled like a wolf, vomited vile fluid from her mouth, and levitated about a foot off the floor while the priests and their assistants tried to hold her down. The second case was that of a woman who had been into drugs and who joined a satanic cult. She spoke in the deep, rough voice of a vulgar, profane man, and she struggled against her exorcists with such strength that seven people could not restrain her. She, too, snarled like some monstrous beast, levitated, and vomited vile fluids.

On December 30, 1998, the London *Guardian* reported that Christian clergy are increasingly being called upon to conduct exorcisms to rid people of evil spirits. The Church of England and the Roman Catholic Church declined the opportunity to make an official comment, but they did admit that every diocese has dedicated staff experienced in dealing with exorcism. While some clerics are embarrassed by critics who claim the entire subject hearkens back to the Middle Ages, priests throughout the Western world are coping with steadily growing demands for exorcism and requests to drive away evil spirits from the afflicted.

Reverend Peter Irwin-Clark, an evangelical Anglican priest in Brighton and a former lawyer, brushes off criticism of such work by reminding his detractors of the frequent references in the New Testament to demonic possession and the commandments of Christ to his followers to cast out evil spirits.

The Church of England has established the Christian Deliverance Study Group for the purpose of examining the issues of exorcism and demon possession. To divert criticism by mental health professionals that evil spirits are more likely to have their origin in psychiatric disorders than Satan, the church has issued guidelines that advise priests to work in close cooperation with medically trained professionals.

Rev. Tom Willis, an authorized Church of England exorcist for more than 30 years in the York diocese, told the *Guardian* that his experiences have convinced him that about one in ten people see a ghost in their lifetime:

People see apparitions, objects moving around, they experience being tapped on their shoulder, doors opening or strange smells. I've seen objects disappearing and re-appearing in a neighboring room. It's not clear to me whether this is an offshoot of the human mind—some sort of stress leaking out—or if it is something using human energy. I've had the experience of poltergeists reading my mind. It can be quite frightening.

In their remarkable book *Werewolf: A True Story of Demonic Possession*, Ed and Lorraine Warren recount the exorcism of Bill Ramsey, a man possessed with the spirit of a werewolf, by Bishop Robert McKenna. The Warrens were in attendance, along with a number of journalists and four off-duty policemen, especially hired by the bishop to defend him from the werewolf's violent attacks. During the course of the exorcism, when Bishop McKenna placed his crucifix against Ramsey's forehead,

the werewolf inside him went berserk. He came up from his chair snarling and growling and grasping at the Bishop. ... The Bishop had no choice but to retreat beyond the altar gate. Bill, spittle flying from his mouth, eyes wild, began to rush through the gate. ... But the priest stood absolutely still now, holding his cross up once again and beginning to speak in Latin. ... Bill felt suddenly weak. ... He felt his desire to attack the Bishop begin to fade. ... The werewolf's power was slipping quickly away. A faint roar sounded in Bill's chest, and then faded. He brought up his hands, but they were no longer clawlike. They were merely hands.

Father Pellegrino Ernetti, an exorcist with the Vatican, has stated that some people actually do make pacts with Satan to become powerful werewolf-like creatures and to gain material success on Earth. He tells of a young French boxer who made such a pact after his career in the ring had proven to be very disappointing. After he allowed the beast to come into him, he was soon winning bout after bout—but then he still had the conscience to realize that his opponents very often were severely injured or disabled after fighting with him.

Father Ernetti said that the young boxer had the courage to come to him for help, and after a difficult series of exorcisms, he was able to drive the beast from his body. Now the man leads a happy, normal life as a garage mechanic in Paris.

For the first time since 1614, the Vatican issued new guidelines for exorcisms in January 1999. The new rite of exorcism is written in Latin and contained in a red, leather-bound, 84-page book, and it reflects Pope John Paul II's efforts to convince a skeptical, materialistic generation that Satan is alive, well, and very much in the world. As Cardinal Jorge Medina Estevez, a Vatican official, put it, "The existence of the devil isn't an opinion, something to take or leave as you wish."

Although the revisions do not drastically alter the words or the gestures to be used by the exorcists, the update does provide optional texts that may be utilized by the priests. And the new guidelines stress that the priest must be certain that the afflicted is not suffering from a mental illness or the excesses of his or her own imagination.

Sources:

"Clergy Responds to an Increasing Demand for Exorcisms." *Guardian*, December 30, 1998.

D'Emilio, Frances. "Vatican Updates Rules for Exorcisms." Associated Press, January 26, 1999.

Steiger, Brad, and Sherry Hansen Steiger. *Demon Deaths*. New York: Berkley Publishing, 1991.

Warren, Ed, and Lorraine Warren. *Werewolf: A True Story of Demonic Possession*. New York: St. Martin's, 1993.

F

Fairy Lore: Selkies and Dryads

Within the history of fairy lore, there exists a tradition of these magical—and sometimes manipulative, dangerous, and even deadly—entities having the ability to shape-shift into a near-dizzying number of forms. We'll begin with one of the lesser-known creatures that falls into the fairy category. It is the Selkie, a beast that is most associated with the people and the old folklore of northern Scotland, the Shetland and Orkney islands, Ireland, and Iceland. It is fair to say that the Selkie is not too dissimilar from the legendary mermaid, although, as will become apparent, there are significant differences.

Like the mermaid and merman, the Selkie is an animal that dwells deep in ocean waters and has a long-standing connection to the human race. Also like mermaids, the Selkie is said to be a seducer supreme. Whereas mermaids and mermen, in times past, were perceived as being half-human and half-fish in appearance, they were not shape-shifters. Rather, they were a combination of creatures. The Selkie, however, has the unique ability to take on two specific forms, that of a seal and that of a human, both male and female. Whereas mermaids are limited to living in the oceans, the Selkie exists as a seal in the water and as a human on land. It achieves the latter by discarding its seal skin and taking on human form—that of a beautiful, alluring woman or a handsome, muscular man.

> *One theory suggests that Selkies are the souls of drowned seafarers, such as sailors and fishermen.*

While the Selkie is certainly a manipulative creature—as all fairies are said to be—it is not a malicious one, for the most part. Not only do Selkies have a deep affinity for the human race, but they are also attracted to us—physically, emotionally, and sexually. A Selkie may live in the seas of our world for an extraordinarily long period of time. Should, however, one of these magical things develop an attraction to a human, they will cast off and carefully hide their sealskin and take to the land in human guise. A twist on this aspect of the legend maintains that if the person in question can locate the hidden hide, then the Selkie will remain with that person, and its love will last as long as its human companion lives.

Even when the Selkie stays on the land with its lover, the time may come when the yearning to return to the sea becomes overpowering and, finally, irresistible. Generally speaking, the Selkie—which, in typical fairy style, has an extremely long lifespan—will only do so when its human partner has passed on. When the grieving process is over, the Selkie will seek out the sealskin that it discarded and hid years earlier, take on its original seal form, and spend the rest of its life traveling the seas.

As for what the Selkies really are, that is very much a matter of conjecture. Most people would likely relegate the entire matter to the world of folklore. Just maybe, however, *most people might be wrong*. One theory suggests that Selkies are the souls of drowned seafarers, such as sailors and fishermen. The notion that the human dead can return to our plain of existence as animalistic shape-shifters is widespread. Then there is the theory that the Selkies represent an ancient group of humans who, in the distant past, chose to return to the seas in which life began: they gradually took on new forms as they became more accustomed to living in the water.

A sixteenth-century engraving depicts dryads dancing around an oak tree. In ancient Greece the Dryads were both guardians of the trees and the trees themselves: every tree had its own spirit, which could appear in tree form or as a sprite-like fairy being.

A more down-to-earth scenario concerns an ancient Hebrides clan, the MacCorums. They were said to display one specific and unusual characteristic, a genetic anomaly that affected their hands, giving them a webbed and flipper-like appearance. This led to the creation of a rumor—one that eventually became accepted as hard fact—that the waters off the Scottish mainland were the collective domain of animals that were part human and part seal.

Whatever the truth of the matter, it is intriguing to note that despite having centuries-old origins, beliefs in the Selkie still exist in certain parts of Scotland, including its surrounding isles, and Iceland. By contrast, mermaids now are almost universally seen as mythological entities. Indeed, David Thompson's 1954 book, *The People of the Sea*, which is a full-length study of the Selkie saga, makes it abundantly clear that well into the twentieth century, the Selkie was perceived by Scottish folk as a real, living shape-shifter.

Of the many and varied kinds of fairies that were said to possess the awesome powers of shape-shifting, certainly one of the most mysterious, and strangest of all, was the Dryad. It was a definitive elemental of magical proportions that took shape-shifting to a unique level. The

Dryad was a supernatural entity that featured heavily in ancient Greek mythology and was exclusively associated with forests and woods. There was a very good reason for that: the Dryad had the uncanny and eerie ability to transform itself into a tree!

In essence, the Dryads were what we would consider today to be nature spirits—nymphs, one might be justified in saying. While in ancient Greece, the Dryads were seen as the guardians and protectors of trees and of the woods, there was a related belief that they *were* the trees: that each and every tree had its own spirit, which could appear in the form of the tree itself or as a sprite-like fairy being.

While in ancient Greece, the Dryads were seen as the guardians and protectors of trees and of the woods, there was a related belief that they were *the trees.*

Different trees were possessed by—or could shape-shift into—different elementals and vice versa. For example, according to the Greeks, ash trees were the domain of the Meliai, well known within Greek mythology as the protectors of the mighty Greek god Zeus during his earliest years. Mulberry bushes were cared for by a subgroup of Dryads known as the Morea. The Syke did likewise for fig trees, the Balanos for the oak, and Ptelea for the elm tree. There was a good reason why so much care and dedication went into protecting the trees: should a tree die, then the elemental within it—or, depending on one's belief system, the entity that could shape-shift into the tree—would die, too. Just like the Selkie of Scotland and Iceland, the Dryads possessed the magical ability to transform themselves into beautiful women and handsome men, with the female entity being the most often reported.

Despite the ancient origins of the Dryads, and just like the trees and forests around us, they have never really gone away. For example, they appear prominently in C. S. Lewis's classic *Chronicles of Narnia* books and movies, demonstrating that despite the passage of time, the old traditions and beliefs continue.

Sources:

"Dryades & Oreads." Theoi Greek Mythology. 2016. http://www.theoi.com/ Nymphe/Dryades.html.

"The Dryads." Roman and Greek Gods. 2016. http://www.talesbeyondbelief.com/nymphs/dryads.htm.

Evans-Wentz, W. Y. *The Fairy-Faith in Celtic Countries*. Wayne, NJ: New Page Books, 2004.

Gifford, Elisabeth. "The Secret History Hidden in the Selkie Story." Elisabeth Gifford (blog). May 3, 2014. http://www.elisabethgifford.com/blog/2014/5/3/the-secret-history-hidden-in-the-selkie-story.

"A Selkie Story." Education Scotland. 2016. http://www.educationscotland.gov.uk/scotlandsstories/aselkiestory/.

Thomson, David. *The People of the Sea*. Edinburgh, Scotland: Canongate Classic, 1996.

Towrie, Sigurd. "The Selkie-folk." Orkneyjar. 2016. http://www.orkneyjar.com/folklore/selkiefolk/.

Fenrir

When Garmr, the hound of hell, breaks free and begins its awful baying, Fenrir, the wolf child of the giantess Angrboda and the god Loki, will snap its fetters and devour the father of the gods, Odin, before Vioarr can protect him. All of these events signal the onset of Ragnarok (in Old Norse, "the final destiny of the gods"), the destruction of the old world and the old gods. Vioarr, the strongest of the gods after Thor, appears soon after Odin has been killed by Fenrir, and he avenges him by grasping the wolf's jaws in his hands and ripping its mouth apart. Fenrir dies, and Vioarr joins the generation of gods who will live in the new world.

After Loki fathered Fenrir with Angrboda, the gods decided to rear the wolf. But when Fenrir grew too strong for them to handle comfortably, they bound him.

In some accounts of the myth of Ragnarok, Loki fathered three children by his dalliance with the giantess Angrboda—Fenrir, the wolf child; the Midgard serpent; and Hel. The gods decided to rear the wolf, but when Fenrir grew too strong for them to handle comfortably, they decided to bind him. The werewolf easily broke his fetters until dwarfs at last managed to create a chain that he could not shatter until he regained his freedom at Ragnarok, the end of the old world.

In certain tellings of the onset of Ragnarok, Garmr and Fenrir become one wolf that rips free of its chains and kills Odin. In other accounts, Garmr is also a wolf, and when Fenrir is freed, one of them swallows the sun, the other the moon. Still other versions allow Garmr and Fenrir to assume their traditional roles in the drama and assign the names Skoll and Hati to the two wolves who devour the sun and the moon.

Sources:

Davidson, Ellis H. R. *Gods and Myths of the Viking Age*. New York: Barnes & Noble, 1996.

Simek, Rudolf. *Dictionary of Northern Mythology*. Translated by Angela Hall. Rochester, NY: Boydell & Brewer, 1993.

Fortune, Dion (1890–1946)

Dion Fortune, the British occultist and author of the occult classic *Psychic Self-Defense*, defines the "psychic parasitism" and "psychic vampirism" that can result from any relationship in which one of the partners "feeds" upon the energy of the other. Such a psychic drain may occur in a pair of friends or lovers, between marriage partners, between parent and child, and even in the office or workplace. Fortune was a pupil of J. W. Brodie-Innes, one of the leaders of the Golden Dawn, and she later formed the Fraternity of the Inner Light.

In her book *Psychic Self-Defense*, she tells how on one occasion she inadvertently created a werewolf with a powerful projection of her will. She had been lying in bed in that familiar altered state of consciousness wherein one is half-awake and half-asleep, brooding over her resentment against someone she was convinced had deliberately slandered her. In an interesting flow of thought progression, she considered throwing off all restraints and going berserk, like the Viking warriors of old. Then came the thought of Fenrir, the powerful and evil "judgment day" wolf of Norse mythology.

"Immediately I felt a curious drawing-out sensation from my solar plexus," she writes, "and there materialized beside me on the bed was a large wolf."

When she appeared about to move, the wolf snarled at her, and she admitted that it required all of the courage she could muster to order it off her bed. At last, the creature went meekly from the bed, turned into a dog, and vanished through the wall in the northern corner of the room. The next morning, Ms. Fortune said, someone else in the house spoke of dreaming of wolves and having awakened in the night to see the eyes of a wild animal glowing in the dark.

Sources:

Cavendish, Richard. *The Powers of Evil*. New York: G. P. Putnam's Sons, 1975.

Fox Maidens of Japan

The seventeenth-century scholar P'u Sung Ling devoted his life to collecting and recording accounts of the fox maidens of Japan. One such story tells of the encounter of a young man named Sang.

Late one night Sang heard a knock at his door. When he allowed the unexpected visitor to enter his home, he was astonished to behold a girl of such great beauty that his heart began immediately to pound. When she identified herself as Lien Shiang, a singing girl from the red-light district of the village, Sang allowed his passion to take full control of his senses and he made love to the beautiful girl until dawn. Lien Shiang left at sunrise, but she promised to return to him every fourth or fifth night.

On one of those nights when Sang was not expecting Lien Shiang, he sat alone, deeply engrossed in his studies. When he glanced up from his work, he was startled to see that a very young, very elegant girl with long, flowing hair stood watching him. For a nervous moment, Sang wondered if she might be one of the fox maidens about whom he had so often heard eerie tales. The lovely girl laughed and promised him that she was not such a creature. Her name was Lee, and she came from a very honorable family.

When Sang took her proffered hand and led her to a sitting cushion, he could not help noticing how cold she felt. She quickly explained that she had been chilled by the evening frost as she walked to his house. Lee went on to astonish Sang by her admission that she had fallen in love with him from afar and that she had decided to sacrifice her virginity to him that very night. Hardly able to believe his good fortune, the young student enjoyed an evening of rapture with the beautiful and highly responsive girl.

Before she left the next morning, she forthrightly asked Sang if there were any other women in his life. The student admitted his liaison with Lien Shiang, and Lee became very serious when she stated that she must be careful to avoid the other girl, because they were of very different classes. Then she presented Sang with one of her shoes, whispering that whenever he touched it, she would know that he was thinking of her. But before she left in the mist of dawn, she admonished him never to take the shoe out when Lien Shiang was there with him.

The next evening, when he paused in his studies, Sang took the shoe from its hiding place and began to stroke it lovingly, his thoughts filled with the memory of the lovely Lee. Within moments, she was at his side. After their embrace, Sang wondered aloud how she had come to his home so quickly, but Lee only smiled and evaded the question.

A few nights later, when Lien Shiang was visiting Sang, she looked at her lover carefully and bluntly told him that he did not appear to be well.

When the student replied that there was nothing wrong with him, Lien told him that she would not return for ten nights.

During that period, Lee came to Sang's home every night, and on the tenth night, she hid herself nearby to see what her rival, Lien Shiang, looked like. She was near enough to the house when Lien told Sang that he looked terrible and that he must be suffering from spirit sickness. She could perceive that he had been making love to a ghost.

And now the two different classes of spirit entities were revealed. Lee appeared and warned Sang that Lien Shiang was a fox maiden. Lien admitted the charge, and she confidently informed Sang that there was no danger in a human making love to a fox-woman every four or five days. On the other hand, if he were to make love to a ghost, his health would soon be debilitated, and he would eventually die. Lee, Lien Shiang accused, was a ghost—and Sang's life was in great danger.

Sang, who truly had weakened his body by making love to both a fox maiden and a ghost, collapsed and fell desperately ill. But this story from old Japan is not a tale in which the werefox and the ghost gleefully claim their victim. Both of the supernatural women set about nursing the young student back to health. Lee confessed that even though she was a ghost, she had fallen deeply in love with Sang. Because she realized that her presence was detrimental to her lover, she would make the great sacrifice and leave his house forever.

The story by P'u Sung Ling has a happy, if somewhat bizarre, ending. Having left Sang's house, Lee came upon a household in which a beautiful young girl had just died. She took over the body and returned to Sang as a flesh and blood woman. As soon as Sang was fully recovered, he married Lee. Lien Shiang remained in the household until she bore a son. Once she delivered the child, she died and returned to her true form of a fox. Ten years later, though, following Lee's example, Lien Shiang's spirit found the suitable body of a young woman, and she returned to Sang and Lee — and the three of them lived happily ever after.

Sources:

Hurwood, Bernardt J. *Vampires, Werewolves, and Ghouls*. New York: Ace Books, 1968.
Larousse Dictionary of World Folklore. New York: Larousse, 1995.

Fox People

Northern China has a tradition of werefoxes who inhabit the netherworld between the material plane and the unseen dimensions. In their human form, they appear as very attractive girls and young men — occasionally betrayed by their tails popping out of their clothing. The male werefoxes and the female werevixens can mate with human partners, but for the human it may result in zombie-like servitude. The werefox's animal shape is often revealed as they sleep or when they have had too much to drink.

In Japan, the werefox, *nogitsune*, is a shape-shifter that can assume any form that suits its nefarious purposes.

In Japan, the werefox, *nogitsune*, is a shape-shifter that can assume any form that suits its nefarious purposes. The werefox is always betrayed by its reflection in a mirror or a pool of water. Some werefoxes, however, manage to keep their identity secret for quite some time.

A favorite Japanese folktale tells of Abe No Yasuna, a poet and hero who rescued a white fox from a hunting party and allowed it to go free. Not long after this humane act, he met and fell in love with the beautiful Kuzunhoa, who professed her admiration for him and agreed to marry him. Tragically, a year later, she died giving birth to their son, Abe No Seimei, who would one day become magician and astrologer to the emperor. Three days after Kuzunhoa's death, she came to her grieving husband in a dream and revealed herself as the white fox that he had so nobly saved from the hunters.

In many Native American cultures, the fox is the form most favored by shape-shifting sorcerers who are on their night rounds to do evil to their enemies. Consequently, among many tribes, the fox is regarded as an instrument of negativity and Witchcraft. While a werefox may not slash, rip, or eat those who get in its path, it would most certainly place a terrible curse upon their heads.

Sources:

Larousse Dictionary of World Folklore. New York: Larousse, 1995.

Steiger, Brad. *Totems: The Transformative Power of Your Personal Animal Totem.* San Francisco: HarperSanFrancisco, 1997.

Fox Strap

It was widely believed that certain sorcerers and Witches possessed a strap of wolf or fox hide that could transform them into the beast of their choice. In the village of Dodow near Wittenburg, Germany, there lived a Witch who owned such a strap, and through its magic, she could transform herself into a fox whenever she wished and keep her larder well stocked with geese, ducks, and chickens. One day, her grandson, who knew that his grandmother was a Witch and was fully aware of how it was that their table never lacked for tasty poultry, even though they owned none of their own, sneaked the fox strap from its hiding place and brought it with him to school.

As it so happened, the schoolmaster that day was discussing magic and Witchcraft, and the eager child volunteered that his grandmother was a Witch and that he had her fox strap with him. Amused by such childlike

The Poacher

In the village of Dodow near Wittenburg, Germany, there lived a Witch who owned a fox strap she used to transform herself into a fox to hunt geese, ducks, and chickens.

belief, the schoolmaster politely asked to examine the strip of animal hide. Unfortunately, as he strode back and forth in front of the class, gesturing broadly to make his points, the strap brushed against his forehead, adhered to his flesh, and instantly transformed him into a fox.

The children began to scream loudly in terror at what their young eyes had beheld, and the schoolmaster, a mild-mannered gentleman who was unaware of his transformation, became frightened at whatever it was that had so terrified his students. As they all ran screaming from the classroom, the schoolmaster's new animal nature assumed command, and he found himself jumping out the open window in a single leap.

Confused and bewildered to find himself running across the countryside on all fours, the schoolmaster had no choice but to make the best of a most peculiar situation. Trusting in his newfound instincts, he found a suitable hill and made himself a den.

Several days later, a group of local sportsmen organized a hunt, and the confused schoolmaster found himself among the other animals running to escape the huntsmen. A bullet struck him in the heart, and the stunned hunters found themselves staring at the meek schoolmaster lying bleeding on the ground. Another bullet had severed the fox strap and returned the schoolmaster to his human form.

Sources:

Bartsch, Karl. *Sagen, Märchen und Gebrauche aus Meklenburg.* Translated by D. L. Ashliman. Vienna, Austria: Wilhelm Braumuller, 1879.

Gargoyle Shape-Shifter

Colin Perks, an Englishman who died prematurely from a heart attack while walking around the fence line of Stonehenge in 2009, was, for years, possessed by a definitive obsession. As a child, Perks became fascinated by the legends pertaining to one of the most cherished figures of British folklore: King Arthur. For Perks, however, Arthur was far more than mere myth. Perks, like so many other students of Arthurian lore, came to believe that the stories of King Arthur were based upon the exploits and battles of a very real ruler of that name. This Arthur held sway over significant portions of ancient Britain from the latter part of the fifth century to the early part of the sixth. He and his fearless soldiers bravely fought off invading hordes of Germanic Saxons and, as a result, left major marks upon British history and mythology.

By the time Perks reached his thirties, he was the proud possessor of a huge library of King Arthur–themed literature. His research by then was not just focused on the past, however. Rather, Perks, following clues that he believed were hidden in a series of complex codes and ciphers that had been provided to him by a fellow Arthur enthusiast in 1978, was a man on a mission to find the final resting place of King Arthur. The location, Perks concluded, was somewhere in the vicinity of the old English town of Glastonbury.

Late one evening in September 2000, after a day and evening spent digging in the woods, Perks received a very weird, somewhat disturbing phone call. It was from a woman who made it clear that she wanted to discuss with Perks his studies of an Arthurian nature. She also made it clear she would not take "no" for an answer.

Several nights later, and at the arranged time of 7:00 p.m., there was a knock at the door. Perks took a deep breath and opened it. He was confronted by what can only be described as a Woman in Black. Standing before him was a beautiful woman, 35 to 40 years of age. She was dressed in a smart and expensive-looking outfit, had a long and full-bodied head of black hair, and pale, smooth skin. For a moment there was silence. Perks simply stared, feeling to various degrees captivated, intimidated, and downright frightened. Although the woman's face appeared utterly emotionless, Perks detected a hard-to-define air of hostility, and perhaps even hatred, toward him. This was hardly a good start to the evening. It proceeded to get even worse.

Wasting no time, Sarah Key got straight to the point and informed Perks that she and those she described as her "colleagues" had been carefully watching him for years. She added, in no uncertain terms, that the purpose of her visit was to request that Perks cease his research. A suddenly defensive Perks loudly responded that there was no way he would ever stop his work to find King Arthur's burial site. On top of that, he scoffed at the very idea that shadowy figures were watching his every move, whether in Glastonbury or in the heart of the old woods. That is, he scoffed until Sarah Key reeled off fact upon fact about where Perks was on specific days and nights, even down to which local pubs he visited for dinner and a pint of Guinness after his nightly work in the woods was over. That's when the scoffing came to a shuddering halt.

As Colin Perks sat silently, Sarah Key continued that Arthur's grave — or his "chamber," as she specifically described it — was no ordinary resting place. Rather, it was built atop a paranormal gateway or portal to other dimensions where there dwelled hideous and terrible beasts of the kind that H. P. Lovecraft would have been forever proud. The chamber had been constructed to prevent the foul things of this strange realm from entering our world. Perks's dabbling and digging, Key told him, might have been innocent and earnest, but he was playing with fire that could result in catastrophe and carnage if the magical "gateway" were opened.

Sarah Key's tone became downright menacing and her face turned grim in the extreme. She explained that if Perks did not give up his quest, he would receive yet another visit. From who or what was not made entirely clear, but Perks knew it was destined to be nothing positive or friendly.

It was roughly two months later, and late at night, when Perks had a truly terrifying encounter. He was driving back to Glastonbury from the city of Bath, which, like Glastonbury, is also located in the English county of Somerset. On one piece of road that lacked illumination and was curiously free of any other traffic, a bizarre figure suddenly materialized in the road ahead. Luckily, as the road was a small and winding one, Perks's speed was barely 25 miles per hour, which gave him time to apply the brakes and stop. In front of him was what appeared to be a gargoyle—that is to say, a tall, man-like figure sporting nothing less than a large pair of bat-style wings. A pair of blazing red eyes penetrated Perks's very soul. Hysterical with fear, Perks hit the accelerator, and the creature vanished before his eyes just before impact could occur. Matters weren't quite over, however.

Perks was awakened from his sleep by the horrific sight of the gargoyle looming menacingly over his bed.

One week later, and not long after the witching hour, Perks was awakened from his sleep by the horrific sight of the gargoyle looming menacingly over his bed. Paralyzed with fear, and with the creature gripping his wrists tightly, Perks could only stare in utter shock as the beast delivered a telepathic message to stay away from the woods and to cease looking for the chamber of King Arthur. An instant later, the monstrous form was gone. Perks wondered for a few seconds if it had all been a horrific nightmare. In his heart of hearts, however, he knew it wasn't. In fact, Perks ultimately came to believe that Sarah Key—Perks's very own Woman in Black—and the gargoyle were not just interconnected but that Key was a hideous and supernatural shape-shifter, one that could take on any form it desired, including that of something akin to a gargoyle.

Colin Perks did not—despite the traumatic nature of the encounters with the gargoyle—give up his research. Nevertheless, he remained a shell of his former self for the rest of his days, living on his nerves and fearing that the gargoyle lurked around every darkened corner.

Sources:

Redfern, Nick. Interview with Colin Perks, 2001.

Garlic

Use garlic to ward off vampires, Witches, or the evil eye. Use garlic to ward off hunger by putting it on toast and eating it with your spaghetti. Use garlic for health reasons, such as improving your circulation. But don't think it does anything to ward off werewolves or shape-shifters. They'll probably even join you in a hearty Italian meal with lots of garlic—before they start looking at you for dessert.

There are some areas in southern Europe in which garlic is held to be effective against werewolves as well as vampires. It is possible that the tradition of garlic as an agent capable of warding off creatures of the night grew out of the simple fact that heavy consumers of garlic are never welcome in any kind of intimate contact. In the ancient mystery religions, with an emphasis upon the goddess and fertility rites, those who had eaten heavily of garlic were ostracized from worship.

Garnier, Gilles (d. 1573)

Over a period of several months in 1572, the small French village of Dole lost two boys and two girls to the attacks of a pitiless werewolf. Each of the four children had been found nude and gruesomely mutilated. One of the boys had one of his legs completely ripped from the torso, and all those villagers who dared to look could see the marks of teeth on the arms and legs of all the little victims.

The mystery of the werewolf's identity was quickly solved, for more than 50 witnesses claimed to have seen the peculiar vagrant that everyone referred to as the "hermit of Dole" in various stages of committing the perverse acts on the children. Gilles Garnier was arrested on the grounds that he was a loup-garou, a werewolf, and that he had been seen tearing apart the bodies of the murdered children with his teeth, gulping down pieces of raw flesh.

Before he "freely confessed" his crimes and was executed in 1573, Garnier told how shortly after the Feast of St. Michael, he, "being in the form of a wolf," seized a ten-year-old girl in a vineyard and "there he slew her with both hands, seemingly paws, and with his teeth carried some of her flesh home to his wife."

A German woodcut from around 1512 depicts a werewolf savagely devouring children, much as Gilles Garnier would do 60 years later.

Eight days later, after the Feast of All Saints, Garnier attacked another young girl at about the same place. "He slew her, tearing her body and wounding her in five places on her body with her hands and teeth, with the intention of eating her flesh, had he not been hindered and prevented by three persons."

Seven days later, the wolfman seized yet another child, a boy of ten years old. The sickened court recorded that upon the Friday before the Feast of St. Bartholomew, Garnier captured and assaulted a young boy aged 12 or 13 under a large pear tree and "had he not been hindered and prevented, he would have eaten the flesh of the aforesaid young boy, notwithstanding that it was a Friday."

In view of the heinous crimes coupled with Garnier's free confession, the court was quick to decree that the werewolf should be handed over to the Master Executioner of High Justice and directed that "the said, Gilles Garnier, shall be drawn upon a hurdle from this very place unto the customary place of execution, and that there by the aforesaid master executioner, he shall be burned quick and his body reduced to ashes."

Sources:

Masters, R. E. L., and Eduard Lea. *Perverse Crimes in History*. New York: The Julian Press, 1963.

Ghostwolf

The classic definition of a ghost describes it as a nonmaterial embodiment or the spiritual essence of a human being. Many people would argue that animals also have a spiritual essence that survives physical death and may later appear as a ghost. A letter from J. E. D. informed me of his experience with a ghostwolf:

> I have been told many times that there absolutely are no wolves in the vicinity of Missouri where I live. Yet I and people with a certain sensitivity have heard a wolf moving in the brush and have seen and heard the ghost wolf. And always, the authorities insist that there are no wolves in the area. Once my eyes were drawn to lights moving among the trees. I felt uncomfortable and walked away. When I had gone about 150 feet, I heard the unmistakable howl of a wolf.

In addition to the spirits of animals prowling the darkened forests, it may well be that there are a host of multidimensional beings that masquerade as ghosts or are perceived to be the spirits of the dead when they are actually entities of quite a different nature—some benevolent, some malevolent. Some may even appear as grotesque, werewolf-like monsters.

In one particularly vivid account, three young couples, all close friends, decided to economize and decrease their debts by temporarily renting an immense three-story house on the outskirts of a medium-size city on the West Coast. Mrs. M., an avid student of antiques, was overwhelmed by the splendid treasures that had been left in the house. A few days later, they received their first eerie clue as to why the house had so long stood deserted with all its valuables left untouched. They all heard the unmistakable sounds of someone clomping noisily up the stairs, then running the full length of the upstairs hallway. In addition, there were slamming doors, cold breezes blowing past them, and the sight of the huge sliding doors being pushed open by an invisible hand.

One night, Mrs. N. was attacked in bed by an invisible assailant that attempted to smother her. At last she freed herself, only to be thrown to the floor with such force that her ankle twisted beneath her and her head hit the wall. Throughout the incredible attack, her husband could only sit helplessly by, his face ashen with fear.

The three couples held a council to decide whether they should move, but they voted to bear the frightening phenomena and continue to save their money. And so they endured foul, nauseating odors, the sound of something sighing and panting in a darkened corner of the basement, and a remarkable variety of ghostly clanks, creaks, and thuds.

> *After a few days of getting to feel the atmosphere of the old mansion, Grandmother W. said that the place was haunted by something inhuman.*

They received some insight into their haunted home when Mrs. M.'s grandparents came for a visit. Grandmother W. was a tiny woman who possessed great psychic abilities. She told the couples that the blond woman in the portrait that hung above the living room fireplace had been poisoned in one of the upstairs bedrooms. After a few days of getting to feel the atmosphere of the old mansion, Grandmother W. said that the place was haunted by something inhuman. She stated that she was not easily frightened, but the creature had terrified her.

As the elderly couple was preparing to leave, some invisible monster threw Grandmother W. to the floor in front of the fireplace and began to choke her. Grandmother W. was turning blue when her husband called upon the name of God and wrenched her free of the unseen beast and into his arms.

Her voice barely a whisper after the attack, Grandmother W. said that she had been "speaking" with the blond lady in the portrait when she saw an awful creature creep up behind her. It was as big as a large man but like nothing that she had ever seen before. It had stiff, wiry, orange-colored hair standing out from its head, its arms, and its torso. Its hands curved into claws, like those of a wolf. The beast had threatened to kill her, and it had left cuts on her neck where its claws had gouged her flesh. Grandfather W. proclaimed the mansion a place of evil and urged the three couples to move.

They made their final decision to move a few days later after a night in which a huge black bat had crept under the covers and clamped its teeth onto Mrs. N.'s foot. It took two men to beat and pry the monstrous bat off her foot—and even after it had been clubbed to the floor, it managed to rise, circle the room, and smash a window to escape.

The encounters with the grotesque werewolf spirit being did not end with their vacating the haunted mansion. Ten years after Grandmother W.'s death, a number of her kin were living in her old ranch house. One night Uncle J. came downstairs, trembling with fear, claiming that he had seen a monster with bristly, orange-colored hair poke its head out of a storage room, then shut the door. Although the family teased him when he began to claim that "something" was entering his room at nights, the laughter ceased when Uncle J. died after about a week of such nocturnal visitations.

A decade later, Mr. and Mrs. M., one of the three couples who had occupied the haunted mansion, were now themselves grandparents, and they decided to spend their vacation on Grandmother W.'s old ranch. They had their nine-year-old grandson with them, and they were looking forward to a comfortable stay in the old homestead. But on their very first night, Mrs. M. was awakened by something shuffling toward her grandson.

In the moonlight that shone through the window, she could see huge hands that curved into long claws.

Looking the creature full in the face, she saw a grinning mouth with huge, yellow teeth. Its eyes were nearly hidden in a series of mottled lumps. It brushed Mrs. M. aside and lunged at her grandson, who was now wide awake and screaming. She grabbed a handful of thick, long hair and desperately clutched a hairy, scaly arm with the other hand. In the moonlight that shone through the window, she could see huge hands that curved into long claws.

At last her husband was alerted to the terrible struggle taking place and turned on the light. The monster backed away, seemingly irritated by the sudden illumination, but it still gestured toward their grandson. In the light, they could see that the beast wore a light-colored, tight-fitting one-piece suit of a thin material that ended at the knees and elbows. Thick, bristly, orange-colored hair protruded from its flattened and grossly misshapen face, and thick, bulbous lips drew back over snarling yellow teeth. It gestured again toward their grandson, then turned and shuffled through the doorway, leaving behind a sickening odor of decay.

To the M. family, it had been demonstrated that a ghostly entity that haunts one house can follow the family to another domicile. Perhaps Grandmother W. had thrown down a psychic gauntlet and a challenge that the grotesque, werewolf-like entity had accepted. Whatever the explanation for the frightening manifestation, they demolished the old ranch house shortly thereafter.

Ghouls

The ghoul is linked with both the vampire and the werewolf in the traditional folklore of the frightening, but a number of somewhat different entities are included in the category of ghoul. There is the ghoul that, like the vampire, is a member of the unrelenting family of the undead, continually on the nocturnal prowl for new victims. Unlike the vampire, however, this ghoul feasts upon the flesh of the deceased, tearing their corpses from cemeteries and morgues. The ghoul more common to the waking world is that of the mentally unbalanced individual who engages in perhaps the most disgusting of aberrations, necrophagia, eating or otherwise desecrating the flesh of deceased humans. Yet a third type of ghoul would be those creatures of Arabic folklore, the *ghul* (male) and *ghulah* (female), demonic Djinns that hover near burial grounds and sustain themselves on human flesh stolen from graves.

Just as the ghoul is linked with both the vampire and the werewolf in the traditional folklore, Sergeant Bertrand (the infamous "werewolf of Paris") is literally an all-purpose monster.

Sergeant Bertrand, the infamous "werewolf of Paris," is literally an all-purpose monster, for rather than ripping and slashing the living, he suffered from the necrophiliac perversion of mutilating and sexually abusing the dead. R. E. L. Masters and Eduard Lea tell of a similar necrophiliac, the ghoul Ardisson, who exhumed the corpses of females ranging in age from three to 80. On one occasion he removed a woman's head from its body and took it home with him to be his "bride."

It is quite easy to envision how the legend of the ghoul began in ancient times when graves were shallow and often subject to the desecrations of wild animals seeking carrion. Later, as funeral customs became more elaborate and men and women were buried with their jewelry and other personal treasures, the lure of easy wealth circumvented any superstitions or ecclesiastical admonitions that might have otherwise kept grave robbers away from cemeteries and disturbing the corpses' final rest.

Then, in the late 1820s, surgeons and doctors began to discover the value of dissection. The infant science of surgery was progressing rapidly, but advancement required cadavers—and the more cadavers that were supplied, the more the doctors realized how little they knew and, thus, the more cadavers they needed. As a result, societies of grave robbers were formed called the Resurrectionists. These men did their utmost to be certain that the corpses finding their way to the dissecting tables were as fresh as possible. And besides, digging was easier in unsettled dirt.

Ghoulish practices have continued into our own times. Jilted lover Michael Schinkel of Herald, California, was so obsessed with his girlfriend, Sandra Lee Crane, that he stabbed her to death in September 1986 and placed her body in a freezer. For the next five years, until the corpse was accidentally discovered by a landlord, Schinkel kept the body with him wherever he moved. He even continued to cherish the mummified corpse after he was married.

In 1994 in Rochester, New York, Jeffrey Watkins, then 24, a self-proclaimed sorcerer who named himself the Grinch, was found guilty of 19 charges of stealing corpses, digging up graves, and vandalizing mausoleums. Watkins slept in coffins with corpses, desecrated cemeteries, and kept a human skull at his bedside. He explained to police that he felt safe with the dead because he could trust them. He needed their company to enable him to feel peaceful inside.

Sources:

Hurwood, Bernardt J. *Vampires, Werewolves, and Ghouls*. New York: Ace Books, 1968.

Masters, R. E. L., and Eduard Lea. *Perverse Crimes in History*. New York: Julian Press, 1963.

Godfrey, Linda S. (1951–2022)

Author and investigator Linda S. Godfrey was one of the leading authorities on strange creatures, especially the unknown, upright canines some call werewolves. Four of her 13 published books are devoted to that topic, and she was featured on many national TV and radio shows such as History Channel's *MonsterQuest: Lost Tapes*, AMC's *Fang or Fiction*, Sean Hannity's *Inside Edition*, the *Jeff Rense Radio Show*, Canada's *Northern Mysteries* and *Coast to Coast AM*, National Public Radio, and Wisconsin and Michigan Public Radio. A former award-winning newspaper reporter, she lived in Wisconsin with her husband until her death on November 27, 2022, at the age of 71.

The Beast of Bray Road: Tailing Wisconsin's Werewolf (2003) documents the events surrounding her breaking 1991 news story about sightings of a werewolf-like creature near Bray Road in Elkhorn, Wisconsin. It describes the impact on the town, explores related local and world history, and speculates on possible explanations for the many eyewitness accounts, including Native American traditions such as the Navajo skin walker.

Hunting the American Werewolf (2006) picks up the trail with many new sightings across the United States and expands not only the many Native American connections—including a surprising relationship to ancient effigy mounds—but also a slew of alternative theories ranging from relict Ice Age species to multidimensional creatures.

The Michigan Dogman: Werewolves and Other Unknown Canines across the USA (2010) adds an astonishing new collection of modern-day sightings from coast to coast and examines not just the witness reports but also the geographical characteristics and socio-cultural artifacts of each location. Godfrey shows eerie similarities between many of the modern American werewolves and takes another look at the many possible

Author Nick Redfern stands with legendary investigator and author Linda Godfrey at the Dogman Symposium of 2016.

theories, including marked links between these sightings and the world-wide phenomenon of phantom black dogs.

Werewolves: Mysteries, Legends and Unexplained Phenomena (2008) takes a broad-ranging look at werewolves throughout history and the world, starting with the earliest cave paintings of transformed animals. It includes case studies from medieval to modern, legends from many cultures, and examples of werewolves in contemporary media. The final chapter provides a how-to on conducting a creature investigation.

Godfrey's work constitutes a unique contribution to the field of cryptozoology because of its large body of contemporary sightings of unknown, upright canines. This topic is also included in many of her other books, including:

- (With Richard D. Hendricks) *Weird Wisconsin: Your Travel Guide to Wisconsin's Local Legends and Best Kept Secrets*, Sterling, 2005.
- *Weird Michigan: Your Travel Guide to Michigan's Local Legends and Best Kept Secrets*, Sterling, 2006.
- *Strange Wisconsin: More Badger State Weirdness*, Trails, 2007.
- (With Lisa Shiel) *Strange Michigan: More Wolverine Weirdness*, Trails, 2008.
- *Mythical Creatures: Mysteries, Legends and Unexplained Phenomena*, Chelsea House, 2009.
- *Haunted Wisconsin: Ghosts and Strange Phenomena of the Badger State*, Stackpole, 2010.
- *Monsters of Wisconsin*, Stackpole, June 2010.

Sources:

"Linda Godfrey" (obituary). *GazetteXtra*, November 29, 2022. https://www.gazettextra.com/obituaries/linda-godfrey/article_3d47e954-adad-5db8-86a0-1783177cddcd.html.

Gordon, Harry (?–1941)

William Johnston, alias Harry Meyers, alias Harry Gordon — the sadistic killer of three women — did not claw or bite his victims to death but earned the title "the Werewolf of San Francisco" with a straight razor. In the manner of London's Jack the Ripper, Johnston chose prostitutes for his victims.

On the night of April 6, 1935, Betty Coffin turned a corner and started to walk down San Francisco's Market Street. It was 2:30 a.m., and her feet hurt. It was time to call it a night.

Then she saw him. She walked right up to the heavy-set, slightly drunk man, who was dressed like a seaman, and propositioned him. Fifteen minutes later, "Mr. and Mrs. Harry Meyers" had registered in a cheap waterfront hotel.

Two hours later, Meyers came down alone and asked the sleepy night clerk where he could get a beer and a sandwich. The clerk directed him to an all-night greasy spoon diner on the corner.

At eight o'clock the next morning, the maid entered the Meyers' room using her passkey and found the nude, bloody, and battered body of Betty Coffin sprawled on the bed. Her face had been beaten savagely. Her mouth was taped shut. Her body had been ripped open again and again with gaping wounds in a regular pattern, as if she had been raked over and over by the claws of a wild beast, a werewolf. Blood-stained fragments of clothing were strewn about the room.

Inspector Allan McGinn of the San Francisco police told the press that the kind of monster who murders in such a fashion is the type to strike repeatedly. Newspapers headlined stories of the Werewolf of San Francisco and his brutal and bloody savagery. But the most arduous of police work failed to turn up any clue of the murderer's identity.

Five years passed without another werewolf murder in San Francisco, but Inspector McGinn had been correct about the sadistic human monster working according to some inner cycle of bloodlust. On June 25, 1940, the moon was right for the San Francisco Werewolf to strike again.

The body of Irene Chandler was found in another waterfront hotel in the same condition as that of Betty Coffin. Official causes of death were listed as strangulation and loss of blood, but the corpse bore the same terrible beastlike slashings. The victim was known to the police as a "seagull," a streetwalker who catered to seafaring men. And this time the werewolf had left his "claws" behind — a rusty, blood-stained razor.

The Sailors' Union of the Pacific supplied the police with a picture of the man whom they felt fit the werewolf's general description. On July 8, 1940, a detective confronted Harry W. Gordon at a sailors' union meeting. Gordon was a big, blond man, and the manner in which he had mutilated the two women indicated that he was bestial, cruel, and most likely a psychopath. The detective braced himself for a struggle.

Keeping his voice quiet, hoping to avert violence and to defuse the situation, the detective told Gordon that the police wanted to talk with him at headquarters. Amazingly, the brute who had so hideously carved up two women slumped his shoulders and offered no resistance. Later, after intense questioning, he broke down and confessed to the murders of Betty Coffin and Irene Chandler. The officers were unprepared for Gordon's next confession: "And I killed my first wife in New York, too!"

On September 5, 1941, Harry W. Gordon took his last breath in San Quentin's lethal gas chamber. The savage hunger of the Werewolf of San Francisco was quieted at last.

Sources:

Masters, R. E. L., and Eduard Lea. *Perverse Crimes in History*. New York: The Julian Press, 1963.

Steiger, Brad. *Demon Lovers: Cases of Possession, Vampires and Werewolves*. New Brunswick, NJ: Inner Light, 1987.

Green Wolf

The celebration of the Green Wolf marks an ancient custom that commemorates the times past when outlaws, wolves, and werewolves would hide in the fields, sometimes camouflaged with green leaves and moss. At harvest time, farmers would come upon "werewolves' nests," where the creatures had trampled down the crop to make a more comfortable sleeping spot. In many sections of France, the children were warned about the loup-garous (werewolves) that crouched in the fields.

In the Normandy region of France, *le loup vert*, the Green Wolf, is chosen each year to lead the other members of the farming community in dance during the harvest festival. The climax of the dance comes when a group of husky farmers make a pretense of tossing the Green Wolf—the man who has been selected to masquerade as the wolf at next year's observance—into the roaring bonfire. The burning of the werewolf clothed in leaves and moss symbolizes the farmers' triumph over hidden menaces in their land that might threaten their families or their crops.

Sources:

Eisler, Robert. *Man into Wolf.* London: Spring Books, 1948.

Greifswald Werewolves

According to old records, around 1640 the German city of Greifswald became overrun with werewolves. The lycanthropic population had become so large that they literally took over the city, working outward from their principal hovel in Rokover Street. Any human who ventured out after dark was in certain danger of being attacked and killed by the large company of werewolves.

At last, as the story goes, a group of bold students decided that they had had enough of living in fear and staying indoors at night, cowering before their hearths. One night they banded together and led a charge against the monsters. Although the students put up a good fight, they were virtually helpless against the powerful werewolves.

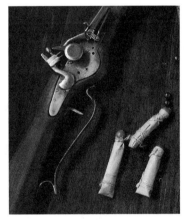

But then a clever lad suggested that they gather all their silver buttons, goblets, belt buckles, and so forth, and melt them down into bullets for their muskets and pistols. Thus reinforced, the students set out once again to challenge the dominance of the werewolves—and this time they slaughtered the creatures and rid Greifswald of the lycanthropes.

The German city of Greifswald, overrun with werewolves, fought back by melting down their silver buttons, goblets, belt buckles, and so forth into bullets for their muskets and pistols.

Sources:

Temme, J. D. H. *Die Volkssagen von Pommern und Rugen.* Translated by D. L. Ashliman. Berlin: In de Nicolaischen Buchhandlung, 1840.

Grenier, Jean (c. 1589–1610)

In 1610, Pierre de Lancre, a noted judge of Bordeaux, France, visited the Monastery of the Cordeliers personally to investigate a werewolf that had been confined to a cloister cell for seven years. The werewolf, Jean Grenier, had viciously attacked several victims, and eyewitnesses to the assaults swore that Grenier had been in the form of a wolf when he made the attacks.

In his *L'inconstance* (1612), Lancre writes of Grenier that he possessed glittering, deep-set eyes, long, black fingernails, and sharp, protruding teeth. According to the jurist's account, Grenier freely confessed to having been a werewolf, and it was apparent that he walked on all fours with much greater ease than he could walk erect. The judge writes that he was horrified when Grenier told him that he still craved human flesh, especially that of little girls, and he hoped that he might one day soon once again savor such fine meat.

The nights and days as a werewolf began for Jean Grenier in the spring of 1603 in the Gascony region of France when small children began to disappear. Then, during a full moon, witnesses watched in horror as a 13-year-old girl named Marguerite Poirer was attacked by a monstrous creature resembling a wolf.

When the fear of a stalking werewolf was reaching fever pitch in the villages of Gascony, a teenage boy whom everyone had believed to be mentally deficient began to boast of having the ability to transform himself into a wolf. As if that announcement were not disturbing enough to his neighbors, the boy, 13-year-old Jean Grenier, also confessed to having eaten the missing children and having attacked Marguerite.

When he was questioned by the authorities, Grenier told of having been given the magical wolf's belt that could transform him into a wolf. This awesome gift had been presented to him by the Master of the Forest, who revealed himself as a large man dressed entirely in black. Although Grenier was content merely to accomplish such a powerful transformation, the very act of doing so caused him to crave the tender, raw flesh of plump children. He tried to stifle the perverse hunger by killing dogs and drinking their warm blood, but such measures were only temporary. He was driven to steal children and eat their flesh.

What is perhaps most remarkable about the case of Jean Grenier is that the court elected not to have him burned at the stake for being a werewolf but instead determined that his claims were the result of his mental deficiency. They decided that his supposed powers of transmutation were but lycanthropic delusions, and because the lad was insane, he could not be held accountable for his terrible crimes. Rather than enduring the tortures of the Inquisition and the usual transformation into ashes at the stake, Grenier was given a life sentence to a cell in a monastery in Bordeaux.

Sources:

Eisler, Robert. *Man into Wolf.* London: Spring Books, 1948.

Hurwood, Bernardt J. *Terror by Night.* New York: Lancer Books, 1963.

Guilbert's Werewolf

Loup-garou is the traditional French name for the werewolf, and struggles with the man-beast were a standard of French folklore as early as the sixth century. Most often the werewolves in these stories were horrid monsters that tore their victims to bloody shreds. Occasionally, however, someone would enter an account into the records in which the werewolf was not all that bad. One popular story of a werewolf that used his lupine talents for good is that of the Abbot Guilbert.

Guilbert was the abbot of a monastery on the banks of the Loire who had one day granted himself the indulgence of saddling his horse and riding into a village to attend a fair. While he was there inspecting the fruits of a bountiful harvest, he also granted himself the indulgence of drinking rather too many glasses of good French wine. As he rode home to the monastery, the effects of the wine and the warm sun made him groggy, and he fell from the saddle.

Quickly regaining his senses somewhat after the shock of the fall, Abbot Guilbert realized that he had cut himself quite badly when he struck the ground—and that the scent of fresh blood had attracted a pack of wildcats. As the snarling, hissing cats surrounded him, he felt all was lost, and he crossed himself and awaited a cruel demise.

Just as the moment seemed darkest, however, a ferocious werewolf appeared and attacked the cats with his flashing fangs and savage claws.

The creatures were driven off, but the werewolf's victory was not without price, for the abbot saw that the beast had received a number of bloody wounds. Guilbert did not dare approach the werewolf for fear the monster might turn on him, so he managed to get back into the saddle and spur his horse back to the monastery. He was curious to note that the werewolf followed him right up to a waiting group of monks, who eagerly dressed the beast's wounds after they heard of Abbot Guilbert's frightening encounter and the daring rescue.

The next morning, Abbot Guilbert and his fellow monks were astonished to see that the werewolf had resumed its normal human shape, and they were beholding the person of a very well-known, high-ranking official of the church. Then, to Guilbert's humiliation, the dignitary proceeded to give him a severe tongue lashing for having besotted himself with wine the day before when he attended the village fair. The werewolf ordered the abbot to do such harsh penance that he resigned his position and left the monastery.

Sources:

Hurwood, Bernhardt J. *Terror by Night*. New York: Lancer Books, 1963.

"Guillaume de Palerme" (poem, c. 1200)

This French romance poem, composed sometime around the year 1200, introduces a benevolent werewolf into a mythology that primarily features savage shape-shifters. The verse was commissioned by Countess Yolande, the daughter of Baldwin IV, Count of Hainault (now in the province of Wallonia in Belgium). In 1350, Humphrey de Bohun, Sixth Earl of Hereford, commissioned a poet named William to translate the romance into English. A surviving manuscript of William's version, written in alliterative verse, is kept at Kings College in Cambridge.

Guillaume is not the werewolf of the romance but a foundling raised at the court of the Emperor of Rome. Of low societal status, Guillaume falls in love with Melior, the Emperor's daughter, even though he knows his chances of marriage to the lovely girl are nonexistent. The situation becomes even more painful to bear when it becomes clear to Guillaume that Melior also loves him. Their romance appears to be forever doomed when the Emperor promises Melior to a Greek prince.

Desperate for a life together, the young lovers disguise their identity with bear skins and escape into the forests of Italy. There they encounter a wolf who recognizes Guillaume as his cousin. The werewolf reveals himself as Alfonso, a Spanish prince who was turned into a wolf by his evil stepmother's magic. Guillaume, Alfonso says, is actually the rightful heir to a kingdom in Spain, which has been usurped by Alfonso's father. The young lovers survive in the woods due to the ministrations of the benevolent werewolf, who provides them with food and protection. Eventually, the three conspirators overcome Alfonso's father, and Guillaume becomes the rightful ruler of the kingdom and Melior his proud queen. The kind and protective werewolf is freed from the magic

The main protagonists of the poem "Guillaume de Palerme" are benevolent werewolves who triumph over cruelties and curses to win romance and a rightful throne.

spell and returned to his human form. All ends happily as Alfonso marries Guillaume's sister.

Sources:

Hibbard, Laura A. *Medieval Romance in England.* New York: Burt Franklin, 1963.

Haarmann, Fritz (1879–1925)

Some years ago, an examination of the terrible crimes of Fritz Haarmann, otherwise known as the "Hanover Vampire," led some to conclude that his acts were those of a sadistic werewolf, since they involved his biting victims to death and cannibalistically eating their flesh. In their *Perverse Crimes in History*, R. E. L. Masters and Eduard Lea agree with such an assessment by stating that in a book about vampires, such as Augustus Montague Summers's *The Vampire: His Kith and Kin*, it is permissible to characterize Haarmann as one of that breed, but it is "somewhat more accurate to regard him as a homosexual sadist and lust murderer—and of course as a cannibal." Haarmann had at least a six-year reign of terror (1918–1924) before he was apprehended by the authorities.

Some of his posthumous analysts and biographers have characterized him as a dull and stupid youth who served a number of jail sentences for child molestation, indecent exposure, and homosexuality. Haarmann's antisocial acts graduated from the petty to the perverse when he became enamored with a young male prostitute, Hans Grans, who also appears to give evidence of werewolfism. Haarmann, then in his forties, had made a token effort to work at gainful employment and had opened a small combination butcher shop and restaurant. With the gleeful urging of Grans, Haarmann would lure a young man to his shop, overpower him, and begin biting and chewing at his throat. In some instances, he did not cease his bloody attack until he had nearly eaten the head away from the body.

Both Haarmann and Grans ate regular meals from their private stock of human flesh. What they didn't eat, Haarmann sold in his butcher shop.

After Haarmann had satisfied his werewolfism and both men had been erotically stimulated by the brutal murder, the body of the victim would be butchered and made into steaks, sausages, and other cuts of meat. Both Haarmann and Grans ate regular meals from their private stock of human flesh. What they didn't eat, Haarmann sold in his butcher shop. His patrons never questioned how it was that his shop always had choice cuts of meat for sale when fresh meat became scarce in other stores throughout the city. When the sensational news of Haarmann's werewolfism and butchery came to light, there were no doubt a good many citizens of Hanover who had cause to wonder if by their patronage of his butcher shop they had become unwitting cannibals.

After his conviction at about the age of 46, Haarmann was beheaded with a sword and his brain removed from its skull and delivered to Göttingen University for study. Hans Grans received a sentence of life imprisonment, which was later commuted to 12 years. The estimated total of Haarmann's victims ranges from 24 to 50. But the newspapers of the city noted that during the year 1924, when the monster's crimes were first revealed, some 600 boys had disappeared in Hanover, at that time a city with a population of about 450,000.

Sources:

Masters, R. E. L., and Eduard Lea. *Perverse Crimes in History*. New York: The Julian Press, 1963.

Hare

One animal that has long been associated with Witchcraft, sorcery, and shape-shifting is the hare, a larger member of the same family as the rabbit. They are widespread, with large populations throughout Eurasia, North America, and Africa. On top of that, they are a most mysterious animal. When it comes to the matter of shape-shifting and hares, there's no doubt that one of the most famous cases on record revolves around a woman name Isobel Gowdie. In contrast to the image that most people have of Witches—namely, old, wizened hags with hooked noses—Gowdie was a young woman, a housewife from the twelfth-century Scottish village of Auldearn.

So the story went, Gowdie had secret and regular late-night meetings with the Scottish ruler of the fairies, the Queen of Elphame, as she was known, a supernatural elemental who had the ability to appear as young and beautiful woman and as an old, menacing woman. They were meetings said to have occurred deep underground, far below an ancient hill near Auldearn. They were also meetings that led Gowdie to become exposed to the secrets of shape-shifting.

"I shall go into a hare, with sorrow and sych and meickle care; and I shall go in the Devil's name, ay while I come home again."

Unlike so many alleged Witches who suffered terribly at the hands of so-called Witch-finders—but who, in reality, were often merely sadistic characters who took pleasure in inflicting brutal pain and even death—Gowdie didn't have to be tortured to be convinced to spill the beans about her meetings with the fairies and her shape-shifting activities. She was wide open about her antics of the after-dark variety. She even shared with her interrogators the specific spell she used to transform herself into a hare. It went as follows: "I shall go into a hare, with sorrow and sych and meickle care; and I shall go in the Devil's name, ay while I come home again."

And, when she wished to return to human form, Gowdie would mutter: "Hare, hare, God send thee care. I am in a hare's likeness now, but I shall be in a woman's likeness even now."

The history books do not record Gowdie's fate; however, given the savagery of the widespread Witch hunts that went on throughout England and Scotland at the time, the likelihood is that the outcome was not a positive one. Drowning or burning at the stake were the most probable outcomes for poor Isobel.

Sources:

Mastin, Luke. "Famous Witches—Isobel Gowdie (?–1662)." *Witchcraft: A Guide to the Misunderstood and the Maligned*. 2009. http://www.lukemastin.com/witchcraft/witches_gowdie.html.

Tinker, Fiona. *Pagan Portals: Pathworking through Poetry*. Winchester, UK: Moon Books, 2012.

Hexham Heads of Horror

This story begins in spring with a pleasant home in the north of England and a pair of young brothers. The two knew nothing of the terror that was awaiting them and their neighbors—and just about anyone who dared to touch a creepy-looking ancient pair of carved stone faces. They became infamous as the Hexham Heads, named after the town of Hexham, Northumberland, where much of the chaos and horror went down. The whole affair would never have occurred if it hadn't been for those two pesky kids.

The culprits were Colin and Leslie Robson, who spent a lot of childhood in the backyard digging deep in the soil, having fun and unearthing mysteries. It was February 1972 when the brothers had the biggest shock of their lives. For whatever reason, the brothers had decided to dig up parts of the yard. In doing so, they stumbled on what seemed to be a pair of ancient, carved heads.

One looked female, and the other appeared to be male. Looking at the heads, anyone could see they appeared extremely aged—possibly even thousands of years old, some experts would later suggest. The boys couldn't wait to show their parents the amazing booty they had found deep in the soil. That evening, all the family scrutinized the prized find. They didn't know what was coming along the horizon, though.

Neither did the next-door neighbor, a woman named Ellen Dodd, who was good friends with the Robson family. It turned out that Ellen's daughter was up all night: the cause was a thumping headache that had to be fixed the next day. In the dead of night (when else?), mother tended to daughter, and in the process, she received the worst shock of her life.

This was a tall, hair-covered, bipedal beast with huge jaws and a head and face that resembled a German shepherd.

What could only be called a deadly, violent werewolf suddenly manifested in the house. This was a tall, hair-covered, bipedal beast with huge jaws and a head and face that resembled a German shepherd. Half human and half wolf, the monster rampaged around the house in the darkness of the rooms. Just as suddenly, the hairy thing left the bedroom, where mother and daughter were curled up on the bed and in a state of hysteria. From another room, Mr. Dodd leaped out of the bed and would later say he heard the creature "padding down the stairs as if on its hind legs."

The hideous man-beast then fled the house out the front door and vanished into the dark shadows of the night. The story, and the mayhem, quickly got out, something that was all but inevitable in the tight community. Indeed, Hexham only has a population of around 13,000 to this day.

Things got even more amazing when the media got involved in the story. It wasn't just the local press that covered the incident; it was also on the BBC's prime-time show *Nationwide*, a program that covered the entire country. Just about everyone learned about the two kids, the girl with the toothache and her mom, and Hexham's resident werewolf that was now on the loose.

Not long afterward, one Anne Ross, Ph.D., was on the scene. At the time, Dr. Ross was one of the U.K.'s leading figures in archaeology and the author of a number of books on the subject: *Folklore of Wales*, *Druids: Preachers of Immortality*, and *Folklore of the Scottish Highlands*. Having driven up to the north of England from her home down South, the doctor was sure that what the kids had inadvertently dug up in their yard were artifacts around two thousand years old, carved by ancient Celtic tribes. This was, to say the least, an incredible development. It didn't end there. Dr. Ross herself became one of the key players in the story—and not in a good way. The doctor herself was about to meet a monster.

Before that, though, Dr. Ross saw one of the heads briefly float in one of the rooms of her house and then drop to the carpeted floor. Startled, the doctor knew she was getting out of her depth.

The night after the amazing sight of the moving stones, Dr. Ross was woken up not long after midnight to a monstrous, hair-covered beast looming over her bed. She saw the pointed ears, long muzzle, and body covered in hair and could barely move; there was nothing less than a werewolf in her bedroom. Almost paralyzed in terror, the doctor forced herself to at least try to flee the house. The thing was soon gone.

To start with, Dr. Ross admitted to the media that she had, indeed, seen either a werewolf or something resembling one in her own home. What she kept quiet—for the most part—was that there "had been a sexual event" in the bedroom, albeit very brief. This sounds very much like a case of sleep paralysis. Of this frightening phenomenon, which is not at all rare, *WebMD*'s Beth Roybal states: "Over the centuries, symptoms of sleep paralysis have been described in many ways and often attributed to an 'evil' presence: unseen night demons in ancient times, the old hag in Shakespeare's *Romeo and Juliet*, and alien abductors. Almost every culture throughout history has had stories of shadowy evil creatures that terrify helpless humans at night. People have long sought explanations for this mysterious sleep-time paralysis and the accompanying feelings of terror."

It is not impossible that Dr. Ross had a hideous, frightening experience of sleep paralysis. But why did the Dodd family and Dr. Ross both see werewolves? Why not ghosts, ghouls, or vampires? On every occasion when the Hexham Heads were around, so were werewolves—and in the dark of the morning. Dr. Ross gave an excellent image of the creature she encountered, and it mirrored the one depicted by the Dodd family. She wrote: "It was about six feet high, slightly stooping, and it was black, against the white door, and it was half animal and half man. The upper part, I would have said, was a wolf, and the lower part was human and, I would have again said, that it was covered with a kind of black, very dark fur. It went out and I just saw it clearly, and then it disappeared, and something made me run after it, a thing I wouldn't normally have done, but I felt compelled to run after it. I got out of bed and I ran, and I could hear it going down the stairs; then it disappeared toward the back of the house."

Dr. Ross soon decided to leave the stones, which may have been a wise thing to have done. She never really touched the stones again, but she did at least continue to follow the developments over a period of a couple of years. After the doctor chose to walk away, the heads were given to a man named Don Robins, who had a Ph.D. in chemistry and magnetism. He was fascinated by ancient stones and, in 1985, wrote a book titled *Circles of Silence*. Unsettling activity in his home led him to give the stone heads away.

At that point, a dowser by the name of Frank Hyde looked after the heads for a few years. He, too, decided to get rid of those old carved Celtic heads. Like just about everyone else in this werewolf-driven saga, they all wanted to see the old, carved heads—*but they didn't want to see them too much.*

To this very day, within the fields of cryptozoology, ancient stones, the occult, the paranormal, and the supernatural, the Hexham Heads are still talked about. The same goes for those accompanying attacks in the night. Answers? There are none. Just mysteries. And a werewolf that, one day, just might return.

Sources:

Redfern, Nick. On-site investigations and witnesses.

Roybal, Beth. "Sleep Paralysis." *WebMD*. November 17, 2022. https://www.webmd.com/sleep-disorders/sleep-paralysis.

Screeton, Paul. *Quest for the Hexham Heads*. Woolsery, U.K.: CFZ Publications, 2010.

Horror Hounds

In his definitive book *Explore Phantom Black Dogs*, the author and researcher Bob Trubshaw wrote the following: "The folklore of phantom black dogs is known throughout the British Isles. From the Black Shuck of East Anglia to the Mauthe Dhoog of the Isle of Man there are tales of huge spectral hounds 'darker than the night sky' with eyes 'glowing red as burning coals.'" While a number of intriguing theories exist to explain the presence and nature of such spectral beasts, certainly the most ominous of all is that they represent some form of precursor to—or instigator of—doom, tragedy, and death.

A ſtraunge.

and terrible Wunder wrought
berp late in the pariſh Church
of Bongay, a Toun of no great di-
ſtance from the citie of Bozwich, named
ly the fourth of this Augoſt, in ý yeare of
our Lozd 1577. in a great tempeſt of bi-
olent raine, lightning, and thunder, the
like wherof hath béen ſel-
dome ſéene.

With the appearance of an hozrible ſhap-
ped thing, ſenſibly perceiued of the
people then and there
aſſembled.

Drawen into a plain method ac-
cozding to the written coppe,
by Abraham Fleming.

The black dog manifests throughout the British Isles, bringing portents of ill luck or outright violence even in modern times.

One of the most infamous horror hound encounters in the British Isles occurred at St. Mary's Church, Bungay, Suffolk, England, on Sunday, August 4, 1577, when an immense spectral hound from hell materialized within the church during a powerful thunderstorm and mercilessly tore into the terrified congregation with its huge fangs and razor-sharp claws. In fact, so powerful was the storm that it reportedly killed two men in the belfry as the church tower received an immense lightning bolt that tore through it and shook the building to its ancient foundations.

According to an old local verse, "All down the church in midst of fire, the hellish monster flew, and passing onward to the quire, he many people slew." Then, just as suddenly as it had appeared, the beast bounded out of St. Mary's and was reported shortly thereafter at Blythburgh Church, about 12 miles away, where it allegedly killed and mauled even more people with its immense and bone-crushing jaws—and where, it is said, the scorch marks of the beast's claws can be seen to this day, infamously imprinted upon the ancient door of the church.

Even more intriguing is the fact that Bungay's legend of a satanic black hound parallels that of yet another local legend: that of Black Shuck, a giant spectral dog that haunts the Norfolk and Suffolk coasts. Such is the popularity of the Bungay legend that it has resulted in an image of the beast being incorporated into the town's coat of arms—and the Black Dogs is the name of Bungay Town Football Club.

The stark, disturbing, and memorable image that the infamous devil dog or phantom hound conjures up is that of a definitively sinister beast that stealthily prowls the towns and villages of ancient England by the silvery moonlight or to the accompanying background of a violent, crashing thunderstorm. It is, however, a fact little known outside of dedicated students of the phenomenon that sightings of such creatures have also taken place in modern times, as is evidenced by the following reports from my files.

First, there is the story of the Bradley family of the city of Leeds who had the very deep misfortune to encounter one of the now-familiar hounds of hell in early 2009 at Lichfield's famous and historic cathedral, which has the distinction of being the only English cathedral to be adorned with three spires.

> *Their attention was rapidly replaced by overwhelming fear when the dog allegedly "charged the wall" of the cathedral and summarily vanished right into the brickwork as it did so!*

According to the Bradleys, while walking around the outside the cathedral one pleasant Sunday morning, they were startled by the sight of a large black dog racing at high speed along one side of the cathedral. The jaw-dropping fact that the dog was practically the size of a donkey ensured their attention was caught and held. Their attention was rapidly replaced by overwhelming fear when the dog allegedly "charged the wall" of the cathedral and summarily vanished right into the brickwork as it did so! Perhaps understandably, the Bradleys chose not to report their mysterious encounter either to cathedral officials or to the police.

Then we have the account of Marjorie Sanders. Although Sanders's account was new to me, in the sense that it only reached my eyes and ears in August 2009, it actually occurred back in the closing stages of World War II, when the witness was a girl of ten or eleven. At the time, Sanders was living in a small village not too far from England's Tamworth Castle, which overlooks the River Tame and has stood there since it was built by the Normans in the eleventh century (although an earlier, Anglo-Saxon castle is known to have existed on the same site, constructed by the forces of Ethelfreda, the Mercian queen and the eldest daughter of King Alfred the Great of Wessex).

According to Sanders, "probably in about early 1945," her grandfather had "seen a hell-hound parading around the outside of the castle that scared him half to death when it vanished in front of him." For reasons that Sanders cannot now remember or comprehend, her grandfather always thereafter memorably referred to the animal in question as "the furnace dog." Whether or not this is an indication that the spectral dog had the seemingly ubiquitous fiery red eyes that so many witnesses have reported remains unfortunately unknown, but it would not surprise me at all if that was one day shown to be the case.

There is also the brief but highly thought-provoking account of Gerald Clarke, a Glasgow baker, whose father claimed to have briefly seen a large black phantom hound with bright, electric-blue eyes on the grounds of an English military base—the Royal Air Force Stafford—while on patrol late one winter's evening in the late 1950s. As was the case with so many other witnesses to such disturbing entities, the elder Clarke quietly confided in his son that the creature "just vanished: first it was there and then it wasn't." In view of all of the above, one can only say: "Beware of the Dog!"

Up until the end of season four of *The Walking Dead*, we were familiar with seeing our straggling bunch of heroes hunkered down in a fortified Georgia prison, doing battle with both the dead and their archvillain, the one-eyed Governor. But the resurrected dead, people feeding on people, and prisons also have a place in the real world. Our story, however, revolves around monsters, rather than virally created zombies of the undead variety.

In the latter part of the sixteenth century, London, England's Newgate Prison was the site of a horrific series of deaths that would have made even the average walker proud in the extreme—if such creatures possess significant amounts of brains to be proud. Due to a pronounced lack of regular food, on more than a few occasions the prisoners targeted the weakest members of the pack and turned them into food. It was very much a case of having to eat the living to avoid becoming one of the dead. We are, then, talking about cannibals in the cellblock.

One of those savagely killed and partially eaten by the prisoners was an unnamed man who did exactly what the bitten and semi-devoured of the prison of *The Walking Dead* did on so many occasions: he rose again. Not, however, as a voracious devotee of raw human flesh but as a ghastly and ghostly black dog with a pair of blazing red eyes.

The actions of this undead man-hound were not unlike those of its television-based equivalents. The creature violently slaughtered all who had taken its human life by savagely biting down on their necks with its immense and powerful jaws. Death swiftly followed for the guilty parties. Reanimation, however, did not. When the deed was done, the man—in spectral dog form—vanished, never to be seen again.

> *William, a Scottish farmer, was hard at work in his fields and heard an unearthly shriek that was accompanied by a brief glimpse of a large, dark-colored dog possessed of a pair of glowing red eyes.*

Then there is the similar, and very weird, tale of a pair of brothers from an earlier century: William and David Sutor. The dark saga began late one night in December 1728 when William, a Scottish farmer, was hard at work in his fields and heard an unearthly shriek that was accompanied by a brief glimpse of a large, dark-colored dog, far bigger than any normal hound, possessed of a pair of glowing red eyes—just like the beast from Newgate Prison.

On several more occasions in both 1729 and 1730, the dog returned, always seemingly intent on plaguing the Sutor family. It was in late November of 1730 that the affair reached its paranormal pinnacle. Once again the mysterious dog manifested before the farmer, but this time, incredibly, it was supposedly heard to speak in rumbling tones and directed William to make his way to a specific, nearby piece of ground within 30 minutes.

William did as he was told, and there waiting for him was the spectral hound of hell. A terrified William pleaded to know what was going on. The hideous hound answered that he was none other than David Sutor—William's brother—and that he had killed a man at that very spot some 35 years earlier.

As David had directed his own dog to kill the man, David had himself—as punishment—been returned to our plane of existence in the form of a gigantic hound. The dogman instructed William to seek out the buried bones of the murder victim and then place them within consecrated ground, which William duly did, in the confines of the old Blair Churchyard.

The ghostly black dog—the spirit of David Sutor in animal form—vanished. Like the beast of Newgate Prison, once its work was done, it never made a reappearance.

Sources:

"Bowerman's Nose." *Dartmoor Walks*, 2016. http://www.richkni.co.uk/dartmoor/bower.htm.

Burchell, Simon. *Phantom Black Dogs in Latin America*. Loughborough, U.K.: Heart of Albion Press, 2007.

Conan Doyle, Sir Arthur. *The Hound of the Baskervilles*. London, U.K.: Cox & Wyman, Ltd., 1961.

"Dog with a Human Face." *Register*, June 15, 1905.

Faery Folklorist. "Wisht Hounds Part 1—Wistman's Wood." *Faery Folklorist* (blog). October 4, 2011. http://faeryfolklorist.blogspot.com/2011/10/wisht-hounds-part-1-wistmans-wood.html.

Rowlands, Samuel. *The Discovery of a London Monster, Called the Blacke Dogg of Newgate: Profitable for All Readers to Take Heed By*. EEBO Editions, 2010.

Salkeld, Luke. "That's Not the Beast of Dartmoor ... It's My Pet Dog." *Daily Mail*, August 3, 2007. http://www.dailymail.co.uk/news/article-472909/Thats-Beast-Dartmoor--pet-dog.html.

"Strange Animal: Has an Almost Human Face and a Red Mustache." *Pittsburgh Press*, May 3, 1905. Reprinted, 2016.

Trubshaw, Bob. *Explore Phantom Black Dogs*. Loughborough, U.K.: Heart of Albion Press, 2005.

Incubus

According to ancient tradition, there are two main classifications of demons that lust sexually for humans—the incubi that assault women and the succubi that seduce men. Both sexual predators were said to have been born as a result of Adam's sexual intercourse with Lilith, a beautiful devil, often said to have been his first wife—or in some traditions, a fantasy wife created to assuage his great loneliness before the advent of Eve. If Lilith were but the personification of our first father's erotic imagination, then his intercourse with her would really have been nothing more than masturbation. In such an interpretation, the incubi and the succubi would have been born of Adam's spilled semen. Modern occultists theorize that the lustful human imagination, when excited by powerfully erotic daydreams and fantasies, ejaculates an ethereal sperm that provides the seed for succubi and incubi.

In the Middle Ages, theologians warned against masturbation on the grounds that waiting demons stood ready to transport the spent semen for

The lusty incubi often seduced unsuspecting women in the guise of their husbands or lovers with persistent advances that inspired the women, "ragingly lustful and naturally inclined to vice," to put up only a feeble defense.

their own nefarious purposes. Nocturnal emissions were interpreted as the work of succubi, who excited sleeping males to the point of ejaculation.

The lusty incubi often seduced unsuspecting women by appearing to them in the guise of their husbands or lovers, and as one might suspect, the incubi played an important role in the history of the Inquisition. We might suppose that the Tribunal listened with both disgust and fascination as a female Witch told of the pain of having intercourse with her incubus's large, cold penis that set her belly aflame. Even pious nuns appeared before the Inquisition, attesting to their affliction by persistent incubi that tried to persuade them to break their vows of chastity. The epidemics of demon possession and erotomania that swept such convents as those of Loudon, Louviers, Auxonne, and Aix-en-Provence have become classic cases of sexual hysteria.

In his *Eros and Evil*, R. E. L. Masters remarks on the scant amount of records from the Inquisition concerning the experiences of men who succumbed to seductive succubi in contrast to the enormous number of recorded instances in which women yielded to the sexual attentions of the incubi:

> This did not, of course, imply that succubi were less seductive than incubi, and in fact the reverse seems to

have been the case. The stories rested on the belief that women, ragingly lustful and naturally inclined to vice, would always put up defenses more feeble than those offered by males.

The incubus could prove to be a very jealous lover. In April 1533, according to old church records, an incubus became enraged when he discovered his human mistress in the arms of the son of the tavern keeper at Schilttach, near Freiburg. In his furious state of mind, the incubus not only set the tavern ablaze but burned the entire village to the ground.

An oft-repeated case to demonstrate the sexual possessiveness of the incubus is that of the mother of Guibert of Nogent in the eleventh century. The good woman was possessed of an incubus, but she spurned her demon lover and married a human husband. This act of disobedience caused the incubus to become so furious that he cursed her husband and made him impotent for seven years. During those years when her husband was unable to perform his marital duties, the demon sat on the marriage bed and either laughed at the incapacitated human male or obscenely volunteered to perform in his stead.

It is recorded that the good Christian husband managed to break the demon's curse by nightly prayers and devotions, but shortly thereafter he was sent off to war and was forced to leave his wife vulnerable. The incubus wasted no time. On the very first night of her husband's absence, the demon was trying to resume his sexual hold on the woman. With the help of fervent prayers to the Holy Mother, the good woman was able to keep her demon lover at bay until her husband returned to the marriage bed.

Church authorities dealt with the corporeal condition of the incubus by advancing such theories as these: incubi fashion temporary bodies out of water vapor or gases; they have no actual physical bodies but possess the power of creating an illusion of corporeality; they inhabit recently deceased corpses and animate them for the purpose of sexual intercourse with the living; they actually have material bodies that they can shape-shift into any shape they so desire.

Father Montague Summers, that indefatigable pursuer of Witches and werewolves, theorized that such demons as the incubi might be composed of that same substance, known as ectoplasm, from which the spirits of the dead draw their temporary body during materialization séances. He reasoned that such a psychic drainage could occur if a frustrated young person encouraged the attentions of an evil entity by longing thoughts and concentrated willpower.

Sources:

Masters, R. E. L. *Eros and Evil*. New York: The Julian Press, 1962.

Spence, Lewis. *An Encyclopedia of Occultism*. New Hyde Park, NY: University Books, 1960.

Steiger, Brad. *Demon Lovers: Cases of Possession, Vampires, and Werewolves*. New Brunswick, NJ: Inner Light, 1987.

Indochina's Vicious Swamp Demons

As medical doctors and psychiatrists have discovered, some individuals who suffer from lycanthropy have contracted the condition after a violent physical or mental shock. Often, the individual recovering from temporary lycanthropy, having been temporarily possessed by demons, will explain the desire to bite, tear, and slash at an opponent.

Author Ed Bodin tells of the possession by a vicious, ripping, biting swamp demon of the beautiful Yvonne Marchand, the daughter of Colonel Jean-Baptiste Marchand, the French officer who had been sent to take command of the French detachment in Indochina in 1923. The lovely blond 18-year-old had become the belle of the military colony, and Colonel Marchand's troubles seemed few. Although he was of the old military school and contemptuous of native beliefs concerning jungle monsters and demons, the native people, for the most part, tolerated him.

The colonel's principal error in public relations lay in what he adjudged native trespassing on military property. A native corporal did his best to explain to the officer that the reason for such regular trespassing could be found in the people's desire to avoid going through a certain demon-inhabited swamp to get to the hills beyond. According to local legend, those who passed through the swamp at night would be in extreme danger of becoming possessed by fiendish demons. As an

According to local legend, those who passed through the swamp at night would be in extreme danger of becoming possessed by fiendish demons.

WEREWOLF STORIES

intelligent Frenchman educated in the best schools, Colonel Marchand found only amusement in such tales.

One day a local thief surrendered to the authorities rather than risk escaping capture by running into the accursed swamp. Colonel March-and saw this as an opportunity to demonstrate the qualities of French justice, so rather than having the man shot, he ordered the man cast into the midst of the swamp so that he would have to wade through the very area that he so feared.

The terrified felon begged the colonel to reconsider, and he attempted to throw himself at the feet of the colonel's daughter to beseech her intercession. All he accomplished by such a gesture was to trip Yvonne. In a rage, the colonel had the man forced into the swamp at bayonet point.

Late that night, Yvonne's maid rushed to the colonel with the news of the thief's terrible revenge. He had managed to creep back into the military camp, and he had carried off the colonel's daughter. A search was organized immediately, but the native corporal feared the worst when the trail led to the swamp.

The search party was met by a soldier at the edge of the swamp. The thief had been found bleeding to death, his face and body covered with teeth marks and scratches, his jugular vein torn open. With his dying words he gasped that the beautiful Yvonne had wrenched herself free of his grasp and had turned on him with her teeth and nails. The colonel took some satisfaction that his daughter had escaped from her kidnapper—but who or what had ripped open the man's jugular vein?

The men searched for an hour with powerful spotlights and lanterns before they caught sight of something white moving ahead of them in the swamp. It was Yvonne, naked except for a strip of cloth about her thighs. The searchlights caught the streaks of blood on her body, but her father was most horrified by the fiendish grin that parted her lips. Yvonne stood there before them, her teeth flashing as if she were some wild thing waiting for prey to fall within reach of her claws and fangs.

Yvonne stood there before them, her teeth flashing as if she were some wild thing waiting for prey to fall within reach of her claws and fangs.

To the astonishment of the entire search party, the girl rushed the nearest soldier, ready to gouge and bite.

Colonel Marchand ran to his daughter's side. She eluded his grasp, seemed about to turn on him, then collapsed at his feet. Her shoulders and breasts were splotched with the indentations of dozens of tooth marks. The colonel covered his daughter's nakedness from the curious gaze of the soldiers, and he called for a litter to carry Yvonne home.

Later, when the girl regained consciousness, she told a most bizarre and frightening story. The thief had clamped a rough hand over her mouth and dragged her into the swamp. When they stopped to rest, Yvonne became aware of hideous, fanged demonic faces bobbing all around them.

"A terrible sensation came over me," she said. "Never before have I felt anything like it. I wanted only to kill the man, to bite his throat, to tear at his face. I have never had such strength before. I ripped and slashed at the man and mangled him as if he were but a small child cowering before me. I gloried in tearing away his flesh, in hearing him scream, in seeing him drop to the ground and crawl away.

"Then the faces summoned me on into the swamp. I tore off my clothes and began to bite myself. The faces laughed at me, and I laughed too."

When Yvonne had seen the lights of the searchers, she became furious and had wanted to kill them. "And, Father," she went on, "I knew you, but I wanted to kill you too. I kept trying to think of you as my father, but something terrible kept tearing at my brain. Then, when you reached out to touch me, the awful fire that was burning inside me seemed to fall away."

After that horrible incident, Colonel Marchand was much more sympathetic to the hill people who trespassed across a small portion of military property to avoid the swamp. His daughter had said over and over again that if there were truly a hell, that swamp must be it. Eventually the swamp was completely filled in by earth and stone from a more godly part of ground. Yvonne Marchand bore no lasting ill effects of her awful ordeal, and she later married and produced healthy children. But when friends got her to tell about her night of possession in the Indochinese swamp, few walked away as skeptics.

Sources:

Bodin, Ed. *Scare Me!* New York: Orlin Tremaine Company, 1940.

Jackal People

Perhaps since the days of ancient Egypt and because of their close association with Anubis, god of the souls of the dead, jackals have been regarded as entities somehow connected with the underworld. In Hebrew tradition, jackals become symbols of destruction, and throughout a good portion of Asia, a jackal represents cowardice. Indian folklore dictates that if you hear the howl of a jackal and it appears to be coming from somewhere over your left shoulder, you have been given an omen of very bad luck.

In many parts of Africa, the jackal is regarded as a not very brave, but very wise, trickster figure. Those who become werejackals do so

In many parts of Africa, the jackal is regarded as a not very brave, but very wise, trickster figure.

by wearing a strip of its hide across the forehead or about the waist. A witchdoctor who has the ability to shape-shift will often choose the form of a jackal to travel secretly at night.

Sources:

Larousse Dictionary of World Folklore. New York: Larousse, 1995.

Steiger, Brad. *Totems: The Transformative Power of Your Personal Animal Totem.* San Francisco: HarperSanFrancisco, 1997.

Johnson, Jeremiah (?–1899)

Liver-eating Johnson is the same dude that ruggedly handsome Robert Redford portrayed in *Jeremiah Johnson* (1972), a beautifully photographed tribute to the Mountain Men. The real Johnson had flaming red hair and beard, stood over six feet tall, and weighed a solid 250 pounds.

The plot of the movie was fairly accurate. In 1847, Johnson married Swan, a girl from the Flathead tribe, and took her with him to his cabin on the Little Snake River in northwestern Colorado. After making certain that Swan was comfortable and had plenty of food and firewood, Johnson left for his winter trapping grounds with his .30 caliber Hawken rifle, tomahawk, knife, and backpack. He was unaware that Swan was pregnant with his child.

When he returned as soon as the spring thaws permitted, he was horrified to see vultures circling over his cabin. Inside he found the bones of Swan scattered by birds and animals. Beside her lay the skull of an unborn baby. The markings on a feather lying among the skeletal remains told him that the assassins had been members of the Crow tribe. At that same moment of recognition and rage, Johnson vowed a vendetta to the death—a personal feud that would take the lives of three hundred Crow braves.

Such savagery inspired great terror among the Crow, for it seemed as though they were dealing with a wild beast, something much more terrible than a mere man.

As portrayed in the Redford film, during all the years of Johnson's one-man war against the Crow, they never once managed to catch him unaware. What they did not show in the motion picture was Johnson's method of revenge. Whenever Johnson triumphed over a Crow warrior, he would slash open the fallen brave's chest with his knife, rip out the warm liver from within, and eat it raw. Johnson had peeled away centuries of civilization and allowed the unbridled lycanthrope within his psyche to assume control. Such savagery inspired great terror among the Crow, for it seemed as though they were dealing with a wild beast, something much more terrible than a mere man.

Once Johnson was captured by a group of Blackfeet who saw a chance to sell him to the Crow and receive a rich reward. Bound with leather thongs and placed under guard in a teepee, Johnson managed to gnaw through the straps, disarm one of his captors and amputate one of his legs. Fleeing into the deep snows and freezing cold of winter, it required superhuman strength and endurance to survive. But he had food in the form of the Blackfoot brave's leg to sustain him until he reached the cabin of a fellow trapper.

Johnson finally made peace with the Crow and lived to a ripe old age, passing away in a Los Angeles veterans' hospital in 1899.

Sources:

Hurwood, Bernardt J. *Vampires, Werewolves, and Ghouls.* New York: Ace Books, 1968.

Kaplan, Dr. Stephen (1940–1995)

For many years the late Dr. Stephen Kaplan and his wife, Roxanne, conducted worldwide research on the number of real-life vampires and werewolves. Kaplan was interviewed for the book *Hollywood and the Supernatural*; he said that when he served as the consultant on the cable television series *Werewolf*, more than half a million telephone calls were received on their "werewolf hotline."

According to Kaplan, "People were invited to call in if they thought they knew a real werewolf or if they felt they had ever seen one in real life. They were also invited to call if they were werewolves."

Most of the callers simply requested additional information, but Kaplan said that about 5,000 of them insisted that they had seen actual werewolves apart from the motion picture or television screen. An astonishing number of callers claimed that they, themselves, were real werewolves, with some describing very convincingly how they had killed their victims. Others claimed to be "latent werewolves," the result of werewolves who had mated with normal humans.

"It was great," Kaplan laughed at the memory. "Television was helping me research werewolves!"

Kaplan said that he had actually had his first encounters with real were-wolves—both females—in the late 1970s, but he chose not to go public with that aspect of his research until 1985. He was always very cautious in conducting interviews with self-professed werewolves: "Many of them have spent time in mental institutions. Many have killed as teen-agers and were committed. And the full moon really does affect them."

Although he said that he had never observed an actual metamorphosis from human to werewolf or to wolf in the manner of Lon Chaney Jr. in *The Wolf Man* or David Naughton in *An American Werewolf in London*, many of the self-professed werewolves do have unusually long canine teeth. "Many of them said that they are affected about two days before the full moon," Kaplan said. "Then it's two days during the full moon and two days after—so for six days, they are werewolves."

Because of their obsession with becoming wolves, Kaplan said, male were-wolves may go for those six days without shaving, thus adding to their hairy effect. A six-foot male may walk on his toes—wolf-style—thus adding to his height and appearing three or more inches taller. Kaplan explained:

> The voice, the posture, the personality changes. In some cases, even eye color changes. They become full-blown schizoids. Some of them will actually use artificial hair to give a stronger emphasis to their were-wolf appearance.

Kaplan said that he had received angry threats from werewolves:

> A couple of werewolves in Pittsburgh were disturbed because I had maligned their kind. They took excep-tion to hearing me on a radio talk show state that werewolves ripped, mutilated, raped, and sometimes devoured a portion of their victims. How dare I say such terrible things? So they threatened to kill me as an object lesson.

Stephen Kaplan has a theory that werewolves may be the genetic result of the more aggressive Yeti—the so-called Abominable Snowman—who came down from the mountains and eventually crossbred with humans. Werewolfism may skip a generation or lie latent in many people.

"One of the most common causes of accidents on the playgrounds, in nursery schools, in primary schools, is kids biting each other," he commented. "How many latent werewolves do we have out there among us?"

Sources:

Kaplan, Stephen. *In Pursuit of Premature Gods & Contemporary Vampires.* Privately printed, 1976.

Steiger, Brad, and Sherry Hansen Steiger. *Hollywood and the Supernatural.* New York: St. Martin's Press, 1990.

Kelpies at Loch Ness

Not only do shape-shifters prowl the woods and forests, but some lurk in the lakes and rivers of our world. Indeed, many people don't know that shape-shifting isn't just for werewolves. The deadly things are

The Loch Ness Monster, As Sketched by Mr. A. Grant From Lieut.-Commander Gould's Interesting Monograph Upon the Subject.

The vast majority of centuries-old reports of Kelpies — shapeshifting beasts with the ability to transform into numerous forms — emanated from Loch Ness. Could the Nessies of today, and the Kelpies of yesteryear, be one and the same?

everywhere. Let's have a look, for example, at the body-changing monsters of Nessie's home—Loch Ness.

For centuries, Scottish folklore and legend have told tales of a wild and deadly beast known as the Kelpie. The terrible beast, which has the ability to transform itself into numerous forms, including people, was greatly feared throughout the 1600s and 1700s, when reports of the Kelpie were at their height. As for its curious name, *Kelpie* is an ancient Scottish term meaning "water-horse."

As its name strongly suggests, the water-horse spent much of its time lurking in the waters of Scottish lochs, particularly in the shallow, marshy areas. It would coldly and callously wait for an unwary passerby to appear on the scene and then strike, mercilessly and without any hint of a warning. The beast's mode of attack was, admittedly, ingenious, even if the result for the victim was not a good one. In fact, it was almost always fatal.

Very much creatures of the night, Kelpies were said to dwell in the waters of literally dozens of Scottish lochs. As creature seeker Roland Watson demonstrated in his book *The Water Horses of Loch Ness*, however, the vast majority of reports of such beasts emanate from none other than Loch Ness, the home of what is arguably the world's most famous lake monster, Nessie—to which we shall return shortly.

We may never know the real form of the Kelpie—only the guise that led to its name. But what we can say for certain is that the small number of witnesses who encountered the beast and lived to tell the tale described it as a large black or white horse. In most cases, the victim was a late-night traveler, walking along an old, well-known pathway near the water's edge of the relevant loch. Suddenly, the huge horse would rise out of the water, dripping wet, and make its way to the shore, with its coat shining under the light of the moon.

Under such strange circumstances, many might be inclined to make a run for it immediately. A strange aspect to many of the Kelpie stories prevented this, however. Namely, the people who crossed a Kelpie's path felt as if their free will had been taken from them and that they were deliberately prevented from fleeing the scene. Today, we might justifiably suggest that the beast had the power to control the minds of those in its deadly sights, perhaps even by a form of supernatural hypnosis. Those fortunate enough to escape the icy clutches of the Kelpie described how they felt driven, despite a sense of dread, to climb on the back of the horse and grab its reins. It was at that point that the Kelpie made its move.

With the entranced person now atop the monster, it would suddenly launch itself into the cold, deep waters of the loch, with the poor soul unable to let go of the reins. Death by drowning was all but inevitable, aside from the lucky few who were fortunate enough to have survived to relate their stories—hence why we know of the creature and its terrible modus operandi. As for the reason behind these deadly attacks, it was said that the creatures sought one thing more than any other: the human soul.

When word of the murderous monster got out, the Kelpie cunningly chose to take on another form, given that its cover as a large horse had now been blown.

When word of the murderous monster got out among the people of the small hamlets and villages of ancient Scotland, the Kelpie cunningly chose to take on another form, given that its cover as a large horse had now been blown. Its new form was of a beautiful woman with long hair, dressed in a flowing robe. Her (or, rather, its) targets were always men, again walking home late at night, perhaps after a few pints of beer at a local inn or after toiling in the fields until dark. The she-devil would, just like its horse-based form, beckon the entranced man to the water's edge. She would then take his hand and slowly lead him into the loch, careful step by careful step. Then, when the man was about waist-deep, she would violently drag him below the water, drowning him in seconds and mercilessly stealing his soul.

Legend also tells of the Kelpie taking on the form of a large, hairy, ape-like animal. Notably, Scotland has a long history of Bigfoot-type creatures in its midst—which may not be a coincidence, given what we know of the Kelpie, its shape-shifting skills, and its Scottish origins. All of which brings us back to the dark heart of Loch Ness.

Nessie authority Roland Watson has determined that the vast majority of centuries-old reports of Kelpies emanated from Loch Ness. This, obviously, provokes an important question: could the Nessies of today, and the Kelpies of yesteryear, be one and the same? It's a valid question, since it would seem unlikely for the loch to be populated by two different kinds of unknown animals. As for the answer, it is almost certainly the case that Nessies, far from being flesh-and-blood beasts, are in fact Kelpies in a modern incarnation.

The image that any mention of the Loch Ness Monster provokes is almost always that of a long-necked, hump-backed animal with four flippers and a powerful tail. Certainly, that's how the media and moviemakers portray the Nessies, and even how numerous witnesses have described them. Such descriptions provoke images of long-extinct marine reptiles known as plesiosaurs—animals that became extinct around 65 million years ago. It is a little-known fact, however, that the unknown animals of Loch Ness come in all shapes and sizes, which adds even more weight to the theories that they are shape-shifting Kelpies and not merely unknown animals or surviving relics from times long past.

Contrary to the popular assumption that the Nessies closely resemble plesiosaurs, more than a few eyewitnesses to the monsters have described them in an astonishing variety of different ways—for example, as giant frogs, as tusked, as camel-like, as crocodile-type entities, as beasts that completely lack the long neck that so many people have reported, as animals closely resembling salamanders, and as creatures with feet rather than the oft-reported flippers. In many cases, such descriptions were made by people who were able to see the monsters at very close quarters, strongly suggesting they were not mistaken in what it was they encountered.

It is beyond absurd to try to assert that Loch Ness might harbor not just one but six or seven different types of amazing animals! There is only one reasonable conclusion available to us: the Nessies of today and the Kelpies of the past are one and the same. Constantly shifting their shapes, as they see fit, is the name of their ominous game. Their motivation: the stealing of the human soul.

Sources:

"Kelpie." *Mysterious Britain and Ireland*, October 27, 2008 (updated January 2, 2019). http://www.mysteriousbritain.co.uk/scotland/folklore/kelpie.html.

"Kelpies and Water-Horses." *Education Scotland*. http://www.educationscotland. gov.uk/scotlandsculture/lochness/kelpies/introduction.asp.

Klein-Krams Werewolf

In earlier times there were extensive forests rich with game in the vicinity of Klein-Krams near Ludwigslust, Germany. Great hunts were held in the area by sportsmen who came from all over Germany to test their prowess at bringing down their choice of game. For years, however, the hunters had been stymied by the appearance of a great wolf that seemed impervious to any bullet. Sometimes the beast would taunt them by approaching within easy shooting distance, on occasion even adding to the mockery by snatching a piece of their kill before dashing away without a bullet having come anywhere near it.

Now it happened during one great hunt that one of the participants, a young cavalry officer, was traveling through the village when his attention was captured by a group of children running out of a house, screaming. Seeing nothing pursuing them that would cause such panic, he stopped one of the youngsters and inquired whatever could be the matter. The child told him that no adult from the Feeg family was at home—just their young son. When he was left alone, it was his custom to transform himself into a werewolf and terrorize the neighbor children. They all ran from their playmate when he achieved this transformation because they didn't want him to bite them.

The officer was bemused by such a wild play of the children's imagination, and he assumed that they were playing big bad wolf after the sheep or some such game. But then he caught a glimpse of a wolf in the house—and a few moments later, a small boy stood in its place.

Now greatly intrigued, the officer approached the boy in the house and asked him to disclose more about his game of wolf. At first the boy refused, but the young cavalry officer was persistent. Finally, the lad confessed that his grandmother possessed a wolf strap and that when he put it on, he became a werewolf. The officer begged for a demonstration of such a remarkable transformation. After much persuasion, the boy agreed if the officer would first climb into the loft and pull the ladder up after him so he would not be bitten. The officer readily agreed to the conditions.

The boy left the room and soon returned as a wolf, once again chasing away his little playmates who had gathered in the doorway to watch. After a few minutes of pleasuring himself by frightening his friends, the werewolf disappeared for a few moments and then returned as the boy. Although the astonished cavalryman carefully examined the magic wolf belt, he could not discover any properties of transformation in the strip of wolf hide.

Not long after his experience at the Feeg house, the officer told a local forester about the demonstration. Perhaps the child had fooled him with a large dog of wolflike appearance. The forester said nothing, but he thought at once of the large wolf that could not be brought down during any of the great hunts. He resolved to test both the bizarre tale told by the cavalry officer and the strength of the wolf by making a bullet of silver for the next hunt.

A few weeks later, during the hunt, the wolf showed itself in its usual taunting manner. Many of the hunters were determined to bring the beast down, but their bullets appeared to miss the mark or to have no effect on the great wolf. Then the forester fired his rifle. To everyone's astonishment, the wolf spun to the ground, wounded, then scrambled back to its feet and ran off toward the village.

The huntsmen followed the trail of blood to the Feeg household, where they found the wolf lying bleeding in the grandmother's bed. In her pain she had forgotten to remove the wolf strap, and she was at last revealed as the werewolf.

Sources:

Bartsch, Karl. *Sagen, Märchen und Gebrauche aus Meklenburg*. Translated by D. L. Ashliman. Vienna, Austria: Wilhelm Bramuller, 1879.

Kornwolf

When wolves were numerous in Europe, farmers warned their children to stay out of the dangerous fields, and to this day festivals celebrate the harvest by disposing of the corn wolf's corpse in a ritual bonfire.

In those days in Europe when wolves were numerous, they would run through the cornfields after hares and other small game, completely hidden by the tall stalks. Because of the possibility of coming upon a hunting wolf or a wolf nest without warning, farmers warned their children to stay out of the fields and away from the corn wolves. And in those same days of old when wolves were plentiful, so were escaped prisoners of war, fugitives from justice or injustice, and outlaws—all of whom took refuge in the temporary safety of the cornfields. Until the harvest, someone on the run could remain out of sight for days and not go hungry, eating the ripening grain and peas and beans from the garden.

In some rural areas of France, Germany, Lower Hungary, Estonia, Latvia, Poland, and other countries, festivals celebrating the harvest are often structured around the corn wolf and the disposing of his corpse in a ritual bonfire. While some folklorists speak of the commemoration of a vegetation spirit, most experts agree that the phrase *le loup est dans les bles* ("the wolf is in the grain") refers to the real wolves and werewolves (outlaws) who once haunted the cornfields.

Sources:

Eisler, Robert. *Man into Wolf.* London: Spring Books, 1948.

Kushtaka

Dennis Waller is one of the leading experts in the field of the Kushtaka. He notes in his 2014 book *In Search of the Kushtaka: Alaska's Other Bigfoot* that the word *Kushtaka* equates to "Land Otter Man," which is highly appropriate, taking into consideration that this is precisely how the Kushtaka is described. It is important, however, to note that the creature is not, literally, half human and half otter. Rather, it can take on both forms. In addition, the Kushtaka can manifest in the shape of a giant wolf—often a bipedal, upright wolf—or of a large, hairy humanoid, not unlike Bigfoot. In the Bigfoot-seeking community, Waller observes, this has given rise to the thought-provoking theory that the Kushtaka may well be an Alaskan Bigfoot—one that, over time, has been incorporated into Native lore and legend. On the other hand, Waller also notes, for the Tsimshian and the Tlingit, the creatures are monsters with the power to morph. In that sense, the jury is very much out when it comes to their true identities.

The otter angle is an intriguing one and is born out of the fact that otters are highly intelligent animals, that they have structured communities and even leaderships, that they are occasional tool users, and that they even hold each other's hands. These parallels between the societies and actions of otters and humans are among the reasons the Tsimshian and Tlingit people associate the Kushtaka with otters. There is, however, yet another aspect to the otter issue.

Otters are perceived by most as being good-natured and friendly animals. This is not the case, however, for the two tribes that fear the

Kushtaka. For these people, the engaging outward character of the otter is merely a ruse designed to deceive and manipulate people, in particular to lure them into stressful and even deadly situations. Notably, tribal history maintains that every otter is secretly part human, which allows it to jump from form to form as it sees fit.

It is eye-opening to learn that the Kushtaka has a notable way of luring its human prey into darkened forests, where it can work its evil ways: it mimics the cry of a baby or young child in distress. As we have seen, similar activity has been reported in Bigfoot encounters in Texas and Pennsylvania, and also at Bridge 39 on England's Shropshire Union Canal, the home of the hair-covered shape-shifter known as the Man-Monkey. Clearly, there is a connection here, made all the more fascinating by the fact that these stories span not just countries but continents. This begs an important question: how, centuries ago and from lands separated by thousands of miles, could such tales proliferate? Is it just coincidence? Doubtful. Far more likely, the people of those widely varied areas and eras encountered extremely similar shape-shifters that utilized the same skills of mimicry and supernatural powers.

One of the primary activities of the Kushtaka is to steal the soul—or the supernatural essence—of its targeted victim. This, too, is something we have seen elsewhere, specifically in relation to shape-shifters. When a tribesperson loses his or her soul, it is the responsibility of the tribe's medicine man, or shaman, to seek out the specific Kushtaka that made its victim soulless and then to wrestle it from the Kushtaka and reunite body and soul into one. And, just like the water-based Selkies of Scotland's Shetland Islands, the Kushtaka is known for its cunning and callous ability to lure sailors to watery graves, deep below the high seas. Interestingly, as in the tales of shape-shifting fairies, despite its malignant and dangerous reputation, the Kushtaka is sometimes helpful, even to the extent of saving someone in dire peril. It should be noted, however, that such positive cases are few and far between.

Although the majority of reports of the Kushtaka come from the Tlingit and the Tsimshian people, there have been other sources. A particularly spine-tingling story, dating from 1910, came from the late Harry D. Colp. It is cited in Maddy Simpson's article "Kushtaka: The Alaskan Half-Otter Half-Man Bigfoot."

Colp was an adventurer and a gold prospector who firmly believed that he encountered a colony of Kushtaka at Thomas Bay, which is located in the southeastern part of Alaska. It is also known as the "Bay of Death" as a result of a huge landslide that occurred at the bay in the mid-eighteenth century. And even more chilling name is "Devil's Country," on account of the Kushtaka legends and encounters.

According to Colp, as he climbed a particular ridge on the day in question, he developed a sudden sense of being watched. As Colp quickly turned around, he was terrified to see an entire group of horrific-looking monsters carefully and diligently pursuing him. In eye-opening fashion, he described them as creatures that appeared to be half-human and half-monkey. He also described them as being sexless, by which, in all probability, he meant that no genitalia could be seen. This would not be surprising since Colp said that the entire pack was covered by long and thick hair — aside from those areas showing oozing, infected sores. As the monsters moved closer, howling and screaming in the process, Colp wretched at the foul odor that emanated from their forms, to the point where he almost passed out. Fortunately, after hurling his broken rifle at them, Colp managed to outrun his hideous pursuers, ensuring that he did not fall victim to this grisly band of hungry beasts.

There is no doubt that the tale of Harry D. Colp has more than a few Bigfoot-themed overtones attached to it: the strange howling, the stinking smell, and the description of the animals appearing to be semi-human and semi-monkey are all part and parcel of what today appears in much of Bigfoot lore. Add to that the aforementioned ability of the Kushtaka to imitate the stressed cries of a baby, just as Bigfoot does, and what we have is an undeniable connection. That the Tlingit and the Tsimshian people are firmly of the belief that the Kushtaka is a shapeshifter, however, suggests something potentially mind-blowing: that Bigfoot may not be the flesh-and-blood beast that so many cryptozoologists believe it to be but instead has the ability to morph into multiple forms — apparently, all of them monstrous.

Sources:

Redfern, Nick. Interview with Dennis Waller.

Lamia

Lamia became a monstrous shape-shifter because of the jealousy of Hera, the consort of Zeus, the father of the Greek hierarchy of gods. Lamia was a beautiful woman who, like so many other humans, bore a number of Zeus's children. The furious Hera kidnapped those hybrid offspring and bundled them off to Olympia, far out of the reach of their mother's arms.

Distraught with grief and helpless in her wrath, Lamia knew that she was powerless to combat the wiles of Hera and to win back her children. In desperation, she began to entice any mortal child to serve as substitute for her own progeny.

Regretfully, such wrongful actions transformed her into a beast with the head and breasts of a woman and the writhing, scaly body of a great serpent. And rather than mothering the human children she lured into her presence, she began to feast upon them.

Isobel Lilian Gloag's c. 1890 painting The Kiss of the Enchantress *was inspired by John Keats's poem "Lamia."*

In time, Lamia reproduced and gave life to other creatures such as herself, beautiful women with the power to seduce and to suck the vital essence from those men who fell under their spell. In certain applications of the ancient legend, the so-called Lamiae become very much like vampires or succubi, stealing the life force from their victims.

Sources:

Gordon, Stuart. *Encyclopedia of Myths and Legends*. London: Headline Books, 1993.

Larousse Dictionary of World Folklore. New York: Larousse, 1995.

Lawton, Oklahoma

On the evening of February 27, 1971, 35-year-old Donald Childs of Lawton, Oklahoma, suffered a heart attack when he looked out in his front yard and saw a wolflike creature on its hands and knees attempting to drink out of a fish pond. When he was released from the hospital two days later, Childs told police officer Clancy Williams that the werewolf had been tall, "with a lot of hair all over his face … and dressed in an indescribable manner."

Childs was not the only one who saw the werewolf of Lawton, Oklahoma. Other witnesses who viewed the incredible creature told police investigators that the thing was wearing pants "which were far too small for him."

The first reports of the werewolf came from west Lawton. Police officer Harry Ezell said that the precinct received calls describing "something monstrous" running down the street, dodging cars, hiding behind bushes, then getting up and running again.

Twenty minutes after the initial reports, Officer Ezell stated that they received a call from a man who had seen the monster sitting on a railing outside of his apartment. According to Ezell, the man told him that he saw the thing when he opened his curtain about 11:15 p.m.:

> He thought it was all a practical joke because the thing was perched on the railing. It looked like some monkey or ape. He thought it was a joke until it turned its head and looked at him, then jumped off its perch on the second floor railing and onto the ground seventeen feet below.

> Once it hit the ground, it ran from the area on all fours, running something like the man thought an ape or monkey would run. He described it as wearing only pants, which covered its leg to its knee, as if it had outgrown them. He said that it had a horribly distorted face, as if it had been in a fire. It had hair all over its face, the upper parts of its body, and the lower parts of its legs.

A group of soldiers from nearby Fort Sill encountered the werewolf 15 minutes later, and they freely admitted that the thing had frightened them.

The monster was sighted on Friday and Saturday nights in Lawton. Sunday night was quiet, and on Monday night, Major Clarence Hill, commander of the police patrol division, sent out an alert, ordering his men to be on careful watch for the wolf man.

But the nightmarish creature—whoever or whatever it might have been—had already moved back into the strange dimension from which it had come—or else it traveled east to make its den under an old farmhouse near Fouke, Arkansas.

On May 1, 1971, Bobby Ford, 25, moved into the old Crank place outside of Fouke. He had lived in the home for less than five days when he had a face-to-face encounter with a six-foot-tall, hairy monster. An Associated Press release quoted Ford as saying that the hideous creature had frightened him so badly that he had run "right through the front door—without opening it."

Sources:

Steiger, Brad. *Monsters among Us.* New York: Berkley Publishing Group, 1989.

Leopard Men, 1930s

On the huge continent of Africa, which covers more than 11.5 million square miles, tales abound of violent and deadly so-called Leopard Men. The phenomenon is especially prevalent in West Africa's Sierra Leone and Nigeria. It's important to note that for the people of the area, the leopard has long been perceived as a revered and feared entity. For the most part, this comes from the fact that, according to certain teachings, the leopard directs the human soul, after bodily death, into the domain of the afterlife. When the leopard comes calling, death is rarely far behind. The leopard, those teachings maintain, has the ability to perform this act because it is what is called a totem animal. This is a creature that can effortlessly transform itself from flesh and blood to spirit—and while it is in that spirit state, the leopard has the ability to travel from our physical, three-dimensional world to that domain where the soul resides after death.

Belief in the transformative nature of the leopard has led some humans to do their utmost to emulate the supernatural leopards. They do so by effectively *becoming* leopards themselves. Very few people, aside from those who secretly practice the ritual, have experienced this strange

An exhibit at the Tervuren Museum in Bruxelles displays the statues of a leopard man, complete with artificial claws, and his imminent victim.

form of transformation. One who did experience it was Pat O'Dwyer, a man who held a position of significance in the area in the 1930s. He recounted his story in an essay titled "The White Man's Grave."

At the time, O'Dwyer held the position of assistant district commissioner in Port Loko, in northern Sierra Leone. For the most part, O'Dwyer's job was routine and bureaucratic. There were exceptions, however, some extremely disturbing. On one particular day, the rotting and putrid corpse of a slain man was brought to Port Loko, having been found on a back street in Makeni, a major city in Sierra Leone. "Slain" barely began to describe the situation, however. The unfortunate soul was torn to pieces, and large claw marks covered his body. The chief of the tribe to which the dead man belonged sent a messenger with the body, who told O'Dwyer that not only was this a case of cold-blooded murder, but it involved a secret society that worshipped leopards of both the physical and the supernatural variety.

Despite strongly doubting the murder theory—the claw marks seemed like a clincher—O'Dwyer quickly contacted a local doctor who, in turn, performed an autopsy. There was no doubt that the violent cuts to the body and the attendant massive blood loss were the causes of death. But who—or what—was the culprit? While the doctor couldn't rule out the possibility of someone having mimicked the attack of a leopard, such was the decaying state of the body—which had been left outside in the equatorial heat for more than a day before reaching O'Dwyer—it was hard to say anything definitive. It was down to O'Dwyer to try to reach a conclusion. He did that by suggesting the killer was indeed a leopard. O'Dwyer's conclusion was understandable: the man was a farmer whose land backed onto a large area of dense forest that was known to be the home and hunting grounds of numerous savage leopards. He had, then, unfortunately been in the wrong place at the wrong time. That, however, was not the end of the story. As it transpires, it had scarcely gotten started.

When word got around that the death of the man had been relegated to the attack of a leopard, and nothing more, O'Dwyer was quietly contacted by various people in the Makeni Court who had much to say on the matter, all of it controversial and suggestive of menace. They suggested that while O'Dwyer was not exactly on the *wrong* track, he was certainly not on the *right* track, either. Puzzled, O'Dwyer asked what they meant. Their answers both shocked and amazed him.

Thus was O'Dwyer introduced to the world of the Leopard Society. It was a murderous group that not only worshipped the totemic leopard but also mimicked leopards by becoming them. The group would take the skins of slaughtered leopards, stitch them together, and then wear them as one would wear clothes. The transformation didn't end there. They created vicious-looking claws out of steel, which they would attach to their hands and feet, and then attack their victims in horrific, homicidal fashion.

> *Thus was O'Dwyer introduced to the world of the Leopard Society. It was a murderous group that not only worshipped the totemic leopard but also mimicked leopards by becoming them.*

According to O'Dwyer's sources, the murdered individual was not chosen at random: a great deal of planning went into the matter of determining who would become the sacrificial victim of the Leopard Society. Then, when chosen, the person would be torn to pieces by the Bati Yeli — that is, the executioner — who made expert use of those razor-sharp steel claws.

The secret cult then went one step further: they engaged in full-blown cannibalism, drinking blood and eating the internal organs. This was not done out of hunger, however. They would boil the intestines, creating a gruesome cocktail in the process. It was called Borfima, and it was believed to give them the ability to shape-shift into — of course — leopards. There was another aspect to this ritual, too: ingesting Borfima was said to permit a person's mind to enter that of a leopard, thus taking control of the animal's character and personality.

So, what we have here is a complicated situation involving allegedly real shape-shifting and people supernaturally taking control of the minds of leopards, dressing and disguising themselves as leopards, and acting out deadly rituals and killings to appease their leopard gods. And the weird story is not quite over.

As O'Dwyer looked further into this issue and gained the confidence of more and more of the people of Port Loko, he learned of other, very similar cults whose actions revolved around shape-shifting. They, too, required the drinking of human blood and eating of the intestines as a means to allow the shape-shifting process to proceed. However, these additional cults worshipped not leopards but baboons, lions, and even alligators — animals the followers believed they could transform into, given the right conditions and providing one followed the occult-driven rites properly.

Pat O'Dwyer was not the only person who spoke out on such mysterious matters. Another man who did likewise was Dr. Werner Junge, whose account is told in his book *African Jungle Doctor*, published in 1953. He was German but spent a great deal of time in Liberia, a country on the west coast of Africa. In 1933, while in Liberia, Junge had the distinct misfortune to come across the body of a teenage girl who had been mutilated and killed in terrible fashion. Word soon got around that she was the victim of the Leopard Society, who had killed and partially devoured her as a means to achieve the ability to shape-shift.

According to Junge, the girl's neck was all but destroyed, her pelvis was shattered, her intestines were gone, and one of her thighs was torn out. It was Junge's initial thought that a wild leopard was the culprit. The closer he looked, however, the more he realized that some of the slashing to the girl's body did not resemble the attack of a wild animal. It was more like the work of some sort of weapon—such as something metallic fashioned into claws, which accorded very closely with the findings of Pat O'Dwyer. And like O'Dwyer, Junge soon came to realize that in certain portions of Africa, even as late as the 1930s, belief in shape-shifting was not only widespread but was provoking cold-blooded murder on a significant scale.

Sources:

Downes, Jonathan. *Monster Hunter*. Woolsery, U.K.: CFZ Press, 2004.

Hallowell, Mike. "Cleadon BHM." December 10, 2009. http://forteanzoology.blog-spot.com/2009/12/mike-hallowell-cleadon-bhm.html.

Hallowell, Mike. "Is There a Hairy Humanoid in the Hills?" March 8, 2012. http://www.shieldsgazette.com/news/offbeat/is-there-a-hairy-humanoid-in-the-hills-1-4326022.

Harpur, Merrily. *Mystery Big Cats*. Loughborough, U.K.: Heart of Albion Press, 2006.

Hay, Mark. "The Leopard Man Murders of Africa." November 21, 2014. http://modernnotion.com/leopard-man-murders-africa/.

Junge, Werner. *African Jungle Doctor*. London, U.K.: George G. Harrap & Company, 1953.

O'Dwyer, F. G. (Pat). "The White Man's Grave." 2016. http://www.britishempire.co.uk/article/whitemansgrave.htm.

Remington, Xavier. "What Is a Werecat?" 2016. http://mysticinvestigations.com/paranormal/what-is-a-werecat/.

Swancer, Brent. "The Mystery of the Murderous Leopard Cult." Feb. 24, 2016. http://mysteriousuniverse.org/2016/02/the-mystery-of-the-murderous-leopard-cult/.

van der Kraaij, Fred. "1900–1950: The Leopard Society in 'Vai Country,' in Bassaland." *Liberia: Past and Present of Africa's Oldest Republic*. 2016. https://archives.liberiapastandpresent.org/RitualKillings1900_1950b.htm.

Leopard Men, 1940s

In ancient Egypt, the leopard was regarded as an aspect of divinity and associated with the god Osiris, the judge of the dead. For many African cultures, the leopard is a totem animal that is believed to guide the spirits of the dead to their rest.

A deadly cult whose members expressed their were-leopard lust for human blood and flesh has been in existence in West Africa for several hundred years. Particularly widespread in Nigeria and Sierra Leone, its members regularly eat human flesh in their religious ceremonies. Those who aspire to become initiates in the cult would bring back a bottle of their victim's blood and drink it in the presence of the assembled members.

The cult killed the way leopards do: by slashing, gashing, mauling their victims with steel claws and knives. They prepared a magical elixir known as Borfima, brewed from their victim's intestines, which they believed gave them superhuman powers and allowed them to become leopards.

After a serious outbreak of systematic murders and human sacrifices by the cult shortly after World War I, the authorities believed that they had rounded up its leaders and broken the strength of the Leopard Men. In spite of the executions of numerous key cult members, the Leopard Men only went underground and conducted sporadic human sacrifices.

The cult's principal executioner in its ritual sacrifices was known as the Bali Yeli. This grim individual wore the ritual leopard mask and a leopard skin robe, and after the selected victim had been dragged to the jungle shrine, he performed the act of ritual murder with a deadly, two-pronged steel claw.

In 1948, there were 48 instances of murder that the police were forced to attribute directly to an upsurge in the leopard cult. After two decades of lying relatively low, the Leopard Men had returned to work savage, full-scale carnage on the people of Sierra Leone and Nigeria. During the first seven months of 1947, there were 43 known killings that bore the bloody, unmistakable marks of the Leopard Men.

When the police fired upon a cult member in the act of murdering a victim and killed him with their bullets, the people of the region began to accept the reality that the Leopard Men were only vicious humans, not supernatural beings. Witnesses began to come forward with clues to the identity of cult members and the possible location of their secret jungle shrine.

The shrine itself was discovered deep in the jungle, cunningly hidden and protected by a huge boulder. The cult's altar was a flat stone slab that was covered with dark bloodstains. Human bones were strewn over the ground. A grotesque effigy of a were-leopard, half man and half beast, towered above the gore-caked altar. During February 1948, 73 initiated members of the cult were arrested and sent to prison. Eventually, 39 of them were sentenced to death and hanged in Abak Prison, their executions witnessed by a number of local tribal chiefs.

Sources:

Lefebure, Charles. *The Blood Cults*. New York: Ace Books, 1969.

Leroy, Francis (c. 1940–)

On June 24, 1989, court officials in Paris sentenced Francis Leroy, the "werewolf of the Dordogne" to life imprisonment. Leroy had previously been imprisoned for the full moon rape and murder of a woman, but he was freed in 1973 after having served nine years of a twenty-year sentence.

Leroy acknowledged that he was unable to control his bloodlust during the full moon, and he wished that he had been able to convince doctors to experiment on him to determine why he was compelled to murder when the moon madness seized him. He was convicted of murdering one woman and raping two others in the Paris area. He was also convicted of eight other attacks in southwest France.

Prosecutor Gerard Aldige told the court at Perigreux that Leroy was a "jackal who prowled by night, seeking his prey."

Sources:

Commercial Appeal (Memphis), June 25, 1989.

Lion Men

Few animals inspire as much awe as the lion, the "King of Beasts," for centuries linked with royalty, strength, and courage. As might be supposed, the lion is a favored totem animal for many African cultures, and

Some individuals so identify with the lion that they believe they can achieve the power to shape-shift and become a lion.

its flesh is considered a potent food and a medicinal cure for a host of illnesses. From time to time, however, there will be those individuals who so identify with the lion that they will believe that they can achieve the power to shape-shift and become a lion.

In 1947, London newspapers carried accounts of lion-men in Tanganyika who claimed the lives of more than 40 victims before their killing spree was stopped by the authorities. Twenty-six men and women were arrested in Tanganyika in connection with the "lion-men" murders.

According to law enforcement officers, the lion people believed that their ritual murders would help to obtain such blessings as good weather. They wore lion skins and left wounds on their victims that resembled the marks of a lion's claws. The London *Evening Standard* of January 10, 1948, stated that three women were hanged in Tanganyika for the first time in the country's recorded history. They died with four men for their part in the "lion-men" murders in the Singida district when more than 40 locals were slaughtered by people dressed in lion skins.

Sources:

Daily Telegraph, April 9, 1947.

Evening Standard, January 10, 1948.

Lobo Wolf Girl of Devil's River
by Pastor Robin Swope

According to Feralchildren.com, in May 1835 the Wolf Girl of Devil's River was born to Mollie Dent, who had gone with her husband to the Beaver Lake area to trap. Mollie was having problems with the birth, so her husband, John Dent, rode to get help from a Mexican-run goat ranch on the Pecos Canyon, but he was struck and killed by lightning before he could return with a Mexican couple to help. By the time the Mexicans reached Mollie, she had died, apparently in childbirth. Wolf tracks in the vicinity suggested that the newborn infant had been devoured by the lobo wolves—Mexican gray wolves—of the area.

Ten years later, however, a boy saw a girl in the company of a pack of wolves. They were attacking a herd of goats. Less than a year later, a Mexican woman at San Felipe saw two large wolves and a girl devour a freshly killed goat. She watched the girl run off—first on all fours, and then on two legs.

A hunt was mounted, and after three days the Lobo Girl of Devil's River was caught after fighting wildly to keep her freedom. She was taken to a ranch (really just a two-room hovel) and locked in. Her howling attracted answering cries from wolves far and wide, and a large pack of wolves rushed the corrals, attacking the goats, cows, and horses. Shooting started, and in the confusion the girl managed to remove the board nailed over the window and make her escape.

In 1852 a group of frontiersmen surveying a better route to El Paso saw a girl suckling two wolf cubs on a sand bar in the river; she ran off, carrying the cubs. She would have been 17 in that year, but she was never seen again. Was the creature merely a grown feral child who was mistaken for an animal because of its method of walking on all fours and disheveled appearance? Or was it a skin walker who manifested itself on those late spring nights so long ago?

Luceres

The *Luceres* were one of three possible tribes of lycanthropes that roamed a region near Rome and were considered to be wild or mad people by their neighbors. *Lucumones* may be translated as "mad people," and a derivative, *loco*, in Spanish and in American slang means "crazy." Numerous scholars have theorized that the original *Luceres Lucumones* consisted of tribes of lupine werewolves with powerful, brutal chiefs that systematically terrorized the native people of the area.

Some authorities on the subject have connected the Luceres with *Lokroi*, whose legend may have been brought to ancient Italy by Greek colonists. *Lokroi/Lokros* was said to be the son of Zeus and Maira, one of the she-wolves in the pack of the Great Hunter god and goddess, Hermes and Artemis.

Sources:

Eisler, Robert. *Man into Wolf*. London: Spring Books, 1948.

Lupo, Michael (1953–1995)

Michael Lupo took great delight in the fact that his last name in Italian meant "wolf," and he boasted that he truly was the "Wolf Man." Lupo also bragged that he had taken over 4,000 homosexual lovers and that he had murdered four of them.

In May 1986, the London police realized that a serial killer was stalking the homosexual communities. Twenty-four-year-old Tony Connolly's body had been found on April 6 by children playing near a Brixton railway embankment in south London. Connolly was determined to be HIV positive, and the police soon linked his death to that of another gay man who had been strangled in west London, as well as another attempted murder in the same area.

On May 18, police arrested Michael Lupo, an Italian-born ex-commando who now worked as a makeup artist and the manager of a fashion shop in Chelsea. The 33-year-old Lupo had not been all that discreet in boasting of the murders and his prowess as the Wolf Man, and he had been heard to state that he would continue killing until the police were able to catch him. Lupo was charged with the murder of Tony Connolly, as well as that of railway guard James Burns. Police also accused him of the attempted murder of a man in south London.

Three days after his arrest, the police were able to add the death of Damien McClusky, a 22-year-old hospital worker, to the Wolf Man's list of murders. Before Lupo was brought to Central Criminal Court, a new murder charge, that of an unidentified man in his sixties, strangled near Hungerford Bridge, brought the tally to four murders and two attempted murders.

On July 10, 1987, Lupo pleaded guilty to all charges, and he was sentenced to life imprisonment on each of the murder charges and to consecutive terms of seven years on each of the counts of attempted murder.

Sources:

Lane, Brian, and Wilfred Gregg. *The Encyclopedia of Serial Killers*. New York: Berkley Publishing, 1994.

Lycanthropy

Quite understandably, contemporary medical professionals will seek to offer rational explanations for the werewolves that have scourged the past and haunted the present. The term *lycanthropy* (from the Greek; literally, "wolfman") was used by Reginald Scot in his *The Discovery of Witchcraft* (1584) to denote an extreme form of violent insanity in which the individual may imitate the behavior of a wild beast, especially a wolf. Scot argued against the church and the Inquisition and its institutionalized program of torturing and burning Witches, werewolves, and other shape-shifters, and he nearly ended up bound to a stake for his heretical efforts on behalf of reason. Scot used the term in the same manner as a modern health professional when referring to the mental disease that manifests itself in ways applicable to werewolfism.

The term *lycanthropy* was also applied to those individuals afflicted with a form of dark melancholy, a deep depression that gave rise to a violent form of insanity. In his *Anatomy of Melancholy* (1621), Robert Burton writes that those men and women who are suffering from an advanced form of melancholy that graduates into werewolfism lie hidden throughout the daylight hours, then "go abroad in the night, barking, howling, at graves and deserts; they have unusually hollow eyes, scabbed legs and thighs, very dry and pale."

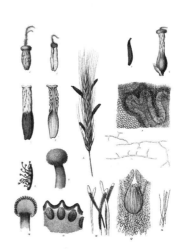

Dr. Mary Matossian theorized that the 30,000 peasants who were condemned as werewolves between the years of 1520 and 1630 had eaten rye bread contaminated by ergot, a grain fungus that acted as a powerful hallucinogenic.

Dr. Mary Matossian, professor of history at the University of Maryland, viewed such statistics as those from France, which proclaimed that 30,000 individuals were condemned as werewolves between the years of 1520 and 1630 and wondered how such a mental aberration could possibly have been so widespread. As she researched the phenomenon, she derived a theory that the peasants were eating a rye bread that was contaminated by a fungus that acted as a powerful hallucinogenic. In essence, Dr. Matossian suggested that thousands of men and women were suffering from "bad trips" from a potent fungus that caused them to have delusions that they were magical beings capable of transforming themselves into werewolves.

According to Dr. Matossian:

> The fungus was ergot, a parasite that attacks rye. The ergot produces sclerotia which grow on the rye plant, taking the place of its natural seeds. The wind blows and the fungus latches onto other rye plants. … During harvesting, the ergot was collected along with the grain and became part of the bread. Since ergot is like today's LSD, some individuals suffered bad trips and imagined themselves being transformed into animals, such as wolves. Others saw themselves with special powers, like flying on a broomstick. They were the Witches.

> The ergot caused them to act in other bizarre ways, even committing murder and injury. As a result, numerous victims of ergot poisoning were tried as wolves and werewolves—and executed. With the advent of modern methods of cleaning and processing grain, ergot was eliminated—along with the appearance of werewolves and Witches.

An interesting theory, but Dr. Matossian should take a better look around the contemporary scene if she believes there are no Witches gathering in covens in the twenty-first century. And she had better look carefully over her shoulder if she believes that werewolves no longer prowl the night—whether in the embodiment of the mentally ill, serial killers, or true lycanthropes.

In the *Canadian Psychiatric Association Journal* in 1975, psychiatrists Frida Surawicz and Richard Banta of Lexington, Kentucky, published their paper "Lycanthropy Revisited," in which they presented two case studies of contemporary werewolves.

Their first case, that of Mr. H., obliquely supported Dr. Matossian's hallucinogenic hypothesis in that he had ingested LSD before he saw himself changing into a werewolf. He saw fur growing over his hands and face, and he craved flesh and blood. Even after the effects of the drug had supposedly worn off, Mr. H. still believed himself to be a werewolf. He was treated as a paranoid schizophrenic, treated with antipsychotic medication, and, after about five weeks, released from a psychiatric unit.

Surawicz and Banta's second case study was that of a 37-year-old farmer who, after his discharge from the Navy, allowed his hair to grow long and began sleeping in cemeteries and howling at the moon. Although there was no indication of drug abuse or misuse in Mr. W.'s case, he was freed from his delusion after treatment with antipsychotic medication.

Although she finally received daily psychotherapy and antipsychotic drugs, she still beheld herself as a wolf woman with claws, teeth, and fangs and believed that her werewolf spirit would roam the earth long after her physical death.

Psychiatrist Harvey Rosenstock and psychologist Kenneth Vincent discuss their case history of a 49-year-old woman who underwent the metamorphosis into a werewolf in their paper "A Case of Lycanthropy," published in the *American Journal of Psychiatry* in 1977. Although she finally was admitted to a locked psychiatric unit and received daily psychotherapy and antipsychotic drugs, she still beheld herself as a wolf woman with claws, teeth, and fangs and believed that her werewolf spirit would roam the earth long after her physical death. Medical personnel would manage to get the woman under control until the next full moon. At that time, she would snarl, howl, and resume her wolflike behavior. She was eventually discharged and provided with antipsychotic medication, but she promised to haunt the graveyards until she found the tall, dark, hairy creature of her dreams.

And speaking of hairy creatures, according to Brian K. Hall, a developmental biologist at Dalhousie University in Nova Scotia, Canada, a team of scientists have discovered a gene that may make certain people extra hairy and appear very much like the classic Hollywood werewolves. Doctors at the Baylor College of Medicine in Houston, Texas, took blood samples from 19 people whose faces and upper bodies were entirely covered with thick, dark hair. The samples spanned five generations of a single family and revealed that their DNA included a mutant gene that was responsible for a condition known as congenital generalized hypertrichosis.

While all humans possess the "hairy gene," Hall stated, in most people it is dormant. The tendency to produce hair that covers the entire face and upper torso may be "an evolutionary trait left over from our animal ancestors." The discovery that the gene still exists in a dormant state in all people and manifests as super hairiness in a small number, Hall said, "tells us that our body stores a lot of genetic information for a long time."

In his *Bizarre Diseases of the Mind*, Dr. Richard Noll lists the traditional traits of the clinical lycanthrope:

- The belief that they are wolves or wild dogs.
- The belief that they have been physically transformed into animals with fur and claws.
- Animal-like behavior, including growling, howling, clawing, pawing, crawling on all fours, offering one-self in the sexual postures of a female animal.
- The desire to assault or kill others.
- Hypersexuality, including the desire to have sex with animals.
- Use of a hallucinogenic substance to achieve the metamorphosis of human into a wolf.
- A desire for isolation from human society (stalking the woods, haunting cemeteries).
- The belief that "the devil" has possessed the afflicted werewolf and provided the power that causes the transformation from human to wolf.

The March 1999 issue of *Discover* magazine reported the hypothesis of neurologist Juan Gomez-Alonso of the Xeral Hospital in Vigo, Spain. He suggests that old tales of vampires and werewolves could have been inspired by people who suffered from rabies. He traced the connection between a rabies outbreak in central Europe in the early eighteenth century to tales of the undead and shape-shifters that began circulating soon after.

According to Gomez-Alonso: "Some of the symptoms, such as aggressiveness and hypersexuality, would not have been seen as manifestations

Neurologist Juan Gomez-Alonso suggests that old tales of vampires and werewolves could have been inspired by people who suffered from rabies, citing an eighteenth-century rabies outbreak in central Europe shortly before tales of the undead and shape-shifters began circulating.

of a disease. Uneducated people could have thought all this was the work of a malign being. Moreover, the bizarre rejection of some stimuli—odors, light, water, and mirrors—shown by rabid humans must have been quite puzzling."

Sources:

Jones, Linda. "Werewolf Gene Found." *Science World*, October 20, 1995.

Noll, Richard. *Bizarre Diseases of the Mind*. New York: Berkley Books, 1990.

Rosenstock, Harvey A., and Kenneth R. Vincent. "A Case of Lycanthropy." *American Journal of Psychiatry*, October 1977.

Surawitz, Frida, and Richard Banta. "Lycanthropy Revisited." *Canadian Psychiatric Association Journal*, November 1975.

Mad Gasser of Mattoon

Only a couple of years before he died, Brad Steiger (1936–2018) was making connections between strange and sinister characters who surfaced during World War II and in the small Illinois city of Mattoon. It's a story that combines a secret society, the FBI, occultist Aleister Crowley (1875–1947), mayhem in a small city in Illinois, and … wait for it … werewolves. But before we get to the matter of shape-shifting wolfmen, let's get our grips into the story of that grim gasser. Back in the 1940s, the people of Mattoon, Illinois, were plagued by a sinister character who became known as the Mad Gasser of Mattoon.

The name was an apt one. The mysterious figure gassed his victims, usually in their bedrooms, as a way to gain entry to their property and take advantage of whatever caught his eye. His actions followed the pattern of a similar wave of attacks that took place in the 1930s in Botetourt County, Virginia. To focus on the later events: On the night of August 31, 1944, a man named Urban Raef was overcome by a mysterious gas that provoked sickness, weakness, and vomiting. Despite Mr. Raef's fear that there was a gas leak in the house, such was not the case. Raef's wife, to her horror, found herself briefly paralyzed.

Also among the Gasser's victims was Mrs. Bert Kearney, who also lived in Mattoon. On September 1, 1944, approximately an hour before the witching-hour struck, Mrs. Kearney was hit by what was described as a "sickening, sweet odor in the bedroom." As was the case with Mrs. Raef, the "gas" caused temporary paralysis in her legs. It also resulted in a burning sensation to her lips and a parched feeling in her mouth.

Mrs. Kearney cried out for her sister, Martha, who came running to see what was going on. She too was unable to avoid the powerful smell. In no time, the police were on the scene, but the Mad Gasser was nowhere to be found—at least, not for a while. As Bert Kearney drove home after his shift as a cab driver was over, he caught sight of a man dressed in dark clothes peering through the window of the Kearneys' bedroom. The man was thin and wearing a tight, dark cap on his head. He quickly fled the scene.

In the wake of the curious affair, other reports of the Mad Gasser's infernal activities surfaced—to the extent that both the local police and the FBI got involved. The townsfolk were plunged into a state of paranoia. While some cases were put down to nothing more than hysteria, that was not the end of the story. For example, Thomas V. Wright, the commissioner of public health, said: "There is no doubt that a gas maniac exists and has made a number of attacks. But many of the reported attacks are nothing more than hysteria. Fear of the gas man is entirely out of proportion to the menace of the relatively harmless gas he is spraying. The whole town is sick with hysteria."

The mystery was never resolved to the satisfaction of everyone. One theory offers that the Mad Gasser of Mattoon was actually nothing stranger than a bunch of kids. Writer Scott Maruna suggests that the Gasser was a University of Illinois student, Farley Llewellyn, who had a deep knowledge of chemistry and who went to school with the initial victims. Other theories include burglars and even extraterrestrials.

Perhaps the most intriguing explanation for the Mad Gasser of Mattoon appears in the now-declassified files of the U.S. government. Thanks to the provisions of the Freedom of Information Act, we now know that one particularly notable theory being secretly pursued by U.S. law enforcement officials was taken very seriously: that the Gasser was not a solitary individual but an entire group of Mad Gassers. A secret society, one might say. According to Illinois authorities, they had heard disturbing stories of a clandestine cult operating in northern Illinois that was inspired by the work of the "Great Beast" himself, Aleister Crowley—and specifically by Crowley's position on the matter of sacrifice (human and otherwise) and on provoking the presence of deadly werewolves that were said to have come from other realms of existence.

> *A number of the victims of the Gasser were woken up in the dead of night by what can only be termed savage, hair-covered, fanged, howling werewolves.*

This is where Brad Steiger began to dig into the matter of the diabolical gasser. According to Steiger, while they were reluctant to come forward at the time, a number of the victims of the Gasser were woken up in the dead of night by what can only be termed savage, hair-covered, fanged, howling werewolves. At least five of the town's women had savage sex with them—and kept everything quiet in the aftermath. Were the werewolves brought forth from other dimensions and engaging with Crowley himself?

Crowley himself said of this issue: "It is necessary for us to consider carefully the problems connected with the bloody sacrifice, for this question is indeed traditionally important in Magick. Nigh all ancient Magick revolves around this matter. In particular all the Osirian religions—the rites of the Dying God—refer to this. The slaying of Osiris and Adonis; the mutilation of Attis; the cults of Mexico and Peru; the story of Hercules or Melcarth; the legends of Dionysus and of Mithra, are all connected with this one idea. In the Hebrew religion we find the same thing inculcated. The first ethical lesson in the Bible is that the only sacrifice pleasing to the Lord is the sacrifice of blood; Abel, who made this, finding favour with the Lord, while Cain, who offered cabbages, was rather naturally considered a cheap sport. The idea recurs again and again. We have the sacrifice of the Passover, following on the story of Abraham's being commanded to sacrifice his firstborn son, with the idea of the substitution of animal for human life. The annual ceremony of the two goats carries out this in perpetuity. And we see again the domination of this idea in the romance of Esther, where Haman and Mordecai are the two goats or gods; and ultimately in the presentation of the rite of Purim in Palestine, where Jesus and Barabbas happened to be the Goats in that particular year of which we hear so much, without agreement on the date."

"It would be unwise to condemn as irrational the practice of those savages who tear the heart and liver from an adversary, and devour them while yet warm."

Crowley continued: "Enough has now been said to show that the bloody sacrifice has from time immemorial been the most considered part of Magick. … It would be unwise to condemn as irrational the practice of those savages who tear the heart and liver from an adversary, and devour them while yet warm. In any case, it was the theory of the ancient Magicians that any living being is a storehouse of energy varying in quantity according to the size and health of the animal, and in quality according to its mental and moral character. At the death of the animal this energy is liberated suddenly.

"The animal should therefore be killed within the Circle, or the Triangle, as the case may be, so that its energy cannot escape. An animal should be selected whose nature accords with that of the ceremony—thus, by sacrificing a female lamb one would not obtain any appreciative quantity of the fierce energy useful to a Magician who was invoking Mars. In such a case a ram would be more suitable. And this ram should be virgin—the whole potential of its original total energy should not have been diminished in any way.

Illinois authorities heard disturbing stories of a clandestine cult inspired by the work of the "Great Beast" himself, Aleister Crowley, and his position on human sacrifice.

"For the highest spiritual working one must accordingly choose that victim which contains the greatest and purest force. A male child of perfect innocence and high intelligence is the most satisfactory and suitable victim. For evocations it would be more convenient to place the blood of the victim in the Triangle—the idea being that the spirit might obtain from the blood this subtle but physical substance which was the quintessence of its life in such a manner as to enable it to take on a visible and tangible shape."

It was Crowley's words that prompted the "Illinois sect," as the group is referenced in the files, to explore the issue of human sacrifice for personal gain. From a budding author in Decatur, Illinois (whose name is deleted from the declassified papers), there came a long and rambling letter in which he claimed personal knowledge of the group in question. Supposedly, its members had engaged in the ritualistic sacrifice of animals from 1942 to 1943 and were, by 1944, ready to do the unthinkable: namely, kill people according to ancient rite and ritual. Our unnamed author further claimed that the "gassing attempts" were undertaken by group members as a means to try to render unconscious, and kidnap, the largely female victims, and then end their lives according to infernal, occult beliefs.

Although the matter was taken seriously by the authorities, the odd and controversial saga fizzled out when suspicions rose that Crowley was lying and was simply trying to insert himself into the saga of the Mad Gasser of Mattoon, and for a less-than-admirable reason: to whip up the controversy and then write his very own book on the subject. On the other hand, perhaps there was some truth to the matter, after all, and the Mad Gasser was actually nothing less than a cult of Mad Gassers with human sacrifice on their minds.

Sadly, much of the story is still embedded in mystery: Steiger is gone. The FBI files that Steiger said he had in his hands—as of 2011—have not been found. And what was the connection between the great magician and packs of monstrous werewolves? The best scenario is that Crowley managed to open a "doorway" that allowed the werewolves to enter our domain. Rather notably, in one of the notes he sent to me, Steiger wrote that he had "a twist between the Gasser and the wolf-men here, but beyond us for now. Let's talk again." On this particular subject, though, we never did talk again. There is no doubt that a connection can be made. It just needs the threads. Sadly, Steiger couldn't put all those threads together. Maybe you will.

I should stress that there is another fascinating, creepy, and relevant part of all this: at the height of the dangerous affair, one of the women in Mattoon reported to the local police that around three o'clock one morning she had seen a "man" over her bed, dressed in a purple cloak and with the face of a huge wolf. The creature terrified the woman with its large muzzle, fangs, and red eyes. The thing bounced out of the woman's home. How this plays in with the Mad Gasser of Mattoon, no one knows—except that the woman was so terrified she stayed elsewhere for the next few nights. A werewolf and a gassing maniac? You bet!

Sources:

Klickna, Cinda. "The Case of the Mad Gasser of Mattoon." May 1, 2003. http://illinoistimes.com/article-70-the-case-of-the-mad-gasser-of-mattoon.html.

Magnus, Olaus

Bishop Olaf Magnussen (1490–1557) of Sweden, who signed his treatise *History of the Goths, Swedes and Vandals* with his Latinized name, Olaus Magnus, declared that the residents of Prussia, Lithuania, and Livonia often lost their livestock to bands of roving wolves, but their losses from the creatures of nature were not nearly as severe as those they suffered from the depredations of the werewolves.

According to Magnus, large numbers of werewolves prowled the outlying districts, attacking humans as well as livestock. The monsters besieged isolated farms, broke into homes, and devoured every living thing. Their favorite haunt was said to be a ruined castle near Courland, a place avoided by all reasonable people and where the werewolves were equally ferocious with their own kind, slaying their weaker fellows.

The bishop also asserted that in Scandinavia, devils come nightly to clean the stables and feed the animals. Devils also work the mines, enjoying a work environment like the labyrinths of their own hellish habitation. Scandinavians have learned to pay little attention to the devils working among them, Magnus states. The indiscreet who might insult or molest the devils are in danger of having their heads twisted backward.

Many a practical sea captain has gainfully employed a devil as a navigator, for a devil, possessing control over the elements, can always induce favorable sailing weather. Bishop Magnussen does worry, however, that those who make such profitable deals with devils might be in danger of losing their souls in the bargain.

Sources:

Seligmann, Kurt. *The History of Magic*. New York: Pantheon Books, 1948.

Man-Monkey and Mermaid of Shropshire Union Canal

In the summer of 1976, there was an encounter with the legendary and much-feared Man-Monkey that lurks around the centuries-old Bridge 39 on the Shropshire Union Canal in England. Despite the name, the creature looks far more like a wolfman. At least, that's what witnesses have said in their descriptions of the muzzle and huge fangs that they saw up close.

One witness was a man named Paul Bell, a keen fisherman who, in July and August 1976, spent several Saturdays out at the canal with his rods, reels, bait, cans of beer, and favorite beef and onion sandwiches, soaking in the intense heat. Bell told me that on one particular Saturday afternoon, he was sitting near the water's edge on a small wooden stool that he always carried with him when he was "literally frozen solid" by the sight of "what at first I thought was a big log floating down the cut, about sixty or seventy feet away."

Bridge 39 over Shropshire Union Canal, where a werewolf-like creature known as the Man-Monkey has been sighted.

According to Bell, however, it was no log. As it got closer, Bell was both astonished and horrified to see a large "dark brown and black-colored" eel or snake-like creature—possibly ten feet in length or a little bit more—moving slowly in the water, with its head, which "looked like a black sheep," flicking rapidly from side to side.

Although he had an old Polaroid camera with him, said Bell, he never even thought to take a photograph. Instead, he merely stared in both awe and shock as the animal cruised leisurely and blissfully past him before finally vanishing out of sight. Bell stressed that the creature apparently did not see him ("or, if it did, it never attacked me") and did not appear to exhibit any outright hostile tendencies.

> *Peering across the width of the canal,*
> *Bell was both horrified and petrified to see a*
> *dark, hairy face staring intently at him out*
> *of the thick green bushes.*

What elevated Bell's story to a far stranger level was the fact that he claimed, in quite matter-of-fact fashion, that the following Saturday he was fishing in practically the same spot when he had a sudden, out-of-the-blue feeling of being watched. He was not wrong. Peering across the width of the canal, Bell was both horrified and petrified to see a dark, hairy face staring intently at him out of the thick green bushes. The head of the animal was unmistakably human-like, said Bell, who added that "as soon as it saw me looking at it, up it went and ran right into the trees and I lost it." He further explained: "That was it; a second or two was all at the most. But as it got up and ran, I knew it was a big monkey. There's nothing else it could have been. But what flummoxed me more than seeing it, though: Was what was it doing there?"

A similar story that takes place not far from the old canal comes from Eileen Gallagher, who told me how a friend of hers, named Janice, underwent some sort of very traumatic, late-night encounter with a British man-beast in the picturesque English village of Child's Ercall some decades ago. Found in north Shropshire, Child's Ercall has origins that date right back to Celtic times and a church, St. Michael's, to the twelfth century. But in all of its many years, the village surely never before, and maybe never since, encountered such a strange beast as that in the tale told to Eileen by her childhood best friend. So the story went, it took place back in 1971, when Janice was 15 and living in a nearby village. Something abominable was about to radically upset the usual tranquil calm of old Child's Ercall.

After an evening spent with her then-boyfriend at the home of his parents in Child's Ercall, Janice was happily riding her bicycle back home when she was shocked to see a large, hairy animal dash across the road directly in front of her, while simultaneously glaring at her in a distinctly menacing fashion. Eileen Gallagher recalled that Janice told her that the animal was no more than 40 feet in front of her, was human-like in shape, was covered in long flowing dark hair, possessed a pair of bright yellow eyes that twinkled, and had a black-skinned and shiny face.

> *Janice was happily riding her bicycle back home when she was shocked to see a large, hairy animal dash across the road directly in front of her, while simultaneously glaring at her in a distinctly menacing fashion.*

Rather bizarrely, the Bigfoot-style entity seen by Janice in Child's Ercall was not the only weird creature said to have inhabited this otherwise utterly normal and pleasant little English village in times past. Legend has it that centuries ago a deadly mermaid was believed by many to inhabit an old pool there.

In 1893, the writer Robert Charles Hope, the source of the story, described the case as follows, in his book *The Legendary Lore of the Holy Wells of England, Including Rivers, Lakes, Fountains and Springs*: "There was a mermaid seen there once. It was a good while ago, before my time. I dare say it might be a hundred years ago. There were two men going to work early one morning, and they had got as far as the side of the pond in [a] field, and they saw something on the top of the water which scared them not a little."

A careful, closer look revealed that the "something" was indeed a mermaid, as Hope noted. Fearful that the mermaid might drag them down in the depths, the men backed away—almost running. When, however, they heard her soothing, inviting voice, they had a sudden turn of thought. There was clearly some kind of hypnotic mind-control at work here, as the pair were said to have instantly fallen in love with the mermaid—who told the men that there existed at the bottom of the pond a veritable treasure trove of gold. If the men would only come into the water and relieve her of the gold, they could have as much of it as they liked. It seemed too good to be true. It was.

The men, said Hope, carefully made their way into the water—practically up to their chins in it—and, as they did so, the mermaid headed below the water and suddenly resurfaced with a huge piece of gold, which led one of the men to cry out, "Good God!" It was an exclamation that caused the mermaid to scream in ear-splitting fashion and then to vanish beneath the waters of the old pond. Neither she nor the gold was ever seen again, the inference being that, in reality, the mermaid was a malevolent shape-shifter who was doing her utmost to lure the men to their deaths, when she was forced to flee at the mention of God.

Examples of United Kingdom–based cases, where hairy humanoids have been seen in the same precise vicinities as strange water-based beasts, absolutely abound. The idea that two very different, entities could inhabit the same locales seems close to impossible. Far more likely is the scenario that these creatures are one and the same—a shape-shifter.

Sources:

Redfern, Nick. Interview with Paul Bell, 2001.

Man Wolf of Stagecoach Road
by Lisa Lee Harp Waugh

This beast was often described by people as a half-human, half-wolf creature. It has been noted by many that the monster was over six feet tall when it stood upright. The Man Wolf had large yellow-orange eyes, a long blunt snout, and long, sharp white teeth. His face was always seen as not quite a man and not quite a wolf. Though some report that the Man Wolf is covered with a full coat of hair, others tell of the coat being sparse and patchy. Reports can differ, with some saying that the werewolf's face is flat and blunt, yet others describing it as pointed and grotesquely long.

The Man Wolf was often encountered along Stagecoach Road, one of the most haunted hotspots in Marshall, Texas. Others say it was Dead Woman's Road, or Sedberry Street, as it is now known.

This were-beast, or "dogman" as some call it, was known for slaying a sheep or a cow in the blink of an eye. Some say there is more than one Man Wolf and that the thousands of chickens they kill could feed the whole state

Following an especially vicious livestock predation, Ethel Briggs's husband set out at night to trap and kill what he thought was a large coyote or mountain lion, but he met a similarly gruesome fate.

of Texas for a year. There are also many stories of them killing a man, woman, or child or two for good measure.

One of the old stories heard most often is that of poor old Ethel Briggs. She was a lonely widow whose husband and young son were reportedly killed by the Man Wolf.

Ethel's husband used to raise all the normal things it took to survive the daily life of the time. Then one day he found a place where something had broken into his many pens and killed his livestock or carried them away. He then found chewed-up pieces of his chickens and animals that showed real signs that they were being killed and eaten.

He set out to trap and kill what he thought was a large coyote or mountain lion. Ethel's husband knew what he had to do. He went out that night and, as the story goes, never returned. They found his foot lying by the front door the next morning with the toes chewed off. They found his left arm missing three fingers and half a thumb near the old barn. His head was by the creek, missing its nose, ears, and tongue. His lips were chewed off, and his cheeks showed deep large punctures and tooth gouge marks.

The very next night, Ethel's youngest boy was taken before her eyes. He was the red-headed one, who had set off looking with his mother for the rest of his dad's chewed-up remains to bury on that cold February day. The very next morning a large part of his upper torso was found nearly five miles away. The sheriff was called to come and investigate the deaths, and Ethel said she and the four surviving children had seen the beast. What they saw, she said, was neither a man nor a mangy, rabies-infected dog. It was very large, and it walked like a man with a strange limp. She also stated that it had run off on all fours with her husband's left leg in its mouth. The next day, she went on to say, she saw it plainly again in the bright winter night's full-moon light. And she watched and froze in terror again as her youngest boy of six was taken before her eyes. She said she screamed as her boy was dragged off by his privates into the dark woods by a huge, half-naked man sparsely covered with long dark hair or fur who had grabbed him. This, she says, happened as they searched for parts of his poor daddy's carcass.

Many say Ethel's ghost still haunts the spot where the old Briggs farm once stood, still searching for the Man Wolf that stole away her husband and youngest son.

Monsters of the Woods

In 2007, I penned an article for my blog *There's Something in the Woods*. The article — "Do Werewolves Roam the Woods of England?" — focused on a strange wave of sightings of hairy, upright bipedal creatures that looked like hair-covered humans and were seen in the heart of England's Cannock Chase woods. Notably, the heads of the terrible beasts closely resembled those of wolves. No wonder, then, that word quickly got out that a pack of deadly werewolves was on the loose in the area.

Such is the strength with which the old traditions and folklore still prevail in the U.K. that even the local newspaper, the *Chase Post*, gave the reports significant coverage. And it did so in a serious, rather than mocking, tone. That the vast majority of the encounters occurred in the vicinity of an old cemetery only served to increase the anxiety that quickly spread throughout the local villages and hamlets.

The road through Cannock Chase leads to a World War II cemetery for German soldiers in Staffordshire, UK, where people have claimed to see werewolves or other shape-shifting creatures.

When my article appeared online, it quickly provoked numerous comments. One of those comments came from a former member of the U.S. military who, in 1970, was stationed at a British Royal Air Force facility in the U.K. Using the name of "Wes," he related the following:

> I encountered a werewolf (for lack of better description) in England in 1970. I was 20 yrs. old when I was stationed at RAF Alconbury. I was in a secure weapons storage area when I encountered it. It seemed shocked and surprised to been caught off guard and I froze in total fright. I was armed with a .38 and never once considered using it. There was no aggression on its part. I could not comprehend what I was seeing.
>
> It is not human. It has a flat snout and large eyes. Its height is approx. 5 ft. and weight approx. 200 lbs. It is very muscular and thin. It wore no clothing and was only moderately hairy. It ran away on its hind legs and scurried over a chain link fence and ran deep into the dense wooded area adjacent to the base.
>
> I was extremely frightened but the fear developed into a total commitment of trying to contact it again. I was obsessed with it. I was able to see it again a few weeks later at a distance in the wooded area. I watched it for about 30 seconds slowly moving throughout the woods and I will never forget my good fortune to encounter it … and to know this "creature" truly does lives among us.

As incredible as it may sound, and taking into consideration the bizarre events of 2007 in the mysterious woods of the Cannock Chase, Wes is undeniably correct in his stance that such infernal monsters are "among us." It's a chilling thought that werewolves are not merely the product of horror writers, Hollywood, and ancient folklore and mythology. It would be wise to remember that if, late one night, you find yourself walking through dense and ancient woodland or taking a shortcut through a creepy old graveyard—particularly so on a night when the moon shines bright and full. Pray you don't hear a loud, animalistic howl.

Sources:

Redfern, Nick. Interview with "Wes," former U.S. Air Force employee, 2007.

Montague Summers, Augustus (1880–1948)

Augustus Montague Summers, the author of *The History of Witchcraft and Demonology* (1927), *The Vampire: His Kith and Kin* (1928), and *The Werewolf* (1929), is also known for his scholarly work on seventeenth-century English drama. He also produced the first English translation of the infamous fifteenth-century Witch-hunters' manual, *The Malleus Maleficarum*.

Born on April 10, 1880, in Clifton, Bristol, Montague Summers was the youngest of the seven children of a wealthy banker. He attended Clifton College before he went on to study theology at Trinity College, Oxford. In 1905 he received a bachelor of arts degree and pursued his goal of becoming a priest in the Church of England by attending Lichfield Theological College.

Although Montague Summers was ordained a deacon in 1908 and served as a curate in Bath and Bitton in Greater Bristol, his pursuit of higher orders was sharply curtailed when he published his first book, *Antinous and Other Poems* (1907), which had as its central theme the subject of pederasty. Rumors spread of Montague Summers's interest in Satanism and his sexual predilection for young boys, and the Church of England strongly discouraged his desire to become a priest. Montague Summers and another clergyman accused of an interest in altar boys were tried and acquitted of any wrongdoing. In spite of his being declared innocent of any acts other than literary interest in homosexual activities, Montague Summers left the Church of England and converted to Roman Catholicism.

Montague Summers also accepted the physical reality of vampires and werewolves, and he wrote of the night terrors performed by these monsters as accurate historical records.

In 1909, after he had joined the Catholic Church, Montague Summers declared himself the Reverend Alphonsus Joseph-Mary Augustus Montague Summers. It is disputed that Montague Summers had so quickly attained the position of a Catholic priest and been properly ordained as such. There seems to be no record that he was ever a member of any Roman Catholic order or diocese. What is well known, of course, is that Montague Summers became interested in medievalism, the occult, Witches, vampires, and werewolves.

While he wrote with passion and belief in the works that he produced about Saint Catherine of Siena and Saint Anthony Maria Zaccaria, Montague Summers also stated that he fully believed in the evil reality of Witches, werewolves, and their kith and kin. Writing with both erudition and a classic style, he portrayed Witches as followers of an obscene and loathsome creed. In 1928, when he published the first English translation of Heinrich Kramer's and James Sprenger's *Malleus Maleficarum, The Hammer of Witches*, Montague Summers believed completely that the fifteenth-century priests had produced an admirable work, which detailed how the church should combat Satanic influences.

Montague Summers also accepted the physical reality of vampires and werewolves, and he wrote of the night terrors performed by these monsters as accurate historical records. While his contemporary, the notorious Aleister Crowley, with whom he was acquainted, assumed the persona of a contemporary magician and occultist, Montague Summers adopted the character of a medieval Witch and monster hunter.

Sources:

Frank, Frederick S. *Montague Summers: A Bibliographical Portrait*. London: The Scarecrow Press, 1988.

Jerome, Joseph. *Montague Summers: A Memoir*. London: Cecil and Amelia Woolf, 1965.

Moon in Full

Since the very earliest accounts of werewolves, those who would seek to explain the onset of such frightening behavior have stated with authority that it is the light of the full moon that serves as the catalyst for the transformation of human into wolf. The ancient Greeks and Romans associated the moon with the underworld and those human and inhuman entities who used the night to work their dark magic. Witches, werewolves, and other shape-shifters received great power from the moon—and just as the moon changed its shape throughout the month, so could these servants of the underworld transform their shapes into bats, wolves, dogs, rats, or any creature they so chose. In addition, they could also change their hapless victims into animals.

The moon goddesses—Hecate, Diana, or Selene—surveyed the world below them and awaited the summons from their disciples who wished to draw down the power of the moon (i.e., the goddess). The moon is nearly always associated with the feminine vibration. Egyptians gave the moon a prominent role in the act of creation, naming her "Mother of the Universe." The Babylonians gave the moon dominance over the sun, and numerous Asian cultures worshipped the moon over the sun, for the goddess of the moon gave her light at night when humankind really needed it, while the sun chose to shine only by day.

A number of studies have indicated that the full moon does make people more violent.

A number of studies have indicated that the full moon does make people more violent. In 1998 researchers observed prisoners in the maximum-security wing at Armley jail in Leeds, England. Claire Smith, a prison officer on the A wing, carried out the psychological study of all 1,200 inmates for more than three months, and the researchers found that there was a definite rise in the number of violent and unruly incidents recorded during the first and last quarter of each lunar cycle, the days on either side of a full moon.

Smith expressed her opinion to journalist David Bamber that she believed her study proved that there is a link between the moon and human behavior. "The best theory I have heard to explain why this happens is that we are made up of 60 to 70 percent water," she commented. "And if the moon controls the tides, what is it doing to us?"

Of course, as with every theory regarding human behavior, there are other points of view and varied opinions. While some researchers agree that there is more crime during a full moon, they attribute the rise in antisocial statistics to the simple fact that there is more light by which to commit mischief. As for dogs and wolves howling wildly at the full moon, animal control officers and park rangers disagree. They say that a full moon appears to calm the canines because they can see more of their surroundings on those nights when there is a full moon.

The Morbach Monster

According to legend, Wittlich was the last town in Germany where a werewolf was killed, but it would appear that something very much in the werewolf tradition still stalks the area.

D. L. Ashliman, author of *Werewolf Legends from Germany*, received the following account in 1997 from a respondent who first learned of the legend while he was stationed at Hahn Air Force Base circa 1988. Morbach is a munitions site just outside the village of Wittlich.

> There is a shrine just outside of town where a candle always burns. Legend has it that if the candle ever goes out, the werewolf will return. One night a group of security policemen were on the way to their post at Morbach when they noticed that the candle was out at the shrine. They all joked about the monster.
>
> Later that night, alarms were received from a fence-line sensor. When the security policemen investigated the call, one of them saw a huge "dog-like" animal stand up on its back legs, look at him, and jump over the seven-a-half-foot chain-link fence. A military working dog was brought to the area where the creature was last seen, and the dog went nuts, not wanting anything to do with tracking the creature.

Sources:
Ashliman, D. L., as told to Brad Steiger.

Mowgli

Although he was in no way a werewolf, Mowgli, the jungle boy, was reared by wolves in the classic Rudyard Kipling story *The Jungle Book*. And just as Tarzan, who was reared by apes, could speak the language of all creatures, so did Mowgli share this extremely useful survival skill.

Mowgli, the jungle boy in the classic Rudyard Kipling story The Jungle Book, *was reared by wolves and could speak the language of all creatures.*

Kipling's highly romanticized tale has proven to have lasting power to fire the imagination of each succeeding generation since its publication in 1895. Scholar Robert Eisler described the advent of the "wolf cubs" in the Boy Scouts as a "curious and harmless revival of atavistic lycanthropic ideas" inspired by the wolf-child Mowgli. Eisler attributed the worldwide success of Kipling's stories to the appeal they make to "archetypal ideas of the human race."

Eisler speaks of such legendary figures as Romulus and Remus but states that there are a number of cases of exposed South Asian children who were cared for by she-wolves with their cubs. He was also familiar with the two wolf sisters rescued by the Rev. J. A. L. Singh and with numerous other cases.

Mowgli was first portrayed in motion pictures in 1942 by Sabu, a former stable boy from Karapur, Mysore, India, who went on to play numerous exotic roles in British and American films. In 1967, Disney Studios applied the magic of animation to *The Jungle Book*. In 1998, the studio released a direct-to-video sequel entitled *The Jungle Book: Mowgli's Story*. Four years prior to its second animated treatment of Mowgli, Disney released a live-action film, *Rudyard Kipling's The Jungle Book*, with Jason Scott Lee as an excellent personification of the wolf-boy grown to young adulthood. And in 2016 Disney released a live action/CGI remake of its 1967 animated film, starring Neel Sethi as Mowgli.

Nagual

In ancient Aztec lore, the Nagual is essentially the form that shape-shifting shamans assume to perform their secret assignments—good or evil.

The name *Nagual* (a were-creature), which comes from the Aztec *Naualii* (sorcerer of dark powers), can also be applied to a shaman's familiar spirit or an individual's guardian spirit. In a fashion similar to the vision quest of the North American tribes, the traditional youth of Central America leave their villages to spend a night in a solitary place away from all other tribal members. The animal that appears to them in their dreams is their Nagual, or guiding totemic spirit.

In Mexican folklore, the Nagual is one of the most feared of all supernatural beings. Some have described the phantom as standing about seven to eight feet tall. The monster is covered with hair and has long arms and the feet and claws of a wolf. It has the ears and mouth of a wolf, but it bears the expression of an evil human. While it howls

In Mexican folklore, the Nagual is one of the most feared of all supernatural beings. The tall, hairy monster has long arms, the feet and claws of a wolf, and the ability to shape-shift into the form of a snake, a puma, or a wild dog.

like a wolf, the Nagual also has the ability to shape-shift into the form of a snake, a puma, or a wild dog.

Sources:

Bierhorst, John. *The Mythology of South America*. New York: William Morrow, 1988.

Nakh

Shape-shifting water demons who appear most frequently as handsome men or beautiful women, the Nakh, like the Greek Sirens, lure their victims into the river or sea with the sound of their sweet, seductive singing. Very often, according to old Estonian folklore, the spirits of the drowned may also become Nakhs, seeking to entice the living into watery graves. Even if one should escape the enchantment of their singing, the very sighting of a Nakh is a bad omen, usually a sign that either the witnesses or someone dear to him will die soon in a river, lake, or ocean.

Sources:

Larousse Dictionary of World Folklore. New York: Larousse, 1995.

Netherlands' Werewolves
by Theo Paijmans

In the sixteenth century, a number of men were prosecuted for claiming they had lived "as wolves for many years and had torn apart cows in their pastures." A man was brought to a doctor who had claimed to have the "wolf's disease," as he said himself. "I am a wolf and if you don't run away I will spring unto you and devour you." This man got off lightly; another was not so fortunate. In 1541 a man was brought before the magistrates. Since it was believed at the time that a werewolf's hairs would grow inward, the man's arms and legs were skinned. The man did not survive his horrible ordeal.

On May 15, 1595, 13-year-old Elbert Folkens was dragged before the court at Utrecht. He told how he and his father had transformed themselves into wolves, his sister and brother into cats, and how they danced "paw to paw" at night on a field somewhere in the vicinity of the city of Amersfoort. The evil one was present in the middle of the dancing circle, "also in the shape of a wolf."

The transcript of the court proceedings was uncovered by accident three and a half centuries later by a genealogist researching the histories of certain families. The transcript is chilling reading. The father, of course, denied the allegations, but as was customary in those days, he was sent to the torture chambers three times and subjected to the cruelest tortures. Broken in the end, he confessed.

Torture was the legal instrument and a very effective method of making people confess the most ludicrous things, of which they were innocent, and implicating other innocent people in these made-up accusations. An entire family—a mother, a daughter, and two sons—was dragged into this nightmare out of which there was no escape. They were put to torture as well. Finally, they all "confessed" to the accusations of having been involved in a satanic crime. Two were thrown in jail after having received a whipping "until the blood flows," and all were put to the stake.

There was a flap of alleged werewolvery going on that year. At Arnhem, for instance, a man named Hans Poeck was garroted at the stake and then burned. He had confessed how, three years before, he had met a mysterious man in black one night whom he held as "the evil one" and who had made him forsake God and make a pact with the devil. Afterward, he was forced to haunt as a werewolf.

In fact, werewolf sightings were once so commonplace that, as a reminder, they were sometimes woven into place or street names.

There are many stories like the ones above, including in the many musty files hidden away in city archives all over the Netherlands that describe the terrible Witch and werewolf crazes where many men and women ended on the stake, to be burned alive. In fact, werewolf sightings were once so commonplace that, as a reminder, they were sometimes woven into place or street names. For instance, in the city of Arnhem, through the center of which the river the Rhine flows, there still exists a small, long alley in the old part of town that descends toward the Rhine. This alley is named Wolvetrappen ("Wolf Stairs"), since, as a Dutch book on local folklore explains, it was especially here that werewolves were sighted so many times in the old days: "The werewolves made life miserable for the neighborhood, so that they dared not venture outside at evenings."

Wolvetrappen is a particularly foreboding alley. It is a narrow passage descending downward, with bushes and trees overhanging the walls on both sides blocking the end from sight and making the alley somehow seem longer than it actually is.

There is one curious and recurring detail in all these early werewolf tales; nowadays we would immediately classify these as shape-shifters. These werewolves were not only men turned into wolves; they also could change themselves into cats or rabbits, thus having a perfect camouflage when stalking a victim.

The mysterious Ura Linda book, written in Frisian and "discovered" in the 1860s, was said to have been an ancient manuscript that chronicles the rise and fall of Atlantis, but is generally considered to be a hoax.

Werewolves were sighted and attacks reported well into the nineteenth century at various places in the Netherlands. Sightings of werewolves in the now-urbanized Netherlands have not been reported in the late twentieth and early twenty-first centuries. So then are there no modern accounts of werewolves or, more generally, shape-shifters prowling the night? There is one curious incident that occurred in the mid-1990s in a remote place in the province of Friesland, named Jubbega. Jubbega is a small village, one of many that are still to be found in this province. There are but two cities in Friesland; the rest consists of small villages, ancient towns, and sometimes even a locality so small that it has just a couple of farmhouses on a lonely road seldom visited by traffic. There are still ancient tumuli to be found with small, crumbling churches built on top, and in many small villages a horse with cart or rider traveling down the road is a familiar sight. So I know something of this beautiful and enchanting countryside that has become so rare nowadays.

I also note that this province for some reason has always been in the limelight when it comes to anomalous phenomena. In 1974, a UFO flap was active in Gorredijk, another part of Friesland, and going back even farther, there are various mentions of other strange aerial phenomena. There is the church at Wiewert that holds mummified bodies in its cellars, the last remaining members of a mystical Christian sect that called itself the Labadisten. There never has been an adequate explanation as to how these corpses became mummified.

Then there is the mysterious *Ura Linda* book, the original manuscript of which rests in a safe in a library there. This book was said to have been an ancient manuscript that chronicles the rise and fall of Atlantis. Commonly believed to be a forgery or satire by a nineteenth-century Dutch writer, it was the subject of two English books, one appearing as early as the nineteenth century, and it managed to capture the fascination of certain occult elements in the Third Reich for a while.

The Frisians still speak a language recognized and acknowledged by the Dutch government and linguists worldwide as a very ancient and original language and not a dialect. It is even older than the English language. In fact, several Frisian words are found in the early English language. Some Frisian traditions are found in England as well, including that of the Green Water Dweller, a woman-like creature that haunts certain waterways and canals and lures the unsuspected to a watery grave. In short, the Frisians, although of Dutch nationality, belong to their own and very old tribe. This is the brief backdrop for a truly anomalous December 1994 incident for which I and others still have not been able to find a rational explanation. The incident, fascinating as it is, never made it to the Dutch national newspapers, but it was fortunately recorded by two provincial dailies.

> *Some Frisian traditions are found in England as well, including that of the Green Water Dweller, a woman-like creature that haunts certain waterways and canals and lures the unsuspected to a watery grave.*

It all happened on the night of December 24, 1994. Twenty-five-year-old Rink de Jong, his uncle, and two aunts were driving home, doing a leisurely 30 kilometers an hour. They drove through a lonely, wooded area locally known as the Belgische wijk. Suddenly, de Jong heard a thundering sound. Before they had the time to find out where the noise came from, the backside of the car was pushed downward. It was as if somebody or something had jumped on the back of the car.

De Jong's first reaction was to get out of there, but no matter how he pushed the gas pedal, the car would only slowly crawl forward. Finally, however, he was able to speed out of the area.

Arriving at home, de Jong checked the backside of his car, where he discovered two immense imprints of hands on the trunk. "It seemed as if the giant had slowly slid toward the fender of the vehicle." These imprints would be wiped away by the rain that fell that evening. The pulley at the backside of the car was dislodged.

De Jong delivered his aunts to their homes and proceeded on his journey with his uncle. His mother had now entered the car, and de Jong, his uncle, and his mother proceeded with their journey home. Then he saw the giant again. "I said: 'That's him.' He came straight at us."

But as quickly as the giant appeared, it disappeared again. De Jong's uncle took courage and left the car in search of the giant. De Jong said: "I should have never done that; that place is haunted." De Jong called the police twice. They came once and found nothing but a number of broken branches.

When interviewed a day later by a newspaper, he was still visibly frightened. He could not exactly describe the thing he had seen. It was a giant, estimated at three meters tall by de Jong. It wore clothes and was loosely described in the article as "a hulklike being." Nothing could move de Jong to visit that place again: "We hear strange sounds there more often."

It was a giant, estimated at three meters tall by de Jong. It wore clothes and was loosely described in the article as "a hulklike being."

WEREWOLF STORIES

Judging from de Jong's words, that particular spot somehow had a bad reputation. Since this was never explained in detail, one wonders what the local lore would have been able to tell about this area, had it been given a voice. As is often the case with accounts of anomalous experiences, an initial report may stir a community, and other people come forward who then feel comfortable telling of their strange experiences. Articles of de Jong's encounter that appeared in Friesland's two leading newspapers were objective in tone. Since the news reports at no time attempted to ridicule the witness, the media created a platform where other people could now tell of their strange experiences.

For two days the local police at the city of Heerenveen were deluged by phone calls. The callers related their experiences in which they had been suddenly confronted with "beings of abnormal size." A man from Oostermeer told how years ago he had also seen two giants. He and his wife were driving home at night. It was windy. Suddenly, he saw two men of exceptional size standing next to the road. "I thought they were hitchhiking and considered taking them along, but my wife was terrified," he told the police. "When we arrived home I dropped my wife off and returned to the spot, but they had already disappeared."

A resident of Leeuwarden told how in her youth she had been confronted with giants: "Forty years ago I stayed with my grandmother at Suameer. On a nice summer evening I decided to pluck some berries in the garden of my grandmother. I was just starting when a giant stood in front of me. I was so frightened that I ran back into the house. Afterward I realized that that giant had saved me from stealing." She further theorized that de Jong might have had "something in his trunk for which the giant tried to warn him."

But there the strangeness doesn't stop. Early January 1995 somebody—a hoaxer, undoubtedly—claiming to be the "Giant of Jubbega" sent a postcard from Paris, France, to the police in Heerenveen. The card read that the Tom Thumbs of the local police had nothing to fear anymore, as the giant had now emigrated.

As time passed, the Giant of Jubbega entered local folklore, as a recollection published in a local newspaper in 2007 demonstrated. Some theories were offered, but as the header of the article shows, the giant still was a mystery. At that time, so many years after the actual occurrences, de Jong's story was laughed at in good humor by his neighbor across the street, who said that she did not believe in such things. But, she added, it made for a great story at elementary school where she taught.

So what was the giant of Jubbega, and what about the tales of a wooded area that for reasons lost to us now had acquired such an unsavory reputation? And what about the recollections of all these other people involving uncanny encounters with giants?

The Netherlands is a small country, and in my research and investigations I have never encountered reports of sightings of Bigfoot-like beings. Our geography simply is too small to house these creatures unseen and undisturbed when we are talking of Bigfoot as a biological species. Also, we do not have a tradition of big hairy men stalking the woods, so it is safe to say that these creatures were not the cause of what de Jong and others saw. What we do have in abundance, however, is a rich tradition of werewolves and shape-shifters, those zooform entities that suddenly materialize out of nothing to frighten unsuspecting eye-witnesses and then disappear into the great unknown again. As the late writer John Keel noted, a werewolf can presumably pop up anywhere, and these uncanny creatures are known to chase cars down deserted lanes or roads at night. With this, the giant of Jubbega was no exception.

The Dutch Tradition of Mind-Shifters

The Giant of Jubbega may be seen as a new variant of an age-old Dutch-European tradition of werewolves and shape-shifters. The Giant

The term mind-shifter *has been used to describe compulsive behavior of dressing up like a werewolf and running around town, which may not be a hoax in the true sense. In this type of event, a person's behavior is compelled for some dark inner fulfillment.*

of Jubbega may have been a hoax. While evidence as to this may yet come to light—and it hasn't so far—a number of werewolf sightings in America clearly featured human involvement. Just like those poor devils Elbert Folkens and Hans Poeck of the sixteenth century, it is as if some compulsion to behave like this has actually struck even in our times. The compulsive behavior of dressing up like a werewolf and running around town—to disappear from the scene a week or so later—may not be a hoax in the true sense. Rather, the term "mind-shifter" has been used to describe this type of event, where a person's mind shifts toward another reality, where there apparently is an absolute need to run around dressed up as a monster or werewolf, not for the hoax and the notorious fame but for some dark inner fulfillment.

In June 1977, something like that puzzled the police of Federalsburg, Maryland. They received reports of a werewolf on the loose. "We got a call that a man with a wolf's head had knocked on a woman's door and scared her son so bad that he jumped on the stove and kicked pork chops on the floor," Lt. Harvey Williamson said. The police investigated and found 18-year-old Ronnie Lathum, who told officers that he was playing around with a large, hairy wolf's head with hair down the neck and along the arms. Williamson also stated that Lathum "apparently jumped in one car and scared the driver who stepped on the accelerator, throwing the 'werewolf' in the path of another car. As for the rest of the mystery, the wolf's head is still at large," Williamson said. No reason was given for Lathum's strange behavior.

> "We got a call that a man with a wolf's head had knocked on a woman's door and scared her son so bad that he jumped on the stove and kicked pork chops on the floor."

In May 1972, residents of Lakeland, Florida, were surprised by a man dressed as a werewolf. "Wearing a grotesque rubber mask, he has appeared twice in the last days—once darting among stalled rush-hour traffic on a main street, another time running through the parking lot of a hamburger stand, sticking his head into car windows and growling." Local resident David Weed called the police to tell them he was going home one night when "a man dressed as a werewolf jumped out of the bushes and then ran off quickly." The werewolf ran too fast for Weed to get a description of its clothing. At another time it was seen on

Lakeland Hills Boulevard, "standing in the middle of the road across from the Foxfire Inn, attempting to stop motorists." One time it actually ran in front of a Greyhound bus. The driver later said that he avoided hitting the man but almost lost control of his vehicle. A spokesman for the police commented that "the wolfman's antics are becoming more dangerous and could result in serious injury to someone." But we read no more of the Lakeland Werewolf. So where did he go?

In September 1965, a seven-foot-tall, wolf-headed monster chased three girls in Bensenville, Illinois. "The alleged monster jumped out at Cindy Miller, her sister Eibby and Sue Jackson from behind a tree around 9:20 p.m. and chased them making growling noises. The girls said the monster was human-shaped with a white sweatshirt pulled up over its head and a wolf's head on top."

And sometimes the compulsive hoaxer, the mind-shifter laboring under mysterious impulses, occupies the same geographical space as a true unknown. The police of the city of Lawton, Oklahoma, cleared up one of four reports of a hairy wolfman haunting the town in 1971. Captain Crawford Hawkins said that "three teenagers told him they had been playing in a yard with an ape mask." But it was added that the police "didn't have any firm explanation of three other reports."

A resident told neighbors that a werewolf creature had been spotted in the area at night. The story was repeated, and each telling added various particulars about description and activity.

In 1961, residents of Chester, Pennsylvania, were frightened out of their wits by recurrent rumors of a werewolf stalking their neighborhoods. A resident told neighbors that a werewolf creature had been spotted in the area at night. The story was repeated, and each telling added various particulars about description and activity. One version had a hair-covered monster leaping from ground level to rooftops. After reassurances by the local police that a werewolf had not been sighted, tempers calmed down, and the story quickly faded from view.

What was described as a wolfman, a werewolf, or a peeping tom in a rubber mask terrorized the residents of Tujunga, California, in December

1960. He turned up three times at the home of Arnold McGurdle. His last visit ended when he struck and tore off the shirt of 18-year-old Michael Eubanks. Said Eubanks: "I bumped into him near the garage. ... I thought his face was a mask, and tried to grab it, when he hit me with his right hand and ripped my shirt with his left hand." Another newspaper mentioned how Eubanks had described the thing as "a character with a Halloween face mask, a long coat and gloves. ... Police said they received more than 20 calls from jittery residents after the Eubanks sighting. Eubanks then admitted how he and two pals bought a mask and other makeup as a joke because a friend earlier reported sighting the "wolf."

Guys like Ronnie Lathum and Michael Eubanks were very lucky not to have lived in the sixteenth century, where the sense of humor was slightly different, to say the least. Mocking these demonic creatures from hell meant certain death, so big was the fear of werewolves and shape-shifters. Writers like John Keel and especially Linda Godfrey have chronicled the saga of true modern werewolves and shape-shifters in America. But long before creatures like the Michigan Dogman or the Beast of Bray Road shambled forth under a full moon, the stakes and fires in the old world darkened the air with the smoke and smell of burning flesh.

Sources:

De Bot, H. *Van Heksen en Weerwolven in 1595*. Rotterdam, Netherlands: privately printed, 1951.

De Jong, Marcel, "Raadsels in Jubbega rond de Reus van Rink." *Leeuwarder Courant*, December 29, 1994.

"De reus Blijft Een Mysterie." *Leeuwarder Courant*, January 2, 2007.

"Jubbegaster Reus Stuurt Kaartje." *Leeuwarder Courant*, January 9, 1995.

"Jubbegaster ziet reus van 3 meter." *Leeuwarder Courant*, December 28, 1994.

Knipscheer, F. S. *Bijgeloof Uit Alle Tijden, IV, Demonen*. Baarn, Holland: n.d.

"Man Seen in Lakeland Dressed as Werewolf." *Lakeland Ledger*, May 30, 1972.

"'Monster' in Wolf Guise Chases Girls." *Bensenville Register*, September 2, 1965.

"One Sighting of Wolfman Is Explained." *Wichita Falls Record News*, March 4, 1971.

"Peeping Werewolf Exposed as Hoax." *Eureka Humboldt Standard*, December 24, 1960.

"Prank Startles Driver." *Lakeland Ledger*, June 1, 1972.

"Reus van Jubbega zorgt voor consternatie. 'Ik Dacht Dat Die Reuzen Daar Stonden te Liften.'" *Heerenveense Courant*, January 4, 1995.

Sinninghe, J. R. W. *Geldersch Sagenboek*. Zutphen, Netherlands: W. J. Thieme, 1943.

"This Werewolf Learned Lesson." *The Capital*, June 10, 1977.
"Werewolf Go Home." *Delaware County Daily Times*, October 5, 1961.
"Werewolf Haunts Rush-Hour." *Montreal Gazette*, May 29, 1972.
"Werewolf Pretender Sought." *Palm Beach Post*, June 3, 1972.
"'Wolf Man' Ceases to Prowl." *Pasadena Independent*, December 23, 1960.

New Orleans' Werewolves
by Alyne Pustanio

In the 1970s the area east of New Orleans was experiencing amazing growth, fueled by the phenomenon of "urban flight" sweeping people out of the older sections of the city. The influx of new residents created a neighborhood typical of the time, one of cookie-cutter brick homes, neatly paved streets with bright lights along every block, and a shiny new shopping mall where the "upwardly mobile" spent their time and money. East New Orleans was the last place one would expect to come into contact with the palpable reality of an ancient fear: werewolves.

Several individuals living in East New Orleans during the 1970s and into the early 1980s were forced to come to terms with the apparent existence of something they had all been taught existed only in fairy tales and movies. In short, although the modern landscape of East New Orleans was the last place anyone would expect to encounter a monstrous being, for a time a very ancient fear became a very frightening reality for the residents there.

By all appearances a werewolf or perhaps even a pack of werewolves had staked a claim on East New Orleans in those days; what follows is just a sampling of stories about encounters with these preternatural beings.

Ouija Wolf Girl

Most of the experiences centered on a particular group of friends, a group that had known each other since early childhood and had grown up in the East New Orleans area. These events followed this group through school and into acquaintances and friendships that lasted beyond the school years. The neighborhoods of East New Orleans were close and clustered together, with new ones abutting the more established areas, and as with neighborhoods elsewhere across America, East New Orleans had its common archetypes. There were the jocks and cheerleaders, the brains and the stoners, the bikers and the bums, and always another caste, one that was often a combination of other types all brought together by a common thread—an attraction to the occult and supernatural.

Many from that era will recall the girl, an "army brat" around 14 years old, who moved into a neighborhood off Chef Menteur Highway with her family. By all appearances she and they were quite normal. But it soon became the talk of the neighborhood that while Dad was serving his country at the nearby U.S. Army Reserve installation and Mom was busy with her PTA duties, the kids were finding interesting ways to amuse themselves.

The harmless fun began with impromptu séances, until the day a new kid joined the group with a Ouija board. Soon a dominant spirit began focusing all its attention on one person in the group, who found her dreams turning dark.

The fun seemed harmless enough. It began with impromptu séances. The kids and a group of friends would gather in the bedroom of the eldest daughter and sit in a circle, trying to contact everyone from Cleopatra to Al Capone. The only thing they ever accomplished was scaring themselves silly, until the day a new kid joined the group.

He was dark-haired, quiet, and for the most part unhindered by any kind of parental influence. When he came to the séances he brought the hippest music, the coolest incense, and the best pot. One day he brought a black light bulb to enhance the atmosphere. Not long afterward he brought a new toy and introduced the group to its first experience with the Ouija board. Before long, as they started to get results, the group started using the board more and more.

At first the spirit contact seemed as random as that of the disorganized séances. But soon a dominant spirit began making itself known. Moreover, it seemed to be focusing all its attention on one person in the group—the army brat. This frightened almost everyone, except for the boy who owned the Ouija board and the girl herself, who found it intriguing that a spirit would be trying so obviously to make direct contact with her. Eventually, the other members of the group trickled away, and, perhaps for lack of an audience, the quiet boy lost interest as well; he left his Ouija board with the girl, who now found herself the center of its attention.

The messages had always seemed disjointed, but as the girl continued to use the board alone, things began to make more sense. Unfortunately, the messages coming through soon took an ominous tone. Words like "family," "curse," and "you" kept being spelled out; before long these were being augmented with phrases like "past reborn" and "came back." The girl found herself completely mystified and told the board as much. That's when it told her to "true dream."

In one dream she looked down at her swiftly moving feet and to her astonishment saw massive animal paws there. It was after this dream that she woke to find her feet caked in mud and grass.

Not long afterward, the girl's dreams turned dark. As she slept, a state of complete anxiety took over. Her dreams became especially vivid: most of them began with a feeling of flying or floating, as if she were floating out of her body. Soon she was able to look down and see her body asleep on the bed beneath her; in the dream state she was free to fly, but it seemed she always preferred running and the feeling of the earth under her bare feet. In every dream she found herself running through deep, impenetrably dark forests, but without any fear. Her every sense seemed heightened, and she could distinguish the smell of the resinous woods, the mossy, heavy air of the underbrush as she moved about it, the rush of fresh air as she jumped and bounded in her dream form. Before long she began to feel a strange connectedness to the dreamy landscapes; she experienced it from an almost feral point of view. In one dream she looked down at her swiftly moving feet and to her astonishment saw massive animal paws there. It was after this dream that she woke to find her feet caked in mud and grass. In a moment she realized that this was the curse: she was turning into an animal!

Seeking answers from the Ouija board, she found it completely mum. It would not respond in any way to her attempts at communication; the planchette, and apparently the spirit, remained unmoved. With the spirit of the board aloof from her, the girl sought out other sources that might explain what was happening to her. First she went to the boy who had been the original owner of the board. She almost expected him to be amused, and when she had poured out her story and her fears, he didn't disappoint her; when he called her "crazy," she realized for the first time that to him the board had always been just a game. He hadn't believed in it at all.

She next approached a group of slightly older girls who had made no secret of their practice of Witchcraft and the fact that they operated as a coven. For the first time the girl found sympathetic ears and learned that she was experiencing "lycanthropic" events: she was turning into a werewolf. They gave her constructive suggestions for how to lift the curse, but then it was the Witches' turn to be astonished when the girl begged them to help her permanently transform into her werewolf shape. The Witches balked and refused, telling her that it was against the natural order of things for them to interfere and that if the girl was meant to live permanently as a werewolf, the transformation had to happen in its own time.

Needless to say, the girl was dissatisfied when she left the coven. Soon she began to formulate a plan in her mind. Secreted in her room, she once again consulted the Ouija board, and to her surprise it began to respond once again. In messages that would have seemed garbled and unclear to anyone else, the girl read what she wanted to hear. "Blood" and "eat" meant she needed to eat blood; the nearest source for this was the raw meat kept in her family's refrigerator. The word "mirror" sent her to the mirror, where she spent hours studying her own face, contorting it into animal-like grimaces and movements. She broke her dental retainer into pieces, knowing her parents would refuse to replace it, thus allowing her already prominent underbite to become even more

Making her way to the French Quarter, she found The Witches' Workshop, where a warlock may have given her the token, talisman, or spell that allowed her to realize her dream of attaining her werewolf form forever.

pronounced. She ceased wearing makeup or grooming herself properly, and when her classmates began to make fun of her at school, she simply stopped going and instead spent her days in nearby Joe Brown Park.

Sometimes she would take a bus or walk all the way to the French Quarter, where she spent time exploring the little occult bookshops that seemed to be everywhere in those days. Ultimately this led her to the most famous of these shops, The Witches' Workshop, owned by Oneida Toups, the great Witch Queen of modern New Orleans, and her husband, the warlock "Boots." Although nobody really knows what she learned there, everyone who knows the story generally agrees that it was Boots who gave her the token, talisman, or spell that allowed her to realize her dream of attaining her werewolf form forever.

Back home, the girl's parents were hearing strange complaints from her siblings. She would scratch the walls, they said, and growl, making horrific sounds that kept them petrified in their beds. The parents were mystified until the other children told them that their eldest daughter might be getting out through the window at night. Astonished and angry, and thinking they knew very well the explanation for the "growls" and other sounds being heard, the parents confronted their daughter with accusations of bringing boys back to her room at night. The girl laughed wildly, a response neither parent expected, but the result was that bars were placed on her window and a heavy lock on her bedroom door. This, of course, only made the situation worse. Locked up, the girl would yammer the night away, and if the moon happened to be full, the yammering was interspersed with doleful howling.

She would scratch the walls, they said, and growl, making horrific sounds that kept them petrified in their beds.

Desperate, her parents did the only thing any loving parents would do in the same situation: they turned to medicine. But multiple doctors gave second, third, and even ninth and tenth opinions, and all were in agreement that there was nothing physically wrong with the young girl. In unison the doctors all suggested that the parents find a good psychiatrist for their daughter because what was wrong with her was obviously all "in her head." Dutifully, the parents followed the instructions of the doctors and put their daughter into treatment with a psychiatrist whose first course of action was to place the young girl on medications to treat everything from depression to psychosis. As often happens, this course of action only exacerbated the girl's apparent "illness," and, as she was soon to discover, instead of treating her symptoms, the medications tremendously enhanced her physical senses as well as her strength. At the very first opportunity, the girl tore the bars from her bedroom window and escaped.

All of East New Orleans was in an uproar. The girl was missing for days. Former friends and classmates let loose with a torrent of all the strange knowledge and assumptions they had collected in their minds about the girl until at last they were all scared to death. Every kid was filled with mortal terror at the prospect of waiting at the school bus stop or walking home from school, not to mention being asked to perform simple chores like putting the garbage out after nightfall. Parents blamed everything from bad parenting to hippie culture for the strange behavior of "that girl." Oddly enough, however, when the missing girl was ultimately found, no one felt any better. Local police had cornered her in Joe Brown Park and taken her to Charity Hospital's infamous third floor mental ward. The neighborhood never saw her again.

The Army transferred the little family to some other town in some other state where, it can be assumed, they were able to leave the past behind. One thing the family did leave behind was their daughter, who, hopelessly and completely convinced she was a wolf, was brought screaming, biting, and howling into the halls of a prominent mental asylum located outside New Orleans.

According to all accounts, she is still there to this day, a woman of 60-plus years who only eats meat, attacks doctors, nurses, and attendants on a regular basis, and, whenever the moon is full, howls wildly like the caged animal she believes herself to be.

Dreamcatcher Transformation

Less than two miles away from where the army brat turned wolf girl lived with her family resided another out-of-state "transplant"—a preteen boy originally from Mississippi who came to the neighborhood when his mother settled there after a divorce.

His father still lived in Mississippi on a working farm located north of the little town of D'Iberville, and the boy would go there to visit on a regular basis. His grandparents also lived on the farm. The place was a successful pig farm and had been in the family for generations; and from an early age the boy had been exposed to the grim reality of animal slaughter in his environment. His mother had tried to shield him from the activity, but after his parents divorced that shield was lifted, and his father saw no harm in teaching the boy what he called the "family business."

At first upset and uncooperative, eventually the boy began to find ways to detach from the slaughtering process and actually gained an appreciation for what his father called his "craft." When the time came for the boy to slaughter his first pig, instead of approaching it with dread, he found himself actually looking forward to it. Something about wielding the power to kill over another creature, even if it was a helpless pig, entranced the boy and awakened something in him that probably would have been better left undisturbed.

> *When the time came for the boy to slaughter his first pig, instead of approaching it with dread, he found himself actually looking forward to it.*

Back at home, with her caring eye, the boy's mother noticed almost imperceptible changes in her young son. He had become more withdrawn and secretive, and he was asking to visit his father and the farm more frequently. In an effort to placate him, she gave in to his sudden desire to have pets, bringing home a dog and two kittens from a local animal shelter. She hoped this would entice her son to want to stay home more, and in fact, it worked for a while. But the visits to Mississippi were inevitable, and since there was no obvious harm being done, his mother could not refuse.

During one particular visit the boy accompanied his grandparents—the sort of strong, sturdy, country people found in the wooded country north of the Mississippi coast—to a local flea market. While they shopped, the boy amused himself among the many booths of local craftsmen until at last he came upon a withered old man selling strange objects made from animal materials. There were belts and bags made of fine tanned hide, and wallets, purses, and decorative items, including a strange object that the boy had never seen before. The old man called it a "dreamcatcher" and explained that it had been made from the hide of a wolf; feathers and bits of fur hung from it on strings of wolf sinew, and its complicated circular web was dotted with wolf's teeth.

The boy knew he had to have it, and after much begging and pleading on his part, his grandparents finally gave in and bought it for him. When he arrived back at the farm, he immediately went to his room and hung it over his bed, just as the old man had instructed, hoping it would catch good dreams. On his return to New Orleans, the boy delicately held his dreamcatcher the whole way. When he was deposited at home, once again he immediately went to his room and hung the dreamcatcher above his bed there, just as he had done in his Mississippi bedroom.

By all accounts, the wolf dreamcatcher definitely caught dreams, but to some these dreams might best be called nightmares.

The boy's mother first began to hear stories of mutilated pets in the fall, when children were returning to school. Neighborhood dogs and cats were being found cut open and skinned, and the contents of their lower abdomens were always missing, along with the genitals. Hoping to shield her son yet again from what she felt was too harsh a reality, the mother mentioned nothing to him about the awful happenings. But she knew kids talked and that he might ultimately hear something from his friends or classmates, so she steeled herself for the time when her son would come and ask her about the horrible mutilations. To her great surprise, he never asked her or even mentioned the subject.

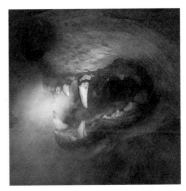

Every night that he slept under the dreamcatcher, he moved astrally through the darkness, killing with a preternatural swiftness.

The truth was that the boy knew all about the animal killings. Every night that he slept under the dreamcatcher—whether in Mississippi or in his New Orleans home—he experienced vivid dreams in which he moved astrally through the darkness, and with a preternatural swiftness was able to overtake and kill the common animals that crossed his path. At first, he used knives in his dreams, the instruments his father had taught him to use in the slaughtering at the farm. Soon, however, he was aware that he had no more need for weapons of any kind; in his dream state, at least, he knew himself to be a predator, and the help-less animals he chased down were his prey. He enjoyed these dreams immensely, especially the hot, metallic pungency of animal blood as it snaked down his throat. He was one with, but also separate from, the animals he killed; he was more powerful, and he knew it, and it certainly beat any mundane thing he did in his waking life.

The mother watched her son become more and more withdrawn. When his two pet cats went missing, presumed dead, and he showed no emo-tion, the boy's mother knew something was wrong with her son. Eventu-ally, she began to refuse to allow him to visit his father, opening a whole new round of legal issues and family fighting. But she did not care. Something had happened to her son on those visits; something, at least it seemed to her, had replaced the son she knew and left—she didn't know what. To her, he now seemed like an empty shell.

Nothing that goes bad and unchecked ever really gets better, and this is exactly how the story of this East New Orleans boy turned out.

With the cats gone, and confined to his New Orleans home while his parents fought things out again, the boy began to occupy himself with his dog. His mother saw this as an encouraging sign, and certainly her son's disposition was improving; she credited his time with man's best friend for the change in him. One evening when she came home early from work, she found out just how friendly her son was being with his pet.

Her son had devolved into a slathering, howling, snapping miniature imitation of a wild wolf. By all appearances, his human nature had completely left him.

By the time she tearfully signed the papers committing him to the boy's mental asylum at Jackson, Louisiana, her son had devolved into a slathering, howling, snapping miniature imitation of a wild wolf. By all appearances, his human nature had completely left him; though the doctors could not pinpoint exactly when this had happened, they suspected it was probably the moment the boy started forcing himself sexually upon his unsuspecting dog.

The pet was mercifully put to sleep. The boy remains committed—and in a devolved animal state—to this very day.

No Ordinary Disappearance

It was around 1972 that a local kid had run afoul of the leader of a local magical coven, a pale teenage boy of about 15 years of age who always dressed in black, wore sunglasses day and night, had numerous vixen-like girlfriends who all resembled Morticia Addams, and kept a full skeleton in a coffin in his mother's parlor. According to all accounts, a local preteen did something to offend this budding Satanist, and although several attempts were made on both sides to smooth over whatever had been done, what kept trickling down to the kids on the street was that the coven leader was planning to go "ape-shit" on the offending kid and that the coven was going to "take care" of the boy.

Later the child's picture appeared on "Missing Child" posters on telephone poles and supermarket bulletin boards.

Certainly, it could have been coincidence; and certainly, parents and other adults didn't put much stock at the time in what they considered teenage "posing." But the kids knew better. Something very bad had happened, just as had been promised. The police were called, reports were filed, and police cruisers made prominent sweeps of all the nearby neighborhoods in the days and nights following the boy's disappearance. But, as usually happens among those closest to the source, it was immediately obvious that all such efforts were in vain, and this knowledge kept everyone silent. Magic had been performed, and a kid had disappeared.

As days and weeks passed and the autumn season when the event had occurred passed into a wet winter, the disappearance became less immediate, replaced by other things in kids' minds. In the missing boy's neighborhood and others nearby, life turned back to a normal routine of school, homework, and whatever pastime got everyone through the night. It was at this remove that word leaked from the dark side that the coven leader had finally spoken about what had happened. Although he told only those closest to him, someone leaked the information into the flow of the neighborhood scuttlebutt, and that's when it was heard that the missing boy hadn't just disappeared into the blue. In fact, the teenage warlock had cursed the boy and turned him into a werewolf—and although it strained credulity, there wasn't a kid within a five-mile radius who doubted the veracity of this pronouncement.

Neighborhood cats began disappearing, then small dogs. Other dogs, left out overnight, were heard fighting with something in their yards.

What made the young warlock's admission even more chilling was the fact that curious, at first seemingly unrelated, things had started to happen. Neighborhood cats began disappearing, then small dogs. Other dogs, left out overnight, were heard fighting with something in their yards. When the owners went out to investigate, the intruding animal—for it was obvious it had been an animal—was nowhere to be seen, and the family dog was usually mauled; several pets had to be put to sleep after these attacks. Groups of children waiting at school bus stops reported sighting a large, strange-looking yellow dog hiding in the morning shadows or snuffling around in brush nearby as the winter afternoon shadows grew long. The last straw was when the mangy feral animal was seen trying to pry its way through a window into a home — the home of the missing boy's family. The father had taken out his squirrel rifle and shot at the wild dog but had missed. Everyone in the vicinity was in an uproar.

Concerned adults turned to the police department and animal control, who showed up and took copious notes, walked around the neighborhood poking into backyards and vacant lots, set some traps, resumed frequent patrols, and reassured everyone that everything would be fine. For a time, this prediction was accurate. But the kids knew better; they knew exactly what — or rather, who — that wild dog was.

Despite all the best efforts of animal control to capture the animal and the police to prevent its reappearance, it did eventually reappear when, around the Christmas season following the time when the curse had been laid out, the animal was spotted on the lawn of the local warlock tearing up a huge black cat; it then attacked the house itself, clawing at the windows and baying like a wild beast at the front door. The parents and siblings of the teenage magician watched in fright from windows inside his house, but no one — not even the warlock, apparently — would come outside.

The police returned just as the feral dog had moved on to chewing at the tires of a pickup truck in the driveway. As the police jumped from their cruiser, the ravenous dog turned to confront them, teeth bared and bloody from rending tire rubber, every wiry yellow hair on end, blue eyes flashing.

"That was the strange thing," said the cop who had fired the fatal shot. "I never saw a dog with blue eyes like that. Couldn't even tell you what breed it was — some kind of mix."

Northumberland Werewolf

In Northumberland County, Pennsylvania, circa 1899, many rural residents had their suspicions about a reclusive old man being a werewolf. While some scoffed at such stories as nonsense and superstition, the

Paul family became uneasy when they noticed that the old fellow had taken an apparent liking to their 12-year-old daughter, May.

Although they had never seen the man do the slightest thing that anyone could consider improper, it made them uncomfortable when he would sit some distance from May while she tended the family's sheep. They knew that their little girl was a lovely, cheerful child who seemed to lift the spirits of all those she encountered, and the elderly gent simply seemed to gain pleasure from watching her performing her daily tasks with the flock. From all they could ascertain, he never even spoke to her or disturbed her duties in any manner whatsoever.

Other shepherds found it strange, though, that while the wolves in the area were so bold that they could attack flocks of sheep in broad daylight, they never bothered the sheep that were tended by little May. Some had witnessed the wolves approaching her flock, then turn tail and run away. Such bizarre behavior on the part of the beasts only increased the gossip about the old man being a fierce werewolf that could frighten normal wolves away.

One night when the moon was full, a hunter spotted a gaunt old wolf skulking out of the underbrush and preparing to cross the road. Thinking of the 25-dollar bounty on wolves, he took aim and fired. He could tell from the yelp of pain that his bullet had struck home, but the wolf staggered into the thicket. Deciding it was too dark for pursuit of a wounded wolf in such tangled growth, the hunter went home, resolving to return at the first light.

The Paul family had never witnessed anything improper in the behavior of the reclusive old man. But they became uncomfortable when he began sitting some distance from their young daughter May while she tended the family's sheep.

The next morning, he returned to the spot, followed the trail of blood, and instead of the carcass of a wolf, he found the body of May Paul's elderly admirer lying stiff and cold. This confirmed the local rumors about the man being a werewolf, and according to regional tradition, he was buried on the spot, which became known as *die Woolf man's grob* ("the wolf man's grave").

As the story goes, May Paul continued to tend her family's flocks in the same area for the next 25 years. Although wolves and other predators continued to harass the flocks of the neighboring farmers, May's sheep were never troubled. She claimed that the spirit of her werewolf protector still watched out for her and drove away the beasts of prey.

Sources:

Hurwood, Bernhardt J. *Vampires, Werewolves, and Ghouls.* New York: Ace Books, 1968.

Organization Werewolf

In 1923, a secret terrorist group known as Organization Werewolf was established in Germany by Fritz Kappe. Its banner was essentially that of the pirates' old Jolly Roger — a black flag with a skull and crossbones in stark white contrast. At first the movement spread rather quickly across Germany, but as a result of a number of arrests by the Weimar government, the Werewolves never became a force that caused any real threat to the establishment. Quite likely, the more ruthless members of the organization responded to Adolf Hitler's summons for ruthless men to join his Nazi Party and to his admonition that Germany's youth should be like werewolves, cruel and pitiless, prepared to erode thousands of years of human domestication.

Toward the end of World War II when the collapse of Nazi Germany appeared imminent, Joseph Goebbels revived the Werewolves after Heinrich Himmler's rabid speech in 1945 calling for a new *Volksstrum* to harass the Allied lines of communication in occupied Germany. The organization took as its insignia a black armband with a skull and cross-bones and a silver S.S. Its main function was to assassinate and terrorize anti-Nazi Germans and to harass advancing Allied troops. In Leipzig, female Werewolves poured scalding water from the windows of houses onto the heads of Allied soldiers passing below. In Baden, they killed a number of French soldiers by ambushing them as they were resting.

Even after hostilities had ended and the war was officially over, the Werewolves continued their terrorist activities. At the Nuremburg trials, several Nazi leaders testified that the Werewolves were now under the control of the notorious Martin Bormann, who had somehow managed to escape capture by the Allies.

The Werewolves resurfaced in 1994 when Steven Spielberg's master-piece about the Holocaust, *Schindler's List* (1993), was scheduled to open in Russian theaters. Members of the group who were arrested by Russian security forces confessed their plans to firebomb Moscow cinemas showing the film. The Werewolves, estimated at about one hundred members strong, acknowledged that they took their name from the Nazi secret-police operation that went underground once the Allies had defeated Hitler's troops in World War II.

In April 2011, MI5 (British Intelligence) released formerly classified documents that revealed the potential use of poisons employed by Organization Werewolf in their resistance program against the Allies. After the Nazi defeat in 1945, the Werewolves sought to establish a Fourth Reich by sowing chaos among the occupying soldiers by leaving poisoned sausages, chocolate, and Nescafe coffee where they could be found by British and American troops.

MI5 discovered a wide range of deadly poisons and devices that were developed by the Nazi Werewolves:

- "Aspirin" tablets that could kill in ten minutes
- Lozenges that would explode upon contact with a wet glass, thereby blinding anyone nearby with shards of glass
- A poison powder to be placed on door handles, books, desks, and other surfaces
- A deadly powder that would cause death either by inhalation or by swallowing to be dusted on food by Werewolf waiters in restaurants
- Tiny pellets that were designed to be scattered in ash-trays and would explode when heated by cigarette ash

- Bacterial agents that could be secreted by female Werewolves in their handbags and doused upon top-ranking Allied officials.

Sources:

Eisler, Robert. *Man into Wolf.* London: Spring Books, 1948.

Singer, Natasha. "'Schindler' vs. the Werewolves: Spielberg Opus Stirs Controversy in Moscow." *Forward: Ethnic News Watch*, July 22, 1994.

Paulin, Thierry (1962–1989)

From 1984 to the end of 1987, a modern werewolf sought his prey among older women, suffocating, strangling, stabbing, or beating to death a toll of victims that may have reached as high as 50. For three anguished years, women over 65 in France's capital city lived in terror as the "Monster of Montmartre" struck again and again, torturing and murdering for the sake of a few francs.

At last, in December 1987, the Monster inadvertently left one of his victims, a 70-year-old widow, with a spark of life remaining in her cruelly beaten body. She provided the police with a detailed description of the beast who had attacked her, and the police recognized Thierry Paulin, a petty thief who already had a record of theft and drug offenses. When his fingerprints matched many of the 150,000 prints the police had accumulated during the three-year death prowl of the werewolf, there could be no mistake — Paulin was the Monster of Montmartre.

When arrested, the 25-year-old, tall, athletic Paulin readily confessed to the brutal murders of 21 women in a manner the police found chillingly detached. While he was confined to Fleury-Merogis prison to await trial, Paulin's health rapidly began to deteriorate. It soon began apparent that his drug abuse and sexual practices had placed him at risk from AIDS. Transferred to the prison hospital at Fresnes, Paulin died on April 16, 1989, from the tuberculosis and meningitis, which his AIDS-impaired immune system could not combat.

Sources:

Lane, Brian, and Wilfred Gregg. *The Encyclopedia of Serial Killers.* New York: Berkley Publishing, 1994.

Pentagram

In the werewolf tradition, it is said that the sign of the pentagram is to be located somewhere on the person of the lycanthrope.

In true magic, the pentagram, the five-pointed star, represents the sign of the Microcosm and is considered the most powerful symbol of conjuration in any magical rite. As a symbol of the Microcosm, the pentagram may represent evil as well as good. If one point is held in the ascendant, it assumes the character of Christ. Some traditions maintain that it was such a star that led the three Magi to the birthplace of the infant Jesus. However, if two points are in the ascendant, the pentagram is the sign of Satan. By such a simple alteration, the pentagram may be used to summon the powers of Light or the powers of Darkness.

In the werewolf tradition, it is said that the sign of the pentagram is to be located somewhere on the person of the lycanthrope, most often on the chest or the palms of the hand. It is also stated in some traditions that the werewolves choose their next victim when the sign of the pentagram appears to their vision alone on either the person's palm or forehead.

Sources:

Spence, Lewis. *An Encyclopedia of Occultism*. Hyde Park, NY: University Books, 1960.

Petronius (c. 27–66 CE)

The Roman satirist Gaius Petronius Arbiter, the Arbiter of Elegance, was well known among his contemporaries as an intimate companion to the emperor Nero. In his classic work *The Satyricon* (c. 50 CE), Petronius deals with the seamier side of Roman life, chronicling a series of loosely related episodes detailing the adventures of three young men as they wander through southern Italy. In one of those picaresque episodes, one of the young narrators describes a man transforming himself into a werewolf:

> Niceros tells of his soldier friend who stripped off his clothes and addressed himself to the stars. Then he [removed his vestments] and all at once became a wolf, which ran howling into the woods. Niceros next heard from a widow whom he visited that a wolf had been worrying her cattle and had been wounded in the neck. On his return home [he] found his friend bleeding at the neck, and he knew then that he was a *versipellis* [werewolf].

Sources:

Eisler, Robert. *Man into Wolf.* London: Spring Books, 1948.

Phantom Black Dogs

Few people who have read Sir Arthur Conan Doyle's classic Sherlock Holmes novel *The Hound of the Baskervilles* can forget those immortal words uttered by Dr. James Mortimer to the world's most famous fictional detective: "Mr. Holmes, they were the footprints of a gigantic hound!"

It may come as a surprise to some that Conan Doyle's novel was based upon real legends of giant, devilish hounds that were said to haunt Britain's villages and countryside, bringing doom, tragedy, and death in their spectral and demonic wake. Yes, Britain has a long, rich, and varied history of encounters with what have generally become known as phantom black dogs.

Usually much larger than normal dogs, they are said to possess a pair of large, glowing eyes (very often red); they frequent graveyards, old road-ways, crossroads, and bridges; and they are associated with the realm of the dead. In some cases, the beasts appear to be demonstrably evil, while in other reports evidence is exhibited of a helpful—perhaps even concerned—nature. But whatever these critters are, they are not your average flesh-and-blood animal. In fact, they might just be your worst nightmare.

While the image of the phantom black dog is most associated with the British Isles and mainland Europe, the beast has been seen in many other locations, too, including throughout Latin America. The leading researcher in this field is Simon Burchell, the author of *Phantom Black Dogs in Latin America*. Although the booklet is brief, its pages are packed with case after case, each offering the reader little-known and seldom-seen information on the definitive Latin American cousin to Britain's more famous counterpart.

Notably, Burchell's publication details the truly startling wealth of similarities between those creatures seen centuries ago in England and those reported throughout Latin America in the last 100 years. These include the diabolical, glowing eyes; the association that the phantom hound has with life after death; how seeing the beast may be a precursor to doom and tragedy; its occasional helpful and guiding qualities; the fact that the animal is usually witnessed in the vicinity of bridges, crossroads, and cemeteries; its ability to shape-shift and change in size; and most important, its perceived paranormal origins.

Burchell also reveals how the legends of the phantom black dog of Guatemala and other Latin American nations have been exploited by those with draconian and outdated morals. For example, there are widespread tales of people who enjoy having a drink (or several) incurring the dire wrath of the phantom black dog—which, as Burchell says, "was certainly popularized by the Catholic Church which used this legend and others as moralizing tales."

Winged hounds—whose appearance and activities smack strongly of the modern-day chupacabras of Puerto Rico—are discussed, as are copious amounts of data linked to tales of a truly dark and satanic nature. Burchell also reveals intriguing information suggesting that at least some tales of the black dog might be based upon cultural memories and stories of very real, large and ferocious hounds brought to the New World by the conquistadors centuries ago — "savage and ferocious dogs to kill and tear apart the Indians."

That said, it is clear that the overwhelming majority of reports of the phantom black dog in Latin America parallel those of Britain to a truly striking degree, in the sense that the creatures appear to be something other than flesh-and-blood entities. As Burchell states:

> Although the Black Dog may appear at first glance to be a British or north European phenomenon, it exists in essentially the same form across the entire length and breadth of the Americas. Much has been written upon the presumed Germanic, Celtic or Indio-European origin of the legend but such an origin would not explain how a highland Maya girl can meet a shape-shifting Black Dog at a Guatemalan crossroads. It appears that the Black Dog, much like the poltergeist, is a global phenomenon.

Sources:

Burchell, Simon. *Phantom Black Dogs in Latin America*. Wilts, U.K.: Heart of Albion Press, 2007.

Poligny Werewolves

According to legend, the werewolves of Poligny, France, were exposed in 1521 when a traveler passing through the town was attacked by a wolf. The wayfarer managed to injure the animal on one of its forelegs and drive it off. The traveler, not wishing to leave an injured wolf that would undoubtedly attack another person — perhaps this time a small child that could not fight it off — began to follow the trail of the wounded wolf's blood so that he might kill it. Puzzled, he discovered the drops of blood led to a house on the edge of the village.

Fearing that the residents inside were being viciously set upon by the injured wolf, the man pushed open to the door to bring his assistance and was shocked to discover a man with a wound on his arm being cleaned by a woman, quite likely his wife. The traveler fled the village in terror, knowing that he had escaped the fangs of a werewolf. He went directly to the authorities and reported that the man, whose name he had learned was Michel Verdun, was most certainly a shape-shifter.

The authorities arrested and tortured Verdun until he confessed to worshipping Satan, murdering a number of men and women, and feasting on their flesh. Under several more sessions of torture, Verdun named two other men who were shape-shifters, Pierre Bourget and Philibert Montot. After enduring days of torture, the two confessed to their power to transform themselves into wolves. Bourget told the inquisitors that he had committed many heinous crimes, including that of snapping a nine-year-old girl's neck and consuming her flesh. All three of the werewolves were executed and burned.

Sources:

"Werewolves of Poligny." April 16, 2010. https://www.werewolves.com/the -werewolves-of-poligny/.

Psychedelics and Mind-Altering Substances: Creating Monsters

Many might find the idea that shape-shifting is somehow connected to the worlds of secret agents, bizarre secret experiments, and the manipulation of the mind way too extreme to accept. But they would be wrong. Sometimes truth really is stranger than fiction—and in ways that are scarcely imaginable. The story in question begins on a hot summer's day in the early 1950s in a little French town called Pont-Saint-Esprit, which is located in the southern part of the country. The town is a tranquil one, filled with a great deal of history dating back to the 1700s. Today, however, it is a decidedly infamous locale, chiefly as the result of a series of events that began on August 15, 1951. That was when all hell broke loose around Pont-Saint-Esprit, and numerous townsfolk took on the guise of marauding animals—in their minds, at least.

The official story is that the people of the town were the victims of a certain fungus called ergot, which can affect rye. For the person who eats the infected rye, it provokes graphic and terrifying hallucinations, as shape-shifter authority Linda Godfrey made clear. In her 2006 book *Hunting the American Werewolf*, she writes that "ergot is now widely regarded as a possible cause of the bestial madness. According to this theory, it was not demonic influence but the ingestion of *Claviceps purpurea* (which contains a compound similar to LSD), which led to the demented behavior and thus, executions, of many alleged witches, werewolves, and vampires."

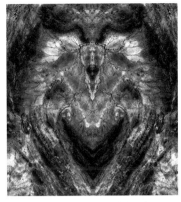

On a hot summer's day in the early 1950s, all hell broke loose in a usually tranquil French town when numerous townsfolk took on the guises of marauding animals—in their minds, at least.

The day began as a normal one for the people of this laid-back, picturesque old town. By sundown, however, it was like a scene out of *The Walking Dead*: what seemed to amount to raging infection was everywhere, and those free of that apparent infection cowered behind locked doors, fearful of becoming the next victims of whatever it was that had cursed Pont-Saint-Esprit. Hundreds of people rampaged around town in bestial states, growling, howling, and causing havoc and mayhem. Others swore they saw their fellow townsfolk change into hideous creatures, such as werewolves, gargoyles, and demons. All told, close to 260 people were affected. Seven died, and more than four dozen were so psychologically traumatized that they were temporarily held at local asylums—for the good of themselves and of the unaffected people of the town, too.

But was ergot really the cause of the devastation and death? Here's where things become controversial. One of those who have dug deep into the mystery of what erupted on August 15, 1951, is H.P. Albarelli Jr. He is the author of a huge book titled *A Terrible Mistake*. It's an immense, 826-page-long investigation of the mysterious 1951 death of a man named Frank Olson, a brilliant chemist who, in the early 1950s, worked for the U.S. Army's Special Operations Division at Camp Detrick, Maryland. Today, it's called Fort Detrick, and it is where the military undertakes research and studies into such issues as chemical warfare, biological warfare, and deadly viruses.

Back in the early 1950s, however, the matters of so-called mind-control and Manchurian Candidates were very much staple parts of Camp Detrick's work. But for Olson, who was at the forefront of the mind-altering technology, his work was not destined to last. Nor was his life. Olson died on November 28, 1953, ostensibly as a result of a "fall" from the tenth floor of the Statler Hotel in Manhattan. Today, the overriding theory is that Olson—who had begun to regret working on the controversial programs—was forcibly thrown out of the window of the room by agents who were fearful Olson was about to blow the lid on the sheer extent to which unwitting people had been dosed with psychedelics, chemical concoctions, and various other mind-manipulating substances, all in the name of national security. But what does any of this have to do with shape-shifters? Let's see.

It is a fact that Frank Olson, while liaising with French intelligence counterparts, traveled to France in both 1950 and 1951, the latter being the year in which the town of Pont-Saint-Esprit became a Bedlam, as Albarelli Jr. notes in his book. The French were as interested as the Americans (and the Russians and the Brits, too, as it transpired) in how the human mind could be clandestinely manipulated. In view of all this, it is notable that Olson's name turns up in previously highly classified CIA documents on the events at Pont-Saint-Esprit. One such document, which has surfaced through the terms of the U.S. Freedom of Information Act—the title of which is blacked out for national security reasons—states: "Re: Pont-Saint-Esprit and F. Olson files. SO Span/France Operation file, including Olson. Intel files. Hand carry to Berlin—tell him to see to it that these are buried."

While this communication is couched in cagey and careful language, it clearly links Olson to Pont-Saint-Esprit, and it abundantly demonstrates that whatever really happened—and led people to believe they and their friends were changing into wild beasts—had to be kept hidden at all costs. "Buried," even. Maybe one of those costs was Frank Olson's life. Albarelli Jr. makes it clear that, in his opinion, the town of Pont-Saint-Esprit was deliberately targeted by powerful and shadowy figures who wanted to know the extent to which the human mind could be messed around with on a large scale—and they chose August 15, 1951, as the date to initiate the experiment. Theories include a powerful psychedelic inserted into the town's water supply, a more than liberal amount of LSD utilized in similar fashion, and possibly even an airborne-based aerosol that was utilized to spray the town, in crop-dusting-style.

Whatever the answer, the people of Pont-Saint-Esprit have not forgotten that terrible day when the people of the town became monsters—in their minds, if not physically.

Sources:

Albarelli, H. P., Jr. *A Terrible Mistake*. Walterville, OR: Trine Day LLC, 1968.

Fuller, John G. *The Day of St. Anthony's Fire*. New York: Macmillan, 1968.

Rakshasas

A Rakshasa is a sort of demon in Hindu tradition. Many scholars of mysticism and the esoteric declare one type of Rakshasa as the Hindu equivalent of the Nephilim, the giants of the Bible who declared war on the greater gods. The evil Rakshasas often appear as beautiful women who drink the blood and feed off the flesh of men and women. The Rakshasas also possess shape-shifting abilities, and they take great delight in possessing vulnerable human hosts and causing them to commit acts of violence until they are driven insane.

In appearance, the Rakshasas are most often described as being yellow, green, or blue in color with vertical slits for eyes. They are feared as blood-drinkers and detested for their penchant for animating the bodies of the dead and stalking new victims.

The *Ramayana* and *Mahabharata*, two ancient Sanskrit literary epics, portray the Rakshasas as a populous race of powerful, supernatural

Ravana, depicted in an eighteenth-century sculpture, is a Rakshasa king known from the Ramayana, *an ancient literary epic.*

humanoids, numbering both good and evil among their ranks. Because they may also become fierce warriors, the Rakshasas are recruited by the armies of both good and evil. As shape-shifters capable of assuming many physical forms, some debate exactly what their true physical form may be—or if they are primarily spirit beings adapting various material images. Scholars and monks are well aware that the Rakshasas are master illusionists, creating appearances that appear real and three-dimensional to all they may confront.

Abbot Ralph (1150–?)

Many ancient chronicles contain accounts of monsters and demons that leap from dark ambush to kidnap or devour unsuspecting victims. These demons are frequently described in words that bring to mind the appearance of the classic werewolf—"dark and hairy creatures" with eyes that glow in the dark and "the devil's bestial look on their faces."

In his *Chronicles*, Abbot Ralph of Coggeshall Abbey, Essex, England, wrote about a raging thunderstorm that lashed the countryside on the night of St. John the Baptist in June 1205 and of the lightning that struck and killed "a certain strange monster" at Maidstone in Kent:

> This monster had the head of a strange being, the belly of a human and other monstrous members and limbs of animals unlike each other. Its black corpse was scorched and a terrible stench came from it and very few were able to go near.

Abbot Ralph recorded another incident that occurred during a storm on the night of July 29, 1205:

> Horrible thunder and lightning raged during the night … many thought the Judgment Day had arrived. … Next day, certain monstrous tracks of [large, pointed]

feet were seen at several places. The prints were of a kind never seen before and many claimed they were the tracks of giant demons.

Sources:

Hurwood, Bernardt J. *Terror by Night*. New York: Lancer Books, 1963.

Ramsey, Bill (c. 1950–)

The first time the eerie sensation overcame him, Bill Ramsey was only nine years old, playing in the backyard with his toy airplane. Suddenly he felt a strange coldness move through him, as if he had walked from the warmth of a summer's afternoon into a frigid meat locker. Later he remembered the sensation as if he had somehow stepped into another dimension, some unearthly place with a terrible, foul odor to it.

The sight of the cross caused the werewolf within Bill Ramsey to go berserk.

Then the peculiar feeling passed, but the boy felt different, as though something frightening had happened to him. He began to perceive of himself as a wolf, and he suddenly felt himself filled with a monstrous rage. To his parents' horror, their little boy began to growl and snap his teeth. He pulled a large fence post out of the ground as if it were a stick, and he tore at the wire fencing with his teeth, pulling it free of the posts. And then the bizarre incident was over. At least for that night. From time to time the "wolf seizures" would take him, but most of the time, Bill was in control.

In 1983, Bill Ramsey was a London carpenter with a wife and a family. On a Monday evening, December 5, he was headed for his second job with the taxicab company when he felt a severe pain in his chest. He tried to get his breathing under control, but the pain got worse. He had a sense that he was dying, that his entire system was shutting down.

Ramsey ended up in the emergency room at Southend Hospital. He clutched at his chest, feeling disoriented and in awful pain. The image of a wolf kept recurring in his thoughts, and he prayed that he wasn't having another one of those seizures.

Two nurses were pushing him on a gurney when Ramsey suddenly began to growl and roar, his hands curling into powerful paw-like claws. Before he could check himself, he had bitten one of the nurses just below the elbow.

> Ramsey was crouched in a corner, growling like a wolf and holding the two nurses captive.

When a policeman arrived, Ramsey was crouched in a corner, growling like a wolf and holding the two nurses captive. The policeman attempted to intervene, and Ramsey attacked him, trying to bite his arm, growling fiercely all the while. After an intense struggle, the policeman and an intern managed to force Ramsey onto a gurney and restrain him with straps until a doctor arrived to inject the wolfman with Thorazine, an antipsychotic sedative.

Bill Ramsey regained consciousness in the ambulance that was transporting him to Runwell, the mental hospital. He was terrified. He had no memory of what he had done.

At last the strange case of the modern-day "Werewolf of London" came to the attention of Ed and Lorraine Warren, directors of the New England Society for Psychic Research. They were experts on the supernatural and demonologists, and they assessed Bill Ramsey's plight as that of possession by a werewolf-like demon. Once contact had been made with the Ramseys and the proper authorities, the Warrens suggested that they arrange an exorcism for Bill with Bishop Robert McKenna, a cleric who had performed more than 50 exorcisms.

The People, a London newspaper, paid the fares for Bill Ramsey and his wife, Nina, to fly to the United States, accompanied by David Alford and John Cleve, a writer and a photographer from their staff.

During the ancient rite of exorcism, holy water, a crucifix, and a relic of a saint are applied to various parts of the victim of the demon while the priest prays in Latin in a strong and loud voice. In addition to the instruments of his holy office, Bishop McKenna had added four off-duty policeman—just in case the werewolf took control of Bill Ramsey's body.

Ramsey remembers that the demonic spirit within him began to trouble him the moment they walked into the church. It made him feel very negative toward the bishop and convinced that such an absurd old ritual would end in failure. He mumbled something to Nina about the whole business being a bunch of mumbo-jumbo.

Bishop McKenna, on the other hand, felt immediately that the exorcism would be successful, but he could sense that the demonic spirit within Ramsey was going to put up a fight. Thirty minutes into the ritual, Bishop McKenna took Ramsey's head in his hands and ordered the werewolf spirit to be banished forever.

> *Two of the burly policemen restrained the werewolf, and the clergyman pushed a crucifix against Ramsey's forehead. The sight of the cross caused the werewolf within Ramsey to go berserk.*

The demon within Ramsey caused him to shake and writhe and to curl his hands into claws to attempt to rip the bishop's face. Two of the burly policemen restrained the werewolf, and the clergyman pushed a crucifix against Ramsey's forehead. The sight of the cross caused the werewolf within Ramsey to go berserk, snarling, growling, and grasping at the bishop. The priest stood his ground, and Ramsey suddenly staggered back to his chair and collapsed.

As the bishop continued his admonitions in Latin, Ramsey felt the demon leaving him. The poison that had been within him was leaving. The werewolf's power was slipping away. A faint roar rose from his chest, then faded away. Bill Ramsey felt purified. The curse of the werewolf had been lifted from his soul.

Sources:

Zaffis, John. "Report from the New England Society for Psychic Research," 1998.

Roberts, Paul Dale (1955–)

Paranormal investigator Paul Dale Roberts often dares to tread where others might exercise a bit more caution. He has interviewed individuals who claim to be real werewolves, true vampires, or actual aliens from outer space, and even a young man who said that he was a mutant chupacabra. Roberts honed his skills as an investigator while serving in the U.S. Army from 1973 to 1976, working with the Criminal Investigation Division's Drug Suppression Team. He reenlisted in 1979, and until 1986 he served with Military Intelligence as an intelligence analyst with the Photo Interpretation Center in Seoul, South Korea. This assignment evolved into Paul's becoming an Opposing Forces instructor, teaching elite troops such as the Navy Seals, the Army's Special Forces, and the Airborne Rangers the intricacies of Soviet-made weapons. Today, Paul's "real" job is as office manager for the Fish and Game License and Revenue Branch in Sacramento, California, but his true vocation is investigating the unknown.

Paul and his friend and associate Shannon McCabe travel across California and most of the United States seeking eerie and astonishing investigations. Halo Paranormal Investigations (H.P.I.; formerly known as Haunted Phenomena Investigations), founded by McCabe, does not limit itself to researching ghosts and haunted houses. During the course of their paranormal adventures, the H.P.I. team has investigated threatening demonic forces, Black-Eyed Boys, werewolves, and vampires. Reporting on their investigations, Roberts has written hundreds of articles on their search for gnomes, pixies, and reptilian shape-shifters. Together, Roberts and McCabe have interviewed victims of UFO abduction, witnesses of phantom mischief, and individuals who claim to be from other worlds. They have also authored a book titled *The H.P.I. Chronicles*.

Romulus and Remus

Romulus and Remus, the legendary founders of Rome, were twin brothers suckled and reared by a she-wolf who filled them with her lycanthropic powers. The jealous Romulus killed his brother, just as Cain

Romulus and Remus, the legendary founders of Rome, were twin brothers suckled and reared by a she-wolf who filled them with her lycanthropic powers.

slew Abel, thus giving us a cross-cultural myth of two great patriarchies being established through an act of fratricide.

Robert Eisler links the Roman she-wolf (*Lupa Romana*) with the *Luperci*, whose priests each year sacrificed a goat at the traditional entrance of the old *Lupercal* (wolves' den) and establishes the original founders of Rome as members of a tribe that bore the name of Wolf. Pursuing even deeper reaches of history in his research, Eisler points out that a *lupanar*, a she-wolves' den, was an old Roman term for a brothel and that the classical poets Livy and Ovid said that the "she-wolf" who gave suck to the abandoned twins Romulus and Remus was really a harlot who dressed in wolf skins. As Romulus matured into the leader of his tribe, he wore a *galea lupina*, a helmet shaped like a wolf's head, and his warriors outfitted themselves as he did, wearing wolf-head helmets and the hides wolves or dogs.

Sources:

Eisler, Robert. *Man into Wolf*. London: Spring Books, 1948.

Rougarou

by Alyne A. Pustanio

Once there was a swamp trapper who used to parade about in the skins of the animals he had caught, terrifying neighbors and friends by pretending to be the loup-garou (werewolf). When the disrespectful trapper fell under the eye of a Louisiana Indian shaman, it is said that the man danced a different dance thereafter—as a real loup-garou under the yellow swampland moon.

The heritage of Louisiana's Native American peoples is rich with tall tales and legends and among these the tale of the werewolf looms large. The Indians know the werewolf as the shape-shifting *Rougarou*, a variation of the Cajun French *loup-garou*. But the name matters little—Rougarou, loup-garou, shape-shifter, or skin walker—these deadly, half-human beasts have been part of the legacy of terror that has haunted the Louisiana swamps for generations. One of the most chilling tales told among the Indian tribes of South Louisiana concerns a warrior tribe of cannibals and how they came to be known—and feared—as man-eating Wolf Walkers. This is that tale.

Where modern-day parish boundaries now exist there were once the mutable limits of the tribal nations of the Opelousas and the Chitimacha, and there exists in the oral tradition of all these tribes a shared memory of vicious and powerful warriors who once held sway over large areas of Native lands, using their powers to instill fear among their own people and to manipulate or control their rivals.

Many believe this dark secret to be evidence of a skin-walking tradition that, if true, would mark the Attakapas as something unique in the annals of lycanthropy: an entire tribe of werewolves.

This was the Attakapas tribe, and they were the source of much fear and loathing among the swamp Indians who shunned them for their reputation as a nation that cannibalized its enemies. But many Louisiana Indian legends hint at something even more sinister at work among the Attakapas. Many believe this dark secret to be evidence of a skin-walking tradition that, if true, would mark the Attakapas as something unique in the annals of lycanthropy: an entire tribe of werewolves.

Only a very few of those who have studied the history of Native Americans in this area of Louisiana are not familiar with the story of these cannibalistic warmongers whose name, Attakapa, in Choctaw means "Man-Eater." The Chitimacha and Opelousas tribes were the traditional enemies of the Attakapas, and it was an unstated fact that any conflict with the Attakapas simply had to be won because the Attakapas were long in the habit of eating their captives.

In one such battle in the 1700s, the three tribes went to war in a low country six miles outside of what is today St. Martinville. The Chitimacha and Opelousas won the day and devastated the Attakapa tribe. Only a half dozen or so were said to have survived the conflict, fleeing to refuge in the area around what is now Indian Bend. Fearing retribution from the victorious tribes and the local people—mostly Cajuns and Spaniards—the Attakapas ran away into the unforgiving swamps.

These swamplands were described by early explorers as "half-solid, half-fluid areas of no agricultural value, but supporting a forest growth so dense with cypress, tupelo, gum, water oaks, ferns, palmettos, and a network of ancient vines, that the appearance is similar to that of the Mayan jungles." The swamps were then (and for the most part still are) only sparsely inhabited by hunters, trappers, and fishermen who lived in palmetto tents and small frame houses or houseboats along the interior bayous.

The renegade Attakapas were unwelcome interlopers in this strange country. Spanish explorer and historian Cabeza de Vaca (c. 1490–c. 1559), who encountered them on his travels, reported that after the great battle, the few surviving Attakapas lived for a while in this environment, subsisting on roots and fish. Some bravely appeared as beggars in the settlements along the edge of the swamplands. But soon they were discovered by members of their fierce rival tribes who chased them back to the swamps—if they could not kill them. In the harsh winter following the great battle, the remnant Attakapas were forced to find a way to survive in the unforgiving environment they now called home.

Some traditions, including Spanish accounts of that time, suggest that the Attakapas, exhausted as subjects of fear and hatred, turned to their shamans for answers. It is said that these elders, once servants of the Great Spirit, now turned aside from the enlightened path and, in desperate search of help and sustenance for their people, began to feel out the heart of darkness for answers. According to all accounts, something responded.

It is said that dark spirits came down and entered into the starving Attakapas. In desperation, they obtained a unique gift: the power of shape-shifting at will. Once notorious as cannibals in conquest, the Attakapas, as other Indian wise men taught, gave over entirely to their animal nature and somehow transcended the deprived state of their humanity, crossing over into the realm of the animals. Not only this, but their numbers grew once again. They were now predatory hunters, and humans were their prey.

> *When the bare winter months came on, sending fish to the bayou bottoms and making other animals scarce, it was believed that all Attakapas lived constantly in their animal forms and were most to be feared.*

Not surprisingly, winter was the time when the shape-shifting Attakapas were most feared. In the summer, it was said, they seemed to live as other human beings, content with small harvests and the food sources provided to them by their environment. Only the most brutal-natured of them remained in their animal forms all the time. But when the bare winter months came on, bringing in the damp Louisiana chill, sending fish to the bayou bottoms and making other animals scarce, it was believed that all Attakapas—men, women, and even children—lived constantly in their animal forms and were most to be feared.

As the short winter days gave on to long, moonlit nights, so the legends say, the Attakapa "Rougarou," driven to frenzy with memories of starvation, would leave the swamp and traverse the low country nearby in search of humans to devour. More frightening still was the knowledge, especially among the Chitimacha and the Opelousas, that the beasts were not driven by fear alone; revenge, too, was ever present in their hearts.

Today the Chitimacha are the only tribe left who prosper in the area, though the Opelousas endure in lesser numbers. This, however, has done nothing to lull these ancient peoples into complacency, especially where the Rougarou is concerned. Fear lingers among them, particularly when a cold, hard winter sets in and the dampness chills the bones. Then their thoughts turn to their long enemy, the Man-Eaters, the Attakapas, and they wonder if—or when—the Wolf Walkers will strike again.

> *Many believe that the Rougarou are once again active.*

Recently, the discovery of the grisly remains of mutilated farm animals and sightings of ghostly figures lurching close to the ground near darkened roadsides have been reported from the Chitimacha reservation near Charenton, Louisiana. Many believe that the Rougarou are once again active. Tribal elders have blamed the strange activity on the series of devastating storms—first Hurricanes Katrina and Rita, and more recently Hurricane Gustav—that have struck the area in the last several years. They say the fragile ecosystem of the nearby swamplands was impacted and may have affected the resources on which the Rougarou have long been dependent. Many fear these natural disasters may have turned the Wolf Walkers back to their predatory ways.

Once again, the Native Americans who live on the edge of the noisome Louisiana swamps are speaking in nervous whispers, and the tale of the killer Attakapas is being retold to a new generation. These tribes know, and must let others know, that as the fortune of the land goes, so goes the vengeance of the dreaded Rougarou.

Rusalki

In the legends of the Slavic people we find that the spirit of a beautiful girl who used her physical charms to work wickedness and consequently was damned for her sins gets another chance to be even nastier when she crosses over to the other side. It is at that time that she may choose to become a *Rusalka*, a sultry shape-shifter who can appear along the river

Famous Czech soprano Růžena Maturová is depicted in the title role of Antonín Dvořák's opera Rusalka, *a telling of the mythological Slavic water sprite.*

banks as an innocent young maiden, singing sweet, seductive songs to smitten young men — before she drowns them.

Some Rusalki are a bit nicer to their victims. They first make love to the men they've seduced and permit them a bit of happiness before they pull them into the water and drown them. In Bulgaria, the Rusalki, known as *Samovily*, are made up of the souls of unbaptized baby girls or of brides who died on their wedding night. They, too, get another opportunity to manifest as tempting shape-shifters who lure men to their watery deaths.

Sources:

Larousse Dictionary of World Folklore. New York: Larousse, 1995.

Santu Sakai

The Malaysian legends of the *santu sakai* have always sounded like something from a Hollywood monster movie to those who doubted the monsters' existence. According to the old stories, the santu sakai are werebeasts—half human and half monster—that the native people refer to as the "mouth men" because of their large fangs and their craving for fresh red meat. When hordes of these savage creatures attack a village, they capture, kill, and eat their victims.

In June 1967, a hunter named Henri van Heerden claimed to have his skepticism regarding the santu sakai removed completely after a near-fatal close encounter with the beasts during a hunting trip near Kuala Lumpur. According to his account, he had bagged a number of birds for his dinner and was about half a mile from his vehicle when he began hearing "ugly growls and strange screams" coming from the other side of the trail. He decided to make a run for his vehicle. When he stopped at one point to look behind him, he saw "two absolute monstrosities" running toward him. They were tall, very large, and looked "like demons from hell."

Van Heerden reached his vehicle, and he could hear that the beasts were close behind him. He turned and raised his shotgun, intending to fire, but it was too late. The hideous "mouth men" were on top of him. One of them bit his arm with its fangs, forcing him to drop his weapon. Somehow van Heerden managed to pick up a good-sized rock and used it to pound one of the monsters on the skull, causing it to fall in a daze. He struck another in the face and managed to get inside his car.

The santu sakai closed around the vehicle, growling, roaring, pounding at the sides and the windows. Van Heerden's shaking hand at last managed to get the key in the ignition just as one of the "mouth men" was smashing the back window and another was crouched on the hood, banging its fist against the windshield. The car's wheels spun into motion, leaving the santu sakai to chase after him. When van Heerden got up speed, he slammed on the brakes, sending the man-beast on the hood flying off the car and into a patch of weeds.

The hunter reported the incident to the police, but they only laughed and told him to go home and sleep it off. The next afternoon, van Heerden talked a number of his friends into accompanying him back to the scene of the attack. Those who had initially doubted his word revised their thinking when they found a number of strange, humanlike footprints and splotches of blood in several places. Van Heerden's expensive shotgun was never recovered, and he speculated whether or not one of the beasts might eventually pull the trigger and blow a hole in one of his fellow "mouth men."

Sources:

Norman, Eric. *The Abominable Snowmen*. New York: Award Books, 1969.

Selkies

The selkies are the seal people who can shape-shift and appear in human form, resuming their true forms only when they wish to travel through the sea. The selkies are among the small number of gentle shape-shifters, desiring to live harmoniously with the fishermen of the Orkney and

Shetland Islands. They often take human spouses and produce children who occasionally have webbed hands and feet and who are always born with a love for the sea. John Sayles, one of the screenwriters for *The Howling* (1981), wrote and directed an enchanting film about the selkie, *The Secret of Roan Inish* (1994).

Sources:

Larousse Dictionary of World Folklore. New York: Larousse, 1995.

Serial Killers

In many cases, plain deranged and evil characters have been lumped in with lycanthropy. Beyond any shadow of doubt, one of the most notorious serial killers of all time was Peter Stumpp, a German farmer who became infamously known as the Werewolf of Bedburg. Born in the village of Epprath, Cologne, Stumpp was a wealthy, respected, and influential farmer in the local community. But he was also hiding a dark and diabolical secret—one that surfaced graphically and sensationally in 1589, when he was brought to trial for the crimes of murder and cannibalism.

Having been subjected to the torture of the rack, Stumpp confessed to countless horrific acts, including feasting on the flesh not only of sheep, lambs, and goats, but also of men, women, and children. Indeed, Stumpp further revealed that he had killed and devoured no less than 14 children, two pregnant women and their fetuses, and even his own son's brain. Stumpp, however, had an extraordinary excuse to explain his actions. He maintained that since the age of 12, he had engaged in black magic and on one occasion had succeeded in summoning the devil, who provided him with a "magical belt" that gave him the ability to morph into "the likeness of a greedy, devouring wolf, strong and mighty, with eyes great and large, which in the night sparkled like fire, a mouth great and wide, with most sharp and cruel teeth, a huge body, and mighty paws."

The court, needless to say, was horrified, and Stumpp was put to death in brutal fashion: flesh was torn from his body, his arms and legs were broken, and finally he was beheaded. The Werewolf of Bedburg was no more. Stumpp was not alone, however.

Under torture, Peter Stumpp — known as the Werewolf of Bedburg — confessed to countless horrific acts, including feasting on the flesh of sheep, lambs, goats, men, women, and children.

Equally as horrific as the actions of Stumpp were those of an unnamed man who, in the final years of the sixteenth century, became known as the Werewolf of Chalons. A tailor based in Paris, France, he killed, dismembered, and ate the flesh of numerous children he had lured into his shop. The man was brought to trial for his crimes on December 14, 1598. Notably, during the trial, it was claimed that on occasion the man also roamed nearby woods in the form of a huge, predatory wolf, where he further sought innocent souls to slaughter and consume. As was the case with Stumpp, the Werewolf of Chalons was sentenced to death and was burned at the stake.

Some reports of werewolves do appear to involve monstrous creatures of unknown origin. But, as the above clearly shows, sometimes the exact opposite is true. And sometimes, regrettably, one of the worst monsters is one of us, the human race.

Serpent People

Nearly every known Earth culture has its legends of wise Serpent People who ruled the planet in prehistoric times and assisted humankind in rising in status from hairless ape to the lords of the planet. Many of these Serpent Kings were said to have come from the sky to promulgate the beneficent and civilizing rule of the Sons of the Sun, or the Sons of Heaven, upon Earth. Quetzalcoatl, the "feathered serpent," the culture-bearer of the Aztecs, was said to have descended from heaven in a silver egg. Ciuacoatl, the Great Mother of the Gods for the ancient people of Mexico, was represented as a serpent woman. Among many African cultures, it is Aido Hwendo, the Rainbow Serpent, that supports the earth.

The Babylonian priest and historian Berossus chronicled the legend of Oannes, an entity described as a serpent-like half man, half fish who surfaced from the Persian Gulf to instruct the early inhabitants of Mesopotamia in the arts of civilization. Before the advent of the serpent master Oannes, Berossus stated, the Sumerians were savages, living like the beasts, with no order or rule.

Like so many accounts of the Serpent People, Oannes appeared to be some kind of amphibious master teacher endowed with superior intelligence but an appearance that was frightening to behold. Oannes had the body of a fishlike serpent with humanlike feet and a head that combined the features of fish and human. Berossus explained that the creature walked about on land during the day, counseling and teaching the Sumerians, but returned to the ocean each evening. The amphibious master gave the once-primitive Sumerians insight into letters and sciences and every kind of art. He taught them to construct houses, found temples, and compile laws, and he explained to them the principles of geometrical knowledge. He made them distinguish the seeds of the earth and showed them how to harvest fruits. In short, Oannes instructed them in everything that could tend to soften the manners and humanize humankind.

Oannes had the body of a fishlike serpent with humanlike feet and a head that combined the features of fish and human.

Because of the respect for the great serpent masters of prehistoric times, the collective unconscious of humankind both fears and reveres the snake. In ancient Egypt the serpent was regarded as both a symbol of immortality and of death, and the pharaoh wore a snake emblem on his headdress as a mark of royalty and divinity. Apollo, the Greek god of healing and medicine, was originally invoked and worshipped as a serpent. Aesculapius, another deity associated with medicine, often materialized as a serpent, and his crest of the double snakes remains today as a symbol of the medical profession.

In the Hebrew account of the fall from Paradise, the serpent is the king of beasts, walking on two legs, who becomes jealous when he sees how the angels honor Adam. For his part in the seduction of Eve, the serpent is punished by having his limbs removed and being forced to crawl on his belly. In the Muslim tradition, it is archangel Michael who chops off the serpent's limbs with the sword of God. In many Native American legends, the great hero Manabozho must battle many serpent people to free his people from bondage.

Father Charlevoix, an early French missionary to the eastern tribes of North America, recorded in his journals that there was no image that the tribespeople marked on their faces or bodies more than that of the snake. According to many tribal legends, in the beginning of time, humans and snakes could converse freely. Shamans and others who were powerfully attuned to the spirit level, it was believed, could still communicate with the serpent and learn the secrets of the future and powerful healing medicines.

Serpent People remain popular as shape-shifting entities in the local folklore of many areas around the world. Some serious-minded researchers have even suggested that an underground race of reptilian beings secretly control all the major events of life on this planet. Other UFO investigators have theorized the Serpent People of prehistoric times are the same beings who today visit Earth in spaceships as overlords surveying the evolution of humankind.

Sources:

Steiger, Brad. *Totems: The Transformative Power of Your Personal Animal Totem.* San Francisco: HarperSanFrancisco, 1997.

Silver Bullet

The agents of the Spanish Inquisition decreed that there was only one way to kill a werewolf: behead it. Then, just to be certain, one must burn both the head and the body.

Creeping up behind a werewolf with an axe with the intent of chopping off the beast's head seems a decidedly injudicious method of attempting to kill the monster. What about a silver bullet?

Curt Siodmak, the scriptwriter who wrote *The Wolf Man* (1941), claimed that he added a number of new details to the werewolf mythology, such as declaring that an object made of silver or a silver bullet was the only thing that could kill the beast. In addition, he composed the famous four-line verse about "Even a man who is pure at heart" becoming a werewolf if bitten by a lycanthrope, and the curse of the full moon signaling the transformation into man-wolf.

Curt Siodmak, the scriptwriter who wrote The Wolf Man (1941), claimed that he added a number of new details to the werewolf mythology, such as declaring that an object made of silver was the only thing that could kill the beast.

In the centuries-old struggle with werewolves, the only known record of a silver bullet slaying a very dangerous predatory shape-shifter occurred during the reign of terror caused by the Beast of Gévaudan. According to Jean Chastel, one of several hundred armed men organized by the Marquis d'Apcher and the man given credit for slaying the monster, he had loaded his double-barreled musket with bullets made from a silver chalice blessed by a priest. In Chastel's view, the bullets were fatal to a thing of evil such as the Beast because they had been made from a chalice that had held "the blood of Christ" during communion and had been blessed by a priest. The fact that the chalice was made of silver was probably incidental in Chastel's view.

Interestingly, in the alchemical tradition, silver represents the moon, the Divine Virgin, purity, and chastity. On some level of consciousness, the use of a silver object or bullet to squelch such an evil as a ravenous werewolf might have been apprehended by both Jean Chastel and Curt Siodmak.

Perhaps, though, the most efficacious method to kill a werewolf remains separating its head from its body and burning both parts in a roaring fire.

Skin Walkers

To many Navajo, a werewolf is called a "skin walker." In the magic of the Navajo, Hopi, and Pueblo, the principal reason that a shaman might shape-shift into a wolf is for the purpose of traversing great distances in a much shorter time than he or she could walk the miles in human form. Those who cover themselves in the skin of a wolf are therefore known as *Yee Naaldlooshii* (those who trot about with it).

In January 1970, four Gallup, New Mexico, youths claimed to have encountered a werewolf on their way to Zuni near Whitewater. All four swore that they saw a two-legged, hairy thing run alongside their car as they were going 45 miles an hour. When Clifford Heronemus later told reporters that he accelerated their vehicle to 60 mph and the creature still paced them, he got scared. The highway section where the werewolf appeared is full of sharp turns, and Heronemus was concerned that the car could skid off the road and they would be easy prey for the monster.

According to Heronemus, one of the four finally got out a gun and shot it. "I know it got hit and it fell down—but there was no blood. It got up again and ran off. I know it couldn't have been a person, because people cannot move that fast."

Heronemus and his three friends were convinced that they had been chased by a werewolf, and they said that they were going looking for the creature with a camera. If they could obtain a photograph of the werewolf, "people won't think I'm half-cracked."

In 1936, anthropologist William Morgan wrote about the werewolf beliefs of the Navajo in Arizona and New Mexico, and he recorded one of his conversations with Navajo who told him that the *Yee Naaldlooshii* could run very fast. They could get to Albuquerque in an hour and a half, the anthropologist was informed. Morgan noted that in those days it took four hours to drive the distance by automobile.

A Connection with Witches

For certain Native American people, the skin walker—tales of which date back centuries—is a definitive Witch, a crone-like thing that has the ability to radically change its form. While a shape-shifting Native American Witch can take on hundreds of forms, the most often reported guises are bears, coyotes, various types of birds, and—at the top of the list—wolves or wolflike animals. This emphasizes that the skin walker is not that dissimilar to the traditional European werewolf, despite being separated by thousands of miles.

There can be no doubt that interest in the skin walker phenomenon soared in 2005. That was when Colm A. Kelleher and George Knapp penned their bestselling book *Hunt for the Skinwalker*. It detailed strange and terrifying activity on a remote ranch in Utah that suggested manipulative skin walkers had descended on the ranch and quickly began wreaking havoc—maybe simply because they could. As well as experiencing countless UFO encounters and sightings of large and hairy Bigfoot-type beasts, the family also had confrontations with a huge, malevolent wolf—a monster-sized animal upon which bullets had absolutely no effect at all.

As George Knapp noted in *Hunt for the Skinwalker*, with regard to the many and varied phenomena that caused chaos and mayhem on the ranch, "Reality isn't what it used to be."

For the Native Americans, however, reality hasn't been what it appears to be for a very long time.

In most cases, however, a Witch will secure the hide of the animal they wish to become and wrap it around their shoulders and back.

The process by which a Witch can become a skin walker is a highly complex one, which involves several different processes. For example, Witches who are both learned and skilled in magical arts can transform themselves into a wide variety of creatures by focusing on its image in their minds. In most cases, however, a Witch will secure the hide of the animal they wish to become and wrap it around their shoulders and back. By effectively wearing the hide, the Witch—slowly and step by step—becomes the very beast it specifically seeks to emulate. That includes, so Native American teachings maintain, adopting its keen senses of smell and sight, its agility and speed, and even its complete, physical form.

Perhaps the most sinister aspect of the skin walker is that it has the ability to supernaturally infect people with deadly diseases and life-threatening illnesses. Strangely, on more than a few occasions, those who have found themselves in the direct, close presence of a skin walker have, in mere days, succumbed to very rare medical conditions. Precisely how the skin walker can perform such a hostile thing remains unknown. It is, however, worth noting that the skin walker is said to have an expert knowledge of medicine, both ancient and modern. No wonder Native Americans avoid them at all costs. And it is not just people who can fall

So-called cattle mutilations, which reached their peak in the 1970s but are still occasionally reported today, are believed by certain Native Americans to be the work of crazed skin walkers.

victim to this dangerous beast. Animals—often farm animals—have also become the targets of these multiformed creatures.

For example, so-called cattle mutilations, which reached their peak in the 1970s but are still occasionally reported to this very day, are believed by some Native Americans to be the work of crazed skin walkers. The approach of the creatures is to remove organs and blood from cattle for use in further rites and rituals designed to enhance their paranormal powers to even greater degrees. This may not be quite as strange, or as unlikely, as it might seem: between 1975 and 1978, police officers investigating dozens of cattle mutilation events in New Mexico, Utah, Colorado, and Arizona found that many such attacks had specifically occurred on Native American reservations, a fact that most assuredly offers food for thought.

Of course, there is one critical issue we have yet to touch upon: namely, why would anyone even want to become a skin walker in the first place? The answer, as you may have already deduced, is not a good one. Adopting the guise of an animal can, quite literally, allow a person to get away with murder. After all, if the target of the skin walker is violently slaughtered by a rampaging bear or a savage wolf, who would ever dream of the possibility that the beast was actually a transformed human?

As for why the skin walker issue is steeped in so much mystery—despite it being the subject of a bestselling book—it is chiefly because Native Americans fear that if they speak openly on the matter, it may well lead those same skin walkers to target them. I (Nick) found this out for myself, to a graphic level, in August of 2010. I was out in the California desert, specifically in Joshua Tree, where a spate of savage attacks on animals occurred in 1982, amid claims that a shape-shifting skin walker was the culprit. In 2009 and early 2010, the attacks began again: vital organs were removed from the animals, as was blood, in massive amounts. My reason for being there was no coincidence: I had been hired by the VH1 channel to make a documentary on the phenomenon for the now-defunct show *Real and Chance: The Legend Hunters*.

On the second day of shooting, the film crew and I headed out to a local animal sanctuary—which specialized in caring for, and rehabilitating, wolves. I quickly learned just how much the skin walker phenomenon was feared in and around Joshua Tree. And, in all likelihood, it still is. I also saw for myself a deep reluctance on the part of the staff of the sanctuary to ever utter that dreaded word. By now, you know the one I mean.

An Encounter with a Skin Walker

Priscilla Garduno Wolf, an Apache medicine woman from New Mexico, told of her encounter with a skin walker when she was a teenager. In Sister Wolf's own words:

> It was a beautiful day, and I was ready for the prom. I caught a ride with a friend, Molly, and the night went very well.

> However, at the end of the prom, Molly told me to catch a ride home with someone else; she was going to Alamosa with her boyfriend. I asked several people, but no one offered to take me home. I lived three miles from the school, and at that time all the roads were dirt.

> I had no choice but to walk home in my formal, holding my heels in my hands. The moon was shining, but it was still very dark.

> I wasn't scared until I got close to the area where people claimed the Wolf Boy was buried. Grandpa said that the old people buried him there in the 1500s. Nearby, there was this huge tree that my grandfather had named the skin walker tree, because of sightings of Skin Walkers in that area.

> I wanted to walk back to my grandmother's home, but I was scared that the Wolf Boy would appear to me, so I continued walking east toward my mother's home.

> When I crossed the old bridge, I heard a noise coming from under it. I looked back, and I saw what appeared to be a calf walking toward me. I started to run, and it began to run, following me.

> It was about 300 feet to my mom's home, and I took off running fast. The animal stood up on its hind legs and almost caught me. I could hear its loud breathing. It sounded not human or animal like, but different.

> I made it to my mother's farm land, and the thing jumped across the fence.

When I got to the door of the house, I banged so hard to wake up Mom. "Open up!" I kept yelling. "Something is chasing me."

Mom made it to the door. I pushed her aside and shut the door, and we locked it. She shut the lights off so no one could look in the house.

My baby brother Adam was sleeping, and after a while I lay down. I was so worn out from running.

> *The monster was tall and skinny — half human and half something that looked like a cow. His hands were rough and hairy, and he had long nails.*

I heard someone turning the knob of the door—and opening it! I could hear what sounded like the footsteps of a horse moving from room to room toward me.

All of a sudden it was next to my bed. I screamed for Mom to turn the lights on, but she was having a hard time getting up. It was like she was in a daze.

I felt the Skin Walker's hand on me, touching my face and throat! His smelly breath and loud breathing were right next to me.

The monster was tall and skinny—half human and half something that looked like a cow. His hands were rough and hairy, and he had long nails.

I couldn't breathe! I screamed again and asked God to help me. It scratched my neck, and I was bleeding.

When Mom managed to turn on the light, it vanished.

Mom saw three scratches on my neck and said it was the devil that had left his claw marks on me. We got up and checked the door. It was still locked, but the door hadn't mattered to the Skin Walker.

By morning the scratches were gone, just vanished. I wrote two stories years later that I called "The Devil's Claws" and "The Skin Walker."

Sources:

"Battle of Palo Duro Canyon, Texas." 2016. http://tripsintohistory.com/2013/05/23/battle-of-palo-duro-canyon-texas/.

Coleman, Loren. "Werewolves of the Southwest." *Strange Magazine* 7, April 1991.

Guie, Heister Dean. *Coyote Stories*. Lincoln: University of Nebraska Press, 1990.

Kelleher, Colm, and Knapp, George. *Hunt for the Skinwalker*. New York: Paraview-Pocket Books, 2005.

"Malicious Myths: The Were-Hyena." 2016. https://inthedarkair.wordpress.com/2015/10/26/malicious-myths-the-were-hyena/.

Myths, Legends, Superstitions of North American Indian Tribes. Lawrence, KS: Haskell Institute, 1995.

O'Brien, Christopher. *Stalking the Tricksters*. Kempton, IL: Adventures Unlimited Press, 2009.

Redfern, Nick. *Chupacabra Road Trip*. Woodbury, MN: Llewellyn Publications, 2015.

Redfern, Nick. "Searching for California's Skinwalkers." October 27, 2015. http://mysteriousuniverse.org/2015/10/searching-for-californias-skinwalkers/.

Redfern, Nick. *Secret Societies: The Complete Guide to Histories, Rites, and Rituals*. Canton, MI: Visible Ink Press, 2017.

Sorcery

In the ancient traditions, there were two basic ways by which a person became a werewolf, and they both involved sorcery. Either one deliberately sought to become a shape-shifter by employing a number of spells, invocations, and secret rituals so that he might have the power and strength of a lycanthrope to perform nefarious deeds, or one was cursed by a powerful sorcerer who used his magic to turn his victim into a werewolf to live the life of the damned. In other words, there were voluntary and involuntary werewolves.

The notion that a victim of a werewolf attack will become a lycanthrope himself because of a bite or a scratch from the beast is largely

An eighteenth-century illustration depicts a woman grappling with the Beast of Gévaudan.

the invention of motion pictures, quite probably beginning with *The Wolf Man* (1941). In all of the accounts of werewolf attacks throughout Europe in earlier times, we never read of the victims returning as lycanthropes. If the thousands of victims of the Beast of Gévaudan had returned as werewolves, all of France would have been overrun by an army of conquering lycanthropes. In point of actual fact, the victim of a werewolf attack is almost always mangled, mutilated, and murdered—not merely bitten and "infected" with the werewolf curse.

> *The notion that a victim of a werewolf attack will become a lycanthrope himself because of a bite or a scratch from the beast is largely the invention of motion pictures.*

Sorcery involves the manifestation of supernatural powers granted by spirits who have been summoned by a skillful magician or sorcerer. Many believe that such manipulation of psychic energy can only manifest evil spirits, who seize such an opportunity to enter the physical dimension to work evil against humankind and the true God of the universe. The French jurist Jean Bodin insisted that only Satan can change the shape of one body into another—and only God grants him that power in the elemental world.

Those who voluntarily became werewolves through sorcery did so most frequently through the use of special ointments, the wearing of the magical wolf belt, or the chanting of various spells and invocations to summon the demonic beings that would implement the shape-shifting process. Those who involuntarily became werewolves were the victims of such incantations, curses, and the sinister work of demons summoned to do the evil work of sorcerers who had given themselves to the Dark Side.

Sources:

Spence, Lewis. *An Encyclopedia of Occultism*. New Hyde Park, NY: University Books, 1960.

Spells to Ward Off Werewolves

A practitioner of magic set up a retail outlet to supply Witches, sorcerers, and magicians with the genuine articles needed for occult research. They had completed worldwide travel and an enormous amount of research and experimentation over more than 20 years to be able to offer potions and mixtures that were absolutely identical to the ancient, original formulas. According to the practitioner, superstition and ignorance had given ceremonial magic a bad name:

> If one approaches the occult from a strictly objective viewpoint, it will prove to be one of the most fascinating subjects which one can study. There are so many ramifications and complexities that no one person could master the occult in one lifetime. In our coven, we had each member specialize in certain aspects of

magic, while, at the same time, maintaining a general knowledge of the entire field. In this way, we always have an expert at hand.

Sorcery does not have to be evil. Sorcery and ceremonial magic does involve the summoning of beings and forces from other planes. As a general rule, sorcery is used for self-gain, but it can serve other purposes just as well. We feel that it is the purpose that counts, assuming no harm is [intended]. The most ideal usage of magic is the gaining of knowledge. Those who are sincere follow this path. Naturally there are pitfalls and dangerous areas, but is this not also true of everyday, mundane life?

For whatever the following may be worth — as werewolf repellents or entertaining curiosities — such spells as these have been used traditionally to keep one's household safe from lycanthropes when the moon is full.

An Invocation to Diana, the Moon Goddess, to Keep One Safe from Evil Entities — Specifically Werewolves

'Tis _____ (name the date) now, and at an early hour

I fain would turn good fortune and safe passage to myself, firstly at home and then when I go forth.

With the aid of the beautiful Diana, Goddess of the Moon, Great Huntress with Her pack of she-wolves,

I pray for protection from evil werewolf fang and claw ere I do leave this house!

May Her guiding and protective hand keep me safe until my return.

Three drops of oil are now required to be slowly fed to the flame of a candle in propitiation to Diana with the supplication that she remove any evil influence that might be lurking about in the shadows of the night.

A Spell to Repel Werewolves

Well-protected may I be as I go forth to roam,
for Diana, beautiful, Diana, I walk abroad with thy blessing.
I do implore thee to keep all evil from me;
I do beseech thee to drive all werewolves away from my
   path.
May you change deadly wolf intent and savage heart
back to the human form of gentle man or woman.
May you quench the lust for blood
And transform it into love for thee.

At this point, slowly drip three drops of oil into the flame of a candle in propitiation to Diana.

A Prayer to Ask Light Beings for Protection

As you recite the following, be prepared to sprinkle drops of perfume over the flame of a candle or a small tin of burning oil.

> I dedicate to you, o ye Angels of Light and all heavenly spirits, these drops of aromatic perfume to send a sweet smell that will inspire all goodness. Receive the prayer from my heart to keep me safe from evil and from those beings who transform their human flesh into the unholy bodies of wolves and monsters. Receive these drops as perfume from my heart to quelch the foul stench of demons and shape-shifters who would do evil to me and to others whom I love. Receive these drops of heavenly perfume to cover the putrid odor of evil and to cleanse my household from demonic influences. Keep our home safe from evil, O Living God of the Universe and all Angelic Beings of Light. Amen and amen.

Stumpf, Peter (c. 1525–1589)

Peter Stumpf—also known as Peter Stumpp or Peter Stubbe—was born in the town of Bedburg near the city of Cologne, Germany, about 1525 and, according to contemporary biographers of this notorious werewolf, gave himself up in his youth to the pursuit of magic and sorcery. Through necromancy, he acquainted himself intimately with many spirits and demons. While other magicians made their pacts with Satan to acquire great earthly riches, Stumpf was interested only in being able to transform himself into a werewolf to work harm on men, women, and children.

After his capture and during his trial, Peter Stumpf told how Satan gave him a hairy girdle or belt, which, whenever he wore it,

> transformed him forthwith into the likeness of a greedy devouring wolf. It was strong and mighty, with great eyes which in the night sparkled like brands of fire. Its body was huge, and the mouth great and wide with most sharp and cruel teeth. No sooner should he put off this girdle, but the mighty paws would again become hands, and presently he would appear in his former shape as if he had never changed.

Until he was revealed as a werewolf, Stumpf had appeared to his fellow townsfolk as quite an ordinary man. Few people suspected that Peter was leading such a ghastly double life. Although he was never a man believed to be concerned with his eternal salvation, few could guess that within his soul lurked a secret nature "inclined to blood and cruelty." Later, it was established that all those individuals who had somehow aroused his anger were stalked and viciously attacked, usually as they traveled beyond the edge of the town. When his victims were discovered, their bodies were so badly mutilated that no one could have imagined that their attack had been accomplished by anything other than a savage beast.

Other than those men who had angered him in some way, Stumpf's favorite victims were women and children. According to the old court records, he would "ravish them in the fields" in human form, then transform himself into a wolf and "cruelly murder them."

To add to his roster of outrageous sins against humanity, Stumpf sexually abused his daughter, who had matured into a beautiful young woman. The horrified judges recorded that "cruelly he committed most wicked incest with her. ... But such was his

A 1589 woodcut depicts the decapitation of Peter Stumpf, the Werewolf of Bedburg.

inordinate lust and filthy desire toward her that he begat a child by her, daily using her as his concubine." And Stumpf's shocking acts of incest did not end with the abuse of his daughter. "Furthermore, this insatiable and filthy beast, given over to works of evil, with greediness lay even with his own sister. He frequented her company long times according to the wicked dictates of his heart."

Stumpf had other women as well. One woman singled out by the court was suspected to be a beautiful shape-shifting demon, rather than an ordinary human female, for Stumpf's "inordinate lust" could hardly be satisfied with any "natural woman."

Grisly acts of cannibalism were added to the many charges against the notorious werewolf of Bedburg. During one brief time period alone, he was accused of having slain 13 young women and having devoured large portions of their bodies. In this same time frame, Stumpf killed two pregnant women and "tearing the children out of their wombs in a most bloody and savage sort, he afterward ate their hearts, panting and raw, which he accounted dainty morsels greatly agreeing with his appetite."

The werewolf killed and badly mutilated the men, but no trace of the woman was ever found, "for she, whose flesh he esteemed both sweet and dainty in taste, the vile monster had most ravenously devoured."

On one occasion, Stumpf ambushed two men and a woman as they were traveling between towns. The werewolf killed and badly mutilated the men, but no trace of the woman was ever found, "for she, whose flesh he esteemed both sweet and dainty in taste, the vile monster had most ravenously devoured."

There seemed no end to Peter Stumpf's outrages against civilized society. Although he had been heard frequently to refer to his firstborn son as his "heart's ease," nonetheless, when he was in the form of a wolf, he killed the youth and "next ate the brains out of the boy's head as a most savory meal to assuage his greedy appetite."

Stumpf was finally captured when a party of men with dogs set out to track down a wolf that had been seen carrying away a small boy tending his family's cattle. As they neared a thicket to which the dogs had led them, the men heard the child crying hysterically. Then, they swore to a man, they saw first a wolf appear, and as they watched in astonishment, the beast shape-shifted into the form of Peter Stumpf. Since the men recognized the human image before them as a citizen of Bedburg, they at first thought that Satan may have presented them with some kind of an illusion. Cautiously, they followed Stumpf back to his house, then they decided to take him to the authorities for questioning.

> *Stumpf was threatened with the rack, and he startled the authorities by immediately confessing to be a sorcerer, a werewolf, a cannibal, a rapist, and an incestuous adulterer.*

During the questioning, Stumpf was threatened with the rack, and he startled the authorities by immediately confessing to be a sorcerer, a werewolf, a cannibal, a rapist, and an incestuous adulterer. Stumpf's daughter and his mistress were tried with him as accessories, and all three were condemned to death. As the "principal malefactor," Stumpf was given the severest punishment.

On October 31, 1589, in the town of Bedburg, Stumpf was stretched on the wheel, and flesh was torn from his body in ten places by red hot pincers. His arms and legs were severed with an axe, he was decapitated, and his body was burned. Some time afterward, the city erected a memorial of the Werewolf of Bedburg, which consisted of a pole supporting the wheel on which Stumpf was broken, a plaque bearing the image of a wolf, 15 wooden portraits representing the monster's verified victims, and impaled at the very top, the lycanthrope's head.

Sources:

Bores, George. *The Damnable Life and Death of Stubbe Peeter*. London Chapbook of 1590.

Hurwood, Bernardt J. *Vampires, Werewolves, and Ghouls*. New York: Ace Books, 1968.

Masters, R. E. L., and Eduard Lea. *Perverse Crimes in History*. New York: The Julian Press, 1963.

Summers, Montague. *The Werewolf*. New York: Dutton, 1934.

Succubus

According to certain mystical traditions, the lustful demons known as the incubi and the succubi were the children of Father Adam's intercourse with a beautiful fallen angel named Lilith, who, in the view of certain Jewish mystics, was Adam's wife before the creation of Eve. Succubi appear to men as beautiful, sensual women, tempting and promising.

The heavy cloud of sexual guilt that hung over the Middle Ages undoubtedly spawned a million succubi every night. As might be expected, the Christian hermits and monks in their lonely desert hovels or penitential cells were constantly harassed by sensuous succubi, who sought to tempt them into committing carnal sins.

In the Middle Ages, theologians warned against masturbation on the grounds that waiting demons stood ready to transport the wasted semen for their own nefarious purposes. Nocturnal emissions were interpreted

Fritz Schwimbeck's 1909 illustration "My Dream, My Bad Dream" depicts a succubus-like character mounting a male subject in repose.

as the work of succubi, who excited sleeping males to the point of ejaculation so they might steal away their spent semen.

Sources:

Spence, Lewis. *An Encyclopedia of Occultism*. New Hyde Park, NY: University Books, 1960.

Steiger, Brad. *Demon Lovers: Cases of Possession, Vampires, and Werewolves*. New Brunswick, NJ: Inner Light, 1987.

Taigheirm

Many people with an interest in powerful, secret societies will be familiar with the likes of the Bilderbergers, the Illuminati, and the Freemasons. Relatively few, however, will be conversant with an equally powerful body of people called the Taigheirm (also spelled Taghairm). Like so many other secret societies, the Taigheirm is populated by people who crave absolute power, massive wealth, and elite standing in society. It is, however, the way that the members of the Taigheirm achieve their goals—in a ritual that involves the sacrifice of cats to invoke a certain shape-shifting demon—that places the group in its own unique category.

This centuries-old cult, which has operated in stealth in the highlands of Scotland since at least the seventeenth century, uses ancient sacrificial rituals to get just about anything and everything it desires. It is rumored that numerous Scottish politicians, police officers, bankers, actors, doctors, judges, and landowners are counted among the Taigheirm's many and varied members.

Merrily Harpur, a British researcher who has studied the history of the Taigheirm, says that key to the success of the members is "an infernal magical sacrifice of cats in rites dedicated to the subterranean gods of pagan times, from whom particular gifts and benefits were solicited. They were called in the Highlands and the Western Isles of Scotland, the black-cat spirits."

The process of sacrifice was, and still is, gruesome in the extreme. Isolated and lonely places high in the mountains of Scotland are chosen, chiefly to ensure privacy. Secrecy is paramount. Members arrive, in black cloaks and pointed hats, at the chosen spot in the dead of night, determined at all times to protect their identities and presence from outsiders. Then comes the main event. Huge spits are built upon which live cats placed and slowly roasted for up to four days and nights, during which the operator of the spit is denied sleep or nourishment, aside from an occasional sip of water. Supposedly, when the ritual is at its height, from the paranormal ether terrifying, huge black cats with glowing red eyes appear before the conjurer, demanding to know what it is that he or she wishes to have bestowed on them: money, influence, or something else. In return, and in a fashion befitting the likes of Faust, on his or her death the conjurer agrees to turn over their soul to those ancient, mighty gods worshipped by the Taigheirm.

Without doubt, the one person, more than any other, who was conversant with the terrible rituals of the Taigheirm was J. Y. W. Lloyd, who penned an acclaimed 1881 book titled *The History of the Prince, the Lord's Marcher, and the Ancient Nobility of Powys Fadog and the Ancient Lords of Arwystli, Cedewen, and Meirionydd*. Lloyd became fascinated by the Taigheirm after reading Horst's *Deuteroscopy*, which was the first published work to expose the actions of this heartless group. Lloyd recorded that "the midnight hour, between Friday and Saturday, was the authentic time for these horrible practices and invocations."

Horst presented a terrible image: "After the cats were dedicated to all the devils, and put into a magico-sympathetic condition, by the shameful things done to them, and the agony occasioned to them, one of them was at once put alive upon the spit, and amid terrific howlings, roasted before a slow fire. The moment that the howls of one tortured cat ceased in death, another was put upon the spit, for a minute of interval must not take place if they would control hell; and this continued for the four entire days and nights. If the exorcist could hold it out still longer, and even till his physical powers were absolutely exhausted, he must do so."

> "Infernal spirits appeared in the shape of
> black cats. There came continually more and
> more of these cats; and their howlings,
> mingled with those roasting on the spit, were
> terrific."

It was after that four-day period, said Horst, that "infernal spirits appeared in the shape of black cats. There came continually more and more of these cats; and their howlings, mingled with those roasting on the spit, were terrific. Finally, appeared a cat of a monstrous size, with dreadful menaces. When the Taigheirm was complete, the sacrificer demanded of the spirits the reward of his offering, which consisted of various things; as riches, children, food, and clothing. The gift of second sight, which they had not had before, was, however, the usual recompense; and they retained it to the day of their death."

As the nineteenth century reached its end, Lloyd came to believe that while the legend and cruel and cold reputation of the Taigheirm still existed, the group, as a fully functioning entity, no longer did. He recorded that one of the very last Taigheirm rituals was held on the Scottish island of Mull in the early 1800s. Lloyd added that the folk of Mull "still show the place where Allan Maclean, at that time the incantor, and sacrificial priest, stood with his assistant, Lachlain Maclean, both men of a determined and unbending character."

Theirs was reportedly a frightening ritual held on a cold winter's night and under a full moon. Lloyd noted: "Allan Maclean continued his sacrifice to the fourth day, when he was exhausted both in body and mind, and sunk in a swoon; but, from this day he received the second-sight to the time of his death, as also did his assistant. In the people, the belief was unshaken, that the second-sight was the natural consequence of celebrating the Taigheirm."

There is, however, intriguing data strongly suggesting that the Taigheirm are still with us, lurking in the shadows and still extending their power and influence. In 1922, Carl Van Vechten commented on post–nineteenth century Taigheirm activity in a footnote contained in his book *The Tiger in the House*. It reads: "The night of the day I first learned of the Taigheirm I dined with some friends who were also entertaining Seumas, Chief of Clann Fhearghuis of Stra-chur. He informed me that to the best of his knowledge the Taigheirm is *still* celebrated in the Highlands of Scotland."

Texas Taigheirm

In early 2008, rumors circulated to the effect that a U.S.-based equivalent of the ancient Scottish order of the Taigheirm was operating deep in the heart of Dallas, Texas. As was the case with the original Scottish members, those tied to this Lone Star State–based equivalent were using the rites and rituals to achieve two things: power and wealth. While such rumors were never conclusively proved to be real, the fact is that from 2008 to 2011, there were numerous cases of cat mutilation in the heart of Dallas. And they clearly weren't the work of coyotes or bobcats. There was method in the grisly, city-wide madness.

It all began in the summer of 2008 when two cats were found "dissected," as the local media reported, in the city's Lovers Lane. Almost one year later, a cat was found dead, with organs removed with surgical precision, in Dallas's Lakewood Heights. The unfortunate man who stumbled on the remains of the poor animal said: "The cat was literally cut in half at its midsection. There was no blood on our front lawn, so it appears that the mutilation probably occurred elsewhere and the remains were dumped on our lawn by the perpetrator."

Two more cats were found within days, also mutilated in fashions that suggested the culprits were all too human. As a result, the Dallas SPCA offered a $5,000 reward for anyone who could help solve the disturbing mystery. There was not a single taker. A couple of weeks later, Dallas's Midway Hollow was targeted. The local police said: "We used to think it was a juvenile up to no good. But now we think it might be an older guy who lives nearby, snatches these cats, mutilates them, then takes them back to where he finds them."

Then, in August, NBC-DFW reported on the discovery of six dead and mutilated cats in the northwest part of Dallas.

Although 2010 was quiet, 2011 was anything but. It all began again in April of that year when a "surgically mutilated" cat was stumbled on in Wilshire Heights, Dallas. Yet again, a substantial reward was on offer. There was, however, nothing but silence and not a single lead in sight.

Without doubt, the most controversial theory surfaced in May 2011. The story, from a local conspiracy theorist, Bob Small, was that the Taigheirm group was allied to the better-known Skull & Bones group, which was founded in 1832 at Yale University in New Haven, Connecticut. Small believed—and continues to believe—that it's no coincidence that former president George W. Bush, himself a member of Skull & Bones, lives in the Preston Hollow neighborhood of Dallas, not far from where the cat killings took place from 2008 to 2011.

Sources:

Spence, Lewis. *An Encyclopedia of Occultism*. Hyde Park, NY: University Books, 1960.

Taw: Jungle Werewolves

For many years, Harold M. Young, an official of the Burmese government during the period of British control, was stationed among the remote tribes of the Shan of the Lahu. It was among these peoples that Young first heard of—then saw for himself—the strange mountain werewolves that terrorize the Lahu tribe, whose people live in the jungles bordering Northern Thailand and Burma (now Myanmar).

Manifestations of the supernatural, Young discovered, were daily occurrences among the Lahu. The government official expressed his opinion that the more humanity retreated from nature and hid behind the barrier of civilization, the farther we remove ourselves from the basic powers that are the natural heritage of the "uncivilized" human.

Working among the native people, Young had heard about the Taw for many years. They were always described to him as strange, fearsome creatures with furry hides that at certain times of the month would raid a village and either kill or carry off a victim. He had dismissed all such comments referring to the strange creatures as native superstition, an excuse for carelessness in allowing a wild beast to get past the sentries and into the village. Young was secure in his "educated and civilized" opinion until he was actually confronted by the bloody deeds of a jungle werewolf.

The eerie confrontation occurred in 1960 while he was on a hunting party. His expedition had taken him into Lahu country, high in the mountains that lie to the north of the Burma-Thailand border. The trek had been wearisome, but the thought of some nighttime hunting had

Manifestations of the supernatural were daily occurrences among the Lahu people of Burma (now Myanmar), including a werewolf-like tiger creature known as the Thaman Chah, or Taw.

adrenalin pumping through his system. As he neared a Lahu village, he foresaw no difficulty in obtaining rights for a night shooting; the Lahu and he had always been on friendly terms.

On this night, however, the chief shook his head firmly in denial of his request. He warned Young that the Taw were near to the village. It was dangerous to hunt now.

Young was just opening his mouth in protest when a terrible shriek filled the night. His hunter responses were well-conditioned. His hand grasped his pistol firmly as he ran to the thatched hut standing close to the jungle's edge from which the cry had issued. His mind and body alert, he could not help noticing that the chief and other of the men followed him at a distinctly slower pace. He was puzzled by their reluctance to dash after him. He had seen these same men face a snarling tiger without fear, yet now they seemed strangely hesitant about rendering aid. Over and over he heard the whispered word, "Taw."

As Young approached the hut, he cautiously slowed his pace. An experienced hunter and adventurer, he could smell danger in the atmosphere of the now ominously silent hut. He tiptoed up to the window and squinted through the aperture.

Later, recalling the incredible experience for writer Ormand McGill, Young said, "There was bright moon that night, and as my eyes became adjusted to the light in the hut, I saw a sight that I will never forget to my dying day—one that literally lifted the hairs on my head."

> *The hideous beast could only be described as half human, half beast. Its body was covered with coarse hair. Its face was grotesque; its eyes small and red.*

Inside the hut was a ghastly creature, chewing slowly on the slashed neck of a dying woman. The hideous beast could only be described as half human, half beast. Its body was covered with coarse hair. Its face was grotesque; its eyes small and red. Its mouth showed cruel fangs, dropping blood and spittle as it worked deeper into the woman's flesh.

Young had seen enough. His hand automatically brought up the pistol to the window and blasted several slugs at the monster. The beast spun crazily, leaped to its feet with a wild cry, and dashed past the men gathered outside the hut. Within moments it had disappeared into the night.

Young shook his head in confusion. He was an expert marksman, but apparently he had missed the creature at point-blank range, for the thing had vanished into the jungle. Resolved to bring the beast down, he shouted for the men to follow him, and they plunged into the darkness after it.

Hours later, their search unsuccessful, they gathered back at the village and huddled around a fire. Talk was scarce; the embers were low. Their nocturnal encounter with the half-human, half-animal being caused more than one tribesman to brood in silence as he awaited the dawn.

With the first light of morning, Young and the Lahu renewed their search. In the clear light, a fresh clue was discovered. Splotches of blood were found leading into a thicket. Young hadn't missed the monster after all. The hunters excitedly followed the trail, which circled the village and re-entered it from the opposite end. Young was baffled. How could the creature have crawled back into the village unnoticed?

The blood trail was traced to a certain hut. With a sudden rush, the men tore aside the skin door covering. Inside, lying on a bed was a dead man. The trail of blood had turned into a stagnant pool that had formed from the blood dripping from a bullet hole in the man's side.

Young could barely speak. This was not the thing that he had seen ripping at the poor woman's throat the night before. This was a man.

The chief leaned forward and spat on the man's face. "Taw!" he uttered with revulsion.

That amazing incident was the only time that Harold Young actually saw the hated and feared Taw, but he continued to hear many stories about them during his stay in Burma.

Sources:

Dane, Christopher. *The Occult in the Orient*. New York: Popular Library, 1974.

An artist's rendering of the chupacabra of Puerto Rico, notably different from their homonymic Texas counterparts.

Texas Chupacabras and Their Puerto Rican Cousins

Over the course of the last few years, I have found myself doing more and more radio, newspaper, magazine, and TV interviews on the phenomenon of the so-called Texas chupacabras—those admittedly very strange-looking, hairless beasts that have predominantly been reported within woods and fields in and around the Austin and San Antonio areas but are now being seen with increasing frequency in the vicinity of Dallas, very near to where I live.

One of the questions I am asked frequently during these interviews is how, and under what particular circumstances, these mysterious beasts managed to migrate from the island of Puerto Rico—where the chupacabra reports began to surface in the mid-1990s—to the heart of the Lone Star State. Well, the answer to that question is very simple: they didn't.

While Puerto Rico's most infamous monster may share its name with that which haunts the woods, ranches, and wilds of Texas, that is pretty much where the connection ends. Notably, when I have mentioned this to certain media outlets, there's nothing but outright disappointment in response. So, let's take a look at what is really afoot, and how the creatures of Texas have become entwined with those of Puerto Rico.

I have been on a number of expeditions to Puerto Rico in search of the island's blood-sucking beasts, and there is no doubt in my mind that they exist. I have interviewed numerous ranchers, veterinarians, civil defense employees, and members of the public who have either seen the creatures or have been witness to their blood-sucking activities.

> *The chupacabras of Puerto Rico are described as bipedal creatures with large eyes, vicious claws and teeth, hairless monkey-like bodies, row of spikes running down the backs of their heads and necks, and membranous bat-like wings.*

In most cases, the chupacabras of Puerto Rico are described as bipedal creatures with large eyes, vicious claws and teeth, hairless monkey-like bodies, row of spikes running down the backs of their heads and necks—punk-rock Mohawk-style—and even, occasionally, membranous bat-like wings. As for their mode of attack, most of the interviewees stated that the chupacabras kill their prey by a bite to the neck and then proceed to drink the blood.

Turning to Texas, however, we see something very different. In every case on record, the Texas chupacabras are not described as being bipedal in nature. Rather, they walk on four legs. There are no wings, no huge eyes, and certainly not any spikes running down their heads.

But that doesn't mean that high strangeness is not afoot. It most certainly is. In those cases where we have been fortunate to secure the body of a Texas chupacabra—after it has either been shot or been hit by a vehicle—DNA analysis has proven with 100 percent certainty that these creatures have canine origins. Yes, they look weird, but there is no doubt that they are from the dog family.

> *Yes, they look weird, but there is no doubt that they are from the dog family.*

The story doesn't end there, however. Canine they are, but normal they are not. The lack of hair has led many commentators to suggest that the animals are afflicted by mange—which may be true. However, not only are we now seeing pups with the adult creatures, but young and old all seem to be adapting quite well to living without hair. There's none of the usual intense itching and scratching—to the point of bleeding—that is typical in animals affected by mange, and the lack of hair doesn't appear to have any bearing on their ability to roam quite happily and comfortably in the pulverizing summer heat of Texas. And as someone who shaves his head to the bone daily, I can say with certainty that the Texan sun can certainly do some damage to the skin without adequate protection!

In addition, in some cases the front legs of the animals appear to be much shorter than one would consider normal, which gives them a weird hopping, kangaroo-type gait. Others have elongated upper jaws, many have cataracts, and they act in a highly aggressive nature around people—quite unlike normal wild canines, which will usually steer clear of humans.

And then there is their mode of attack, which a number of ranchers have said involves bites to the neck of farm animals and the draining of a size-able amount of blood from the bodies. It is this latter point—and, argu-ably, this latter point alone—that has led many people to believe that the Puerto Rican chupacabra and the Texan chupacabra are one and the same. But they're not. The term *chupacabra* is a great marketing tool. It provokes intrigue and terror and is thus a journalist's dream come true. The concept by now has gone viral within the media, on the internet, and in monster-hunting circles.

So, in other words, we have two distinctly different phenomena in evidence: one arises from sightings and encounters with truly unknown beasts on the island of Puerto Rico, and the other is focused upon weird-looking Texas canines that may have some extraordinary changes going on at a genetic level. Beyond that, however, all we can say for certain about the real chupacabra is that just like Las Vegas, what happens in Puerto Rico continues to stay in Puerto Rico.

Sources:

Redfern, Nick. Investigations, 2004–06.

Thags Yang

The folklore of Tibet includes numerous accounts of malignant, shape-shifting demons that lurk near trees, rocks, lakes, and many other places to seize men and animals and suck away their vital breath and life force. One of the most vicious of these entities is the Thags Yang, a demon that can appear as a tiger, a man, or a were-tiger. The terrible Thags Yang follow those travelers who are not sufficiently protected by strong spiritual beliefs and drain their life essence from them. They also lurk near villages, seeking out the weak and the foolish who do not utter their prayers of protection.

Sources:

David-Neel, Alexandra. *Magic and Mystery in Tibet*. New York: Dover, 1971.

Theriomorph

A Theriomorph is one who has perfected the ability to shift from animal form to human form and back again whenever he or she wishes. A Theriomorph who has mastered such physical transformations at will would be a true shape-shifter in the classic sense. Many contemporary students of metaphysics and Native American medicine term themselves "spiritual Theriomorphs," recognizing an inner identification with a particular animal as a guide or mentor, much as traditional shamans perceive the transformative powers of their personal animal totem.

Thylacines, Werewolves, and Chupacabras

Now and again, I find myself on the receiving end of a conspiratorial story that is so unbelievable, so downright bizarre, and so utterly implausible that I actually wish it could be true, even though it isn't. Well … it *probably* isn't. Or is it? I still can't be sure. In terms of the chupacabra, I was in just such a position in September 2013. That was when, on the third of the month, I received the first of around 20 emails from a man I'll call Ed. It transpires that Ed, who lived in Utah and claimed to work at the ultra-secret Dugway Proving Ground, had seen the 2004 episode of the SyFy Channel's *Proof Positive* series—not when it first aired but when it was uploaded to YouTube in 2012. Ed said he could tell me *exactly* what the chupacabras were, so I asked him to please enlighten me. He did that and much more.

According to Ed, the creatures that have become known as chupacabras amount to nothing less than relic populations of the thylacine, also known as the Tasmanian tiger or Tasmanian wolf. Its correct title is *Thylacinus cynocephalus*, which translates as "pouched dog with a wolf's head." They are dog-sized, striped marsupials, with jaws that have the ability to open to almost 180 degrees. There are, however, at least two problems with this theory. First, thylacines are believed to have become extinct back in the 1930s; second, they were native to New Guinea, Australia, and Tasmania, not remotely near the chupacabra's home of Puerto Rico. But never mind; these factors do not have a single bearing upon Ed's engagingly odd scenario.

Before I get to Ed's story, a bit of background on the thylacine is in order. Although, as I noted above, mainstream zoology is of the opinion the creature is now extinct, it certainly had a good run: fossilized examples of the creature demonstrate that it lived as far back as the Miocene period, around 23 million to 5 million years ago. While the thylacine is generally accepted to have died out in Australia thousands of years

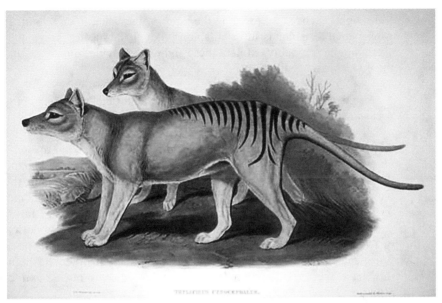

Thylacines, native to New Guinea, Australia, and Tasmania, are believed to have become extinct back in the 1930s. However, thylacine sightings have continued to be reported, though no conclusive evidence of a thylacine has been found.

ago, it survived in Tasmania, roughly 150 miles from Australia, until quite recently. Not everyone, however, is so sure the creature is *completely* gone. How do we know? It's all thanks to the Tasmania Parks and Wildlife Service (TPWS) and the Australian government's Freedom of Information Act, that's how.

Both the TPWS and the Australian government have declassified their files and records on the creature, and they are *filled* with credible sightings of thylacines in Tasmania that post-date the 1930s, in some cases significantly. The TPWS itself states on its website:

"Since 1936, no conclusive evidence of a thylacine has been found. However, the incidence of reported thylacine sightings has continued.

"Although the species is now considered to be 'probably extinct,' these sightings provide some hope that the thylacine may still exist."

Most sightings occur at night, in the north of the State, in or near areas where suitable habitat is still available. Although the species is now considered to be 'probably extinct,' these sightings provide some hope that the thylacine may still exist."

As for the Australian government, it notes at its official webpage on the thylacine:

"Australia is home to some of the world's most unusual and mysterious wildlife. Our native animals, such as the platypus, the koala and the kangaroo, have been a source of wonder and surprise to people the world over. But perhaps our most mysterious animal is the thylacine, or Tasmanian Tiger. There are many reasons why people are fascinated by this animal. Perhaps it is its name and the romantic notion of Australia having its own 'tiger.' Perhaps it is its sad history since European settlement, or the fact that there are many people who claim they have seen a Tasmanian Tiger and believe it may not be extinct after all."

Australian government officials also state:

> Although commonly called the Tasmanian Tiger or Tasmanian Wolf, the thylacine has more in common with its marsupial cousin the Tasmanian devil. With a head like a wolf, striped body like a tiger and backward facing pouch like a wombat, the thylacine was as unbelievable as the platypus which had caused disbelief and uproar in Europe when it was first described.

> The thylacine looked like a long dog with stripes, a heavy stiff tail and a big head. A fully grown thylacine could measure 180cm from the tip of the nose to the tip of the tail, stand 58cm high at the shoulder and weigh about 30 kilograms. It had short, soft fur that was brown except for the thick black stripes which extended from the base of the tail to the shoulders.

Well, that's all very fascinating, but the Puerto Rican chupacabra is almost exclusively described as being a bipedal beast—it walks on two legs, not four. Surely a creature that looks like a wolf and gives the impression of having been crossed with a tiger and a kangaroo couldn't walk on two legs as well as four—could it? Rather amazingly, yes, it actually could, and it did. It's time for a further examination of the Australian government's thylacine files:

> The thylacine was said to have an awkward way of moving, trotting stiffly and not moving particularly quickly. They walked on their toes like a dog but could also move in a more unusual way—a bipedal hop. The animal would stand upright with its front legs in the air, resting its hind legs on the ground and using its tail as a support, exactly the way a kangaroo does. Thylacines had been known to hop for short distances in this position.

All of this brings us right back to the weird words of Ed. Let's begin with his supposed place of work: the Dugway Proving Ground. In February 1942, President Franklin D. Roosevelt signed a piece of legislation that gave what was then called the War Department complete jurisdiction over more than 120,000 acres of land in Utah. It wasn't long before the DPG was up and running. And it is running still, but now with the benefit of almost three-quarters of a million acres of heavily guarded and near-inaccessible land. The best way to describe the base is as an Area 51 that, instead of allegedly researching crashed UFOs and autopsying dead aliens, focuses its top-secret research on deadly viruses and exotic diseases—those pesky things that usually provoke catastrophic zombie outbreaks in the likes of *The Walking Dead* and *Night of the Living Dead*.

As our email exchange progressed, Ed opened up significantly. He claimed that back in the 1980s, staff at the Dugway Proving Ground got its hands on thylacine DNA and secretly decided to try to resurrect the creature using high-tech gene-splicing and cloning. According to Ed, it worked very well. The beast, incredibly, walked—and hopped—yet again. Not in Australia, New Guinea, or Tasmania, but right in the heart of Mormon country.

As for why the creature was resurrected, this is where it gets really controversial. According to Ed, the military wanted to create an army of savage beasts that could be unleashed on the battlefield and tear the

A modern illustration of the thylacine demonstrates the animal's odd proportions and remarkable jaw capacity.

enemy apart, rather than take them out with conventional bullets and the like. The thylacine was seen as the perfect beast, chiefly because of its immense, powerful jaws. There was something else, however: mad scientists at the proving ground had created a terrible virus that plunged the infected into manic states of homicidal rage, as was the scenario in the *28 Days Later* and *28 Weeks Later* movies. Those scientists weren't using their nightmarish virus on people, however. The targets of experimentation were those resurrected thylacines. However, long before the animals could be let loose in war zones, test runs had to be undertaken to see how deadly these creatures, infected with a mind-altering virus, really could be. And which place was chosen for the tests? Yep: Puerto Rico.

A pack of frenzied, resurrected thylacines, causing mayhem and havoc on Puerto Rico, and being responsible for spawning the legend of the chupacabra: is that *really* what happened? It is hard to say. Ed assured me that he was speaking 100 percent truth. He was even careful to comment on the fact that, as the Australian government confirmed, the thylacine had the extraordinary ability to walk like a wolf at one moment and then in "a bipedal hop" in the next. This was why, Ed assured me, some people claimed the chupacabra appeared to resemble a large dog, and others said it walked on two legs. That the thylacine could walk in *both* fashions was the clincher, he said. Admittedly, that did make a degree of sense.

Thylacine/Chupacabra in Russia?

Here we must make a slight diversion to Russia, after which we will return to Ed. In April 2006, Russia's *Pravda* newspaper told a story that strongly suggested the chupacabra had somehow made its way to the heart of the former Soviet Union. It was a story that, when I dug it out of my old files, suggested to me that there just might be some merit to Ed's controversial claims.

"The worries," said *Pravda*, "began at the end of March 2005 not far from the regional center of Saraktash. On the Sapreka farm two farming families suddenly lost 32 turkeys. The bodies of the birds, found in the morning, had been completely drained of blood. None of the farmers either saw or heard the beast that killed them. Then in the village of Gavrilovka sheep fell victim to the night-time vampire. The unknown animal was also in the hamlets of Vozdvizhenka and Shishma. In the course of the night 3–4 sheep or goats perished. All together the losses in the region amounted to 30 small horned cattle."

A farmer named Erbulat Isbasov, *Pravda* reported, got a close look at the creature that was slaughtering his animals: "I heard the sheep start to bleat loudly. I ran up to them and saw a black shadow. It looked like an enormous dog that had stood up on its hind legs. And jumped like a kangaroo. The beast sensed my presence and ran away. It squeezed through an opening in the panels of the fence."

Although I kept a careful watch on this story, it soon died, and the killings in Saraktash ended as mysteriously as they had begun. I have to say, though, that the references to "an enormous dog that had stood up on its hind legs" and "jumped like a kangaroo" sounded astonishingly like the physical characteristics of a thylacine.

August 2012 saw a dramatic development in the Russian chupacabra saga when a creature astonishingly like so many found across Texas popped up in another part of the former Soviet Union, specifically in the Ukraine. It was canid, its limbs were disproportionate, and it was hairless. It would have looked perfectly at home on the property of Devin McAnally or in the freezer of Phylis Canion, to name two Texans who have identified chupacabras. The Ukraine was a hell of a long way from Texas, however.

"The animal doesn't look like a fox or a wolf, or a raccoon," commented Mikhail Ilchenko, the deputy head of the district veterinary service in Mikhailovskoe. He added: "It cannot even be a marten. I have never seen such animal before. But, judging by the fangs, I can definitely say that it is a predator."

Interestingly, in no time rumors surfaced concerning the creature's origins that closely mirrored what I had heard in both Puerto Rico and Texas. The U.K.'s *Daily Mail* newspaper noted the claims that had been made: "It could be a 'mutant' fox poisoned by radiation. ... Another theory was that it may be a hybrid originating from a Soviet plant conducting tests on animals relating to chemical or biological weapons development. 'A creature we were not supposed to see has escaped from a secret defense lab,' said one comment."

Alexander Korotya, of the Zoological Museum of Zaporozhye National University, stated to the press: "I cannot identify what kind of animal it is. For example, its canine teeth are similar to a fox, but smaller in size—like a marten. Yet a marten has a different type of skull. If to compare with an otter's head, then the ears are too small. It has a wide nose and a stretched muzzle. My opinion is that it's most likely a hybrid animal or a mutant."

> *When people reported seeing spikes, Ed explained, they were really catching brief glimpses of the tiger-like stripes that did indeed feature prominently on the backs of thylacines.*

And now, with the Russian conspiracies out of the way, back to Ed. Ed also had an ingenious explanation for that row of spikes that numerous people have claimed run down the necks of so many chupacabras. Ed told me that many of these sightings were made at dusk, or after the sun had completely set, ensuring that visual sightings of the creature were somewhat distorted. When people reported seeing spikes, Ed explained, they were really catching brief glimpses of the tiger-like stripes that did indeed feature prominently on the backs of thylacines. True or not, I thought it was a plausible explanation.

As for how the story ended, Ed said that the thylacines proved to be far too difficult to handle, that the virus made them completely uncontrollable, and that the project was abandoned around 1997. Trying to round up the animals was seen as way too dangerous, as it might have given the game away, suggested Ed. So, they were left alone — to kill, reproduce, and do whatever else it is that the average thylacine does on an average day in Puerto Rico. And it was all successfully hidden behind the veil of myth, legend, rumor, and lore of the chupacabra.

There's something else, too: Ed was quite the enigmatic whistleblower. I have a friend who — how shall I put this? — is what I might describe as being "very good with computers." He offered to take a look at Ed's email address, which was a safe-mail.net account. Safe-mail, based in Israel, is often used by those who wish to protect their real identities and locations. Encryption and cyber-stealth are the combined name of the game. It turned out that Ed's emails *were* coming from Utah — in a fashion. In reality, the emails were merely being routed *through* Utah, via at least two other locations. One was in Maryland and the other was in Langley, Virginia. It transpires that Maryland is home to the National Security Agency, while Langley, Virginia, is the place that the Central Intelligence Agency calls home.

That didn't mean or prove anything, but I found it interesting.

After about four or five days, Ed's emails suddenly stopped. I found that interesting, too. In fact, I found *everything* about the affair interesting. Whether Deep Throat or deeply disturbed nut, I never did find out.

Sources:

Nick Redfern. Personal correspondence, and notes from a two-week expedition in Puerto Rico, 2008.

Tiger People

The Khonds are an ancient people who inhabit eastern Bengal and whose traditions include a kind of voluntary shape-shifting, which utilizes as its imagery a tiger deity. Some years ago, an Englishman who wished to remain anonymous claimed that he had actually witnessed a Khond transforming himself into a were-tiger and swore that his account was true. According to the Englishman, he had spent a good deal of time in India, especially among the Khonds, and had frequently heard stories about the ability of certain individuals to transform themselves into tigers. When he persisted with a number of questions regarding such beliefs, he was informed that there was a place he could go to actually witness such metamorphoses.

Once he had secreted himself at the designated spot in the jungle where such magic was alleged to transpire, he soon began to wonder if he had been played for a fool and tricked into spending the night with snakes, wild boars, big cats, scorpions, and a host of other poisonous vermin. But as things turned out, he didn't have long to wait before the would-be tigerman appeared.

The individual was hardly what the Englishman had expected. Not at all fierce in appearance, the man was very young and almost feminine in his mannerisms. Once he reached the edge of the sacred circle, he knelt down and touched the ground three times in succession with his forehead, looking up all

The Englishman beheld the young man staring directly at him from the circle, not with the eyes of a human but with the "yellow, glittering, malevolent eyes of a tiger thirsting for human blood."

the while at a giant kulpa tree opposite him, chanting as he did so in a dialect that was unintelligible to the spying Englishman.

Suddenly the jungle seemed to become unnaturally quiet. For some reason he could not understand, the Englishman was filled with a penetrating dread of the unknown. For a moment he wanted to turn and run, but he seemed unable to move. The silence was broken by an eerie half-human, half-animal cry, and there followed the sound of something very large crashing through the jungle.

The silence was broken by an eerie half-human, half-animal cry, and there followed the sound of something very large crashing through the jungle.

Whatever the thing truly was, the Englishman saw it manifest before the young supplicant as column of pure, crimson light about seven feet in height. The slim young man knelt before it and scratched a symbol of some kind in the circle and set within it a string of beads. As he began once again to chant, the column of crimson light shot forth a lightning-like bolt of energy to the beads, which instantly began to glow a luminous red. The boy put the beads around his neck, clapped his hands together, and began to chant in a voice that deepened and became more and more animal in tone. There was a shattering roar from the young supplicant's throat, and the crimson column of light vanished.

And then the Englishman beheld the young man staring directly at him from the circle, not with the eyes of a human but with the "yellow, glittering, malevolent eyes of a tiger thirsting for human blood."

The Englishman ran for his life toward a tree about 50 yards away. He could hear the tigerman growling behind him. When he reached the tree, the nearest branch was eight feet above him. Resigning himself to his fate, he slumped against the tree trunk as black, gleaming claws came toward him. Then, to his amazement and relief, the tigerman gave a low growl of terror and bounded away in the jungle. Not bothering to speculate why the tigerman had spared him, he ran as quickly as he could back to the village.

The next morning he learned that an entire family had been found in their home, mutilated, torn, and partially eaten. The horrible manner in which they had died indicated that a tiger had attacked them. Significantly, the Englishman learned through village gossip that they had been blood enemies of the young man that he had seen transform himself into a were-tiger.

When the Englishman asked a village elder why he thought the were-tiger had spared him, the old man asked him for an exact description of where he stood when the beast-man attacked. Listening carefully, the elder explained that he had unknowingly sought refuge at a holy tree that bore an inscription of the name of the god Vishnu's incarnation. Merely touching the tree would protect anyone from attack by animals. The Englishman concluded his account stating that he did inspect the tree later that day and found upon it an inscription in Sanskrit. He never returned to that village again, but he swore that his witnessing of the were-tiger transformation was true.

Sources:

Hurwood, Bernardt J. *Vampires, Werewolves, and Ghouls.* New York: Ace Books, 1968.

Tigre Capiango

Those individuals in the central Argentine provinces of Santa Fe and Cordoba who can change themselves into jaguars through the magical application of great cat skin fragments and incantations are known as *Tigre Capiango.* Such jaguar-people are known as *Runa Uturunco* in the Quechua region and as *Yaguarete-Aba* in the Guarani region. As in the European traditions of lycanthropy, these sorcerers voluntarily seek to accomplish the transformation from human into animal for purposes of individual empowerment.

Sources:

Picasso, Fabio. "South American Monsters and Mystery Animals." *Strange* 20 (December 1998).

Totems

Regardless of our ethnic and cultural origins, almost all ancestors employed animal totems or spirits as tools in reaching the Supreme Being, receiving visions and revelations, and surviving in hostile environments. The spirit helper that will express itself most often in animal form is usually received during the vision quest. Shamans advise the supplicants that while on the quest, they are to fast, deny their physical bodies, and pray to the Great Mystery to grant them a spirit helper.

After a few days on the quest, a forest creature may approach the supplicant and offer itself as a guide. Those individuals on the quest are forewarned by the shamans that the temptation to accept the first animal that approaches as one's spirit helper is great. The shamans advise the supplicants that if they are able to endure greater hunger and exposure, the Great Mystery will be certain to send them a more powerful spirit helper, one especially destined for the individual. If one could endure, according to some traditionalists, the true spirit helper would appear as if it were glowing, as though it were composed primarily of light.

In *Warriors of the Rainbow*, William Willoya and Vinson Brown state that the Native Americans traditionally used the animal spirit to reach the "source of the world" and to purify the soul. This was not idol worship, they insist, "but something far deeper and more wonderful, the understanding of the Spirit Being that manifests itself in all living things."

Grandmother Twylah, repositor of Seneca wisdom, commented on the tragedy that, in the early days of conquest and missionary work, the invading Europeans saw the Native people interacting with their totem animals and became convinced that the tribespeople worshipped idols and a hierarchy of gods. While the traditionalist does most certainly believe that the Great Mystery manifests itself in a variety of forms, it must be understood that to see the expression of Deity in everything is not the same thing as seeing everything as Deity.

As Walking Buffalo attempted to explain in *Tatana Mani, Walking Buffalo of the Stonies*, the white missionaries misinterpreted the Native people's belief that the Great Spirit existed in all things as the worship of idols. "We saw the Great Spirit's work in everything, and sometimes we approached him through our totem animals."

For those early missionaries who truly listened and paid attention to the words of the shamans, there was never any misconception that the Native people were worshipping animals as deities. As early as 1742, missionary David Brainerd stated in his *Life and Travels* that the Delaware did not suppose a divine power in animals, but that "some invisible beings communicate to these animals a great power and make these creatures the immediate authors of good to certain persons." And perhaps those early men of the cloth who understood recalled the passage in the Book of Job (12:7–8): "Ask the animals, and they will teach you, or the birds of the air, and they will tell you; or speak to the earth, and it will teach you, or let the fish of the sea inform you."

In his *Man, God and Magic*, the brilliant ethnologist Ivar Lissner ponders the mystery of why the anonymous Franco-Cantabrian cave artists of over 20,000 years ago painted strange and ghostly two-legged creatures with the heads of animals and birds—what we now call the Lascaux Cave paintings. Despite what appear to be remarkable artistic gifts, our Stone Age ancestors chose not to share a depiction of their own features but confined themselves to portraying entities that were half human, half animal. Lissner speculates that perhaps, after all, the

The 20,000-year-old Lascaux Cave paintings depict half-human, half-animal figures but are most renowned for their surprisingly sophisticated depictions of contemporary animals.

ancient artists were portraying themselves, "but in animal guise, ecstatically or shamanistically." Perhaps these shamans of the Stone Age may have believed that "the road to supernatural powers is easier to follow in an animal shape and that spirits can only be reached with an animal's assistance." Perhaps the totem animals are "intermediary beings," stronger than mere mortals and "able to penetrate more deeply into the mysteries of fate, that unfathomable interrelationship between animals, men, and gods."

Beginning perhaps as early as the second century of the Christian Era, those European shamans who sought their animal totems were condemned as Witches and servants of the devil. By the time of the demon-obsessed Middle Ages, those who expressed confidence in their spirit helpers were actively hunted down and burned at the stake as Witches and heretics. Those shamans who lived deep in the forests and explored other dimensions with the assistance of their animal totems were declared enemies of the church, active members of Satan's minions, and put to the torture and the flames. Those herbalists and teachers of the old ways who wore animal skins for clothing and elected to be close to nature and apart from the congestion of growing cities were branded werewolves.

Sources:

Lissner, Ivar. *Man, God, and Magic*. Translated by J. Maxwell Brownjohn. New York: G.P. Putnam's Sons, 1961.

Steiger, Brad. *Totems: The Transformative Power of Your Personal Animal Totem*. San Francisco: HarperSanFrancisco, 1997.

Willoya, William, and Vinson Brown. *Warriors of the Rainbow: Strange and Prophetic Indian Dreams*. Healdsburg, CA: Naturegraph, 1962.

U

UFOs and Werewolves

It may come as a surprise to many to learn that one of the world's most famous monsters—Bigfoot of the Pacific Northwest and elsewhere—is a shape-shifter. As controversial as it may sound, reports of strange, unidentified apes that have the ability to take on numerous guises—all around the planet, never mind just in the United States—abound.

There is absolutely no doubt that Rendlesham Forest, in the English county of Suffolk, is most famous for a series of sensational UFO encounters that occurred across the period of December 26–29, 1980. Multiple military personnel, from the nearby twin bases of Royal Air Force Bentwaters and Royal Air Force Woodbridge, reported seeing strange lights in the sky; their accounts can be found in an official U.S. Air Force document of January 13, 1981, titled "Unexplained Lights." It was written by Lieutenant Colonel Charles I. Halt, the deputy base commander at Bentwaters. Others saw UFOs beaming lights down to the weapons-storage areas—which were the secret home to nuclear weapons. There are even accounts of some of the airmen seeing small, humanoid figures with cat-like eyes—aliens, perhaps. It's a far less known fact, however, that Rendlesham Forest has its very own shape-shifter. Its name is the Shug Monkey. Like most shape-shifters, it is a creature that terrifies all those who encounter it.

"Sam Holland," who I spoke with in 2001, encountered the Shug Monkey as he walked his little dog through the woods back in 1956. Holland described the monster as a veritable chimera: part monkey, part dog, and part bear. That it had a length of around ten feet demonstrates it was no normal, or even known, animal. Fortunately, neither Holland nor Harry the dog were harmed by the lumbering creature, which, after briefly glaring at the petrified pair, vanished into the woods.

> *Holland described the monster as a veritable chimera: part monkey, part dog, and part bear.*

A near-identical animal was seen seven years later in the same stretch of forest by a woman named Peggy Cushing. The only difference—a very significant difference—was that the animal suddenly changed into the form of a hideous, bat-winged gargoyle, which soared off into the dark skies above. Notably, Cushing said that as the beast changed in shape, there was a shimmering effect surrounding it.

Adding yet another component to the story is an account that comes from monster-hunter Jonathan Downes. He is the director of the British-based Centre for Fortean Zoology and accompanied me on my 2004 expedition to Puerto Rico in search of the legendary chupacabra, a story I told in my 2015 book *Chupacabra Road Trip*. Downes described, in his 2008 book *Island of Paradise*, how in 1996 an old girlfriend of his had shown him a very interesting piece of film footage of unidentified paw prints found a year or two earlier in a certain area of muddy ground in Rendlesham Forest. They closely resembled the prints of a cat, but of what variety no one could say. What could be said, however, is that they were far bigger than the kinds of prints that would be left by even the largest lion, tiger, or leopard. Of course, there is nothing roaming the wilds of the United Kingdom of such a size. Or, at least, there shouldn't be any such beast on the loose. There have been multiple encounters in Rendlesham Forest with what have become known as alien big cats, or

ABCs. But not even they can boast of being the size of the animal that left the prints studied by Jonathan Downes.

Moving on, we have the saga of "Tom Potter," a local man who was witness to a large monkey-like animal seen in Woodbridge in the early hours of a 1987 morning. I met Potter in December 2000 in the heart of Rendlesham Forest, during a twentieth-anniversary party to celebrate the 1980 UFO landing. As Potter drove to work at around 4:30 a.m. and passed the fringes of Rendlesham Forest, he caught sight of a creature that was not dissimilar to a chimpanzee. In fact, that is exactly what he thought the creature was, and he slowed his vehicle to a near-halt and watched it amble along the road at a leisurely pace. Suddenly, however, it stopped and turned to look at Potter, whose vehicle was moving at a speed of barely a couple of miles per hour. According to Potter, the "chimpanzee" dropped onto its four limbs, was briefly lit up by a white light, and took on the form of a sleek and shiny black cat. It then bolted into a nearby field and was not seen again.

The idea that Rendlesham Forest could be home to numerous unknown animals—such as Sam Holland's ten-foot-long beast, Tom Potter's "chimp-cat," and Peggy Cushing's nightmarish gargoyle—is absurd. In all likelihood, particularly when one takes into consideration the testimony of Cushing and Potter, we are dealing with a creature that is not limited to one physical form. A supernatural chimera, one might justifiably suggest.

An intriguing and thought-provoking afterword: with multiple animal forms seen roaming around Rendlesham Forest for decades, what does all of the above say about the famous UFO encounter of late December 1980? While it is not impossible that extraterrestrials from a faraway star system may have touched down in the woods all those years ago, the more logical answer to the riddle is that the UFO events were *also* the result of shape-shifting, but on this occasion the phenomenon chose to take on the form of E.T. Which begs an even more thought-provoking question: *What form will the shape-shifting intelligence of Rendlesham Forest turn into next?*

Sources:

Redfern, Nick. *The Rendlesham Forest UFO Conspiracy: A Close Encounter Exposed as a Top Secret Government Experiment*. Lisa Hagan Books, 2020.

Valhalla's Great Wolves, Geri and Freki

Valhalla (in Old Norse, "hall of the slain") is the name of Odin's stately home in Asgard where the father of the gods gathers the spirits of all the brave warriors who have fallen in battle. Although there are 540 gates to Valhalla, the gate through which the Vikings pass is called Valgrind, and it is guarded by a great wolf and watched by an eagle soaring above. Valkyries escort the einherjar (slain warriors) through Valgrind and seat them at the great banquet table set before Odin. Once the drinking horns have been filled with mead, the Valkyries serve the heroes meat from a boar, tasty flesh that constantly renews itself. In Valhalla, there will always be plenty of meat, mead, and wine in a feast of celebration that continues unabated.

At Odin's side are the great wolves, Geri and Freki, eating only from their master's hand and surveying steadily the warrior spirits arrayed

At Odin's side in Valhalla are the great wolves, Geri and Freki, eating only from their master's hand.

before them. During the day, the einherjar fight among themselves, choosing sides, battling fiercely, perfecting their warrior prowess. At sunset, those who were killed in the intramural battles come alive again, and all return to Odin's banquet hall for more eating and drinking. Valhalla is truly a warrior's dream of a perfect paradise.

Sources:

Simek, Rudolf. *Dictionary of Northern Mythology.* Translated by Angela Hall. Rochester, NY: Boydell & Brewer, 1993.

Vincennes, Indiana
by Tim R. Swartz

In the early eighteenth century, French fur traders making their way south from Canada settled in what is now southwestern Indiana. The area was rich with game such as beaver and buffalo, and even after the French lost their claim on the territory following the French and Indian War (1754–63), the settlers remained and founded the town of Vincennes.

The loup-garou, or Rougarou (as seen here in an Audubon Zoo exhibit in New Orleans) haunted the dreams of early French settlers. The shapeshifter could appear as a monstrous wolf, but it could also be someone who transformed into a cow, horse, or any other animal.

Because of its early French heritage, which is robust with supernatural-based folklore, Vincennes, Indiana, has become a focal point for mysterious creatures straight from the shadowy corners of the human mind. For the eighteenth-century settler, the dark, endless forest that surrounded Vincennes was filled with all manner of unknown dangers. But it was threats of the supernatural that produced the most terror, and the most horrifying of these paranormal nightmares was the loup-garou.

The loup-garou, also known as the Rougarou, haunted the dreams of early French settlers. It could appear as a monstrous wolf, but it could also be someone who transformed into a cow, horse, or any other animal. Once under a spell as a loup-garou, the unfortunate victim became an enraged animal that roamed each night through the fields and forests for a certain period of time, usually 101 days. During the day, he returned to his human form, though he was continually morose and sickly and fearful to tell of his predicament lest even a worse sentence should befall him.

According to some legends, a person could become a loup-garou by breaking Lent seven years in a row. As well, the cursed shape-shifter was especially fond of hunting down and killing Catholics who did not follow the rules of Lent. The main way the loup-garou could be released from its spell was for someone to recognize him as a cursed creature of the night and injure him to the point of drawing blood. Only this would effectively remove the curse. However, both the victim and his rescuer could not mention the incident, even to each other. Anyone who defied this taboo could find themselves possessed and transformed into the loup-garou.

One could also be possessed by the spirit of a loup-garou if they were unfortunate enough to encounter a Feu Follet in the forest. A Feu Follet, also known as a will-o'-the-wisp, was a bright ball of light that would be seen flying and hopping around trees and brush. It was thought that the Feu Follet could bewitch both man and horse to lead them off the trail and into the dark forest.

By the beginning of the twentieth century, memories of the loup-garou were fading with each passing generation. Fortunately, many of these folktales were recorded in the 1920s by Anna C. O'Flynn, a teacher in the old French section of Vincennes. As well, in the 1930s a group of writers with the Federal Writers' Project of the Works Progress Administration also managed to record some of the old tales from a handful of Vincennes' French descendants. These people, who at this point were in their seventies and eighties, clearly remembered the stories of the loup-garou told to them on dark nights in front of the flickering fire of the family hearth.

One story, as recalled by Pepe Boucher, involved a man named Charlie Page who one night, as he was going home, encountered a large black dog with gleaming red eyes. Page, a large man who feared nothing, at first tried to shoo the dog away. When the dog refused to move, Page attempted to kick it in its face. However, the dog, with a stealthy, panther-like movement, sprang at his throat and knocked him to the ground. Boucher recalled:

You bet this time he tried to kick and get his knife to finish the dog whose hot breath was singeing his hair—whose great paws were tearing his shoulders and whose fangs were near his neck. With one of his powerful arms he [grabbed] the neck of the dog until his tongue [hanged] out. The shaggy hair on the dog's neck be lashing his face and his eyes blazing with madness. The loup-garou be trying to bewitch Page. He know now it be loup-garou. He know that nothing but blood could save him. Struggling to use his knife the beast pushed the point against Page to make him draw his own blood. Now had Page not been almost a giant he would have turned right into a loup-garou.

Throwing his whole strength into the struggle, Page managed to push his knife through the shaggy fur, deep behind the forelegs of the savage creature. As its blood spurted from its wound, the loup-garou vanished in a flash of light and flames, and in its place stood Page's best friend, Jean Vetal.

"They look and look at each other," Boucher said. "*Mais* they spoke no word. Soon they part, each going to his own home. The knife had cut Jean Vetal's arm near the elbow, he doctor it and soon it be well, and then he be delivered from the loup-garou power."

According to tradition, for 101 days Page and Vetal never spoke of the horrible animal. After the 101 days had passed, the two men were free to tell their friends what had happened.

Boucher told the researchers that Jean Vetal gave Page a horse and a cow in gratitude from being freed of his curse.

The Loup-Garou Cow

Another tale, again as recalled by Pepe Boucher, shows that the traditional loup-garou was not always a wolf or dog. Around 1780, shortly after General George R. Clark and his troops took Fort Sackville from the British, Vincennes saw an increase in American settlers coming from the east in search of homesteads. The Americans had no time for tales of ghosts, Witches, and loup-garous and openly mocked the French and their superstitions.

Soon, however, one of the new American settlers, a man who had been especially scornful of the French and their belief in the loup-garou, started disappearing from his home every night. When questioned by his friends, he claimed that he had lost his cow and was simply out trying to find it.

This story sounded suspicious to Jean Vetal, who, remembering his own misery as a cursed loup-garou years before, was certain that supernatural forces were at work. Feeling that God had presented Vetal this opportunity to further cleanse his accursed soul, he secured a large, sharp knife and went out into the night in search of the possessed American.

The traditional loup-garou was not always a wolf or dog but could manifest even as a cow.

After searching most of the night, Vetal heard the moan of a cow. Gathering up his courage, Vetal crept softly to the spot where the moaning came. There, lying in a clearing, was a cow, moaning like a person in great pain.

Vetal was convinced that this cow was the missing American, now a loup-garou. The unearthly moaning made Vetal tremble in fear as he reached out with his knife to draw blood and deliver the cursed man. Unfortunately, before Vetal could plant his knife, the cow jumped up, swung her head, and knocked the man onto the ground.

For over a mile the loup-garou ran, with Vetal chasing close behind. Finally he was able to get close enough to stick his knife deep enough into the cow's shoulder to draw blood.

"Oh! Oh!" Boucher said. "The blood spout out and the cow tumble down as Vetal tumble over on the grass in the common right by the side of the American what always make fun on the French loup-garou."

As the two men walked back to town, the American begged Vetal not to tell anyone until he had died or moved away. Shortly afterward, he moved back east and was never heard from again.

Boucher concluded his story with: "When the American be gone Vetal tell, *mais* some not believe, *pourquei. Et quelquesunes ne pas eroire!*" ("It is so whether you believe it or not!")

Curses of the Cauchemars

In Old Vincennes, shape-shifters did not necessarily have to be loup-ga-rous. According to an article published in the January 8, 1891, issue of the *Vincennes Commercial* newspaper, there were also Witches around to cast evil spells upon the early settlers of Vincennes.

It was believed that Witches—called *cauchemars* (nightmares)—could turn men into horses so that they could ride them along the Wabash River Bottoms. In the morning, when the French woke up feeling all worn out and "hag-ridden," they would say, "*C'est mon cauchemar!*" ("It is my nightmare!")

One old man claimed that this had happened to him. The next day he said he could see where he had stood and pawed the earth, at the place where the Witch had dismounted and tied him. And there were marks on the fence rail where he had gnawed as an impatient horse. Even the day after, he still was picking some pieces of wood out of his teeth, the bewitched man said.

It was also believed that Witches could shape-shift themselves into anything that they desired, and in that shape they would torment their neighbors.

At length he made a silver bullet, loaded his gun, and went to a deer-lick. There he killed the Witch that had taken the form of a deer.

One old French farmer said that for years he had experienced nothing but bad luck because of an old hag that had been persecuting him. At length he made a silver bullet, loaded his gun, and went to a deer-lick. There he killed the Witch that had taken the form of a deer. After that his luck turned around, and he was never bothered again.

Nowadays the vast, wild forests that once surrounded Vincennes have been cut down to make way for shopping malls, housing developments, and highways. In the harsh light of modern society, the old superstitions of the early French settlers have been all but forgotten. Nevertheless, the shape-shifters, Witches, and other monsters of times past remain, quietly waiting for their chance to live once again in the nightmares of those foolish enough to travel alone into the dark, forbidding night.

The Volsunga Saga

The Volsunga Saga (c. 1300) tells the story of the Norse king Volsung who had ten sons and one daughter, Signy, who was married to King Siggeir. Siggeir later proved to be a most untrustworthy son-in-law when he murdered Volsung and placed his ten sons in the stocks. Then, to add to the horror, Siggeir allowed his mother, a werewolf, to eat his brothers-in-law. However, Signy, his wife, the daughter of Volsung, was not without magical powers of her own, and she managed to arrive in time to save Sigmund, the tenth son, from being devoured by the voracious she-wolf. Sharing her Witchcraft with her brother, Signy enabled Sigmund to slay the werewolf who consumed the other nine siblings.

Later, after Sigmund went into hiding to escape the revenge of Siggeir, Signy exchanged physical form with a sorceress and had a son, Sinfiotli, by Sigmund. Sigmund and his son, who were outlaws in the eyes of the populace that remained under Siggeir's influence, assumed the wandering life. On one of their journeys, they came upon a hut in the forest where wolf skins hung above two sleeping men. In the Norse tradition, the transformation into werewolf is accomplished by donning the *ulf-har* (lit-

An illustration by Arthur Rackham depicts Sigmund holding aloft his sword Nothung.

erally, "wolf's hair"), a belt of wolf's leather, representing the *ulfhamr*, the wolf's skin. Since Sigmund and Sinfiotli had been following the werewolves, they knew that when the men donned the *ulfhamr*, they would be werewolves for nine days and men on the tenth.

Sigmund and Sinfiotli put on the wolf skins and found that they were unable to remove them. Since they were now werewolves, they made a solemn pact between them to abide by certain rules when they fought other men: They would speak only in the wolf-language that they both understood. While each should be prepared to take on as many as seven men at once, that number should be the limit. If one or the other was ever outnumbered, he must call out for the other's help in wolf-language only.

Later, when Sigmund learned that his son had slain 11 men without howling for his help, he angrily struck Sinfiotli for breaking the vow and wounded him. Dismayed at what he had done and what they had both become, Sigmund stayed with his son until he was healed and until the cycle was fulfilled when they could remove the wolf skins. They agreed to lay them aside forever and burn them in the fire.

Sources:

Davidson, Ellis H. R. *Gods and Myths of the Viking Age.* New York: Barnes & Noble, 1996.

Simek, Rudolf. *Dictionary of Northern Mythology.* Translated by Angela Hall. Rochester, NY: Boydell & Brewer, 1993.

Wales Tales

On April 29, 2009, the U.K. newspaper the *Daily Mail* published an article with the intriguing title: "Police Launch Hunt for 'Wolfman' behind Mini Crimewave Who Lives on Rabbits and Berries in Woods." The *Mail's* article begins by setting the scene:

> He ekes out a solitary existence deep in the woods, surviving by snaring rabbits and foraging for berries. … The one man mini-crimewave is also suspected of a string of thefts of shopping from parked cars and clothes from washing lines during his furtive forays into the civilised world over the last two years.

> Police have tried to catch him during searches on foot and have even sent up a helicopter with heat-seeking equipment to track him down, but he has so far always managed to avoid capture. He knows the miles of paths

through the dense woodland near Ammanford, South Wales, where he lurks, so well that even when officers are on his trail, he manages to give them the slip. Abandoned hideouts made from board with plastic roofs have been found, suggesting he moves around to avoid arrest."

He became known, locally and infamously, as the Wolfman.

In the tiny hamlet of Pantyffynnon, which was one of the mystery-man's favorite hunting grounds, outraged and worried locals planned on taking steps to seek out the strange and elusive man of the woods. Planning a course of attack that included vigilante parties, the people of Pantyffynnon were very nearly baying for the wild man's blood. One villager said, ominously, "We want him caught before something serious happens."

For their part, the local police vowed to apprehend the man "sooner or later"—a decidedly open-ended statement that hardly satisfied many—and loudly appealed to locals not to start scouring the woods themselves. As evidence of this, one Sergeant Charles Gabe sternly warned any would-be heroes "not to take the law into their own hands or approach this man."

Sergeant Gabe added: "We've found one or two hides where we believe he has been sleeping. We think he catches rabbits and eats berries or whatever else he can get his hands on. But although we've had the police helicopter overhead using heat-seeking equipment we've still been unable to locate him. This is a massive thickly-wooded area—and one he obviously knows well. On one occasion a couple of our guys came close to nabbing him but he scarpered back into the woods. But we are sure he will be caught sooner or later."

"The area where he is living is thickly-wooded and forested — the sort of area where it is easy to disappear."

When questioned for comment, local councilor Hugh Evans said: "It's a very strange case and no one seems to know who he is. But he must be a bit of a *Rambo* type and pretty tough to have survived the bitterly cold winter living out in the open. The area where he is living is thickly-wooded and forested—the sort of area where it is easy to disappear." Evoking surreal imagery of some *Stig of the Dump*-type character, the *Daily Mail* added: "The 'Wolfman' lives in the woodland on an area of reclaimed coal slagheaps known locally as 'The Tips.'"

Meanwhile, a Dyfed-Powys police spokesman tactfully said, in typically bureaucratic terminology that was suggestive of far more than they were willing to impart at the time: "We want to question him over several alleged incidents." For a while the wild man and his equally wild antics vanished—perhaps into the underground lair that many believed had become his home. He wasn't destined to stay buried for too long, however. In the latter part of 2010, the mystery man resurfaced from the heart of those dark woods: "The hunt for a West Wales 'wolfman' is back on—after walkers stumbled across what is thought to be his lair," noted *Wales Online* on October 10, 2010.

The "unknown vagrant," it was reported, was up to his old tricks, leading to the revelation that "officers from the Dyfed-Powys force this week confirmed they are looking into possible fresh sightings after walkers reported stumbling across a woodland shack stuffed with food, clothes and electrical equipment."

One of those who was willing to speak publicly on the return of the wild man was John Jones, a builder from Pantyffynnon, who told *Wales Online*: "We've been told that some walkers found a tin shed full of food and clothes, so we assume that is one of his hideouts. Lots of people have been looking for where he is, but the woodland is so dense it's not an easy place to search. There have been one or two sightings of this long-haired, bearded person who is so scruffy and unkempt; *he's like a wild man.*"

There was also talk of milk being stolen, of food taken from freezers in outside storage areas in the dead of night, and of what were intriguingly, but briefly, described as "odd sightings." But was the wild man simply some eccentric, solitary soul that had decided to leave the restrictive boundaries and conventions of society far behind him? Not everyone was quite so sure that's all he was.

A local official said that Wales' elusive Wolfman "must be a bit of a Rambo type and pretty tough to have survived the bitterly cold winter living out in the open."

Gwilym Games, a regional representative for Wales of Jon Downes's Centre for Fortean Zoology, noted correctly, "There is a long history of werewolves in Wales and even an earlier mention in the Amman valley."

Despite this undeniably intriguing aside, nothing else surfaced on this aspect of the mysterious matter, and once again the wild man vanished into obscurity, likely into the heart of the thick woods that dominate the area. As usual, the police continued on their plodding path of "making enquiries." They proved to be utterly fruitless. But there was one further development in the story.

One week after the *Wales Online* article surfaced, a Pantyffynnon solicitor named Peter Rhys Jones said that the wild man was harmless, nothing stranger than an ex-serviceman whom Jones had once represented. Then in 2012, there was a dramatic development in the story that confirmed what Jones had to say about the man's military background. In February of that year, it was revealed that the man living wild was one Wayne John Morgan, aged 37, formerly of the British army and someone well trained to survive in the harsh and unforgiving wilds of the Welsh outdoors.

A Pantyffynnon solicitor named Peter Rhys Jones said that the wild man was harmless, nothing stranger than an ex-serviceman whom Jones had once represented.

A police spokeswoman said: "He has not been seen by his family for four years, but now concerns have been raised about his welfare." She added: "As he is living rough, he may be hungry and on the look-out for food. If you are suspicious that any food items are missing from your stores, or whether any outbuildings such as garden sheds and garages have been disturbed, then please contact us."

Mike Lewis, editor of the *South Wales Guardian*, stated of the latest news on the affair: "One magazine specialising in the paranormal even sent a reporter to assess whether this was a real-life werewolf. ... But strip away the legend and what's left? A missing man, a police appeal and a worried family anxious for news. The *Guardian* has covered some strange stories during my five years at the helm, but the one about 'The Wolfman' of Pantyffynnon tips must rank among the strangest."

By May, with still no news—despite renewed and fairly widespread media publicity—things were looking bleak. The local press highlighted the opinion of people in the area that there was "no chance" Morgan was still hiding out in the woods—citing the recent bitterly cold weather as one reason—while his obviously very anxious family prayed and hoped for good news. At the time of writing, unfortunately, that is where matters stand in this sad affair. While the matter turned out to have been driven by nothing more than a poor man living in the wild—rather than by a real werewolf—the fact that the U.K.'s media chose to use terms like "werewolf" and "wolfman" demonstrates just how powerful the word "werewolf" can be.

Sources:

Beer, Trevor. *Mystery Animals of Britain and Ireland*. Robert Hale, 1987.

Cooper, Rob. "Where Is the Wolfman? Hunt for Wild Man Who Has Been Hiding in a Welsh Forest for Five Years." *Daily Mail*, February 10, 2012. https://www.dailymail.co.uk/news/article-2098634/Wolfman-woods-centre-police-hunt-goes-missing-years-living-like-Rambo.html.

"Face of the 'Wolfman' of Pantyffynnon Tips." *South Wales Guardian*, February 7, 2012. https://www.southwalesguardian.co.uk/news/9516464.face-of-the-wolfman-of-pantyffynnon-tips/.

Misstear, Rachel. "Wolfman's 'Lair' Discovered." *Wales Online*, October 10, 2010. https://www.walesonline.co.uk/news/wales-news/wolfmans-lair-discovered-1890450.

Wilkes, David. "Police Launch Hunt for 'Wolfman' behind Mini Crimewave Who Lives on Rabbits and Berries in Woods." *Daily Mail*, April 29, 2009. https://www.dailymail.co.uk/news/article-1175075/Police-launch-hunt-Wolfman-mini-crimewave-lives-rabbits-berries-woods.html.

Warfare and Werewolves

In May 2007, I penned an article for my blog *There's Something in the Woods* titled "Do Werewolves Roam the Woods of England?" It was a feature prompted by the fact that in that same year, numerous sightings of a werewolf-type beast were reported in the heart of the Cannock Chase, a large area of forest and heath in the English county of Staffordshire. Of note, all the encounters on the Chase occurred within the confines of an old cemetery housing the remains of German soldiers and airmen who died in prisoner of war camps on British soil during World War I and World War II. Six years on, it remains the most popular post at my blog and prompted one commenter to the article, using the title of Wes, to state that he had encountered a werewolf at a weapons storage area at a British military base—Royal Air Force Alconbury, situated in the county of Cambridgeshire—in the 1970s. The beast, said Wes, had a flat snout, very big eyes, a height of around five feet, and a weight in the order of 200 pounds. It retreated into the surrounding woods.

Moving on, in January 2010, I spoke at a New York conference called *Ghosts of Cooperstown*, which was organized by the stars of the SyFy Channel's *Ghost Hunters* series. It was on the Saturday night of the event that an American soldier, who had recently returned from serving with the military in the Middle East, revealed to an audience in the hotel bar that he had heard tales of large, marauding werewolves roaming by night the mountains of Afghanistan and some of the more ancient parts of Iraq.

The U.S. Army secretly knew that the beasts were out there, he said, but didn't know how to handle the situation. They even lacked any real understanding of what the creatures were or from where, exactly,

Numerous sightings of a werewolf-type beast have been reported in Cannock Chase, Staffordshire, with all the encounters occurring within the confines of an old cemetery housing the remains of German soldiers from the First and Second World Wars.

they came. And so the military simply chose to take the easiest of all approaches available to them: they outright ignored the reports or wrote them off as the equivalent of campfire tales told to kids on Halloween.

I asked the man if there were any way I could get his data validated. He replied in the negative but stressed it was true, all the same. His story might well have been the barest bones of what sounds like a much bigger and far more significant saga, and it is made all the more intriguing by the fact that similar stories reached the eyes and ears of the late author and researcher Linda Godfrey (1951–2022), who was without doubt the United States' leading authority on all things of a werewolf nature.

The U.S. Army secretly knew that the beasts were out there, he said, but didn't know how to handle the situation.

One of the most intriguing things that Linda Godfrey learned in her more than 20 years of research into werewolf phenomena in the United States is that, just as appears to be the case in the U.K., Iraq, and Afghanistan, the beasts seem to be unfathomably attracted to locations known for being home to highly active military installations.

Of the various reports that Linda uncovered, one concerns the Fort Custer Recreation Area in Michigan, which amounts to around 3,000 acres of recreation land that fell into the hands of the U.S. government back in 1917 and, as Camp Custer, was utilized as a training center for army inductees. Late one night in 2000, the area had what was quite possibly its strangest visitor of all: a large, fox-like animal that had the ability to run on both two legs and four.

There is more: just like the werewolf-infested cemetery on England's Cannock Chase that is home to the remains of hundreds of German military personnel from long-gone wars, so the old camp in Michigan once housed more than 500 Nazi troops during the hostilities of World War II, 26 of whom died on site and were subsequently buried there. I freely admit I am utterly baffled as to why there should even be a connection between werewolves, military installations, and wartime conflict at all. If anyone has any ideas, let me know!

Sources:

Redfern. Nick. "Wolfmen and Warfare." February 8, 2013. https://mysteriousuniverse. org/2013/02/wolfmen-and-warfare/.

Warren, Ed (1926–2006) and Lorraine (1927–2019)

North America's best known lay demonologist was Ed Warren of Monroe, Connecticut, who, with his talented clairvoyant wife, Lorraine, directed the New England Society for Psychic Research beginning in 1952. They investigated over 4,000 hauntings, as well as cases of real-life werewolves and vampires, such as the astonishing account of the possession that transformed Bill Ramsey into a real "Werewolf of London." The Warrens were the psychical investigators in the famous Amityville Horror haunting, and their book *The Haunted*, about a Pennsylvania family under diabolical attack, was made into a television movie by Fox in 1991.

Ed said that he grew up in a haunted house from the time he was five until he was 12. His father, a police officer, kept insisting that there was a logical reason for the phenomena they experienced, but Ed noted that the elder Warren never quite came up with the logical explanation.

Ed and Lorraine met when they were both 16 and he was an usher at a movie theater in Bridgeport. Ed enlisted in the Navy on his seventeenth birthday. Four months later, after his ship sank in the North Atlantic and he was home for a 30-day survivor's leave, Ed and Lorraine were married. After World War II ended, Ed supported his wife and baby girl by selling his paintings to tourists who visited the New England area. Strangely enough, it was through his paintings and sketches that the Warrens began their psychical research. Whenever he heard of a haunting, they would travel to the location, and he would sketch it. When the homeowners saw his painting of their home, they would invite the young couple inside to investigate the ghostly manifestations. Soon Lorraine would be picking up highly accurate clairvisual and clairaudient impressions of the entities.

When the New England Society for Psychic Research was established in 1952, its initial goal was to investigate reports of haunting phenomena.

Ed and Lorraine Warren, directors of the New England Society for Psychic Research, investigated over 4,000 hauntings, as well as the possession that transformed Bill Ramsey into a real "Werewolf of London" and the famous Amityville Horror haunting.

As their reputation grew, Ed and Lorraine would sometimes research an alleged haunted house with as many as four clairvoyants, a number of physical scientists with state-of-the-art equipment, and an ecumenical assortment of clergy. Some critics have called Ed an eccentric because he believed in devils and demons. He admitted that he had no doubts about the reality of negative entities: "I learned about them as a child, and as a man I have proved beyond a shadow of a doubt that they exist. If you don't want to call them devils and demons, just call them evil, I don't care. Religions are man-made, but spirituality isn't."

The Occult Museum was a special project of the Warrens for many years. Tours are available by appointment, and serious visitors are allowed to study the vast collection of artifacts, books, pictures, masks, and idols they collected during their five decades of investigation into the unexplained. Ed did not recommend, however, that anyone touch the objects they have assembled in the museum. "Some are so dangerous that just in touching them you could be very badly affected. They are the opposite of what you would touch in a church where the statues, the crosses, and the holy relics have been blessed. The things in the museum were used in Witchcraft, black magic, sorcery, and curses."

Sources:

The New England Society for Psychic Research, P.O. Box 41, Monroe, CT 06468. https://tonyspera.com/.

Warrington Man-Beast

Witches, their legendary familiars, and their eerie ability to disguise themselves as a variety of animals cannot be overlooked in a discussion of shape-shifters. Indeed, they are an integral part of the overall phenomenon.

Warrington is a picturesque town located in the north of England, dominated by the expansive River Mersey. Its origins date back millennia to the Roman invasion of England, which began in 43 CE. Like so many old English towns and villages, Warrington has its very own saga of the supernatural kind attached to it. It is a story that goes back to the 1600s and revolves around the malignant machinations of an evil local crone. She was known by the people of the area as Old Peggy Gronach and was described as being "evil, ugly and haggard." The tale is a strange one. It was carefully and independently investigated and chronicled by two English researchers of the paranormal, Neil Arnold and Wally Barnes, the former in an article titled "The Warrington Man-Beast!" and the latter in a 1990 book called *Ghosts, Mysteries and Legends of Old Warrington*.

So the old tale goes, much-feared Peggy had for years managed to successfully stay one step ahead of the many Witch-hunting gangs that roamed the countryside and were determined to see all of England's Witches roasted to death on flaming bonfires. Whether due to good luck or the effects of some dark and disturbing incantation, Peggy was clearly not meant to have a fiery end. She successfully went from hamlet to hamlet, from town to town, and carefully ensured that she never stayed in one place for too long. That included Warrington, which she chose to call her home after skillfully eluding hunters from the eastern England city of Norwich. Although the Witch-hunters failed to catch up with Peggy, her reputation most assuredly preceded her—to the effect that when word got out about who she was, a chilled and ominous atmosphere would descend upon her chosen town.

Because it took weeks or even months at that time for news to travel the length and the breadth of the country, Peggy knew that she was safe from the hunters at least for a while. As a result, she quickly put down roots at what became known locally as Peggy Gronach's Chicken Farm. It was a ruined, spooky old building that no one wished to visit. Not even the local, and usually adventurous, children of the town—at least at first.

It was a hair-covered humanoid that sported blazing red eyes and two huge horns on top of its large, bulbous head.

The day came, however, when that spirit of youthful excitement got the better of a group of young kids, who decided to check out the old farm for themselves. It was something that one and all quickly and bitterly came to regret. As they stealthily crept through the wild, tall grass that surrounded an old and battered cottage that stood next to the farm, a terrible and fierce face appeared at one of the windows. The children were momentarily frozen by the sight of a creature that, with a degree of hindsight, sounds like some unholy combination of a Bigfoot and a demon: it was a hair-covered humanoid that sported blazing red eyes and two huge horns on top of its large, bulbous head. Suddenly, the slavering monster was gone, and old Peggy came screaming through the front door, running wildly in the direction of the hysterical children.

When the kids told their parents of the terrible thing they had just encountered, in no time at all rumors got around that the horned, hairy thing and Peggy Gronach were one and the same—a Witch that understood, and employed, the mysterious secrets of shape-shifting. Others believed that the beast was Gronach's familiar—a familiar being a supernatural entity, such as an imp or a demon, that could take on the form of numerous animals, such as cats, toads, and rats, and monstrous things. No one dared go anywhere near the old farm lest they became a victim of Peggy or her familiar.

Thankfully, things quieted down for a couple of weeks. Eventually, however, a local man, pulling his horse and cart, was attacked by what sounded very much like the same, hideous beast. Luckily, no harm came to man or horse, and both managed to flee the area, never looking back—an incident not unlike the one that occurred at Bridge 39 on England's Shropshire Union Canal in January 1879. Only days later, there was yet another supernatural assault. On this occasion, the outcome was very different: a local farmer found one of his cows savagely mutilated and killed by violent decapitation.

Enough was enough. A band of locals—no doubt waving flaming torches and provoking, for us, imagery of those old black-and-white *Frankenstein* movies of the 1930s and 1940s—headed off to the farm. It was time to bring Peggy Gronach's reign of terror to an irreversible halt. Perhaps anticipating that she had outstayed her welcome, Peggy was nowhere in sight. The only tell-tale sign of her dark presence was the bloodied, half-eaten body of a dead goat.

Although that was the end of the story and the old hag was never seen again, years later rumors swirled around Warrington to the effect that the skeleton of a strange creature had been found semi-buried in a nearby field. It was said to have had the body of a large, four-legged animal and the skull of a human. Could it have been old, wizened Peggy struck down halfway through a terrible transformation from woman to monster? That's exactly what many of the townsfolk of Warrington thought. And who knows? Maybe they were right on the money.

Should you ever find yourself in Warrington and you stumble across an old farm, it may be wise to return the way you came. Peggy the crone, in beastly form, may still haunt the neighborhood.

Sources:

Arnold, Neil. "The Warrington Man-Beast!" Sept. 22, 2011. http://forteanzoology. blogspot.com/2011/09/neil-arnold-warrington-man-beast.html.

Barnes, Wally. *Ghosts, Mysteries and Legends of Old Warrington* Owl Books, 1990.

Werecats

Throughout history, folklore, and mythology, one can find accounts of shape-shifting creatures. The most famous example is surely the werewolf. The deadly monster of the full moon is far from being alone, however. In Africa, there are legends of were-hyenas. Wererats have been reported in Oregon. Cynanthropy is a condition in which a person believes they can shape-shift into the form of a dog. And then there are werecats.

Tales of werecats exist in numerous locations: South America, Asia, Africa, and Europe. Sometimes the werecats are nothing less than transformed humans. Leopards, lions, tigers, and jaguars are typically the werecat forms into which a human shape-shifter mutates. Others are regular cats, altered by dark magic into something hostile and terrible. And there are numerous tales of the werecats of Britain.

The earliest case I have on file dates from August 1953. The location: Abbots Bromley, a village in the English county of Staffordshire, the origins of which date back to at least 942 CE. The witness was a now-deceased man, Brian Kennerly. In 2002, Kennerly's family told me of how he often spoke of the occasion when, as he walked through Abbots Bromley on a warm summer's night, he was confronted by a large black cat—one that he described as the typical "black panther."

Are infernal werecats really roaming the British Isles? Witnesses are adamant that they encountered large, black, upright cats that displayed vaguely human characteristics.

Not surprisingly, Kennerly was frozen in his tracks. His amazement turned to outright fear when the beast suddenly rose onto its back limbs, giving it a height of around five and a half feet. The creature reportedly issued a low growl and flicked its dangling front paws in Kennerly's direction. Notably, Kennerly's daughter told me her father said that as the beast rose up, "its back legs changed shape, probably to support it when it was standing upright." A few seconds later, the creature dropped back to the ground and bounded out of sight.

A similar report, this one from the centuries-old village of Blakeney, Norfolk, occurred in 1967. In this case, the witness, who was driving to Blakeney on a cold winter's night, caught a brief glimpse of a creature standing at the side of the road that was eerily similar to the one seen by Brian Kennerly 14 years previously. In this case, the woman said: "It stood like a person, but stooped, and had a cat's head. Even the pointed ears."

"It stood like a person, but stooped, and had a cat's head. Even the pointed ears."

The final two cases in my files are separated by seven years — 1981 and 1988 — but the location was the same: the German Military Cemetery located within the heavily wooded Cannock Chase, Staffordshire. The Chase has long been a hotbed for weirdness: Bigfoot-type creatures, werewolves, huge serpents, ghosts, UFOs, and much more of a supernatural nature have been reported in the depths of the Chase.

As for the two reports of werecat-type creatures seen at the cemetery, one was a daytime event involving a beast that was black in color, taller than the average man, and seen leaning on one of the gravestones — that is, until it realized it was being watched and dropped on all fours and raced off into the trees.

The second case concerned the driver of a van crossing the Chase late at night who was forced to bring his vehicle to a halt very near the cemetery as a result of the presence in the road of a huge black cat. The cat stared intently at the shocked driver until it "sort of jumped onto its back legs." According to the man, Don Allen, the creature remained in view for no more than about 20 seconds, after which it headed toward the cemetery, making a curious "hopping and bouncing" movement as it did so.

Are infernal werecats really roaming the British Isles? Granted, the number of reports is small. And yet, the witnesses — and in the case of Brian Kennerly, the family — are adamant that what they encountered were large, black, upright cats that displayed vaguely human characteristics. Perhaps the old myths and legends are not just folklore after all. Maybe the monstrous werecat really does roam the old landscapes of the British Isles.

Sources:

Redfern, Nick. *Mysterious Animals of the British Isles: Staffordshire.* Woolsery, U.K.: CFZ Press, 2013.

Werewolf Assassins

During the summer of 1989, something dark and disturbing descended upon the town of Newport, England: farm animals were found dead under mysterious circumstances. They were not the victims of attack by wild animals, however. Rather, they gave every indication of having been ritually slaughtered, even sacrificed. Indeed, they were, and the deadly attackers were nothing less than werewolves. One of those who was determined to get to the bottom of the grisly matter was a man named Rob Lea, on whose farm some of the killings occurred.

According to Lea, in August 1989 his father woke to a shocking sight: five sheep were lying dead in a field and placed in circular fashion. Even worse, the organs of the poor animals had been removed from the bodies and laid out in triangular patterns. Clearly, those responsible were human. But what kind of human would stealthily kill someone's sheep in the dead of night? And why? Those were the questions swirling around the minds of both Rob Lea and his father. In view of all the above, it's very easy to see why the Lea family concluded that a secret band of "devil worshippers" were the culprits. As it transpires, they were not far from the truth. Not only that, it was a cult of devil worshippers who had the power to summon supernatural werewolves.

> *Clearly, those responsible were human.*
> *But what kind of human would stealthily*
> *kill someone's sheep in the dead of night?*
> *And why?*

Rob Lea's father quickly telephoned the local police, who were soon on the scene and took the matter very seriously, suggesting that the family should not discuss the matter with anyone else, lest doing so might provoke deep concern—and maybe hysteria—across Newport and its immediate surroundings. The family, it transpires, was fine with that, as the last thing they wanted was the local media descending on the farm. Despite an intense investigation, the police found themselves with not even a single lead to go on. The outcome was that the matter was eventually dropped, amid apologies to the Lea family that, despite putting more than a few officers on the case, the authorities were at a loss to find the culprit.

That wasn't the end of the story, though: Rob Lea decided to briefly become what we might call an amateur detective. He was determined to find the guilty party or parties, and he may well have done exactly that. I was able to meet personally with Lea in 2000 and listened carefully to his controversial story. Within minutes of us meeting, from a large, padded envelope, Lea extracted seven 35mm color photographs, each six inches by four inches, that clearly and graphically showed the scene

Amateur investigator Rob Lea stumbled upon a sinister group of people who were using slaughtered animals in ancient rites and archaic rituals of a sacrificial nature, and whom Lea grandly dubbed the Cult of the Moon Beast.

of complete carnage at his family's farm 11 years earlier. In other words, if nothing else, that part of the story could at least be firmly validated. But this was merely the beginning.

He admitted to me that when he first began digging into the animal mutilation mystery, he was, for a short while at least, a firm adherent of the theory that deadly extraterrestrials might have been behind the predatory attacks. As time progressed, however, and as he delved ever deeper into the heart of the puzzle, he found that something much more disturbing than alien visitations seemed afoot.

By the late 1990s, said Lea, he had quietly and carefully traveled the length and breadth of the British Isles in diligent pursuit of answers and had inadvertently stumbled upon a sinister, and possibly deadly, group of people based near the English city of Bristol. Lea grandly dubbed them the Cult of the Moon Beast and asserted they were using slaughtered farm animals, and even household pets, in ancient rites and archaic rituals of a sacrificial nature. The purpose of the rites and rituals, said Lea, was to use the sacrificed unfortunates as a means of conjuring up monstrous entities from some vile netherworld that would then be dispatched to commit unknown atrocities on behalf of their masters in the Cult of the Moon Beast.

It transpired that Lea had been stealthily watching the activities of the Cult of the Moon Beast — which, he stressed several times, was merely a term that he alone had applied to this group of around 15 — for approximately seven years by the time we met. He admitted he had no firm idea of the group's real name or even if it had a designated moniker.

Although the cult was firmly based in the city of Bristol, said Lea, its members were spread both far and wide, with at least four hailing from the eastern coastal town of Ipswich; two from the Staffordshire town of Cannock; two from the city of Exeter; one from Tavistock, Devonshire; and five from Bromley, in the county of Kent.

Lea related to me how he had clandestinely and doggedly tracked the movements of the group and had stealthily viewed three of their dark practices, one of which had occurred in early 2000 near the Ingestre Park Golf Club. This was deep in the heart of the Cannock

Chase woods in Staffordshire, which had been the site of numerous encounters with a veritable menagerie of mysterious beasts, including werewolves, Bigfoot-type entities, ghostly black dogs, and huge marauding cats.

> *The Cult of the Moon Beast was engaged in occult rites designed to summon unholy beasts that originated within a realm or dimension that coexisted with ours.*

According to Lea, the Cult of the Moon Beast was engaged in occult rites designed to summon unholy beasts that originated within a realm or dimension that coexisted with ours. He added that certain locales across the country—and, indeed, around the globe—allowed for a doorway or portal to be opened if one followed the correct, ancient rites, rituals, and "rules of animal sacrifice," of which the Cult of the Moon Beast seemingly had a deep and profound knowledge and awareness. Numerous such portals existed in Devon, Cornwall, and Staffordshire, Lea assured me earnestly.

Lea told me that the beasts in question were not physical, flesh-and-blood-style beings—at least, not in the way that we mortals understand things. Rather, they were a form of nonphysical intelligence that could take on the appearance of whatever was in the mind's eye of the beholder—more often than not, that of a large werewolf.

But why? According to Lea: "Mind-power: fright, suggestion. They'll stop your heart in a beat with fear. You want someone dead, you kill them through fear: fear of the unknown, fear of anything. That's much better than risking taking someone out with a gun or a knife; there's less of a chance of getting caught."

Lea added that the Cult of the Moon Beast was linked with some very influential people and that, when needed, the cult was "hired for its services"—and paid very handsomely—by the highest echelons of private industry and even by the intelligence services of the British government. As he explained it to me: "You want someone dead, then you give them a heart attack by having a monster appearing in their bedroom at night. Or you drive them to suicide by making them think they are going mad if they are seeing werewolves."

An ancient cult, working and killing in stealth? Death by conjured-up werewolves? A conspiracy that reaches the heart of the British government? Yes, so Rob Lea has claimed.

Sources:

Redfern, Nick. Story told to Nick by Robert Lea, 2000.

Werewolf at RAF Alconbury

About the Royal Air Force Alconbury, Wikipedia notes: "Royal Air Force Alconbury or more simply RAF Alconbury is an active Royal Air Force station in Huntingdon, England. The airfield is in the civil parish of The Stukeleys, close to the villages of Great Stukeley, Little Stukeley, and Alconbury. … Opened in 1938 for use by RAF Bomber Command, the station has been used from 1942 by the United States Army Air Force and then the United States Air Force." Thus is established the ordinary background for matters of high strangeness.

The wooded perimeter of RAF Alconbury may be home to a moderately hairy werewolf-like creature with a flat snout and large eyes.

In 2007, in response to an article I wrote on werewolves, a man named Wes shared with me the details of his very own sighting, 37 years earlier, of an upright wolflike animal. Wes said: "I encountered a werewolf (for lack of better description) in England in 1970, I was 20 yrs. old when I was stationed at RAF Alconbury. I was in a secure weapons storage area when I encountered it. It seemed shocked and surprised to have been caught off guard and I froze in total fright. I was armed with a .38 and never once considered using it. There was no aggression on its part."

Wes continued: "I could not comprehend what I was seeing. It is not human. It has a flat snout and large eyes. Its height is approx. 5 ft. and weight approx. 200 lbs. It is very muscular and thin. It wore no clothing and was only moderately hairy. It ran away on its hind legs and scurried over a chain link fence and ran deep into the dense wooded area adjacent to the base.

"I was extremely frightened but the fear developed into a total commitment of trying to contact it again. I was obsessed with it. I was able to see it again a few weeks later at a distance in the wooded area. I watched it for about 30 seconds slowly moving through the woods and I will never forget my good fortune to encounter it … and to know this 'creature' truly does lives among us."

Sources:

Redfern, Nick. Interview with "Wes."

Werewolf Rock

Outside the village of Eggenstedt, near Sommerschenburg and Schöningen, Germany, stands a large rock that has been called Werewolf Rock for many centuries. According to the legend, a mysterious figure known simply as the Old Man would venture out from the Brandsleber Forest and offer to perform tasks for the villagers, such as watching over their flocks of sheep. On one occasion, as he herded sheep for a shepherd named Melle from Neindorf, the Old Man asked for a particular spotted lamb as payment for his work. Melle refused, as he particularly prized that lamb. The Old Man repeated his request many times, and Melle always denied his wishes.

When it was time to shear the flock for the wool, Melle hired the Old Man to help out. Later, when the work was completed, the shepherd found that both the mysterious old fellow and his prized, spotted lamb had disappeared.

Many months went by without a trace of either the Old Man or the lamb. Melle concluded the obvious: his hired helper had taken his lamb and eaten it.

One day as he grazed his sheep in the Katten Valley, Melle was surprised by the sudden appearance of the Old Man, who mocked him by sneering that his spotted lamb sent its regards. Enraged, the shepherd raised his crook to give the Old Man a clout, but the strange man from the woods changed his shape into that of a wolf. Melle was frightened, but his dogs came to his rescue and attacked the wolf with fury, causing it to flee.

Melle pursued the wolf until it reached the vicinity of Eggenstedt where the dogs trapped and surrounded it. At that point, the werewolf returned its form to that of the Old Man, who begged to be spared. Melle would not be deceived by such pleas, and he began furiously to beat the man with his crook. An accomplished shape-shifter of the highest prowess, the Old Man assumed the form of a sprouting thorn bush. Knowing now that he was faced with an adversary of great supernatural powers, Melle did not back off but continued to strike away at the branches of the thorn bush.

The shape-shifter, realizing that a mortal had hardened his heart and was determined to kill him, once again changed its form to that of the Old Man and begged for his life. Melle the shepherd continued to ignore his pleas and kept flailing away with his crook. The shape-shifter changed back into a wolf, planning to run away and escape in its four-legged form, but a fatal blow from Melle suddenly snuffed out its life. The spot where the creature dropped dead was named Werewolf Rock.

Sources:

Grimm, Wilhelm, and Jacob Grimm. "Der Werwolfstein." In *Deutsche Sagen*, translated and edited by D. L. Ashliman. 1816–1818.

Weyer, Johann (1515–1588)

All too seldom, amidst the screams of pain rising from the torture chambers and the stakes of the Inquisition, a voice of reason would sound — if only fleetingly and in vain. Such a voice of protest against the ghastly machinery of the Grand Inquisitors was Johann Weyer, a pupil of the famous Platonist Cornelius Agrippa of Nettesheim and a medical doctor who had studied in the humanist France of François I and practiced in Holland when it was under the enlightened influence of the scholar Erasmus. Agrippa had incurred the wrath of the Inquisition by defying it, shaming its "workers in its slaughter houses" for ignoring the baptism in Christ that would prevent the innocent from suffering from the baseless accusations of heresy. Dr. Weyer admired his teacher's courage and his skepticism.

In 1550, Dr. Weyer was invited to accept the protection of the tolerant Duke of Cleves, Julich-Berg-Marck, William V, and encouraged to write a work critical of the terrible ministrations of the Inquisition.

In 1563, at the age of 48, Dr. Weyer published *De Praestigiis Daemonum*, a work that would earn him notoriety throughout Europe and the accusation by famed jurist Jean Bodin that the author of such a foul book was a patrol of Witches and an accomplice of Satan.

While later generations would hail Johann Weyer as the father of modern psychiatry, even the good doctor's friends told him that he must immediately rewrite the book or destroy it before it fell into the hands of the powerful Catholic Church, which championed the Inquisition and the torture and burning of heretics, werewolves, and Witches. While there were a few fellow physicians who hailed him as a prophet of enlightenment, the great majority branded him a lunatic. The book was burned by the Lutheran University of Marburg, denounced by the French Calvinists, and placed on the Index by the Roman Catholic governor of the Netherlands, the Duke of Alba, who finally managed to accomplish Dr. Weyer's dismissal from the Court of Cleves.

> *He by no means denied the reality of Witchcraft, werewolves, demons, and the vast universe of Platonic spirits and entities.*

Lest we paint too fine a picture of Dr. Johann Weyer and portray him as a bold thinker centuries ahead of his time, it must be understood that he by no means denied the reality of Witchcraft, werewolves, demons, and the vast universe of Platonic spirits and entities. In fact, he firmly advocated the existence of the satanic monarchy and its attendant demons, and he catalogued the evil workings of many of them himself, declaring that, not counting Satan himself, there were 44,435,556 demons roaming Earth, seeking whom they might possess and afflict.

Where he displayed his greatest insight was in arguing that the poor wretches who were being dragged to torture chambers by the thousands and burned as Witches and werewolves were not true agents of Satan. On the contrary, they had been deceived by the hellish monarch into believing that they had supernatural powers. They were not heretics, they were fools. Their supposed powers were not based on any true knowledge or gifts from Satan. Their magical abilities were merely works of fantasy. They had no ability to fly through the air, to heal, or to change their human form into animal shapes. They only imagined such things. Or—and here Dr. Weyer presented great psychological acumen—these so-called Witches and werewolves suffered from confused mental states, and they should not be condemned by either civil or ecclesiastical courts, for even a child's or a melancholic's bad and ineffectual wicked intentions are not legally punishable.

Sources:

Russell, Jeffrey Burton. *Witchcraft in the Middle Ages.* Ithaca, NY: Cornell University Press, 1972.

Seligmann, Kurt. *The History of Magic.* New York: Pantheon Books, 1948.

Trevor-Roper, H. R. *The European Witch-Craze.* New York: Harper & Row, 1967.

Wild Hunt

Common folk kept themselves well hidden behind closed and locked doors and windows on those dark and stormy nights when Wodan and his wolves were abroad on their Wild Hunt. While some anthropologists have suggested that this old folk legend can be explained by noting that the simple forest people were merely frightened by the noises of a violent storm moving through the trees, Robert Eisler scoffs at his colleagues' theories. Men and women who lived in huts in the forest would be quite familiar with the sound of wind and lightning in the trees, he states firmly. In his opinion, the legend began when primitive hunting tribes, armed only with sharpened staves, ran through the forests in lupine packs seeking fresh meat. When they found their prey, whether animal or human, they would kill and dismember their victims as much with their teeth and claws as with their weapons. Other, more passive tribes knew that they had better stay hidden in the darkness when the lycanthropic packs were on the hunt.

Centuries later, in complete defiance of the game laws decreed by the lord of the manor, gangs of poachers with their packs of hunting dogs crashed through the night, driving their quarry before them, closing in on it before dawn, then feasting on large sections of their prey in the bloody archetypal way. Once again, the common folk knew enough to stay hidden inside their huts, for they fully realized that the lupine packs of poachers would not hesitate to chase and to kill any humans who happened to get in their way.

On dark and stormy nights, common folk locked their doors to keep out Wodan and his wolves on their Wild Hunt. Anthropologist Robert Eisler believes the legend began when primitive hunting tribes would run through the forests in lupine packs seeking fresh meat.

Interestingly, the German resistance movement raised against Napoleon I in 1813 was known as the Wild Hunt, in an obvious historical allusion to the legend of Wodan hunting at night with his wolves. In the 1930s, the black uniform of the Schutz-Staffeln, the dreaded S.S. of Hitler's troops, with the skull and crossbones on their caps, was inspired by the nightly terror visited on the people by the Wild Hunt and by the skeletons of the dead left in Wodan's wake. Hitler gloried in what he expressed as the brutal, wolflike political measures he would visit upon those who opposed him. His very title, "Führer," denotes the wolf that is the leader of the pack.

Sources:

Eisler, Robert. *Man into Wolf.* London: Spring Books, 1948.

Russell, Jeffrey Burton. *Witchcraft in the Middle Ages.* Ithaca, NY: Cornell University Press, 1972.

Wild Things in Germany

In 1879, Karl Bartsch wrote that in the vicinity of Klein-Krams, near Ludwigslust, Germany, there existed in earlier centuries huge woods that "were so rich with game that the dukes often came to this region to hold their great hunts. During these hunts they almost always saw a wolf who—even though he came within shooting distance—could never be killed by a huntsman. Indeed, they even had to watch as he took a piece of game before their very eyes and—something that was most remarkable to them—ran with it into the village."

Bartsch continued that, on one particular occasion, a hussar from Ludwigslust was making his way through the village to meet with a man named Feeg. When the unnamed hussar arrived at the home of the man in question, he got much more than he bargained for, as Bartsch recorded:

"When he entered the house a flock of children stormed out of the house with a loud cry and hurried out into the yard. When he asked them about their wild behavior, they told him that except for a small boy, no one from the Feeg family was at home, and that he—as was his custom when no one was at home—had transformed himself into a werewolf, and that they were running away from him, because otherwise he would bite them."

Soon afterward, Bartsch continued, the much-feared wolf-boy appeared, but by now he was back in his human form. The hussar demanded that the child tell him what manner of devilry was afoot in the village. Although the boy was initially reluctant to say anything at all, he finally relented. In Bartsch's words: "The child told him that his grandmother had a strap, and that if he put it on he would instantly become a wolf. The hussar kindly asked the boy to make an appearance as a werewolf. At first the boy refused, but finally he agreed to do it, if the strange man would first climb into the loft, so that he would be safe from him. The hussar agreed to this, and to be sure pulled up the ladder with which he had climbed into the loft."

By Bartsch's account, the incredible transformation from boy to monster happened quickly:

"As soon as this had happened the boy ran into the main room, and soon came out again as a young wolf and chased away all those who standing in the entryway. After the wolf had run back into the main room and come back out as a boy, the hussar climbed down and had the Feeg child show him the magic belt, but he could not discover anything unusual about it."

In no time at all, the astonished and concerned hussar went to a forester in the vicinity of Klein-Krams and told him what he had experienced in the Feeg house. On listening to the tale, the forester, "who had always been present at the great hunts near Klein-Krams, immediately thought about the werewolf who could not be wounded. He now thought that he would be able to kill the werewolf."

> *At the very next hunt the forester told his friends, as he carefully inserted a silver bullet into the barrel of his rifle: "Today the werewolf will not escape from me!"*

At the very next hunt the forester told his friends, as he carefully inserted a silver bullet into the barrel of his rifle: "Today the werewolf will not escape from me!" His concerned friends looked on in silence.

According to Bartsch: "The hunt soon began, and it did not take long before the wolf showed himself once again. Many of the huntsmen shot at him, but he remained unwounded. Finally he approached the forester, who brought him to the ground. Everyone could see that the wolf was wounded, but soon he jumped up again and ran into the village. The huntsmen followed him, but the werewolf outran them and disappeared into the Feeg farmyard."

There was, however, an unforeseen ending to this strange saga of shape-shifting in Germany of centuries past. The werewolf killed by the forester was not the young Feeg boy after all. Bartsch revealed the twist in the story: "In their search, the huntsmen came into the house, where they found the wolf in the grandmother's bed. They recognized it from the tail that was sticking out from under the covers. The werewolf was no one other than Feeg's grandmother. In her pain she had forgotten to take off the strap, and thus she herself revealed the secret."

A Grimm Story

Jacob and Wilhelm Grimm, better known as the Brothers Grimm, were born in Hanua, Germany—Jacob in 1785 and Wilhelm in 1786. They are renowned for their popularization of folklore, myths, and legends, and for promoting the likes of *Rapunzel, Cinderella, Hansel and Gretel,* and *Rumpelstiltskin.* They also had an interesting tale to tell of werewolves. In 1816, they wrote:

"A soldier related the following story, which is said to have happened to his grandfather. The latter, the grandfather, had gone into the forest to cut wood with a kinsman and a third man. People suspected that there was something not quite right about this third man, although no one could say exactly what it was. The three finished their work and were tired, whereupon the third man suggested that they sleep a little. And that is what they did. They all laid down on the ground, but the grandfather only pretended to sleep, keeping his eyes open a crack. The third man looked around to see if the others were asleep, and when he believed this to be so, he took off his belt (or, as others tell the story, put on a belt) and turned into a wolf.

Werewolves appear throughout folktale collections such as those arranged by German medievalist Karl Bartsch, famed German lexicographers the Brothers Grimm, and Canadian author Léon Pamphile LeMay, whose Contes Vrais (or True Tales) contains this illustration of a loup-garou.

"However, such a werewolf does not look exactly like a natural wolf, but somewhat different.

"Then he ran to a nearby meadow where a young foal was grazing, attacked it, and ate it, including skin and hair. Afterward he returned, put his belt back on (or took it off), and laid down, as before, in human form.

"A little later they all got up together and made their way toward home. Just as they reached the town gate, the third man complained that he had a stomachache. The grandfather secretly whispered in his ear: 'That I can well believe, for someone who has a horse, complete with skin and hair, in his belly.'

"The third man replied: 'If you had said that to me in the forest, you would not be saying it to me now.'"

The Brothers Grimm also related:

"A woman had taken on the form of a werewolf and had attacked the herd of a shepherd, whom she hated, causing great damage. However, the shepherd wounded the wolf in the hip with an ax blow, and it crawled into the brush. The shepherd followed, thinking that he could finish it off, but there he found a woman using a piece of cloth torn from her dress to stop the blood gushing from a wound.

"At Lüttich in the year 1610 two sorcerers were executed because they had turned themselves into werewolves and had killed many children. With them they had a boy of 12 years whom the devil turned into a raven whenever they were tearing apart and eating their prey."

Stories from Asmus and Knoop

The German writers F. Asmus and O. Knoop tell similar tales. In 1898 they wrote that by using what was called a wolf strap, it was possible for just about anyone to transform themselves into a werewolf. If, however, someone were to call the werewolf by their human name, they would transform back into human form. As for what, exactly, a wolf strap was, the pair noted that it was "a gift from the devil." They continued:

"A person who possessed such a strap could not get rid of it, however much he wanted to. Anyone who accepted a wolf strap also had entered into brotherhood with the devil, surrendering body and soul to him. If real wolves were feared in earlier times, werewolves were feared all the more. A real wolf could be shot dead or lured into a so-called wolf pit, where it would perish from hunger. However, a werewolf could not be brought down with a rifle bullet, nor would it ever fall into a wolf pit."

Asmus and Knoop put this question to their readers: "What is the use of running around as a werewolf?" It was, indeed, a good question, and the pair offered an answer:

"This was not done for no good reason. When the pantries and meat containers were empty, one would only have to fasten on the wolf strap, run off as a wolf, seek out a fat sheep that was wandering off toward the edge of the woods, creep towards it, seize it, and drag it into the woods. In the evening one could bring it home without anyone noticing. Or the werewolf would know when a peasant was going through the woods with a lot of money. He would ambush him, rob him, then run off across the field with the booty."

In earlier times, the writers expanded, after the horses had been unhitched from a wagon or a plow, "they would be driven out to a community pasture where they would be watched until morning by two herdsmen. Even colts were put out for the night. People took turns watching after them."

There was a very good reason for that: the fear the horses would become the victims of the deadly werewolves in their very midst. On this matter, Asmus and Knoop recounted a story that had been told to them: "Now once it happened that one of the two herdsmen had a wolf strap. After both herdsmen had kept watch for several hours they got sleepy and laid their heads down. The first one, however, who had heard that his companion possessed a wolf strap, only pretended to be asleep, and the other one thought that he was indeed sleeping. He quickly fastened the strap around himself and ran off as a wolf. The other one got up and saw how his companion ran up to a colt, attacked it, and devoured it.

"After this had happened, the wolf man came back and lay down to sleep. Toward morning they both awoke. The werewolf man was rolling around on the ground and groaning loudly. The other one asked him what was wrong.

"He said that he had a horrible stomach ache.

"To this the first one said, 'The devil himself would have a stomach ache if he had eaten an entire colt at one time.'

"The werewolf asked him to say nothing about what had happened. He kept silent about it for a long time, but later he did tell me about it, and now I too feel free to tell about it, because both men have been dead for a long time."

Sources:

Redfern, Nick. *The Monster Book: Creatures, Beasts and Fiends of Nature*. Canton, MI: Visible Ink Press, 2017.

Witchie Wolves

David A. Kulczyk provided an account to *Strange* magazine that told of a legend that came to life—to the genuine fear of those who trespassed sacred ground. According to Kulczyk, on the eastern shore of Lake Huron, approximately 34 miles north of Bay City, Michigan, located a few miles from a small town named Omer, is a wilderness area of scrubby pines and swampland known as Omer Plains, the home of the "Witchie Wolves." According to local Chippewa legend, the Witchie Wolves are the invisible guardian spirit dogs that watch over the graves of ancient warriors, attacking all who are foolhardy enough to desecrate the sacred ground.

According to local Chippewa legend, the Witchie Wolves are the invisible guardian spirit dogs that watch over the graves of ancient warriors, attacking anyone foolhardy enough to desecrate the sacred ground.

Kulczyk states that he and friends went twice to Omer Plains, but nobody in his vehicle was brave enough to get out. They could all hear the "hideous, high-pitched laughing bark that came from all directions out of the near total darkness." Visiting Omer Plains became a kind of male teenager's rite of passage, Kulczyk said, but few were foolish enough to get out of their cars. However, he writes:

> Several times a year, a skeptical youth, usually an athlete or an outdoorsman type, would take the car and get out of the car—only to be violently knocked to the ground by what always seemed to be an invisible wolf or dog, snarling and snapping at the victim's head. Screaming and scrambling back into the car, nobody ever stuck around long enough to see what else would happen. I have seen tough guys cry while telling of their experience. I have heard claims of torn clothes, and I have seen scratches and dents on roofs of cars which the owner, straight-faced and sober, would claim weren't there before the Witchie Wolf attack.

Sources:

Kulczyk, David A. "The Witchie Wolves of Omer Plains." *Strange* 15 (Spring 1995).

Wolf Belt

According to the folklore of Northern Europe, one of the most common methods by which one transformed himself or herself into a wolf was to put on a wolf belt. The belt was basically a strip of wolf hide with the hairs still attached. Some men put on such a belt simply to become more wolflike, to summon courage and to display savage prowess in battle or to bring about extraordinary strength while performing tasks of heavy labor. Such applications of the wolf belt were acceptable, even common, and were considered charms or talismans. When, however, the wolf belt had received the magical ministrations of a sorcerer, it bequeathed to the wearer the ability to shape-shift into the form of a wolf. The basic motivations for such transformations were to enable the wearers of the belt to go out into the night and attack their enemies or their enemies' livestock.

Wolf Girl of Texas

When it comes to the matter of mysterious creatures that seem to be part-human and part-wolf, they don't come much stranger than the "Wolf Girl" of Texas, who, for a significant amount of time, was seen prowling around the Devil's River, close to Del Rio in the southwest portion of Texas. It is a strange story that circulated around for many years and, in fact, is still talked about now. The creepy story, steeped in mystery and tragedy, begins back in the early part of the 1800s.

As the tale went, the Dent family, who lived close to the Devil's River, were about to have a baby when, tragically, the mother died. John Dent raced on his horse to summon help form a local doctor, but he was hit by a huge bolt of lightning and killed.

The local people did their best to try to find the baby, which had mysteriously vanished. Years later, in 1845 in that same area, what looked very much like a wild, half-human woman was seen roaming with a pack of wolves at San Felipe Springs. Her hair was long, she was naked, and she was seen savagely attacking a goat for food. That food was for her and for her wolf friends. Realizing that she and the wolves had been seen, the woman raced away with her four-legged comrades.

Over the course of the next year, the woman was seen again, along with that pack of wolves that had clearly "adopted" her. It's almost certain that the little baby had become part of the wolf family and was, by the mid-1800s, a fully grown woman who acted just like a wolf: she howled and grunted and ate food raw.

> *The girl was very young and running with a pair of wolf pups. Clearly, the elders of the pack had embraced her.*

At one point, when the woman was seen near a group of Apache, a band of locals headed out to try to capture her, only to find prints on the ground. Notably, some of them were human prints, while others were nothing less than the prints of wolves—large wolves. There is, however, some degree of confusion, as there were tales of *other* wolf-girls and wolf-women in Texas that went back to the 1700s. Clearly, several legends, spanning a period of close to a century, had blended into one. For example, there was a tale of a girl found as a baby at the Devil's River who had been adopted by wolves. And that was a long time after the original stories began. Another tidbit says the girl lived to be a full-grown woman, still with the wolves.

Another fascinating story surfaced in early 1852. That was when a surveying team, working to plan a new road, saw a pack of wolves in the vicinity who had a girl with them. In the 1852 story, the girl was very young and running with a pair of wolf pups. Clearly, the elders of the pack had embraced her. Attempts were made both day and night to try to capture the girl. It didn't work. The story wasn't over, though. After 1852, locals said that "barefoot tracks of two human beings" were seen frequently in Navidad, Texas. Were there now two girls, or women, who had made their home with wolves in the area? A fascinating and intriguing scenario, to be sure.

Attempts were made to try to capture the wolf girl. It didn't work. Eventually, the skull of a human was found. Was this the original girl, who died as an adult?

It is said that not long after the surveying team had encountered at least one girl and the wolf pack, the skull of a human was found. Was this the original girl, having died as an adult? Or was it yet another girl who became part of the wolf group?

There's something else, too, that may be connected. In 1837, a pair of wild people — one a woman and the other a man — were seen in the aforementioned Navidad area of Texas, specifically around the settlements of the lower Navidad. Guard dogs were no use: the pair eluded everyone, even the dogs. On several occasions, however, the pair were seen running with wolves or breaking into peoples' homes for food. It's clear from the accounts that the two were not just thieves — or escaped slaves, as some suggested at the time. In this story, rather, these were definitive feral people, reared by animals. A couple of years later, there was a story of a skeleton found in the lower Navidad. A connection? The chances are likely, based on the data in hand.

As for that mysterious pair, although groups of locals, law enforcement, and others tried to solve the riddle and find ways to catch the two, nothing worked. Eventually, dozens of local men went hunting — vowing to continue until the two were dead and the area secure and safe. More dogs were brought in to help, and lassos were, too. It became clear the wild ones were hiding out in surrounding woods — the perfect location for people who may have been living in the woods, with wolves, all their lives.

At one point, one of the hunters told the group that he'd seen a woman, covered in dirt, wildly riding a horse and carrying a large club — likely getting ready to kill anyone who came close. Some say she and her comrade were strung up and killed. Others say that the pair fled the area. Was there a direct connection to the wolf-women and the wolf-girls? We cannot know. What we can say, however, is that there are enough threads to suggest that in various parts of Texas, at some point from the 1700s to the 1800s, there were people who lived with wolves — and apparently preferred to live totally wild with animals and not the human race.

Wolf-Headed Beast

Sleep paralysis, if you've experienced it, can be absolutely terrifying. I had it once years ago, a horrifying situation that I will come back to shortly. As for the cause, there are two possibilities: it is provoked either by the human mind or by an external phenomenon of the paranormal kind. For the down-to-earth explanation, here is a good description from Beth Roybal at WebMD: "Sleep researchers conclude that, in most cases, sleep paralysis is simply a sign that your body is not moving smoothly through the stages of sleep. Rarely is sleep paralysis linked to deep underlying psychiatric problems.

"Over the centuries, symptoms of sleep paralysis have been described in many ways and have often been attributed to an 'evil' presence: unseen night demons in ancient times, the old hag in Shakespeare's *Romeo and Juliet*, and alien abductors. Almost every culture throughout history has had stories of shadowy evil creatures that terrify helpless humans at night. People have long sought explanations for this mysterious sleep-time paralysis and the accompanying feelings of terror." Then there is the paranormal angle of all this mayhem and chaos.

The reason why I think there is far more to this than just the human brain playing "tricks" in the night is that so many people see the very same things. If it was all down to the mind and nothing else, people's experiences would differ, and I would say that, yes, we are talking about something that is wholly internal. However, the fact that people all around the world see identical phenomena makes me think there is far more going on.

For example, there's the "Hat Man." It's an entity that surfaces time and again. Sometimes it appears in the form of a shadow. On other occasions, though, it looks just like us, but with one difference: the Hat Man—as its title suggests—wears a hat. Always. And it's almost always of the Fedora type. I've written about the Hat Man in a number of my books and received a lot of feedback in relation to the phenomenon. People who have had no preexisting knowledge of the Hat Man have seen it while in a state of sleep paralysis. The same goes for the "Old Hag," another dangerous entity that surfaces when we sleep.

"I was awake and yet not awake. ... I was frozen. ... Something was slowly heading down the corridor ... a humanoid figure with the head of a wolf."

Now let's take a look at the werewolf angle of this phenomenon. I once experienced something that fits the sleep paralysis profile 100 percent. One night in August 2002, after my ex-wife and I had gone to bed, I had an extremely curious encounter. It was around 4:00 a.m., and I was awake and yet not awake. And I couldn't move. I was frozen. Not only that, but I was aware that something was slowly heading down the corridor of the duplex that linked the bedroom to the living room. *That something was a humanoid figure with the head of nothing less than a wolf.*

It was attired in a long, flowing black cape. It emitted strange and rapid growling noises that seemed to be in an unintelligible language. And the creature, whatever its origin was, seemed to be mightily pissed off about something. As it closed in on the room, I made a supreme effort to move my rigid, paralyzed form and finally succeeded, just as the beast entered the bedroom. In an instant it was gone, and I was wide awake.

It was attired in a long, flowing black cape. It emitted strange and rapid growling noises that seemed to be in an unintelligible language.

I have mentioned this werewolf angle to sleep paralysis on a number of occasions. Here is just one example of many on record: In *Monsters among Us*, author Linda Godfrey tells the story of a man named Paul who, in October 2012, shared with her an intriguing story. Paul states that at the time he was 21, and one week before his traumatic encounter, he had read Ira Levin's novel *Rosemary's Baby*. That Paul thought it relevant to even raise that issue is interesting. According to Paul, he was asleep in the front bedroom of his girlfriend's house when he quickly woke up to a smoke-like odor. In an instant, Paul saw at the foot of the bed what he described as a Dogman. He added: "It was very dark in color, like a German shepherd without the saddle colors but more black, and the presentiment of its intellect was very scary." That was very much like my experience.

Consider the saga of the Hexham Heads and compare that experience with mine: two young boys, playing in their back garden in the old northern England town of Hexham, unearth a pair of creepy-looking stone heads. Believed by some to have ancient Celtic origins, the heads seemingly provoke a wide and unsettling range of paranormal phenomena, including the manifestation of a bizarre beast in the area. Then, when an expert in Celtic history gets involved in the saga, a monstrous werewolf-like creature materializes in her home in the dead of night. Over time, the heads provoke yet more mystery and mayhem, finally vanishing under strange circumstances but never forgotten by those obsessed with, and intrigued by, such terrible things. It is yet another example of a werewolf-like thing appearing in the early hours of the morning.

That there are *certain, specific* archetypes (werewolves, the old hag, and the Hat-Man) that seem to attach themselves to us makes me conclude this phenomenon is not merely a phenomenon of the mind. It demonstrates that when we are in deep, altered states of mind, we can be exposed to supernatural entities that have the ability to enter our realm of existence and even bring us into theirs. As my own experience demonstrated back in the early 2000s, when we are in those strange states, we are also open to absolute danger. That is, unless we find ways to break the terrible, monstrous grip that can cause such terror and turmoil.

Sources:

Redfern, Nick. Own investigations and own experiences.

Roybal, Beth. "Sleep Paralysis." WebMD, November 17, 2022. https://www.webmd.com/sleep-disorders/sleep-paralysis.

Steiger, Brad. *Monsters among Us*. New York: Berkley Publishing Group, 1989.

Wolfman or Wild Man of Kentucky

On March 27, 1907, the Nevada-based *Reno Evening Gazette* ran a story with the eye-catching title of "Wild Man Startles People of Kentucky." The subtitle added even more to the eye-opening and jaw-dropping nature of the story: "Hairy Creature Seen by Farmhand, and Both Are So Scared That They Prepare to Run."

The story began: "Information has been received here that the people in the country around Buena Vista, a village in Garrard County, are much excited over the reports that a wild man has high haunts in the Kentucky River hills near that place. A party is being organized to explore a cave where the creature is believed to have his lair and attempt to capture him."

The saga continued that one Jim Peters, who was a farmhand working for a man named S. D. Scott—the postmaster at Buena Vista, Kentucky—encountered the hair-covered man-thing in Bowman's Woods, in the vicinity of High Bridge. Peters believed that the wild man was attracted by the scent of his dog. Indeed, in the presence of the hair-covered thing, Peters's faithful pet responded by "yelping and showing every evidence of extreme fright." Peters was just as terrified as the dog, particularly when the creature approached to within 60 feet of the pair.

He described it as having long, dark, wild hair, a completely hairy body of a dark appearance, "a coon skin tied about its loins," and claw-like talons instead of fingernails.

The writer of the newspaper article detailed what happened next: "Peters says he was too frightened to run. The apparition kept its eyes on the dog until asked what it was doing there." Unsurprisingly, the hairy man-beast failed to respond in English—or in any known language. Instead, it turned and vanished into the dense woodland. Fortunately, Peters had been able to get a good look at the monster. He described it as having long, dark, wild hair, a completely hairy body of a dark appearance, "a coon skin tied about its loins," and claw-like talons instead of fingernails.

When petrified Peters finally made it back to Buena Vista, he breathlessly told his boss, S. D. Scott, what had just gone down. Scott, seeing that Peters was serious and not pulling a prank on him, quickly whipped up a posse to track down what may have been some type of Bigfoot-like creature. Although the creature was not found, its tracks were seen in the mud of the riverbank. Local women and children were said to be too scared to leave their homes. The most popular theory—albeit an extremely unlikely one, taking into consideration the physical appearance of the thing—was that the man-monster was an escaped lunatic from a nearby asylum. Evidently, the wild man got wind of the fact that he was being hunted down and headed off for pastures new. He was not seen again in Bowman's Woods.

Sources:

"Wild Man Startles People of Kentucky." *Reno Evening Gazette.* March 27, 1907.

Wolfmen in the Woods

Wolfmen prowling around the woods of central England? The saga began in March 2007 when a paranormal investigations group, the West Midlands Ghost Club, found itself on the receiving end of something extremely weird and surely unanticipated: a stash of reports of werewolf-like beasts seen lurking among the old gravestones of the Cannock Chase's German Military Cemetery. It is a large cemetery where the remains of almost 5,000 German soldiers and airmen are interred. During both World War I and World War II, numerous German military personnel were captured and transferred to prisoner of war camps across the U.K. Many of those military personnel died during the hostilities and were buried in cemeteries and graveyards closest to where they had been imprisoned. In 1959, however, the governments of the U.K. and Germany reached an agreement that resulted in the remains of the 4,929 Germans who died on British soil all being transferred to a single location: the then newly constructed Cannock Chase German Military Cemetery.

The reports provoked enough interest that Mike Lockley, at the time the editor of the (now defunct) local newspaper, the *Chase Post*, gave the story a great deal of ink. Such publicity brought in even more reports. For around three months, the good folk of the Cannock Chase found themselves plunged into a controversy that had at its heart sinister

Britain has a long, rich history of encounters with wolfmen, as celebrated in this nineteenth-century engraving.

shape-shifting monsters that dwelled among the long dead. It was a controversy that soon aroused terror and hysteria.

The morphing monsters of the Cannock Chase were not typical of the old legends, however. In other words, this was most assuredly not a case of witnesses reporting people changing into werewolves (or vice versa). No, they were wolflike creatures that had the ability to alter their body structure to walk on either four legs or two.

One of the earliest reports—referenced in the *Stafford Post* newspaper on April 26, 2007, in an article titled "Werewolf Spotted in Stafford"—came from a local postman who, while riding his motorbike past the cemetery on one particular sunny morning, caught sight of what at first he thought was a large dog walking around the cemetery. It was not a dog at all: it was a walking nightmare. The man was amazed, and more than a little concerned, by what he could soon see was a wolf of extraordinary size. That wild wolves have reportedly been extinct in the United Kingdom since 1680 made matters even more amazing. That was the year in which one Sir Ewen Cameron killed a wild wolf in Perthshire, Scotland—quite possibly the very last wild wolf in the entire U.K. Granted, there have been sporadic reports of wolves still inhabiting some of the less traveled parts of the country. Nothing, however, has surfaced conclusively to demonstrate that wolves have lived in the wilds of the U.K. since the seventeenth century. But try telling that to the beasts of a certain cemetery. And good luck telling that to the witnesses, too.

As the man slowed his bike down to a complete stop, he stared in awe and fear as the bulky animal prowled around the gravestones. It was abundantly clear to the man that this was not merely a husky or any other type of large dog. The stone-cold facts hit the man suddenly and hard: there was a wolf on the Cannock Chase. As the witness watched, entranced and with his heart practically pounding out of his chest, something terrifying and unearthly happened. The wolf caught sight of the man, froze, and stared intently in his direction, its eyes firmly locked on him for a few terrifying seconds. It was then that the body of the four-legged animal began to change—to mutate. The postman could only sit and watch, near-paralyzed to the spot, as the hind legs of the wolf started to grow in length. Oddly, for a few seconds, the creature became blurry to the eye as its form began to change. Then, with its legs now very much resembling those of a human in shape, the beast reared up on its morphed limbs and took on a bipedal stance. Not surprisingly, all that the man could think was: *werewolf.* Fortunately for the witness, the creature raced into the heart of the woods, and within seconds, it was gone.

It was soon destined to return, however.

> *The animal shape-shifted into a hairy,*
> *humanoid form, rose up onto its back legs to*
> *a height of around seven feet, and charged*
> *off into the darkened depths of the*
> *surrounding trees.*

Only weeks later, yet another encounter occurred in the cemetery; this time the witness was the leader of a local scout group. He, too, had the distinct misfortune to cross paths with the monster. As was the case with the postman's experience, the witness at first assumed that what he was seeing was a wolf—perhaps one that had escaped from a private zoo, he initially thought. That theory went completely out of the window when the animal shape-shifted into a hairy, humanoid form, rose up onto its back legs to a height of around seven feet, and charged off into the darkened depths of the surrounding trees.

In another case, a woman from the nearby town of Rugeley described seeing such a monster barely a two-minute drive from the cemetery, late one night in July 2007. On this occasion, the creature was in its upright werewolf form and standing near the edge of a tree-shrouded small lane as she approached it. She brought her car to a complete halt and, gripping the steering wheel, watched as it was enveloped in a blue haze, took on that blurry appearance described by the postman of just a couple of months earlier, altered its body shape, and dropped down onto all fours. In seconds it was gone. And so was the woman, who quickly drove home in a state of ice-cold terror. As is so often the situation in cases like this one, the mystery came to a sudden halt: the beast was gone and never returned.

Sources:

Cannock Chase Werewolves, West Midlands, England. 2007. http://www.ghost-story. co.uk/index.php/other-paranormal/188-cannock-chase-werewolves-west-midlands-england.

"Werewolf Spotted in Stafford." *Stafford Post*, April 26, 2007.

Wolf-Rage

Dion Fortune (1890–1946), born Violet Mary Firth, was an occultist, mystic, and the author of a number of acclaimed works. Fortune, who died in 1946 at the age of 55, was skilled at creating monsters in the mind and then unleashed them into the world around her. Fortune made it very clear, however, that creating a mind-monster rarely has a positive outcome. It is a lesson of which every one of us should take heed. Her story is as fascinating as it is disturbing, as she explained:

"The artificial elemental is constructed by forming a clear-cut image in the imagination of the creature it is intended to create, ensouling it with something of the corresponding aspect of one's own being, and then invoking into it the appropriate natural force. This method can be used for good as well as evil, and 'guardian angels' are formed in this way. It is said that dying women, anxious concerning the welfare of their children, frequently form them unconsciously.

Dion Fortune accidentally conjured her elemental wolf in anger by envisioning Fenris, the "Wolf-horror of the North," seen here at battle with Odin.

"I myself once had an exceedingly nasty experience in which I formulated a werewolf accidentally. Unpleasant as the incident was, I think it may be just as well to give it publicity, for it shows what may happen when an insufficiently disciplined and purified nature is handling occult forces.

"I had received serious injury from someone who, at considerable cost to myself, I had disinterestedly helped, and I was sorely tempted to retaliate. Lying on my bed resting one afternoon, I was brooding over my resentment, and while so brooding, drifted towards the borders of sleep. There came to my mind the thought of casting off all restraints and going berserk. The ancient Nordic myths rose before me, and I thought of Fenris, the Wolf-horror of the North. Immediately I felt a curious drawing-out sensation from my solar plexus, and there materialized beside me on the bed a large wolf. It was a well-materialized ectoplasmic form. It was grey and colorless, and had weight. I could distinctly feel its back pressing against me as it lay beside me on the bed as a large dog might.

"I knew nothing about the art of making elementals at that time, but had accidentally stumbled upon the right method—the brooding highly charged with emotion, the invocation of the appropriate natural force, and the condition between sleeping and waking in which the etheric double readily extrudes."

Sources:

Fortune, Dion. *Psychic Self-Defense: A Study in Occult Pathology and Criminality.* The Aquarian Press. 1979.

Wolfsbane

If applied in fatal dosages, wolfsbane would truly repel a werewolf or any other physical being, for it is extremely poisonous. Perennial herbs of the buttercup family (*Ranunculaceae*) are divided into two genera: *Aconitum* and *Eranthis*. The flowering *Aconitum* branch, which includes wolfsbane or monkshood, is the deadly one, for it exudes the substance aconite. In Nepal, where the most poisonous variety grows, warriors used the flower to tip their arrows or to turn their enemies' wells into lethal water supplies.

In the skillful, caring hands of an herbalist, however, proper dosages of wolfsbane can be a very effective pain-reliever or a tonic. Since so many of the Witches of the Middle Ages were accomplished herbalists, it is easy to assume that they knew well how to apply wolfsbane for curative or destructive purposes. While the fabled ointment that could transform the sorcerer into a werewolf is

While an ointment of wolfsbane is sometimes believed able to transform the sorcerer into a werewolf, it is possible that a hallucinogenic effect causes the initiate merely to believe that he has shape-shifted into a wolf.

sometimes thought to be wolfsbane, the potion would need to be mixed with extreme care or certain death would have resulted. It is possible, of course, that the correct proportions could have created a hallucinogenic effect that might have caused the initiate to believe that he had shape-shifted into a wolf.

Sources:

Larousse Dictionary of World Folklore. New York: Larousse, 1995.

Wolf Stone Beast-Woman

In a century long past and in a valley in the Fichtel Mountains, Bavaria, Germany, said Alexander Schöppner in 1874, a shepherd was tending his flock in a green meadow. Several times it happened that after driving his herd home, he discovered that one of the animals was missing. On each and every occasion, the search for the animals ended in complete failure. They were, said Schöppner, "lost and they remained lost."

On one occasion, however, the shepherd spied a huge wolflike animal stealthily exiting the woods and attacking, and quickly killing, a small lamb. The shepherd gave chase, but he was not quite quick enough. The wolf-thing was near-instantaneously gone, as was the unfortunate lamb. Schöppner noted that the shepherd was not going to give up easily, however, and he formulated a plan:

"The next time he took an expert marksman with him. The wolf approached, but the marksman's bullets bounced off him. Then it occurred to the hunter to load his weapon with the dried pith from an elder bush. The next day he got off a shot, and the robber ran howling into the woods. The next morning the shepherd met an old neighbor woman with whom he was not on the best of terms. Noticing that she was limping, he asked her: 'Neighbor, what is wrong with your leg? It does not want to go along with you.'"

The old woman, eying the shepherd with suspicion, replied: "What business is it of yours?" She didn't wait for an answer and quickly went on her way. The shepherd, said Schöppner, took careful note of her reply. The old woman "had long been suspected of practicing evil magic. People claimed to have seen her on the Heuberg in Swabia, the Köterberg, and also on the Hui near Halberstadt. He reported her. She was arrested, interrogated, and flogged with rod of alder wood, with which others suspected of magic, but who had denied the charges, had been punished. She was then locked up in chains. But suddenly the woman disappeared from the prison, and no one knew where she had gone."

That was not the end of the story. Sometime later, Schöppner recorded, the shepherd encountered the wolf again, once more on the fringes of the forestland and late at night. On this occasion it was not the shepherd's animals that the beast had come for. No, it was the shepherd himself that the monster had in its deadly, predatory sights. A violent battle between the two erupted, during which the shepherd "gathered all of his strength together against the teeth and claws of the ferocious beast."

The instant that blood began to flow from the wolf's side, the old woman from the village appeared in the field before them, writhing and twisting terribly.

Despite the shepherd's determination to slay the beast, it quickly became clear that he was overwhelmed when it came to the matter of sheer brute force and strength. The shepherd would have died had it not been for a hunter who quickly happened upon the scene and who "fired a shot at the wolf, and then struck it down with his knife. The instant that blood began to flow from the wolf's side, the old woman from the village appeared in the field before them, writhing and twisting terribly. They finished killing her and buried her twenty feet beneath the earth."

Schöppner concluded his account as follows: "At the place where they buried the woman they erected a large stone cross, which they named the 'Wolf Stone' in memory of these events. It was never peaceful and orderly in the vicinity of the stone."

Sources:

Redfern, Nick. *The Monster Book: Creatures, Beasts and Fiends of Nature*. Canton, MI: Visible Ink Press, 2017.

Wolf Wives

Because of the harmony and partnership between early humans and wolves as they hunted and lived together, it became common among many tribes around the world to believe that their ancestors had once been wolves. At first, the old stories said, humans also walked on four legs. Over time they began to develop more humanlike appendages—a toe here, a finger there, smaller ears every now and then. Although there were advantages to being able to stand upright, sitting upright posed the problem of what to do with the tail, so, gradually, it was eliminated—although one could always borrow one from a wolf, coyote, or fox.

Legends grew, and it was supposed that the greatest warriors had either bears or wolves for mothers. And fortunate was the man who won the love of a spirit that could appear both as a beautiful woman and a wolf. As a wolf, she could use her sharp sense of smell to lead him to the best game. As a beautiful woman, she would be a marvelous lover and bless him with children that would combine the best of wolf and human traits.

Many tribes around the world believed that their ancestors had once been wolves who, over time, became more humanlike.

German legends advise that if a man were to throw a piece of iron or steel over a wolf that is suspected of being a werewolf, if his suspicions were correct, the beast would immediately change into its human form. One man suspected that a particular high-born and beautiful woman was able to transform herself into the same wolf that occasionally stole a lamb from his flock. One night as the wolf was about to snatch a meal from his

If a man were to throw a piece of iron or steel over a wolf that is suspected of being a werewolf, if his suspicions were correct, the beast would immediately change into its human form.

flock of sheep, the shepherd sprang from his hiding place and threw his steel pocketknife over its head. At once the beautiful woman stood naked before him, and he promised to keep her secret if she would marry him.

Another old folktale tells of the poor farmer who lived with his wife in poverty and bemoaned the fate that had made him a pauper even though he worked hard in the fields. At the same time, he counted his beautiful wife his dearest blessing, for she never complained about their crude lifestyle and she somehow always managed to have delicious fresh meat on the table for his dinner.

One day he decided to spy on his good wife to learn just where she acquired the choice cuts of meat. He was astonished when his beloved tied a wolf belt around her waist as she approached a flock of sheep and transformed herself into a wolf. Stunned beyond speech, the farmer watched as his wolf wife selected a fine lamb, then fell upon it. At that point, however, a pack of dogs and a shepherd came running at the wolf, intent upon doing it the greatest harm within their power. The farmer called out his wife's name to warn her, and she immediately changed back into her human form, standing naked before her husband, the shepherd, and the growling dogs. The farmer quickly threw his coat over his wife's nakedness and led her away from the confused shepherd and his baying dogs. The farmer won a promise from his wolf wife never to do such a thing ever again—at least not in the daylight when she could be so easily sighted.

Sources:

Emerson, Ellen Russell. *Indian Myths*. Minneapolis: Ross & Haines, 1965.

Spence, Lewis. *An Encyclopedia of Occultism*. New Hyde Park, NY: University Books, 1960.

World War II Creature on the Loose

From Jonathan Downes, the director of the Centre for Fortean Zoology, comes what is surely one of the strangest of all tales of a hair-covered creature that may very well have been a werewolf. Since the story is a lengthy and complex one that is full of an absolute multitude of twists and turns—not to mention deep conspiracy and World War II–era secrecy and subterfuge—the most profitable approach is to allow Jon, who is one of my closest friends, to relate the extraordinary findings for himself and in his own fashion. They are findings that relate to a turbulent, terrible, and ultimately tragic story told to Jon back in the early 1980s, when Jon was still in his early twenties and working as a psychiatric nurse at Starcross Hospital, Devon—Starcross being a small village on the west bank of the River Exe, Teignbridge. With that said, let us take a close and careful look at this emotion-filled tale of people long gone, shadowy secrets, deep stigma, and a war-torn era immersed in carnage and conflict.

According to the British government's National Archives at Kew, England:

> Originally known as the Western Counties Idiot Asylum, [Starcross Hospital] opened in 1864 in a house and two acres of land at Starcross, rented from W.R. Courtenay, 11th Earl of Devon. A committee appointed to collect donations and subscriptions, and to accept patients into the asylum, was chaired by the 11th Earl who was also its first president, positions he held until 1904.

> By 1870 the building housed 40 residents, and an appeal for funds to build larger premises was launched. A new building, surrounded by 7 acres of grounds, was opened in June 1877. This was able to house 60 boys and 40 girls. Further additions were built between 1886 and 1909, and by 1913 a total of 1,451 patients had been admitted to the institution. In 1914, the asylum was incorporated under the Companies Act. It then became known as the Western Counties Institution, Starcross, and was certified as "a residential special school for mental defectives." Residents were trained in carving, weaving, basketry, lace-making and carpentry, and worked on the institution's agricultural holdings.

> In the 1930s, properties at Dix's Field, Exeter and Steepway, Paignton were purchased for use as domestic training hostels for young women. A farm hostel was founded on Langton Farm at Dawlish and a seaside holiday home was opened. In 1948, the institution was transferred to the National Health Service, and became merged into the Royal Western Counties Institution

Hospital Group, which coordinated all the residential mental deficiency services. The institution came under the control of Devon Area Health Authority from 1974 and of Exeter Health Authority from 1982. In 1986, in keeping with a national policy of transferring the majority of mentally handicapped people back into the community, the Royal Western Counties Hospital was marked for closure.

With that background on Starcross Hospital revealed, let us now focus on Jon Downes, who begins the remarkable tale as follows: "A story, which, I am sure, was told me in good faith, and which even now I do not know whether to believe, apparently took place during the Second World War. There had, apparently, been a number of occasions when captured German aircrew and pilots who had been shot down over South Devon or the English Channel were kept, temporarily, in a remote wing of Starcross Hospital—which is roughly ten miles from the city of Exeter—until they could be transferred to the prisoner-of-war camp high above Starcross on the Haldon Hills."

On one particular occasion, says Jon, what was known in World War II as the Home Guard had been searching for a fugitive German airman in the woods surrounding Powderham Castle, which is about half a mile away from the old hospital, and which was constructed between 1390 and 1420 by Sir Philip Courtenay. They had ventured into the deepest parts of the woods in search of their quarry when, suddenly, the small band of elderly men and boys who were too young to join the army saw what they believed was the fugitive airman running through the woods in front of them. The leader shouted at him to stop but to no avail, as Jon reveals:

> The old man who told me the story was actually one of the Home Guards, and he told me that one of the party had been a teacher in Germany before the war and could speak the language. He ordered the man to stop, but the fugitive ignored him. In 1942, the war was not going well—at least as far as the British were concerned—and Home Guard units, especially in rural areas, were desperately under-equipped. Most of the patrol was only armed with pitchforks, although one had a dilapidated shotgun and the captain—who led the unit—had his old First World War service revolver.
>
> If it had been a normal patrol there would only have been about half a dozen of them, but large parts of

Exeter had been leveled by successive waves of German bombers, and the opportunity for a population of a tiny village like Starcross to actually face the enemy on equal terms was an irresistible lure. According to my informant, the Home Guard patrol had been augmented by a gang of villagers baying for blood and desperate for revenge.

The captain was an educated man and had no intention of using force to capture the fugitive unless it was absolutely necessary. The man with a shotgun—a local farmer, who had lost two of his sons in the desperate weeks leading up to Dunkirk—had no such compunction. He was also drunk. Shouting, *"I'll get you, you bastard!"* he raised his weapon and fired. The dark figure ahead of them let out a grunt of agony and fell to the ground. The captain was furious. He immediately put the drunken farmer under arrest and confiscated his shotgun.

It was at this point, Jon demonstrates, that the group came to a shocking realization: The man who had just been felled by the irate farmer was far stranger than anything that could have come out of Nazi Germany: "The party then ran on towards what they thought was an injured German airman, but they found, to their horror, that it was nothing of the sort. Instead of a proud member of the Luftwaffe, *they found a naked man in his early twenties covered in hair* and plastered in mud."

Even 40 years after the event, says Jon, it was obvious that his informant had been badly shaken by this highly unnerving experience. He was now an elderly retired nursing officer in his early seventies who, spared military service because of his profession, had eagerly embraced the Home Guard as his opportunity to fight "the Hun," and it was equally obvious that that these years had been the happiest of his life. The rest of his professional career had been spent at the hospital, and he intimated to Jon that he had found the increasing struggle with a moribund bureaucracy exponentially tedious. So, when he was offered early retirement, he was quite happy to spend the rest of his days fishing and propped in a corner of the bar in the pub that had been named after Brunel's spectacularly unsuccessful foray into setting up a mass transit system.

You may very well ask: What happened to the hairy man who was supposedly felled all those years ago?

Of his source and his strange and sensational story, Jon states: "Apparently, he told me, the badly injured wild man—hair-covered—was taken to Starcross Hospital in the middle of the night, and all efforts were made to make him comfortable. Then, in the early hours of the morning, apparently an unmarked black van had arrived, and two men in uniform and another wearing a long white coat manhandled the mysterious victim on to a stretcher, loaded him into the back of the van, and took him to an unknown destination."

Jon had more to say: "My informant never heard anything about the case again. He did hint, however, that the authorities warned everybody involved to say nothing. And, in the prevailing culture of careless talk costing lives, they had all concurred. I was, apparently, the first person that he had ever talked to about the incident. And that was only because he had recently found out that sixty years of smoking had taken their toll and that he was doomed to die of lung cancer within the next eighteen months."

> "I had heard of werewolves in Canada — indeed, I had even been on a hunt for it whilst living in Canada — but I had never heard of such things in the United Kingdom. Could it be?"

As Jon's following words make abundantly clear, the revelations of his Deep Throat–like source had a profound and lasting effect upon the young and eager monster hunter: "I sat back on the barstool in the pub we were frequenting at the time, and gulped at my pint. This was possibly the most bizarre thing that I had ever heard—in a life that had already seen several bizarre and inexplicable incidents. I had heard of werewolves in Canada—indeed, I had even been on a hunt for it whilst living in Canada—but I had never heard of such things in the United Kingdom. Could it be? I thought: 'Surely not.'"

Jon added: "But my informant seemed genuine enough. He sat in the corner of the bar puffing away on a cigarette and wheezing gently like a dilapidated steam-engine. His face had the unmistakable translucent aura of somebody struck down by incurable cancer, and he sat telling me of these extraordinary events in a matter-of-fact tone, as if he was recounting the previous weekend's football results. Did he remember the

An aerial view of the River Exe's estuary. Starcross is the small shoreline village at the upper right, just before the peninsula at the river mouth.

exact location? If so, would he be prepared to take me there? I asked these questions diffidently, and to my delight he agreed. There was no time at the present, he told me; and, so, finishing our beers, we went outside and walked towards the castle grounds."

Matters were about to be taken to a whole new level. Jon related: "If you're traveling towards Exeter from Dawlish, go through Starcross village, and when you pass the Atmospheric Railway pub, go on past the large car park on the right-hand side of road, but instead of following the main road round to the left towards Exeter, take the right-hand fork which is sign-posted to Powderham. Carry on down this little road for about half a mile. On the left-hand side you will see an expanse of deer-park, which is bordered by a wide ditch full of brackish water that acts as a moat. Just before you come to a railway bridge, the moat peters out. And although it may not be there now, back in 1982 when I conducted the interview, there was a convenient gap in the fence. This was apparently well known to the local poaching community in the village, and formed their main entry point to the woods where Lord Courtenay and his family raised their pheasants. We wriggled through the gap in the fence to find ourselves blissfully trespassing in the forbidden grounds of the castle."

Realizing that even on such a brightly moonlit night, it would be pretty much impossible to venture any further into the thick and uninviting woodland, Jon and his aged informant decided to turn around and carefully retrace their steps back to Starcross village. Jon says that as he was working for the next three days, he made arrangements to meet his companion once again in the pub the following weekend. This time, however, the atmosphere was distinctly different and profoundly frosty, as Jon makes acutely clear. Commenting on his source, Jon recalls: "He came around, and I rushed down to·the Atmospheric Railway to fulfill our tryst. Sure enough, my friend of a few evenings previously was there, puffing away on a cigarette and drinking his customary pint of light-and-bitter. However, something had changed: I tried to broach the subject of the mysterious wild man, but he was unwilling to talk about it. 'I should not have said anything the other night,' he muttered, 'but I'm an old man and I wanted to share it with you.'"

Jon had more than a few thoughts on the matter of this distinct about-face: "Whether it was the intimation of his imminent demise, or just a memory of the promise that he had made back in the 1940s, I don't know. But, in stark contrast to his verbosity of our previous meeting, on this occasion he was adamant that he didn't want to talk about it. So, I bought him a beer, challenged him to a game of cribbage, and spent the rest of the evening doing the sort of things that blokes normally do in a pub." Not surprisingly, however, for someone whose cryptozoological pursuits were growing dramatically by the day, Jon just could not let the beastly matter drop. In actuality, for a while it's fair to say the whole thing became something of an obsession for Britain's most famous creature seeker: "The whole affair fascinated me. Over the next months I cautiously broached the subject of wolf-men in Powderham woods with a number of the elderly men who drank in the pub, or who hung out in the hospital social club. None of them knew anything. Or, if they did, they weren't saying."

"None of them knew anything. Or, if they did, they weren't saying."

Bad news was looming on the horizon too, as Jon sadly recalled: "The months passed, and the old man who had told me of the events in Powderham woods during 1942 was admitted to the cancer ward at the Royal Devon and Exeter Hospital in Exeter. I visited him on a few occasions—the last, a couple of days before he died. I smuggled him in a bottle of Guinness and sat at the end of his bed as he drank it with relish. However, in view of his condition—and because I truthfully didn't think that I could get anything else out of him—I refrained from asking him any more about an incident which he obviously regretted having shared with me. I attended his funeral. I was one of the few people there. When his lonely black coffin trundled behind the curtain at the Exeter crematorium, I was convinced that the truth about this mystery would go up in smoke along with his elderly, cancer-riddled corpse. How utterly wrong I was."

Of the next chapter in this winding and weird story, Jon kicks off as follows: "Christmas came and went. In the early weeks of 1983, I found myself going through the voluminous filing cabinets that held over a century's worth of patient records at Starcross. This was part of my training as a psychiatric nurse. And although I was supposed to be looking into the distribution of different syndromes of mental and physical handicap from which the patients at Starcross hospital suffered, much to my surprise I found what I strongly suspect to be the solution to my forty-year-old mystery." And it was here that the tragic truth spilled out:

"In amongst some of the older files, I found a number that referred to members of a very wealthy and noble local family. These were not the Earls of Devon; however, as the family is still very wealthy and extremely powerful, I do not feel comfortable with revealing their identity—at least not yet. It appeared that there was a strong vein of mental illness in the family, and possibly more significantly, metabolic disorders running through the line.

"I discovered the details of some terrible human tragedies reaching back over a century. It turned out that an old lady, known affectionately to all the staff as Winnie—and who at the time I knew her, must have been in her early nineties—was a member of this noble family. She had committed the unpardonable sin of becoming pregnant at the age of 13, following her liaison with one of the stable boys. This had happened way back before the First World War, and although history didn't relate what had happened to her boyfriend, she had been forcibly given an abortion and incarcerated for the rest of her life in Starcross Hospital."

Several of Winnie's relatives suffered from congenital generalized hypertrichosis, commonly known as "Wolf-Man Syndrome."

There was far more misfortune to come: "It turned out that, before the Mental Health Act of 1959 was passed, there were three criteria under which a person could be admitted to hospital without any real recourse of appeal. These people were labelled as 'idiots' (nowadays known as people with moderate learning difficulties), 'imbeciles' (individuals with severe learning difficulties), and moral defectives. I looked at Winnie with new respect from then on, and, whenever I had the chance, I would give her a packet of cigarettes or some chocolate."

Now Jon came to the meat of the tale, including the origin of the hairy wild man of Starcross Hospital: "The files also contained details of a number of her relatives. Several of them suffered from congenital generalized hypertrichosis, commonly known as 'Wolf-Man Syndrome.' In extreme cases, this disease not only causes bizarre behavior and radical mood swings, but the body of the victim becomes excessively hairy. Although several people from Winnie's family had been diagnosed as suffering from this syndrome, there were no hospital records absolutely proving that they had been resident at a hospital after the First World War. What I did find out, however, was that the bloodline definitely had not died out. The family was still very important in the Devon area. They were notable benefactors to local charities; and at one time, at least, members of the family had been on the governing board of Starcross hospital itself."

As the condition is an inherited one, it seemed quite probable to Jon that the strain of congenital, generalized, hypertrichosis had not died out in the early years of the twentieth century. Rather, a more enlightened generation of the family had decided to treat these poor unfortunates at home rather than subject them to the rigors of an institutionalized life. Maybe this, Jon mused, was the truth behind the story of the hairy man of Powderham.

In extreme cases, this disease not only causes bizarre behavior and radical mood swings, but the body of the victim becomes excessively hairy.

He added later: "I thought it was quite likely that the unruly rabble that had accompanied the Home Guard on that fateful night in 1942 had actually shot a member of the local ruling family—in the mistaken belief that he was a German airman. This would explain everything. It would explain why the whole affair had been shrouded in secrecy. In those days, the part of the landowner and the patrician establishment was far greater than it is today. There is still a stigma surrounding mental illness, mental handicap, and disability. This poor idiot, covered in hair, was a member of the family who, after all, still paid the wages of most of the members of the posse that had hunted him down. Especially at a time when the nation was facing the deadly peril of the Nazi hordes, the powers-that-be would not have wanted the populace at large to be aware that one of their own was an unstable, dangerous, hair-covered lunatic who had escaped from his care and was wandering, naked and belligerent, across the countryside."

Thus ends the sad, enigmatic, and conspiracy-filled saga of the Starcross wolfman, the decades-old secrets of a powerful family, official cover-ups, frightened figures, a shadowy informant who had hidden the truth for decades, and a young man—Jon Downes—who, more than 30 years ago, found himself so graphically exposed to the story in all its hideous and weird glory.

Another Creature?

Actually, the story is not quite over. The noted British naturalist Trevor Beer had an equally provocative account to relate that might be of some significant relevance to the tale described above. The event occurred in the late 1950s and was reported by a man out walking his dog at the time of its occurrence. Although the year is different to that in the story told to Jon Downes, and the incident reportedly involved a werewolf rather than a wild man (although, to the untrained, terrified eye, is there really that much of a difference?), the location—Devon—was the same. Also the same are two further matters of significance: in the story told to Beer, (a) the hairy man-thing was shot; and (b) it was found to be a member of a well-known family in the area.

Beer described the story of the witness in these words: "Climbing a hedge, he stumbled upon an animal ravaging a flock of sheep, and taking careful aim he shot it; the beast reared onto its hind legs to run off into the woods. The dog followed the animal into the trees where there was much hideous snarling unlike any creature he had ever heard before. Suddenly the dog came dashing out of the woods and bolted past its master who, firing a second shot into the trees, also ran for home in great fear." Beer added that the man "went on to explain his later studies of matters concerning the occult and his realization that the animal he had shot was a werewolf and a member of a well-known local family. [He] further states that he knows the family involved and that they called in help from the church over a decade ago but that they had to withdraw because of the terrible phenomena beyond their comprehension. Now the problem is at a stalemate, the family being aware of the nature of his character and chaining him and locking him behind barred doors every night."

Are the similarities between this case and the one described to Jon Downes actually evidence of a *single* story that, over time, became somewhat distorted into two separate ones? Or, incredibly, could it be that the case Trevor Beer described involved yet *another* member of the affected and afflicted werewolf family to which Jon referred? Maybe, one day, we will know the full and unexpurgated truth of this intriguing and conspiratorial affair. Or perhaps, like so many tales of deep cover-up, it will forever languish in mystery, intrigue, and a closely guarded, locked filing cabinet marked "Top Secret." A hair-covered wild man, or a real-life werewolf? Perhaps someone out there will resurrect the story and solve the mystery.

Sources:

Redfern, Nick. Interview with Jonathan Downes. Woolsery, Devon, England: CFZ Press, 2000.

World War II Monster-Hound

From a woman who, as a young girl, had a traumatic encounter with an infernal, supernatural hound at the height of World War II, we have the following:

During World War II, as the German Luftwaffe bombed London relentlessly, many families left the city for more remote parts of the country, less likely to attract the enemy's attention.

"At the time, because of the war, my mother and I usually stayed with an elderly gentleman, who had kindly taken us in as 'refugees' from London. We only went back to the capital when the bombing ceased. The cottage where we lived is still in existence, in Bredon, Worcestershire. My encounter took place one late afternoon in summer, when I had been sent to bed but was far from sleepy.

"I was sitting at the end of the big brass bedstead, playing with the ornamental knobs and looking out of the window, when I was aware of a scratching noise, and an enormous black dog had walked from the direction of the fireplace to my left. It passed round the end of the bed, towards the door. As the dog passed between me and the window, it swung its head round to stare at me—it had very large eyes, which glowed from inside as if lit up, and as it looked at me I was quite terrified, and very much aware of the creature's breath, which was warm and as strong as a gust of wind.

"The animal must have been very tall, as I was sitting on the old-fashioned bedstead, which was quite high, and our eyes were level. Funnily enough, by the time it reached the door, it had vanished. I assure you that I was wide awake at the time, and sat on for quite some long while wondering about what I had seen, and to be truthful, too scared to get into our bed, under the clothes and go to sleep. I clearly remember my mother and our host sitting in the garden in the late sun, talking, and hearing the ringing of the bell on the weekly fried-fish van from Birmingham as it went through the village! I am sure I was not dreaming, and have never forgotten the experience, remembering to the last detail how I felt, what the dog looked like."

Wulver

Jessie Margaret Saxby (1842–1940) was a well-known folklorist in the 1900s. In 1933 she wrote an excellent book titled *Shetland Traditional Lore*. In the pages of her Scotland-based book, she penned the following intriguing words: "The Wulver was a creature like a man with a wolf's head. He had short brown hair all over him. His home was a cave dug out of the side of a steep knowe, half-way up a hill. He didn't molest folk if folk didn't molest him. He was fond of fishing, and had a small rock in the deep water which is known to this day as the 'Wulver's

Stane.' There he would sit fishing sillaks and piltaks for hour after hour. He was reported to have frequently left a few fish on the window-sill of some poor body."

Unlike the traditional werewolf, the Wulver was not a shape-shifter. Its semi-human, semi-wolf appearance was natural and unchanging. One of the most fascinating, and certainly disturbing, accounts of a Wulver came from Elliott O'Donnell. Shortly after the start of the twentieth century, O'Donnell interviewed a man named Andrew Warren, who had a startling story to tell. In his book *Werwolves*, which was published in 1912, O'Donnell carefully recorded every word that Warren had to say. The priceless account reads:

"I was about fifteen years of age at the time, and had for several years been residing with my grandfather, who was an elder in the Kirk [Church] of Scotland. He was much interested in geology, and literally filled the house with fossils from the pits and caves round where we dwelt. One morning he came home in a great state of excitement, and made me go with him to look at some ancient remains he had found at the bottom of a dried-up tarn [lake].

"It's a werwolf, that's what it is. A werwolf! This island was once overrun with satyrs and werwolves!"

"'Look!' he cried, bending down and pointing at them, 'here is a human skeleton with a wolf's head. What do you make of it?' I told him I did not know, but supposed it must be some kind of monstrosity. 'It's a werwolf [*sic*]' he rejoined, 'that's what it is. A werwolf! This island was once overrun with satyrs and werwolves! Help me carry it to the house.'

"I did as he bid me, and we placed it on the table in the back kitchen. That evening I was left alone in the house, my grandfather and the other members of the household having gone to the kirk. For some time I amused myself reading, and then, fancying I heard a noise in the back premises, I went into the kitchen. There was no one about, and becoming convinced that it could only have been a rat that had disturbed me, I sat on the table alongside the alleged remains of the werwolf, and waited to see if the noises would recommence.

"I was thus waiting in a listless sort of way, my back bent, my elbows on my knees, looking at the floor and thinking of nothing in particular, when there came a loud rat, tat, tat of knuckles on the window-pane. I immediately turned in the direction of the noise and encountered, to my alarm, a dark face looking in at me. At first dim and indistinct, it became more and more complete, until it developed into a very perfectly defined head of a wolf terminating in the neck of a human being.

"Though greatly shocked, my first act was to look in every direction for a possible reflection—but in vain. There was no light either without or within, other than that from the setting sun—nothing that could in any way have produced an illusion. I looked at the face and marked each feature intently. It was unmistakably a wolf's face, the jaws slightly distended; the lips wreathed in a savage snarl; the teeth sharp and white; the eyes light green; the ears pointed. The expression of the face was diabolically malignant, and as it gazed straight at me my horror was as intense as my wonder. This it seemed to notice, for a look of savage exultation crept into its eyes, and it raised one hand—a slender hand, like that of a woman, though with prodigiously long and curved finger-nails—menacingly, as if about to dash in the window-pane.

"Remembering what my grandfather had told me about evil spirits, I crossed myself; but as this had no effect, and I really feared the thing would get at me, I ran out of the kitchen and shut and locked the door, remaining in the hall till the family returned. My grandfather was much upset when I told him what had happened, and attributed my failure to make the spirit depart to my want of faith. Had he been there, he assured me, he would soon have got rid of it; but he nevertheless made me help him remove the bones from the kitchen, and we reinterred them in the very spot where we had found them, and where, for aught I know to the contrary, they still lie."

Dr. Karl Shuker, who is an expert on the Wulver, has studied this closely: "Quite aside from its highly sensational storyline, it is rather difficult to take seriously any account featuring someone (Warren's grandfather) who seriously believed that the Hebrides were '… once overrun with satyrs and werwolves'! By comparison, and despite his youthful age, Warren's own assumption that the skeleton was that of a deformed human would seem eminently more sensible—at least until the remainder of his account is read. Notwithstanding Warren's claim that his account was factual, however, the arrival of what was presumably another of the deceased wolf-headed entity's kind, seeking the return of the skeleton to its original resting place, draws upon a common theme in traditional folklore and legend."

Sources:

Shuker, Karl. "Wulvers and Wolfen and Werewolves, Oh My!! — Tales of the Uninvited." July 28, 2012. https://karlshuker.blogspot.com/2012/07/wulvers-and-wolfen-and-werewolves-oh-my.html.

Zombie Vampires

From time to time, an investigation will take the average adventurer in a direction very different to that originally anticipated. Exactly that happened to Jon Downes, director of the Centre for Fortean Zoology, and me during a visit to Puerto Rico in 2004. We found ourselves plunged into a deeply weird story of nothing less than a *third* breed of island vampire. The chupacabra and the vampire of Moca, it seemed, had a rival in the blood-drinking stakes.

Puerto Rico is a place filled to the brim with dark superstitions, beliefs in all manner of paranormal phenomena, and an acceptance that terrible and savage things lurk deep within the woods and forests. I, too, am inclined to think such creatures live there. One such story that really caught our attention was focused on the alleged existence of an isolated village somewhere on the Rio Canóvanas. It's a river that dominates the municipality of Canóvanas, in the northeast of Puerto Rico, that is noted for its green hills and extensive plains.

According to the tale — which half the film crew and a couple of locals had all heard — the entire population of the village was afflicted by a strange malady. The village folk, we were told, were skinny, pale, and downright anemic-looking. They never surfaced during daylight hours. They only ever dressed in black. The clincher: they fed on nothing but fresh blood. To a pair of English vampire hunters, it all sounded great; it was precisely the sort of thing Jon and I were looking for. That didn't mean it was true, however. Or did it?

None of the people of the village exceeded four and a half feet in height. Their heads were larger than normal and were marked with prominent blue veins. They were completely lacking in hair.

It has been my experience that behind just about every controversial legend or rumor there is usually at least a nugget of truth, even if it is somewhat distorted. We asked our storytellers to expand on what they knew of this infernal tribe of bloodsuckers. They were happy to do so. The picture their words painted was notably unsettling.

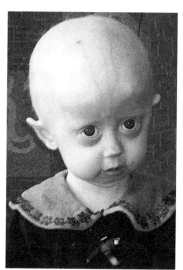

The symptoms of the so-called vampires that dwelled on the Canóvanas River were those of a rare genetic condition called progeria, which provokes rapid aging in afflicted children.

None of the people of the village exceeded four and a half feet in height, we were told. Their heads were larger than normal and were marked with prominent blue veins. They were completely lacking in hair. Some of them had six fingers on each hand. Their noses were almost beak-like. They had skin that gave them a leathery, wrinkled, aged look. Their genitals were supposedly nearly nonexistent. Their voices were oddly high-pitched. They walked with a stiff, robotic gait. And they dined voraciously on human blood.

On hearing all of this, Jon and I looked knowingly at each other. The symptoms that were described to us (aside, that is, from the blood drinking) were not those of vampirism at all but of a distressing, and extremely rare, condition called progeria—a tragic genetic affliction that affects children. It is so rare that, officially at least, only one case exists per every eight million people. Progeria provokes rapid aging and a physical appearance nearly identical to that of the so-called vampires that dwelled on the Canóvanas River. In some cases, those with progeria show signs of polydactylism: an extra digit on the hands or feet. Life spans are usually short, from early teens to (at the absolute extreme) the twenties.

Of course, given the rarity of progeria, this instantly made both of us wonder: how was it possible that an entire village could be affected by this genetic disorder—and across several generations? The answer we got was as amazing as it was controversial.

Back in 1957, something unusual was said to have crashed to earth in the Canóvanas region. Among those we spoke to, opinion was split between a meteorite and a craft from another world. Whatever the culprit, it let loose in the area nothing less than a strange alien virus. This virus wormed its way into the water supply of the village and soon infected the population of 30 or 40. The result was disastrous: every subsequent newborn displayed the awful symptoms of what, to Jon and me, sounded acutely like progeria.

As startling as it may seem, the threat of an alien virus surfacing on our world is one that the National Aeronautics and Space Administration (NASA) takes very seriously.

According to the text of Article IX of the Treaty on Principles Governing the Activities of States in the Exploration and Use of Outer Space, Including the Moon and Other Celestial Bodies, which was collectively signed at Washington, D.C., London, England, and Moscow, Russia, on January 27, 1967, and was put in force on October 10 of that year, "In the exploration and use of outer space, including the Moon and other celestial bodies, States Parties to the Treaty shall be guided by the principle of co-operation and mutual assistance and shall conduct all their activities in outer space, including the Moon and other celestial bodies, with due regard to the corresponding interests of all other States Parties to the Treaty."

Most significant of all is the next section of the document: "States Parties to the Treaty shall pursue studies of outer space, including the Moon and other celestial bodies, and conduct exploration of them so as to avoid their harmful contamination and also adverse changes in the environment of the Earth resulting from the introduction of extraterrestrial matter and, where necessary, shall adopt appropriate measures for this purpose."

The main concern revolved around the fear that a deadly virus would be released into the earth's atmosphere, a worldwide pandemic would begin, and an unstoppable plague would escalate, ultimately killing every one of us.

It must be stressed that the main concern, as described in the document, revolved around the fear that a deadly virus would be released into the earth's atmosphere, a worldwide pandemic would begin, and an unstoppable plague would escalate, ultimately killing every one of us. But what if that same alien pandemic didn't kill us but provoked progeria-style symptoms and a craving for human blood?

Such a possibility sounds manifestly unlikely in the extreme. It's worth noting, however, that the so-called extraterrestrial Grays of alien abduction lore — those dwarfish, skinny, black-eyed, and gray-skinned creatures that are so instantly recognizable to one and all and made famous on the likes of *The X-Files* — do, admittedly, display far more than a few characteristics of progeria.

On the matter of the Grays possibly being affected by progeria, *Flying Saucer Review* magazine noted: "If Grays have progeria, then there is a very serious situation out there. An entire civilization may be threatened with extinction because their children and young people are dying. A possible reason why progeria may be so widespread among Grays and not among humans is probably because the Grays have been around much longer than humans and the DNA replication is probably deteriorating, making room for genetic mutations and serious genetic diseases. ... One reason why they may want to hybridize with *Homo sapiens* is to add healthier DNA to their gene pool and to weed out the progeria gene."

I chatted with Jon about this and had to wonder: Was it feasible that a strange, extraterrestrial plague — or, perhaps, futuristic gene-tinkering linked to the alien abduction phenomenon — had provoked a disastrous outbreak of something that manifested in a combination of progeria and vampirism among the population of a small Puerto Rican village?

It seemed outlandish even to give the matter serious thought. Certainly, when all attempts to verify the story came to absolutely nothing, and even the exact location in question could not be identified, we came to a couple of tentative conclusions. First, perhaps what was being described was not progeria, after all, but the results of decades of in-breeding in a village that was in dire need of new blood (so to speak). Second, the idea that these unfortunate people were vampires was almost certainly born out of superstitious fear of their curious appearance rather than actual proof that they thrived on human blood—which they almost certainly did not.

Unfortunately, regardless of the truth of the matter, everything was against us in this investigation. No one was able to point us in the specific direction of the village. To the best of everyone's knowledge, no photographs of the villagers existed. And the tight schedule we were on meant that there simply wasn't time to pursue this admittedly fascinating tale.

While a down-to-earth explanation was probably the likely one, try as we might, neither Jon nor I could fully dismiss from our minds the dark notion that Puerto Rico might harbor a band of unholy vampires of the outer space kind, a band with a voracious need for human blood. It was a chilling thought.

Sources:

Redfern, Nick, and Jonathan Downes, personal research, 2004–05.

Image Credits

A

Page 2: Lion man statue: Dagmar Hollman, via Wikimedia Commons
Page 5: Scene from Apuleius's *Metamorphoses*: *Master of the Die*, after Michiel Coxie, via Wikimedia Commons

B

Page 9: Angelucci and mysterious orbs: Raggedstone/Shutterstock
Page 14: Sabine Baring-Gould's *The Book of Werewolves*: public domain, via Wikimedia Commons
Page 17: Early New Orleans map: National Archives and Records Administration
Page 22: *Le Loup-Garou* by Maurice Sand, 1857: public domain, via Wikimedia Commons
Page 26: Berserkir: yanik88/Shutterstock
Page 29: Beast of Bray Road: Sergey Mironov/Shutterstock
Page 34: *Beauty and the Beast* by Warwick Goble, 1913: public domain, via Wikimedia Commons
Page 35: Wolf print: stasokulov/Shutterstock
Page 40: Illustration by Sidney Paget for *The Hound of the Baskervilles*: public domain, via Wikimedia Commons
Page 45: Stone bridge: Joanna K-V/Shutterstock

C

Page 48: *Lycaon Transformed into a Wolf* by Hendrik Goltzius, 1589: Los Angeles County Museum of Art, via Wikimedia Commons
Page 51: *Clovelly Harbour, Devon* by Alfred William Hunt: public domain, via Wikimedia Commons
Page 53: Cat people and werecats: Yana Radysh/Shutterstock
Page 59: Illustration by Maurice de Becque from *The Jungle Book*, 1924: public domain, via Wikimedia Commons
Page 64: Chindi/bear walking upright: Eric Mandre/Shutterstock
Page 70: Chupacabra: Dick Langer, via Wikimedia Commons
Page 73: Cleadon Hills windmill: David Elsy, via Wikimedia Commons
Page 74: Coyote: Joshua Fawcett/Shutterstock

D

Page 80: Nick Redfern in Defiance, Ohio: Nick Redfern
Page 84: Unibrow: Z11o22, via Wikimedia Commons
Page 86: *Diana as Personification of the Night* by Anton Raphael Mengs, c. 1765: Steffi Roettgen/James Steakley, via Wikimedia Commons
Page 88: Nick Redfern with *Dogman* head: Nick Redfern
Page 91: The Donas de Fuera of Sicily/*Take the Fair Face of Woman* by Sophie Gengembre Anderson: public domain, via Wikimedia Commons
Page 92: Dwayyo: Krasula/Shutterstock

E

Page 98: Eagle Creek wolf cult: Microgen/Shutterstock
Page 105: Enkidu: Sailko, via Wikimedia Commons
Page 107: Vseslav of Polotsk on silver coin: National Bank of the Republic of Belarus, via Wikimedia Commons

F

Page 113: Dryads, by Pierre Milan after Rosso Fiorentino: public domain, via Wikimedia Commons
Page 115: Fenrir, by Mabel Dorothy Hardy: public domain, via Wikimedia Commons
Page 119: Yako/Werefox, by Sawaki Suushi: public domain, via Wikimedia Commons
Page 121: Fox engraving by T. Landseer after E.H. Landseer: Wellcome Images, via Wikimedia Commons

G

Page 127: German woodcut of werewolf, by Lucas Cranach the Elder, c. 1512: Herzogliches Museum, Gotha, Germany, via Wikimedia Commons
Page 131: Ghouls/*Le Vampire* by F. Avenet and Alexandre Ferdinandus, c. 1880: public domain, via Wikimedia Commons
Page 133: Linda Godfrey with Nick Redfern: Nick Redfern
Page 137: Ancient flintlock musket with bullets: Militarist/Shutterstock
Page 141: Frontispiece from "Guillaume de Palerme," c. 1630–40: public domain, via Wikimedia Commons

H

Page 145: Hare, by Wenceslaus Hollar: public domain, via Wikimedia Commons
Page 150: Horror hound/black dog, 1577: Abraham Fleming, via Wikimedia Commons

I

Page 156: Incubus/*The Nightmare* sculpture by Eugène Thivier, 1894, photographed by Didier Descouens: public domain, via Wikimedia Commons

J

Page 161: Jackal: MZPHOTO.CZ/Shutterstock

K

Page 167: Kelpies at Loch Ness: San Antonio Light, via Wikimedia Commons
Page 172: Cornfield: UMB-O/Shutterstock

L

Page 178: *The Kiss of the Enchantress* by Isobel Lilian Gloag, c. 1890, inspired by "Lamia" by John Keats: public domain, via Wikimedia Commons
Page 180: Leopard man exhibit, illustrated in *Le Monde colonial illustré* by Paul Wissaert, 1934: public domain, via Wikimedia Commons
Page 186: Lion: Atlaspix/Shutterstock
Page 189: Ergot parasite on rye, illustrated by Franz Eugen Köhler, 1897: public domain, via Wikimedia Commons

Page 193: Rabies illustration by Abdallah ibn al-Fadl, c. 1224: public domain, via Wikimedia Commons

M

Page 198: Aleister Crowley, c. 1925: public domain, via Wikimedia Commons
Page 201: Bridge 39 over Shropshire Union Canal: Nick Redfern
Page 204: Mountain lion: Kwadrat/Shutterstock
Page 206: Cannock Chase road: Nick Redfern
Page 212: Mowgli, illustration by Charles Maurice Detmold from *The Jungle Book*, 1913: public domain, via Wikimedia Commons

N

Page 214: Nagual, from Codex Borgia: public domain, via Wikimedia Commons
Page 216: *Ura Linda* book sample, written in Frisian: public domain, via Wikimedia Commons
Page 220: Mind-shifter: leolintang/Shutterstock
Page 225: Ouija board: Couperfield/Shutterstock
Page 227: French Quarter, New Orleans: Josh11566/Shutterstock
Page 231: Wolf fangs: Savvapanf Photo/Shutterstock
Page 235: Shepherdess painting by Carlo Pittara, c. 1891: public domain, via Wikimedia Commons

P

Page 242: Pentagram tattoo: goldeneden/Shutterstock
Page 247: Psychedelic nightmare animal: Munimara/Shutterstock

R

Page 250: Ravana, a Rakshasa king, sculptor unknown: Claire H., via Wikimedia Commons
Page 251: Cross/Bill Ramsey: nito/Shutterstock
Page 255: *Lupa Capitolina* with Romulus and Remus, Capitoline Museums, Rome: Jastrow, via Wikimedia Commons
Page 260: Ruzena Maturová as a Rusalka, 1901: public domain, via Wikimedia Commons

S

Page 264: Beheading of Peter Stumpp: public domain, via Wikimedia Commons
Page 267: Silver bullet: Sir Magnus Fluffbrains, via Wikimedia Commons
Page 270: Cattle mutilation: Gerardo C. Lerner/Shutterstock
Page 275: Beast of Gévaudan, c. 1765: public domain, via Wikimedia Commons
Page 279: Decapitation of Peter Stumpf: public domain, via Wikimedia Commons
Page 282: Succubus depicted in "My Dream, My Bad Dream" by Fritz Schwimbeck, 1909: public domain, via Wikimedia Commons

T

Page 290: Thaman Chah/Taw, 1897: public domain, via Wikimedia Commons
Page 292: Chupacabra drawing by LeCire: LeCire, via Wikimedia Commons

Page 297: Thylacine, illustration by John Gould, 1863: public domain, via Wikimedia Commons
Page 299: Thylacine, modern illustration by Nellie Pease/CABAH: ARC CoE CABAH, via Wikimedia Commons
Page 303: Bengal tiger, painting by William Huggins, 1838: public domain, via Wikimedia Commons
Page 307: Lascaux Cave paintings: JoJan, via Wikimedia Commons

V

Page 314: Odin with Geri and Freki, by Carl Emil Doepler, 1888: public domain, via Wikimedia Commons
Page 314: Rougarou exhibit, New Orleans: XxxJohnDoExxxx, via Wikimedia Commons
Page 317: Cow: Bob Mawby/Shutterstock
Page 319: Sigmund and his sword, illustration by Arthur Rackham, 1910: public domain, via Wikimedia Commons

W

Page 323: Sylvester Stallone as Rambo: Yoni S. Hamenahem, via Wikimedia Commons
Page 326: German cemetery at Cannock Chase, Staffordshire: Nick Redfern
Page 329: Amityville house: Seulatr, via Wikimedia Commons
Page 333: Black panther: apple2499/Shutterstock
Page 336: Full moon: Roadcrusher, via Wikimedia Commons
Page 338: RAF Alconbury border: Michael Trolove, via Wikimedia Commons
Page 343: *Wild Hunt of Odin* by Peter Nicolai Arbo, 1872: Nasjonalmuseet, Norway, via Wikimedia Commons
Page 346: Loup-garou illustration from *Contes vrais* by Léon Pamphile LeMay, 1907: public domain, via Wikimedia Commons
Page 349: Witchie Wolves: SSokolov/Shutterstock
Page 352: Human skull: Antti T. Nissinen, via Wikimedia Commons
Page 354: Hooded figure with wolf mask: Jakub Krechowicz/Shutterstock
Page 357: Nineteenth-century wolfman engraving: public domain, via Wikimedia Commons
Page 360: Fenris battling Odin, by Mabel Dorothy Hardy, 1909: public domain, via Wikimedia Commons
Page 361: Wolfsbane: Anna Light/Shutterstock
Page 364: Man with dog's or wolf's head, by Hartmann Schedel: public domain, via Wikimedia Commons
Page 370: River Exe estuary and Starcross village: steverenouk, via Wikimedia Commons
Page 372: Hypertrichosis, or "wolf-man syndrome": Wellcome Images, via Wikimedia Commons
Page 375: London after the Blitz, photograph by Herbert Mason, 1941: public domain, via Wikimedia Commons

Z

Page 382: Progeria, from "The Cell Nucleus and Aging: Tantalizing Clues and Hopeful Promises," by Paola Scaffidi, Leslie Gordon, and Tom Misteli: PLOS, via Wikimedia Commons

Index

Note: (ill.) indicates photos and illustrations.

WEREWOLF STORIES